S0-BLM-929

Women and the church in medieval Ireland, c.1140–1540

Women and the church in medieval Ireland, *c*.1140–1540

DIANNE HALL

Set in 10.5 pt on 12 pt Bembo
by Carrigboy Typesetting Services for
FOUR COURTS PRESS LTD
7 Malpas Street, Dublin 8, Ireland
e-mail: info@four-courts-press.ie
http://www.four-courts-press.ie
and in North America for
FOUR COURTS PRESS
c/o ISBS, 5824 N.E. Hassalo Street, Portland, OR 97213.

A catalogue record for this title
is available from the British Library.

ISBN 1–85182–656–4

Printed in England by
Antony Rowe Ltd, Chippenham, Wiltshire

Contents

Illustrations

TABLES

GRAPHS

FIGURES

Author's note

Personal names have been standardized when they are of well-attested people. Personal names that appear once or only in contemporary documents are given in the original spelling.

Acknowledgements

My research on this project was assisted by an Australian Postgraduate Scholarship, a Melbourne University Postgraduate Scholarship and a Melbourne University Research Scholarship. Travel grants from the Faculty of Arts, Melbourne University, School of Graduate Studies, Melbourne University, and the History Department, Melbourne University, assisted with travel expenses.

The staff of the inter-library loans department at the Melbourne University Library have remained cheerful, helpful and sympathetic in the face of frequent requests for research materials. The staff of the State Library of Victoria, Joint Theological Libraries, Melbourne University Libraries and the library of Newman College, Melbourne, were all helpful in allowing me access to materials and assisting with searching for obscure references. John Cain, Map Curator of Melbourne University Libraries, explained the mysteries of digital mapping and gave generously of his time and patience. Librarians at Co. Offaly Library, Co. Clare Library and Co. Tipperary Library all responded promptly and generously to my requests for information. On my visits to Dublin, the staff of the libraries of Trinity College, National Library and National Archives were all helpful with their assistance.

Katherine Simms and Mary O'Dowd examined the thesis on which this book is based, and I am very grateful for their helpful comments and suggestions. Mrs Margaret Phelan and John Kirwan of the Kilkenny Archaeological Society both were generous with their time and local knowledge of Kilkenny, St Canice's Cathedral and the tomb of Elicia Butler. Philomena Connolly was encouraging with her advice about this project at a crucial point. Writing this book so far from Ireland has meant that I have had the opportunity to correspond with many people, who have been generous in searching for references and sharing their knowledge of different aspects of this research, so I am grateful to Reginald Barnewell, Maeve Callen, Geraldine Carville, Colm Cullerton, Marie Therese Flanagan, Peter Harbison, Canon K. Virginia Kennerley, Mrs Dorothy Leonard, Fr Michael Lyons, Mary Malone, Colman Ó Clabaigh, Pat O'Hora, Helen Perros, Pete Scherman and Roger Stalley. In response to my queries, Dr M. Haren also kindly supplied me with relevant transcripts from his researches in the Vatican Library.

Margaret O'Flanagan helped with photographs and finding obscure nunnery sites with good humour and patience. Louise Willis has shared many expeditions in rain and sunshine to see nunnery sites and ensured that there were plenty of rest stops along the way. Lee Ann Monk has joined me in many discussions over coffee about this project and also helped with the final editing; her support and friendship over many years has been invaluable.

In the History department at the University of Melbourne, I found congenial intellectual support and wish to thank the "the Melbourne medievalists", Adina Hamilton, Elizabeth Freeman, Lucy Mills, Meagan Cassidy and Megan Street. Ann Trindade has read many drafts of this book, discussed the ideas and always shown great faith that it would be finished. Anne Gilmour-Bryson and Paul Nicholls read earlier drafts and were generous with their comments. Elizabeth Malcolm recently has given generously of her knowledge of Irish history and I am grateful for her support on this project and others.

Finally I want to thank Rowan, for the laughter.

Abbreviations

AClon	*The annals of Clonmacnoise, being the annals of Ireland from the earliest period to 1408*, trans. C. Mageoghagan and ed. D. Murphy (Dublin, 1896).
AConn	*Annala Connacht: the annals of Connacht, 1224–1544*, ed. A.M. Freeman (Dublin, 1844, rpt. 1970).
AFM	*Annála rioghachta Eireann: Annals of the kingdom of Ireland from the earliest period to the year 1616 by the Four Masters*, ed. J. O'Donovan (Dublin, 1851).
AI	*Annals of Inisfallen*, ed. and trans. S. MacAirt (Dublin, 1951).
ALC	*The annals of Loch Cé: a chronicle of Irish affairs, 1014–1590*, ed. W. Hennessy (London, 1871).
AU	*Annála Uladh: annals of Ulster … chronicle of Irish affairs*, 431–1541, ed. W.M. Hennessy and Bartholomew MacCarthy (Dublin, 1887–1901).
AA	Arroasian observance of Augustinian Rule.
Account roll of Holy Trinity	*Account roll of the priory of Holy Trinity, Dublin, 1337–1346*, ed. J. Mills (Dublin, 1891, rpt. 1996).
Alen's reg.	*Calendar of Archbishop Alen's register, c.1172–1534*, ed. C. McNeill (Dublin, 1950).
Anal. Hib.	*Analecta Hibernica*.
Arch. Soc.	Archaeological Society.
Archdall (1786)	M. Archdall, *Monasticon Hibernicum or an history of the abbies, priores and other religious houses in Ireland* (London, 1786).
Archdall (1876)	*Monasticon Hibernicum or an history of the abbies, priores and other religious houses in Ireland*, edited and expanded by P.F. Moran (Dublin 1876).
Archiv. Hib.	*Archivium Hibernicum*
BL	British Library.
Book of Obits	*The book of obits and martyrology of the Cathedral Church of the Holy Trinity, commonly called Christ Church, Dublin*, ed. J.C. Crosthwaite and J.H. Todd (Dublin, 1844). Reprinted in *The registers of Christ Church Cathedral, Dublin*, ed. R. Refaussé with Colm Lennon (Dublin, 1998), pp 37–86.
Cal. Christ Church deeds	*Calendar of Christ Church deeds*, ed. M.J. McEnery and Raymond Refaussé (Dublin, 1999).
Cal. doc. Ire.	*Calendar of documents relating to Ireland* (London, 1875–86).

Cal. inquis. Dublin	*Calendar of inquisitions formerly in the office of the chief rememberancer of the exchequer, prepared from the manuscripts of the Irish records commissioners*, ed. M. Griffith (Dublin, 1991).
Cal. justic. rolls Ire. 1295–1307	*Calendar of justiciary rolls of Ireland, 1295–1307*, ed. J. Mills, (Dublin, 1905–1914).
Cal. justic. rolls Ire. 1307–1313	*Calendar of the justiciary rolls of the proceedings of the court of the justiciar of Ireland, I–VII Edward II*, ed. M. Griffith and prepared under the direction of H. Wood and A.E. Langman (Dublin, 1957).
Cal. papal letters	*Calendar of entries in the papal registers relating to Great Britian and Ireland: papal letters,* ed. W. Bliss et al. (London and Dublin, 1893–).
Cal. pat. rolls	*Calendar of patent rolls* (London, 1906–).
Cal. pat. rolls Ire., Jas. I	*Irish patent rolls of James I: facsimile of the Irish Record Commission's calendar prepared prior to 1830* (Dublin,1966).
Cat. pipe rolls	*Catalogue of great rolls of the pipe of the Irish exchequer.*
Chart. St Mary's, Dublin	*Chartularies of St Mary's abbey, Dublin, with the register of its house at Dunbrody and annals of Ireland*, ed. J.T. Gilbert (London, 1884).
Cist.	Cistercian.
Extents Ir. mon. possessions	*Extents of Irish monastic possessions, 1540–1, from manuscripts in the Public Record Office, London,* ed. N.B. White (Dublin, 1943).
Fiants Ire., Hen. VIII–Eliz.	*Irish fiants of the Tudor sovereigns during the reigns of Henry VIII, Edward VI, Philip and Mary and Elizabeth I* (Dublin, 1994).
Ir. cart. Llanthony	*The Irish cartularies of Llanthony prima and secunda,* ed. E.StJ. Brooks (Dublin, 1953).
Ir. mon. deeds, 1200–1600	*Irish monastic and episcopal deeds, 1200–1600,* ed. N.B. White (Dublin, 1936).
Knox, *History of Tuam*	H.T. Knox, *Notes on the early history of the dioceses of Tuam, Killala and Achonry* (Dublin, 1904).
L.& P. Hen. VIII	*Letters and papers, foreign and domestic, Henry VIII* (London, 1862–1932).
Med. rel. houses Ire.	A. Gwynn and R.N. Hadcock, *Medieval religious houses – Ireland* (Dublin, 1970).
NAI	National Archives of Ireland.
NHI II	*A new history of Ireland – Medieval Ireland 1169–1534,* ed. Art Cosgrove, 1st ed. (Oxford, 1987).
NHI IX	*A new history of Ireland – Maps, genealogies, lists. A companion to Irish history,* Part II, ed. T.W. Moody, F.X. Martin, F.J. Byrne,(Oxford, 1984).
NLI	National Library of Ireland.
OFM	Franciscan.
Ormond Deeds	*Ormond deeds, 1172–1603,* ed. E. Curtis (Dublin, 1932–43).
OSA	Augustinian.
PRI rep. DK	*Public Records of Ireland, report of the Deputy Keeper.*
Pont. Hib.	*Pontifica Hibernica*, ed. M. Sheehy (Dublin, 1962).

RIA Proc. C	*Royal Irish Academy Proceedings,* Part C.
RSAI Jn	*Royal Society of Antiquaries of Ireland, Journal.*
Reg. All Saints	*Registrum Prioratus Omnium Sanctorum juxta Dublin*, ed. R. Butler (Dublin, 1845).
"Reg. Cromer"	"Archbishop Comer's register", ed. L.P. Murray and Aubrey Gwynn.
"Reg. Fleming"	"A calendar of the register of Archbishop Fleming", ed. H.J. Lawlor, *RIA Proc.* C 30 (1912–13), pp 94–190.
Reg. St John Dublin	*The register of the hospital of St John the Baptist, Dublin,* ed. E.StJ. Brooks (Dublin 1936).
Reg. St Thomas Dublin	*Register of the abbey of St Thomas, Dublin,* ed. J.T. Gilbert (London, 1889).
Reg. Swayne	*The register of John Swayne, archbishop of Armagh and primate of Ireland, 1418–1456,* ed. D.A. Chart (Belfast, 1935).
Reg. Sweteman	*The register of Milo Sweteman, archbishop of Armagh, 1361–80,* ed. B. Smith (Dublin, 1996).
Reg. Trist.	*Registrum monasterii B.V. Mariae de Tristernagh … register of the priory of Tristernagh,* ed. M.V. Clarke (Dublin, 1941).
Register of wills, ed. Berry	*Register of wills and inventories of the diocese of Dublin in the time of Archbishops Tregruy and Walton, 1457–83,* ed. H.F. Berry (Dublin, 1898).
Registrum Iohannis Mey	*Registrum Iohannis Mey: archbishop of Armagh, 1443–56,* ed. W. Quigley and E.F.D. Roberts (Belfast, 1972).
"Rep.Viride, Alen"	"The reportorium viride of John Alen, archbishop of Dublin, 1533", ed. N.B. White *Anal. Hib.* 10 (1941) pp 171–122.
Rot. pat. Hib.	*Rotulorum patentium et clausorum cancellarie Hibernicae calendarium,* ed. E. Tresham (Dublin, 1828).

Introduction

In 1236 a group of lay women, nuns and children were burned along with three priests while sheltering in a church at Emlagh, in an act of violence as familiar as it must have been devastating.[1] There is no more information about this episode, but if the incident is put into the wider context of women's interactions within the church in medieval Ireland, it is possible to speculate on what the women were doing in the church and who they might have been. Termonkeelin was the closest convent to the church. The nuns may have been from this convent, and could have been visiting relatives in the area or managing the estates of the convents, both common reasons nuns left their convent walls. The lay women were likely to have been from the local community, women who prayed in the church, buried their dead in its grounds, and contributed to its building and furnishing, and to charitable work organised from its doors. To all these women the church must have seemed a place where they might be safe from attack, a place that would be a focus for religious practice. The record of these women's deaths in a church is unusual in a period where women have left few traces of their presence within religious spaces, as is the record of association of lay women with nuns. The lives of nuns in medieval Ireland have been cloaked with shadows and their lay sisters' devotional activities have emerged just as rarely into the glare of the historical stage. Women, though, were vital participants within most of the ecclesiastical institutions of medieval Ireland: they worshipped in churches, financially supported parishes and monasteries, while some took religious vows, living within convent walls. This book focuses on women and how they negotiated spaces for themselves and their families within the churches and religious communities of medieval Ireland.

The women of medieval Ireland were not a homogenous class who acted only in the interests of their own gender. Generally, propertied women's devotional interests were aligned with those of their family and community; they operated within all the complex systems of loyalty and patronage in which men are found throughout the medieval period in Ireland. Religious women, although marginalised within the ecclesiastical hierarchy, were generally privileged women whose properties and social position would have dominated local communities.[2] As well as being members of families and communities, however, women also

1 *AConn.* 1236. 2 This point is eloquently made by Dyer in "Review article: Gender and

had to operate within gendered expectations, which meant that they did not participate within society or the church in the same way as men did.

There is still a marked tendency for historians of medieval Ireland to concentrate on political and legal history within well-worn limits.[3] This means that the history of women, and the relationships between women and men, in later medieval Ireland has been neglected and has only recently started to be systematically addressed in published work.[4] While there have been a number of detailed studies of the impact on women of some of the important institutions of medieval Ireland, such as marriage, property law and literature as well as some histories of individual women, there has been no extended study of how women participated in the structures and culture of the church, one of the most important institutions in medieval Ireland.[5] Looking for traces of medieval women's religious activities in medieval Ireland means looking with eyes trained for omissions, ellipses and small clues. By reading sources in this way I have assembled a wide range of small references to lay and religious women, some so slight that they had been overlooked previously. These scraps of information have then been assembled together against the patterns historians have established for women's religious activities in other parts of medieval Europe. In this way the brief records of religious practices of women in the different communities of medieval Ireland can be brought together to build a vibrant picture of these otherwise silent women.

The availability of source material has also dictated the broad chronological and geographical limits of this book. Examining women's religious activities, from around the time of the arrival of the Anglo-Normans in the late twelfth century until the suppression of the monasteries in the 1540s and the beginnings of the Protestant reformation, provides a very wide scope for analysis. There are disadvantages with these limits, chiefly that such a broad time scale can telescope events so as to minimise differences which occurred over time, and that, by considering women from all over Ireland, the very real economic, cultural, linguistic and political differences between and among women in different communities may be lessened. These disadvantages, though, must be set against the poor survival of sources, which does not allow continuous chronological or geographical coverage of any one group or area. By casting my net widely both in terms of chronological limits and sources, I have been able to build a frame in which to place these women. Inside this frame, it is possible to see quite clearly how some women participated within the church, while the shadows of others are able to emerge from obscurity, even if only briefly.

Gwynn and Hadcock's collection of the scattered and often contradictory references to the monastic houses of Ireland is an indispensable tool in any study of religion and medieval Ireland. Their chapter on women's religious houses

material culture", p. 124. **3** Bhreathnach, "Medieval Irish history at the end of the twentieth century", pp 260–71. **4** See for example the articles in Meek and Simms ed., "*The fragility of her sex*"? **5** Simms' articles from the 1970s remain crucial; see "The legal position of Irish women", pp 96–111 and "Women in Norman Ireland", pp 14–25; more recently see Cunningham, "Women and Gaelic literature, 1500–1800", pp 147–59; and Fitzpatrick,

highlights the difficulties of studying women's religious history by emphasising the paucity of the records.[6] Other writers on the history of the church in medieval Ireland have taken this warning to heart and have essentially put women's participation in the church into the "too hard basket".[7] While there are studies of individual religious houses for women which have appeared over the past century, with varying degrees of detail and analysis, few have attempted to place the nunneries in the wider context of conventual life for women religious in Ireland or beyond. Part of the reason for this is the uneven nature of the surviving sources for the history of medieval Irish women.

It is soon apparent that the range of source material available for the study of European women does not survive in Ireland. This means that I have gathered together material from a wider range of sources than is usually used in researching women's religious activities. With each set of sources the reasons for women's inclusion or exclusion is important and to some extent dictates how the information can be used. Since there are few published overviews of available sources for the study of medieval women in Ireland, I will detail the groups of sources I have used and the ways that women and their interests were represented. I am sure that future research will unearth more information about women in the diverse remaining material, which can join the pieces I have found and fill some of the empty spaces in our current pictures of the lives and concerns of women in medieval Ireland.

Evidence of women's lives and concerns tends to be found in records originating at a local level – manorial court records rather than royal courts for example. Basic sources for history of women and religion are similarly the records of various local churches and episcopal registers. None of these have survived well in Ireland. The most significant surviving episcopal sources are the fifteenth-and-sixteenth century registers of archbishops of Armagh, but there are very few documents of practice from other dioceses.[8] Wills, donations of land and goods, foundation records and the internal workings of the monasteries themselves must once have been prolifically documented. Few original charters survive from monastic houses in Ireland, although there are some medieval cartularies. Post-medieval destruction is not the only reason for the poor survival rate of charters: these documents were invariably fragile and became worn from use, so many charters must have perished in ordinary use in the medieval period.[9] Nuns themselves may have used charters differently from monks, with some historians of convents in England suggesting one of the reasons for the relative paucity of nunnery sources is that documents in Latin were poorly under-

"Mairgréag an-Einigh Ó Cearbhaill", pp 20–38. **6** *Med. rel. houses Ire.*, p. 307. **7** Watt, *Church in medieval Ireland*, p. 47, gives scant reference to nuns, mentioning them only twice, while adding in an aside that he did not include the origins of houses for nuns as they "present complex problems of origins". Nicholls, *Gaelic and Gaelicised Ireland*, p. 111, uses his paragraph on religious women in Gaelic Ireland to good effect to summarise the histories of St Catherine d'Conyl, Killone and Kilcreevanty. **8** For a summary of the surviving registers of Armagh see Cosgrove, "The Armagh register", pp 307–20. **9** See for example the reference to replacing charters,

stood by the later medieval period and so were not seen as practical documents worth preserving.[10] This may be why so little of this material has survived in Ireland. Nunneries in medieval Ireland did have documents recording details of their estates, but very few have survived and there are few clues as to the reason for their poor survival.[11]

The survival of a large collection of vernacular annals in Ireland provides important additional information, particularly for Gaelic Irish women who are poorly represented in the documents originating from the great Anglo-Irish monasteries and churches. The immediate problem for historians of women using the annals is that women were obviously not particularly significant to the compilers. Women who are included are almost always members of the great Gaelic Irish families and their family connections are almost always the reason for their inclusion. The annals are essentially long lists of obituaries, primarily, though not exclusively, of clerics and kings who died in battle. In this context there are long and valuable descriptions of battles, but little about the daily lives of people or their faith. The deaths of many priors, abbots and bishops are noted with handsome eulogies but only a handful of religious women are given obituaries in the annals. The noblewomen who are mentioned in the annals are usually given enthusiastic notices that emphasise their piety and also often state their place of burial.

Since there are so few surviving traces of the piety and religious practice of Irish lay and religious women, the records that have survived have to be carefully examined for any small clues about the interactions between women and the institutions of the church. So while records of personal faith are scanty, records of the material expression of that faith are more plentiful. Secular records of land ownership and disputes have provided essential information on the estates that lay men and women transferred to religious institutions and how that property was managed through the medieval period. In 1922 there existed hundreds of original rolls generated by the central Dublin administration. Since the destruction of the public records office that year there are now no more than twenty in whole or part.[12] So calendars, manuscript notes and local antiquarian studies made during the previous few centuries have become essential. These calendars, notes and studies are being used for purposes for which they were never intended, and the circumstance in which they were made is particularly important. The compilers of the official Record Commissioners' calendars of these lost deeds, made with precarious government funding in the nineteenth century, for example, were told to compress and edit the material, and eliminate all that was irrelevant or referred to unknown persons and places.[13]

"Irish material in the class of ancient petitions (S.C. 8)", p. 99. **10** Thompson, *Women religious*, pp 13–14. **11** Archbishop Alen refers to the muniments of Hogges and Timolin in the 1530s. *Alen's reg.* p. 185. **12** Connolly, "The medieval plea rolls", p. 9; "The common bench plea roll of 19 Edward IV", pp 21–60 and "Survey of the Memoranda rolls of the Irish Exchequer 1294–1509", pp 49–134. **13** Connolly, "The medieval plea rolls", p. 7 and NAI

Antiquarian scholars from the seventeenth to the nineteenth centuries also had access to material that is now lost.[14] These men all were writing and collecting for their own purposes and their notes are just that – notes – which are not always easily readable, not always complete with details of their sources and not always accurate.[15] Antiquarian notebooks and manuscript calendars are particularly frustrating sources for historians interested in women's lives, as the compilers were interested in the great matters of church and state, landed wealth and succession, arenas which usually focussed completely on men. Some information on women does come through this strong filter and it has proved worthwhile to collect and analyse it.

The final group of sources that shed light on the religious spaces occupied by women is the physical spaces themselves. Recent archaeological attention has been given to burial patterns in medieval cemeteries and monastic precincts, giving valuable information about lay burial practices. As there have been no definitive scholarly archaeological surveys or excavations of nunneries in Ireland to date, my analysis of the physical remains and their significance to the history of the women who lived in them is of necessity preliminary and based on published reports, supplemented where possible by personal observation.

Medieval Irish women have left few indications of their private piety. In order to begin to understand women's piety, I have combined the scant evidence for inner devotions with external signs of women's religious practice. These externals include the places in the landscape such as gravestones, parish churches and convent buildings. The other way that women expressed their piety was by patronage or by donating goods, land and money to favoured churches, monasteries and convents. The medieval period was a time when public demonstration of piety was part of one's communal, familial and personal obligations, so outward signs of devotion are plentiful. This is in many ways a rather narrow measure of religious practice, omitting as it does so much of the personal beliefs of people as well as devotions of those with little of material worth to donate. However, property records are the most likely to have been kept, legal disputes over land and resources the most likely to survive, and in these most secular of records it is possible to glean information about the devotional practice and preferences of otherwise silent people.

This book will examine these external expressions of religious life. It is divided into two parts: the first uses broad measures to assess women's piety and devotions, while the second examines the most obvious public expression of female piety – the convents for women. In the first part I have analysed how lay women publicly expressed their piety and to what extent they participated in the ecclesiastical institutions of their communities. In order to do this as widely as possible in the first chapter I have surveyed the surviving sources for the

RC 7/1, pp 4–6. **14** For a description and discussion of antiquarians and their interests in general see Ní Shéaghdha, *Collectors of Irish manuscripts*, p. 3. **15** Flower and Dillon, *Catalogue of Irish manuscripts in the British Museum, III,* p 13.

categories of evidence of women's devotional practice; much of this evidence is scattered and ranges across time and geography. I have then concentrated on lay women's patronage of six major monastic houses, as this is an element of lay piety that is relatively easy to measure and analyse. These two chapters together demonstrate the range of avenues open to women of the different communities in medieval Ireland to express their piety.

The second part of the book describes and analyses the boundaries within which nuns and other religious women lived: the physical borders of their estates and buildings and the ideological theories underpinning enclosure away from family and community. I argue that these boundaries were permeable; that estates and convent walls built with lay patronage needed continued lay support if the nuns were to continue to survive the often tumultuous circumstances in which they found themselves. I have been interested in how the nuns negotiated these conflicting demands to ensure that they maintained spaces in which they could fulfil the wishes of the lay founders and patrons. Some failed to withstand the pressures of time, changes in lay support and the ravages of violence and war, while others succeeded in maintaining the spaces within which their sister nuns lived quietly throughout the medieval period.

By examining both lay women and those who followed religious vows, I have been interested in establishing a wide-ranging examination of the religious options and choices available to women in medieval Ireland. Many of these choices were specific to different communities at different times. Large areas of Ireland did not have a tradition of separate communities of vowed religious women and those that did were often available only to a privileged few. Patronage of churches and monasteries by lay women was governed by their legal entitlement to property and the communities to which they belonged. The institutions, buildings and structures of the church existed throughout most of the island. The ways women interacted with these institutions is therefore critical to our understanding of both the histories of medieval Irish women and to the histories of the institutions themselves.

CHAPTER 1

Lay women's piety

> In the presence of holy monuments she bows her head and is ever checking her senses; she leaves her psalter unopened till she has first instructed her family in God's love.[1]

This rare description of the personal piety of a fifteenth-century Irish woman stresses her deeply held religious beliefs and pious practices. Significantly it includes her care for her family's devotional needs and she is described as a model of a pious medieval matron. Ólaidh, daughter of Muircheartach Ó Ceallaigh, the subject of this poem, also was described as fasting from Friday until dawn on Sunday, constantly praying and saying psalms. This is a rare insight into the personal religious practices of women in medieval Ireland, though it is clear that women did participate in religious culture and institutions in a variety of different circumstances throughout the later medieval period. There are, however, few records of their personal piety. This is not surprising given the dearth of personal material written in which observations on personal spiritual health and growth were recorded.

The network of parishes begun during the twelfth-century native reform of the Irish church and re-organised by the Anglo-Normans provided for the spiritual well-being of laity throughout medieval Ireland.[2] These parishes included places of worship and were the focus for lay religious practice. Although women were excluded from the priesthood, they were expected to join with their male relatives in following the yearly round of devotional activities and to give material support to parish church buildings. They attended pilgrimage sites and holy wells and asked for prayers when sick or in childbirth. These women, though often hard to find in surviving sources, were active and essential participants in lay religious culture throughout medieval Ireland.

PIETY IN THE LIVES OF MEDIEVAL IRISH WOMEN

Investigating lay piety is a notoriously difficult undertaking.[3] Religious belief is subjective, and how it manifests within different societies requires an almost

1 *Aithdioghluim dána*, vol. 40, p. 26. **2** Smith, *Colonisation and conquest*, p. 17. For the situation in Gaelic Ireland see Mac Mahon, "The charter of Clare abbey", pp 21–8 and Nicholls, "Rectory, vicarage and parish in the western Irish dioceses", pp 53–84. **3** See Corish,

impossible leap of imagination if we are to understand the world-view of people far removed in time and space. Over the past twenty years or so, however, there has been an increase in attention to lay piety in medieval European historiography and in developing sophisticated ways of interpreting the evidence to attempt to understand the religious attitudes of medieval lay people.[4] Some of these insights are valuable for analysing the piety of women in medieval Ireland. Norms of devotion can be seen in the words used to describe some aristocratic Gaelic Irish women. The poets and annalists were fond of praising the piety of women from ruling families. Although these formulaic praises do not give a reliable picture of the women described, they do indicate the characteristics that were seen as important for a woman to be considered pious. Some women emerge from the poets' praise verses with greater reputations for piety than others, suggesting that they were recognised as such by the wider community, and this is certainly the case for Órlaidh – daughter of Muircheartach Ó Ceallaigh.

Other women were honoured with descriptions of piety in their obituaries. Although the phrases used are commonplace, not all women are described as particularly pious, so it is probable that these were women who had reputations for piety. When Christina inghean Uí Neachhtain, wife of Diarmaid Midheach Mac Diarmada, died in 1269, she was commemorated in the annals as "the most hospitable and chaste woman of her tribe, and the most bountiful to the order of Grey Friars".[5] When Gormlaith, wife of Aed son of Niall son of Con, died in 1524, the same year as her husband, she was described as "a charitable, humane, generous woman, to whom God gave a fair good name in this world and surely the true Kingdom hereafter".[6] Clearly a reputation for piety mixed with generosity was valued in later medieval Gaelic societies and meant that there was a well respected space in which wealthy Gaelic women could patronise churches and religious institutions. The piety for which these women were remembered had all the hallmarks of conventional medieval female piety: hospitality, devoutness and charity.

Giving any form of charity or alms to paupers was a form of personal piety for which there are often few records.[7] In medieval Ireland, preachers emphasised the role of charity and alms-giving as part of the duties of Christian life.[8] There are several famous examples of Gaelic Irish women's charity and by extension their personal piety. Mairgréag Ó Cearbhaill's two feasts for the poets of Ireland, given in times of famine at Killeigh, were celebrated by the annalists and poets who were among the recipients of her generosity.[9] Other women also gave alms in their daily lives. In a fourteenth-century account of the founding of a hospital in Cashel, the wife of David Latimer, steward of Mairín Ó Briain archbishop of Cashel (1223–37), gave her daughter bread to give to the people at her door

"Women and religious practice", pp 212–13. **4** See, for example, French, *The people of the parish*. **5** *AFM* 1269; *AU* 1268. **6** *AConn.* 1524. **7** For a general discussion with local examples from England of charity as piety, see Cullum, "And hir name was charité", p. 31. **8** O'Dwyer, *Towards a history of Irish spirituality*, pp 116–17, citing homilies from Mac Donncha OFM, "Seanmóireacht in Éirinn ó 1000 go 1200", pp 77–95. **9** Fitzpatrick, "Mairgréag an-

seeking alms.[10] Women also left charitable bequests in their wills. Joan White, who died in 1472, left a three-legged pan and one trough with two trundles for the use of her neighbours in Leixlip for the health of her soul and her ancestors.[11] Such charitable bequests, when documented, often show that care was taken to ensure that the gifts were to be used by those whom the donors knew and who would keep the memory of the donor alive.

There are also occasional references to personal prayers of women, particularly in ill health or childbirth. A manuscript from Ireland has a copy of the prayer to the Virgin Mary for help to women in childbirth.[12] Órlaidh, daughter of Muircheartach Ó Ceallaigh, whose piety was so extravagantly praised by Tadhg Óg ÓhUiginn in the mid-fifteenth century, was also said to say her seven psalms and to "guide Éire with her constant prayers".[13] Among the possessions of Dame Margaret Nugent who died in 1474 in Dublin was "one small brass pot for holy water" and this suggestion of personal piety is augmented by her donation of all her goods to the chapel of the Virgin Mary in her parish church, where she also requested burial.[14] Another woman noted for her piety was Máire, daughter of Eoghan Ó Máille and wife of Ruaidhri MacSuibhne Fanand, who heard mass at least once a day, and fasted three times a week as well as during Lent and other feast days.[15] Catherine daughter of Maelechlain, son of Maurice Mac Donnchaidh, and wife of Mac Firbisigh, drowned in a "rushing flood" on her way to Sunday mass.[16] Her desire to attend mass in a time of floods certainly suggests a sense of piety and devotion. It also indicates that she was not one of the many women from ruling families in Gaelic Ireland who had obtained permission to have mass celebrated at private altars in their homes. Other women's presence at mass can be assumed by their patronage of church and donation of furnishings, church plate and other essentials for the celebration of services.

From the fourteenth century there was a marked increase in appeals by lay people to have portable altars and private chapels in their houses. These were probably more often status symbols than expressions of deep personal piety, and it has been estimated that by the fifteenth century all knightly families in England had private chapels.[17] In Ireland there was a similar demand for dispensations to have private altars, chapels and private confessors. Women were active participants in this fashion, and obtained licenses from both resident archbishops and Rome. In 1406, Alicia, widow of John Keppok, applied to the archbishop of Armagh for permission to hear mass in her private chapel and her request was granted with the proviso that she also attend mass on Sundays and festivals at her parish church.[18] Between 1344 and 1469, there were 103 requests recorded in the papal

Einigh Ó Cearbhaill", p. 20. **10** Calendar of justiciary rolls, 7 Ed II, 1313 (NAI KB 2/5), pp 35–42. **11** *Register of wills*, ed. Berry, pp 47–8. **12** O'Dwyer, *Mary*, p. 129. **13** *Aithdioghluim dána*, vol. 40, pp 25–6. **14** *Register of wills*, ed. Berry, pp 78–81. **15** *Leabhar Chlainne Suibhne* pp 67 and 69. See discussion in Simms, "Women in Norman Ireland", p. 23, and Meigs, *Reformations in Ireland*, p. 21. **16** *ALC* 1412. **17** Fleming, "Charity, faith and the gentry of Kent", p. 42. **18** "Reg. Fleming", pp 103–4.

records by women alone or with their husbands for permission for private chapels, confessors and plenary remission of sins.[19] The majority, seventy-five out of 103, of these women applied together with their husbands.[20] Only one woman, Alice Stanley of Armagh diocese, was both married and applied on her own in 1399. It is probable that a number of the twenty-four women who were not given a marital status were also married rather than widowed. Although most of the women who applied to the papacy had English names, thirty-four women's names were Irish, indicating that women from Gaelic Irish areas were conversant with fashionable expressions of piety and were able to arrange for the expensive business of the appeal to Rome.

Women were not only associated with conventional piety, although the evidence for heresy or other non-conventional beliefs is often tenuous. The well -documented case of Alice Kytler, the witch from fourteenth-century Kilkenny, is one which is now believed to have been motivated less by heterodox religious views than local politics.[21] In 1300 in Cork, a group of women were associated with three men convicted of false preaching in return for money. There are few details of this case, although the fact that the five women were with them created "great scandal".[22] There are a number of different interpretations that would fit the bare facts as presented in the calendar of court proceedings. Certainly extortion of gullible lay people may have been the reason for this group's conviction. It is also possible that this group genuinely believed in the religious powers that they advertised and, like so many heretical groups throughout medieval Europe, included women in their group to the consternation of secular and religious officials.

Women also expressed their piety in more public ways. One way for lay women and men to access the services performed in the holiest spaces of the church was for special prayers and masses to be said by priests for their benefit. This might be accomplished by joining a confraternity or by arranging for anniversary prayers or masses. Confraternities, literally joining in the prayers of the community, were often attached to monasteries and churches and became popular in Ireland as in the rest of late medieval Europe. Women were members of confraternities and guilds throughout Dublin and probably the rest of Ireland as well. In England there are records of many parish fraternities or guilds, while in Ireland there were fraternities at the parish level as well as confraternities associated with monastic houses.[23] These seem to have been like the confraternities of religious houses in England which were organised to provide the prayers of the religious as well as sometimes food and lodgings in old age.[24] Two of the

19 For this sample, the *Cal. papal letters* were searched for all women's names which were definitely from Ireland. There are a number of names where no home diocese are given and it is not possible to be certain whether the requestors were from England or Ireland; these women were not included. **20** *Cal. papal letters*, 1396–1404, p. 297. **21** Neary, "The Kilkenny witchcraft case of 1324", pp 333–50. **22** *Cal. justic. rolls Ire., 1295–1307*, p. 334. **23** Ronan, "Religious customs of Dublin medieval guilds", pp 225–47, 364–81. **24** Barron, "The parish fraternities of

best-documented are St Patrick's and Christ Church cathedrals in Dublin.[25] Admission to the confraternity of one of these large religious houses was a way of gaining the prayers of the monks and the other members of the confraternity in perpetuity.[26]

The religious houses and churches kept lists for anniversary masses for members of their confraternities, and a good example is the list from Christ Church cathedral in Dublin. The list also records donations bequeathed or given to the cathedral and its community at the time of death. Prominent and wealthy lay people also arranged for special masses to be said for them by the clergy of the cathedral. Although most of these services were intended to speed the soul of the departed through purgatory, the priests might also pray for living patrons in special services or in their own daily masses. When John de Grauntsete, a prominent Dublin citizen, gave significant donations to Christ Church in 1335, he was honoured with daily masses for his health while he lived, and the mass of the Virgin Mary and daily mass before the Holy Cross for the souls of himself and his dead wife.[27] Others who were buried in the cathedral had special masses said for them on their anniversaries.

There are many women commemorated on the surviving list of anniversary masses honoured by the clergy of the cathedral, some with their husbands and others on their own. Over three-quarters of the one thousand entries in the lists of obituaries are for lay people, and of these there are 220 women's names included.[28] Some women would have arranged their admission to the confraternity themselves, others in conjunction with their husbands, and another group would have been admitted at the wish of their surviving husbands or children administering their estates. Some of the donations listed are large, such as the land donated by Johanna Lamkyne who died 1438, and the many donations of Katerina Preston, lady of Tartayne, whose anniversary was honoured with "nine lessons".[29] There are a large number of names from wealthy and important people indicating that it was considered a fashionably pious cause to donate to the cathedral and join its confraternity. However, there are some more modest donations, for example Mariona Flemyng who left 6*d.* and Peter Tympan and Alice Walsh his wife who gave a cow and calf for the works of the church.[30]

Other women and men were listed in the confraternity lists as "conversus"/ "conversa" or lay brother/sister. These undoubtedly refer to the lay brothers who died in the religious communities. The Christ Church confraternity lists for example had twenty-seven conversi listed in the obits, as might be expected from a confraternity attached to a major male monastery. This does not account

medieval London", p. 18. **25** The partial martyrology from Navan survives and contains lists of admission of the laity to the confraternity. Bodl. Rawl. B. 486 ff. 16–23, see description Preston, "The canons regular of St Augustine", p. 243. **26** Barron, "The parish fraternities of medieval London", pp 1–14. **27** *Cal. Christ Church deeds*, no. 225 and discussed in Lydon, "Introduction", *Account roll of Holy Trinity, Dublin,* pp xviii–xix. **28** Refaussé and Lennon, "Introduction", *The registers of Christ Church Cathedral, Dublin*, pp 16–19. **29** *Book of Obits*, pp 47, 49. The saying of the placedo and dirge with nine lessons was a common feature of anniversary masses; see Burgess, "A service for the dead", p. 187. **30** *Book of Obits*, pp 82, 50.

for the female conversa, who may have been pious lay women granted the honour of burial in the robes of a lay sister or even the full habit, or they may have been corrodarians.[31] The purchase of a corrodary may have entitled the pious recipient to be buried in the habit of a lay member of the community. Other lay people were allowed the privilege of being buried in full religious habit, so attaining the spiritual benefits of religious vows after a life lived in the lay world. In the list of obits from the Christ Church confraternity, some of the references to women are ambiguous: Margerta Hakket, for example, is listed as "soror nostre" (our sister) which could refer to her admission as a sister of the fraternity, or it may mean that she was granted the privilege of burial in the habit of Augustinian.[32] Moroc and Eua are both described as "conversa nostra" (our conversa), probably meaning that they were lay sisters at or after their deaths.[33] Another woman who is not given a surname in the lists may also be a "conversa", and that is Matilda, described only as "soror" (sister).[34]

Anniversary masses said by priests on the anniversary of death were a common late medieval way of ensuring prayers were said for the departed soul and were usually arranged by the deceased before their death.[35] The names of other prominent lay people were also recorded in other chantry records so that they could have masses said for their souls.[36] There were other bequests which included very precise instructions for how the pious donations were to be used in the recipient church. Thomas Bennet, a citizen of Dublin, and his wife Elizabeth left a large donation of land to Christ Church cathedral to provide for four precentors to "praise and honour" the Holy Trinity and the Blessed Virgin Mary.[37] Alice Cassell wife of John Calff of Lusk, whose will was recorded in 1474, requested that 10*s* of her estate of just over 20*s* should be provided to the priests of her parish church to celebrate the Trental of St Gregory for her soul.[38] This evidence suggests that for the late medieval Anglo-Irish communities there was a vibrant and lively interest in their personal salvation.

Maintaining the buildings housing the sacred spaces of the church was another public and very practical manifestation of personal piety. Churchmen in Ireland, along with those of other parts of Europe, judged that the responsibility of construction and maintenance of church buildings should be shared with parishioners. The synod of Cashel in 1453 stipulated a detailed code concerning church furnishings. So apart from their traditional responsibility of maintaining the nave, the laity were also to provide the missal, silver chalice, alb, stole, chasuble, surplice, a font and vestries. Each parish church was also to have three statues: Christ on the cross, the Virgin Mary and the patron saint. A church bell was also required to toll three times before services. All these were suitable for lay men and women

31 For discussion of the conversi, see Preston, "The canons regular of St Augustine", p. 102; see also Lydon, "Introduction", *Account roll of Holy Trinity, Dublin*, p. xvii. **32** *Book of Obits*, p. 59. **33** *Book of Obits*, pp 54, 80. **34** *Book of Obits*, p. 54. **35** Burgess, "A service for the dead", pp 183–4, describes the usual form of the anniversary mass. **36** Reg. St Saviour, pp 184, 187–8, 193, 195, 198, 216. **37** *Book of Obits*, p. 68. **38** *Register of wills*, ed. Berry, pp 51–3.

to provide and support materially, thus ensuring their own personal salvation and also their remembrance by the parishioners of the future.[39]

Lay women gave generously to the furnishings of churches, either their own parish church, the cathedral which enjoyed their patronage or the church where they chose to be buried. A study of English lay women's piety argues that providing clothing for statues was seen as a particularly appropriate avenue for women to express their piety, and there is some evidence that providing clothing for statues was also popular with women in medieval Ireland, although providing more general materials needed by local churches was at least as popular.[40] In the early sixteenth century Janet Henry made altar linens for the church of Drumcar.[41] Johanna Roche gave Christ Church cathedral a cup called lenoot and a gold bowl. Margarite Holywood gave to the high altar of the same cathedral a good linen cloth or girdle, while the Lady of Killen gave a gold image of the Virgin Mary.[42] Some women showed definite preferences for where their materials should go within the church and which altar they wished to honour. Olive Whyte gave the chapel of St Mary of Christ Church cathedral a chalice as well as money for the works of that chapel, while Cristiana Gylach gave a linen cloth to the chapel of St Edmund the king.[43] Some women gave money towards the purchase of specified church furnishings, showing that they knew intimately what was required for their churches. In 1473 Alice Whyle of Garristown left 10*s*. in her will to make a chalice for the church of Garristown, while a few years later Joan Drywer of Crumlin gave 3*s*. 4*d*. for the gildings of the chalice in her parish church and an overcloth for the altar of the church at Aderrig.[44] Some of the surviving medieval church plate and decoration are known to have been commissioned and donated by women, such as the late fifteenth-century processional cross from Lislaghtin abbey in Co. Kerry donated by Juliana, wife of Cornelius O'Connor, and the chalice from Kilkenny commissioned by William and Kathleen Archer around 1500.[45]

Contribution of a significant and public part of the church fabric was a way of ensuring the memory of the family was continued. Like donations to monasteries, many of these are in the name of the male head of the family, although there is a significant minority which also mention the wife of the head of the family. Sometimes the wife's family is important enough to be recalled specifically, as when Thomas Archer, mayor of Limerick in 1421 and 1426, and his wife Johanna, daughter of David Murighagh or Miagh, built the eastern front and a window in Limerick cathedral. These were embellished with the arms of both Thomas's and Johanna's families.[46] Wealthy women also contributed substantial donations in their own right, as when Isabella Palmer built an

39 Burrows, "Fifteenth century Irish provincial legislation", pp 65–6. **40** French, *The people of the parish*, p. 105, on the English context. **41** "Reg. Cromer", *Louth Arc. Soc. Jn 8* (1933) p. 47. **42** *Book of Obits*, pp 62, 64, 67, 68. **43** *Book of Obits*, pp 72, 76. **44** *Register of wills*, ed. Berry, pp 63–5, 149–51. **45** Hewson, "Sheela-na-Guira", pp 437–8 and Jackson, "Old Church plate of Kilkenny city", p. 24. **46** Begley, *Diocese of Limerick*, p. 385.

addition to the chancel of St Francis' abbey in Kilkenny which included a new east window. She also chose to be buried there.[47]

Other religious statuary was commissioned by women. Free-standing crosses were erected throughout the English area of Ireland in the latter medieval period and may have been particularly favoured by certain families. The Plunkets of Meath were involved in setting up a number of crosses which still survive. A cross at Killeen was erected by Thomas Plunket and his wife Maria Cruys in about 1470, while twenty years later their daughter Elizabeth was involved in setting up a cross at Sarsfieldstown and their grandson, Christopher, built a cross in 1510 at the centre of the manor village of Rathmore. There are a further six crosses from the period which are not inscribed but were on land either owned by Plunketts or associated with families that the Plunket women married into.[48] The maintenance of family traditions of piety were obviously important to this family and they were continued by their daughters as well as by sons.

Commissioning of religious literature was a public act of piety with a private dimension. The great book known as the Book of Lismore was commissioned by a married couple, Finghin Mac Carthaigh Riabhach and Catherine, daughter of Thomas, eighth earl of Desmond.[49] In return for their commission and patronage, the compilers of the book sought the prayers of all who read the hagiography of Patrick, Brigid and Columcille: "Let everyone who shall read this Life of Brigid give a blessing to the souls of the couple for whom this book is written."[50] The book known as the Leabhar Chlainne Suibhne was compiled for Máire inghean Uí Mháille in 1511. The scribe, Ciothruadh Mág Fhionnghaill, noted that the Life of Columcille had been written especially for Máire, and he also added to his colophon a request for a special prayer for his wife, Black-haired Mór.[51] Both the patron and the scribe were believed to receive spiritual benefits from the composition of such a book, and the scribe felt able to direct the prayers of readers to his wife, so she might share in these benefits. This book is an eclectic collection of religious and secular material. The religious material is diverse and suggests the interests of an educated and pious woman of her times, including hagiography of Patrick, Alexis, and St Catherine, and various homilies and treatises likely to interest a pious lay woman, such as the story of a woman who had used bad language in life having half of her corpse thrown out of her grave by the holy people buried near her.[52] These diverse examples of the religious interests of a variety of women illustrate the range of daily conventional religious experiences open to women in medieval Ireland.

Apart from daily religious practices, Irish women also participated in less frequent pious exercises, such as pilgrimage to local or far-off holy places. Pilgrimages to places of especial piety were attempted either as a public expression

47 *The Annals of Ireland by John Clyn*, p. 34. **48** King, "Late medieval crosses in County Meath c.1470–1635", p. 92. **49** *Book of Lismore*, p. v. **50** *Book of Lismore*, p. 34 (Irish) and p. 182 (translation); Patrick, p. 1 and 149; Columcille, p. 20 and 168. **51** *Leabhar Chlainne Suibhne*, on p. 86 of manuscript. **52** Walsh lists the religious material. "Introduction", to *Leabhar*

of personal piety or as penance for sins. Medieval Ireland abounded with sacred sites which were places of spiritual significance and attracted pilgrims from both within Ireland and from further afield.[53] Those on pilgrimage to the many relics held at Christ Church cathedral were protected by law, including the many Gaelic Irish who were able to enter the "land of peace" in order to visit the relics at Christ Church.[54] In 1462, royal protection was granted to all who wished to visit Christ Church and present alms for the restoration of two windows in the cathedral; this protection included eight days safe conduct for both "English rebels" and "Irish enemies".[55] Another internationally famous pilgrimage site was that of St Patrick's purgatory at Lough Derg.[56] There were famous shrines to the Virgin Mary at Navan and at Trim, and there is evidence from both of lay confraternities.[57] There are many miracles recorded for the statue of Mary at Trim and women were among those who sought out its aid, including one pregnant woman who had been delivered of cats.[58] There were also many churches and monasteries throughout Ireland who obtained licence for special indulgences for pilgrims and penitents who visited their relics and altars on specific days.[59] All of these would have been patronised by women. Even if women did not undertake the long pilgrimages themselves, they probably remained interested in stories of them. In Leabhar Clainne Suibhne, the collection of devotional material compiled for Máire, wife of MacSuibhne Fanad, there are two different accounts of the pilgrimage to St Patrick's Purgatory.[60]

Women also undertook extraordinary pious journeys. Some undertook the harzardous journey to the Holy Land, like Richard de Trum and his wife Helene who prepared for a pilgrimage to Jerusalem in the 1230s.[61] Compostela was a popular destination for Irish pilgrims from all communities, although the long distances involved made it a pilgrimage which could only be attempted by those with sufficient means. Although women may have travelled less frequently than men, there were many women who made vows to go to Compostela. In 1320 Edmund Butler, his wife and son James were absolved of their vows to go, because of the problems with the Irish at home; instead they gave money to the Holy Land subsidy.[62] There were large parties who gathered to sail together on the long and well-established journey to Spain, including the 400 pilgrims who were on the boat *Mary London*, captured by pirates in 1473.[63] In 1445, many Irish went on the voyage with Mairgréag Ó Cearbhaill and Evilin daughter of

Chlainne Suibhne, pp xlivii–lviii. **53** Harbison, *Pilgrimage in Ireland*, pp 53–4, gives one list of pilgrimage places in Ireland mentioned in texts. **54** Lydon, "Introduction", *Account roll of Holy Trinity, Dublin*, p. xvii. **55** *Cal. Christ Church deeds*, no. 297. **56** See *The medieval pilgrimage to St Patrick's Purgatory*, ed. Haren and Pontfancy. **57** Hugh Mac Mahon regained his sight after fasting in honour of the image of Mary at Raphoe and Trim, *AFM* 1397. Other miracles from Trim, see *AFM* 1412. **58** *AFM* 1482, the birth of cats, and other animals, is a common motif for miracles in late medieval and early modern Europe. **59** For a discussion of the Augustinian monastic houses which benefited from pilgrimage to relics held, see Preston, "The canons regular of St Augustine", pp 181–5. **60** Meigs, *The reformations in Ireland*, p. 21. **61** *Chart. St Mary's, Dublin*, I, pp 237–8. **62** *Cal. papal letters, 1305–42*, p. 196. **63** *Cal. pat. rolls, 1476–85*, p. 78, cited and discussed by Stalley, "Sailing to Santiago", pp 397–9.

Edmund Fitz Thomas O Ffeargaill, and while Mairgréag returned after receiving the indulgences of St James, Evilin died in Spain along with several others of their group.[64] When Margaret Athy was involved in establishing the Augustinian friary in Galway, her husband was away in Spain on a pilgrimage. She herself then went on pilgrimage to Compostella and intended to visit the Holy Land.[65]

Lay people were required to accept and follow the rules and precepts of the church in order to continue to access the spiritual benefits of attending mass and belonging to the local community of the faithful. Public performance of penance was the usual result of breaching the rules, although continued knowing transgression of these rules would ultimately result in excommunication from the church and denial of the sacraments and prayers of the priests. The meanings women placed on the sacraments and religious services of the church can then be glimpsed by their willingness or otherwise to avoid penance or excommunication or to remedy the sins that might lead them to ecclesiastical censure. Although not an infallible measure, examining women who were excommunicated gives an indication of women's attitudes to conventional piety and religious practice.

There must have been many sins committed by women that earned the sentence of excommunication. The most common one surviving in the records is that of contracting a marriage not recognised by the church or with a partner who was too closely related and so within the prohibited degrees of affinity.[66] Although excommunication did not eventuate in many instances because the couple had agreed to separation or penance, the threat of being excluded from their community through public excommunication from church services was real and must have acted on many as a deterrent. When penance was asked of the offending sinner, it was usually to be performed publicly and the site of its performance was often the church. In 1412, John Peche and Anne Dardyes were ordered by the archbishop of Armagh to do penance for their sin of marriage within the prohibited degrees, after they had received dispensation from the pope. The penance was to consist of fasting and saying one hundred aves and paters every Friday during their marriage.[67] Michael Hardy and Isabella Wale were found guilty in 1519 of having been married "against the edict of the church"; the couple were ordered to separate for the prohibited period and also to perform the penance of placing a pound of wax before the patron of the church.[68]

Lay people who wished to avoid ecclesiastical censure but found it difficult to adhere to the complex marriage rules applied for papal or episcopal dispensation, indicating a willingness to avoid exclusion from the spiritual benefits of their communities. Irish men and women, particularly of ruling families, found it difficult to adhere to the canonically strict rules of marriage. This was often

64 *Annals of Dubhaltach Mac Firbisigh*, p. 211. **65** Hardiman, *History of the town and county of the town of Galway*, p. 272. **66** See Nicholls, *Gaelic and Gaelicised Ireland*, pp 74–6, for a general summary of Irish marriage customs and ecclesiastical law. **67** "Reg. Fleming", p. 150. **68** "Reg. Cromer", *Louth Arc. Soc. Jn 8* (1933) p. 175.

given as the reason for application for dispensation and seems to have normally been acknowledged as reasonable by the papacy. One example of this was when Maurice Obryn and Joan Ingen Y Concobayr desired to marry, even though they were related in the third and fourth degrees, in order to end the wars between their parents and families.[69] Other less well-connected couples often also found the rules difficult and either through ignorance of their affinity or through blithe disregard for the rules of the church went ahead with uncanonical marriages.[70] The reasons behind the requests for dispensation were probably varied and certainly included a prosaic desire for legal inheritance under English common law: offspring not born within a canonically valid marriage were considered illegitimate and so unable to inherit land and titles. Other couples would no doubt have only applied for dispensation when their priest or bishop discovered their sin and made it more expedient for them to try and remedy the situation than to remain publicly outside the church. Since the rules were complex, it is understandable that some were not aware of their relationships. When Nicholas Fanut and Alice Tykill married they were unaware that they were related too closely because Nicholas was godfather to the illegitimate son of Alice's first husband who had since died.[71]

There also must have been cases of distress at excommunication for sins unknowingly committed. One such may have been Honoria nigen Micguillapadric, whose husband, Odo Ochoncoir, had previously committed fornication with both her illegitimate sister and another relative. The reason given for the application for dispensation is that these facts were unknown to Honoria's friends.[72] Another woman who applied on the grounds that public knowledge of her husband's sin would cause her and her children to be defamed was Joan inyymwyt of Ardfert and Limerick, whose husband had known that she was related within the prohibited degrees to one of his former partners. Once Joan found out, the couple desisted from intercourse, although they still lived together.[73] The details given in these applications suggest concern for the consequences of public excommunication, both from denial of sacraments and the public knowledge of the sins.

A further group of men and women used the rules to escape marriages which they regretted, reporting close affinities they had disregarded or were false to the ecclesiastical authorities. These lay people obviously did not regard the personal religious reasons for abstaining from a profitable marriage to be a sufficient impediment, indicating that threat of exclusion from the sacraments was not important to all lay people. Both men and women used these ploys to escape marriages, although it is possible that men used the tactic more often.[74]

69 *Cal. papal letters 1417–31*, p. 221. **70** Pedersen, "Did the medieval laity know the canon law rules on marriage?" pp 111–52 for a discussion of the ways that lay people could manipulate the rules and the extent to which some of them at least had to have known about the rules so as to bring about the cases which were heard before the courts. **71** *Cal. papal letters, 1396–1404*, p. 246. **72** *Cal. papal letters, 1447–55*, p. 426. **73** *Cal. papal letters, 1455–64*, p. 291. **74** *Cal. papal letters, 1362–1404*, p. 45, for a woman repudiating her husband. Simms, however,

As part of a long and complex judgement concerning the legitimacy of an heir, a reference was made to Nicholas de Inteburge of Tipperary who "after quarrels and insulting words" with his wife, in the archbishop of Cashel's court accused her of fornication with his cousin and so obtained a divorce. Later he suffered a change of heart and, alleging fear of God because of the bad luck and early deaths of the witnesses to the false charges, returned to the archbishop's court to obtain a divorce from his second wife.[75] There is no record of the feelings of the women involved.

The process that couples needed to go through to receive their dispensations could be complex and expensive. Although local bishops did have licence to dispense some uncanonical marriages, this was often uncertain, and could lead to further difficulties. In 1369, William Ohuran and Raganylt Ynymadagyn applied to the papacy for dispensation for their marriage within the third degree of affinity, stating that they had already received a dispensation from the archbishop of Tuam, but there were doubts as to his legal ability to give their dispensation so they were forced to apply to the pope.[76] Other unscrupulous churchmen seem to have profited from forged special licences to give dispensations, such as when John Magoreachdai, archdeacon of Killala, was accused of forgery in allowing Henry Baret and Joan de Burgo of Killala to marry even though they were related in the second degree of affinity.[77] These charges are evidence that lay women and men were trying to adhere to the complex ecclesiastical rules and seem to have gone to considerable lengths to ensure the validity of their marriages and to remain within the sphere of usual lay religious participation. This is suggestive of a pious belief in and respect of religious rules and norms of behaviour.

PIETY IN DEATH

For many Gaelic Irish women there are very few records of any of their preparations for death and afterlife. There are no collections of wills, as there are for fifteenth-century Dublin, and the survival of tombs and burial sites, although important, has been random. The most common reference to the piety of the Gaelic Irishwomen mentioned in the annals is that they received the sacrament or order of penance before their deaths. No doubt many of these descriptions are formulaic, based not so much on the circumstances of the women's deaths but on the scribe's or annalist's interpretation of events. Even if the connection with the "real" women is obscure, however, the sacrament of penance was seen by the annalists as important enough to mention for many of the women they

finds that most of the cases in the Armagh registers were initiated by women who had been repudiated by their husbands. "The legal position of Irishwomen", p. 100. **75** Calendar of justiciary rolls, 1313 (NAI KB 2/4), pp 605–8. **76** *Cal. papal letters, 1396–1404*, p. 139. **77** *Cal. papal letters, 1396–1404*, p. 173.

commemorated in the annals. There are numerous examples, spread over all the extant annals. In 1391, the Annals of Loch Cé record that Bebinn, daughter of O'Maelcondire, died "after great penance".[78] In 1378, Mór, daughter of Ua Ferghail, wife of Diarmait Mag Raghnaill, "died a death of unction and penance" as did Margaret, daughter of Conchobhar Ó Briain and wife of Ó Ruairc, in 1512.[79]

For some Anglo-Irish women there survive wills detailing their preparations for death and afterlife. These are from modest collections of wills, most from the later medieval period and the majority from areas around Dublin.[80] This is a small collection compared to the riches available in England, and is totally unrepresentative of women and men from Gaelic Ireland. The time, late fifteenth century, to which the vast majority of the surviving Anglo-Irish wills belong is consistent with the increased use of wills in England where there is an upsurge in numbers of surviving wills in the fifteenth century.[81] It is also clear that women and men wrote wills that have not survived, as there is ample evidence of disputes over provisions of the wills for which there are no other records.[82] For this study wills, fragments of wills and disputes over wills have been considered. There are thirty-two instances of wills or fragments of wills written by women and 102 by men. The majority of the sample is from later medieval Dublin, though there are records from the Ormond territories and from the archdiocese of Armagh as well as some scattered ones from the rest of the island. In her study of the wills of medieval Dublin, Margaret Murphy used ninety-eight wills, with the majority – seventy-four – coming from the single surviving register of wills and dating between 1457 and 1483.[83]

Recently a significant number of scholarly studies of wills in England have not only illuminated the will-making habits of medieval people of different geographical areas, but have also investigated the methodologies informing previous historical research on wills.[84] These have included some timely warnings on the difficulties and opportunities in using wills as sources for conventional lay piety, one scholar going so far as to describe the problems in using wills as "resembling reefs waiting to sink any venturing unwarily to chart the sea of late-medieval faith".[85] Even the phrases used in the will, which may be thought to indicate whatever level of faith the testator had in the ability of religion to help with the hurdles to come, may be so standard as to be useless, or may indicate genuine individual feeling, with often very little to distinguish the two possibilities.[86]

One of the most obvious problems of using wills to measure the goods left for pious purposes is that the will only lists part of what the testator may have

78 *ALC* 1391. **79** *AU* 1378, *ALC* 1512. **80** From *Register of wills*, ed. Berry; there are also wills in other collections of documents, such as Dublin City Franchise roll; Christ Church Deeds. **81** Heath, "Urban piety", p. 209. **82** For example, in 1444 there was a dispute over the wife of John Lomyng's will which was recorded in the register of the archbishop of Armagh, *Registrum Iohannis Mey*, pp 7–8. **83** For a discussion see Murphy, "The high cost of dying", p. 111. **84** Burgess, "Late medieval wills", pp 14–33, summarises the ways that wills have been used to date. **85** Burgess, "Late medieval wills", p. 15. **86** Heath, "Urban piety", p. 212.

wanted done after death and this may have been only a very small part of what the prudent or pious testator had done for his or her soul during life.[87] There is also the probability that some wills with little detail of bequests to ease the testator's soul on its last journey may actually reflect a person who had organised their estate and communicated their wishes to the parish and executors before death and saw no need to also provide a detailed written record.[88] Wills were also only the instructions given to the executors: they do not reflect what actually happened to the property after death and there were certainly executors who flouted the instructions given to them. It has also not proved possible to measure the wealth transferred to the church or monastic institutions because of the common clause in wills allowing executors to dispose of the residue of estates as they saw fit.

Although married women were not technically able to bequeath goods, custom in England and Ireland seemed to work against this and there are many wills legally executed which were made by married women.[89] In England there were increasing moves in the thirteenth and fourteenth centuries for the restriction by common law of the ability of married women to make wills. The church, though, worked actively against this, encouraging married women to make provision for their own souls. The theological theory behind this was that wills were essentially alms for the good of the soul of the donor: all Christians therefore were entitled to make such provision for their own souls.[90] English common law, however, became increasingly determined to prevent married women from exercising control over property regarded as common to the matrimonial estate, which included alienating any property by testament. This was probably always the case for real estate, although it had not generally been accepted for the moveable goods which the woman may have owned or inherited and wished to dispose. Church authorities did not approve of this method of joining the material assets of married couples, but were not able to prevent the increasing trend in common law away from allowing married women to leave wills. Sheehan in his research found no specific instances of excommunication being used against husbands who sought to prevent their wives from bequeathing their moveable goods, but local studies show that there was a decrease in the number of married women making wills towards the end of the medieval period, suggesting that usage was changing.[91]

There is a general allusion to such a situation in Dublin when, in 1347, the citizens complained to the king that "contrary to the usage of the city" married women have been making wills and bequests of "their husbands' goods without licence" and that those husbands who tried to prevent this were excommunicated

87 Burgess, "Late medieval wills", pp 16–17 and Burgess, "A service for the dead", p. 193. **88** Burgess, "Late medieval wills", p. 21. **89** Sheehan, *Marriage, family and law in medieval Europe*, p. 28, and Helmholz, "Married women's wills in later medieval England", pp 165–82. **90** Sheehan, *Marriage, family and law in medieval Europe*, p. 26. **91** Sheehan, *Marriage, family and law in medieval Europe*, p. 27 and Cullum, "And hir name was charité", pp 183–5.

by ecclesiastics. The king ordered this practice to stop.[92] It does not seem to have lessened the practice of married women making wills, though it may have deterred them from doing so without the consent of their husbands. In the wills in this study, of the thirty-two wills made by women, sixteen are by married women, three by women described as widows and eight by women whose marital status was not mentioned, though many were probably widows. Of the married women, thirteen appointed their husbands as executors, indicating that these wills were being made with their husbands' consent.[93] This is a fairly high proportion of wills from married women, though with such a small sample it is difficult to draw very wide-reaching conclusions. It is also likely that some married women did not make wills but relied on their husbands to carry out their bequests for them. This is probably the case with the bequests of Elena wife of Roger de Moenes, a prominent Dublin citizen. In Roger's will he specified bequests to his children of money and moveable goods that were legacies from their mother.[94]

Women were often named as either sole or joint executors of their husbands' wills.[95] The role of executor could be arduous and involved recovery of credits, payment of debts and control of moveable goods, as well as the delivery of bequests.[96] This is an area where women often would have had significant influence over the distribution of property to benefit the soul of their dead husbands. In the wills from Ireland, most of the men appointed their wives to be executors, with records of forty-seven wills of men who appointed their wives as executors either alone or in conjunction with adult children or others. The common phrase used by these testators was similar to that used in the will of John Holtoun, who appointed his wife Magine Graunt his executor, "to dispose of all my goods for the health of my soul as to her may seem most expedient".[97] This is a very high number of men who appointed their wives as executors, over half on the raw figures, which must represent an even greater percentage in actual terms as some were made by clergy, single men and men whose wives had predeceased them.[98]

There are also numerous references to disputes over wills, recovery of debts involved in last testaments and other business arising from deceased estates in which it is obvious that the wife of the deceased is the executor of the will and involved in the legal action on behalf of the estate. The church, which administered cases of disputes over wills, appears to have approved of wives being appointed as executors of their husbands' estates. In a dispute in 1521 over the will of

92 *Cal. anc. rec. Dublin*, I, p. 145. **93** Married women's wills from *Register of wills*, ed. Berry, pp 1, 3–6, 45–7, 51–3, 55–7, 60–6, 75–66, 102–4, 133–5, 142–4, 155–8, also *Cal. Christ Church deeds*, no. 106. **94** T.C.D. MS 1207/85/26. **95** Burgess, "Late medieval wills", p. 20, and see Archer and Ferme, "Testamentary procedure with special reference to the executrix", pp 3–33. **96** Sheehan, *Marriage, family and law in medieval Europe*, p. 207, and Archer and Ferme, "Testamentary procedure with special reference to the executrix", p. 14, who note that a large number of the more extravagant requests for masses and charity could never have been carried out in full. **97** *Register of wills*, ed. Berry, p. 21. **98** Archer and Ferme, "Testamentary

Bernard McKwyer of Kyllaneyr, there were different witnesses who testified that Bernard had not wanted his wife, Patricia Kelaghpatrick, to be executor, and several priests who testified that this had been his intention. Although there is no record of the verdict, it seems that the churchmen involved all favoured the suit of Patricia.[99] When men died intestate, the church officials also seem to have favoured allowing the wives to be executors.[100]

In one English study it appears that the wills of men are often briefer than the wills of their wives, possibly because they had a chance to talk about the testamentary arrangements and so did not need to write them down in as much detail as their widow did later.[101] There is some evidence of this occurring in Dublin, as emerges from one dispute over a bequest to the Christ Church cathedral in 1467. In this case it appears that over thirty years previously, the wife of James Palmer, alias Tiler, one Alicia Lawless, bequeathed to the cathedral her lands in Rathmore and directed the deed to be given immediately to the prior. Alice stated that Matthew Crumpe, her first husband, had left them to the church after her death.[102] Here Alicia was executor of the earlier will and in turn her will was obviously not followed and only after some time and strenuous pressure was the cathedral finally able to receive the intended donation. However, overall there are not enough surviving wills to fully test the hypothesis that men tended to leave less detailed wills than women. Certainly some men left very brief instructions in their wills and then left their wives as executors, such as Thomas Kelly of Skidoo, who died in 1472 specifying only small amounts for his burial expenses in his will.[103] However, the majority of men's wills did include considerable detail about the destination of pious bequests.

Some women obviously disagreed with their husbands' bequests and failed to discharge their obligations, showing that some women assumed considerable control over the assets of their late husbands and were not averse to redirecting resources. In 1317, there was a court case in which it emerged that Lucy, then wife of Robert Neel, had not paid the bishop of Emly a considerable legacy bequeathed to him in her first husband's will. Andrew de Averton, chaplain for the bishop, broke down the door to her grange and took goods to the value of the legacy. She then sued Andrew for damages to the door and won, although it is not clear from the record what become of the redirected legacy.[104] Another case where the wishes of the married couple were probably different occurred in 1504, when evidence was given that when Robert Wyndon and Alice Isaak his wife were on their deathbeds many years previously, Walter Chamflor, abbot of the monastery of St Mary's, Dublin, was present and tried to induce Robert to leave some land to his daughter Alison on condition that it reverted after her

procedure with special reference to the executrix", p. 4 describe the "regular" choice by medieval husbands of their wives as executor of wills. **99** "Cromer' reg.", *Louth Arch. Soc. Jn.* 8 (1933–6) pp 262–3. **100** Two examples are in *Registrum Iohannis Mey*, p. 388 and *Register of wills*, ed. Berry, pp 61–2. **101** Cullum, "And hir name was charité", p. 185, for differences between men's and women's wills. **102** *Cal. Christ Church deeds*, no. 299. **103** *Register of wills*, Berry, ed. pp 18–20. **104** Transcript of plea roll, 11 Ed II (NAI MS KB 2/9).

death to the monastery instead of the cathedral of Holy Trinity. However, Alice refused to give consent to this, leading apparently to the land being claimed by both the monastery and the cathedral.[105] Besides the rather unedifying standover tactics of the abbot, this does demonstrate that women as wives exercised considerable decision-making power over the common property of a marriage when it came to its disposal after death. In other cases when the wishes of a married couple obviously were not compatible, it appears that the legal rights of the man overruled those of his wife. There is a complex case where Thomas Comyn, Lord of Balgriffin, gave land and an advowson to Christ Church cathedral in 1395. The necessary papal and crown permissions were obtained, yet after his death his widow disputed the donation and tried to recover the land. There followed several years of litigation through crown and diocesan courts before the cathedral won the case.[106]

Aside from bequests for religious purposes, the most important spiritual decisions made by lay people were the choice of burial place and the associated allocation of money for funeral expenses. One historian has noted that:

> The grave provided the focus for a dialogue between this world and the next, and was believed to be only a temporary "resting place", a fundamental aspect of medieval eschatology being the belief in bodily resurrection at the Last Judgment.[107]

The burial place indicated the position that the deceased wished to maintain among his or her community and the company in which they desired to await the resurrection. In this way choice of burial place can indicate many aspects of social order within communities as well as the end point of the spiritual life of the deceased.[108] Local studies of medieval English communities suggest that people were most likely to request burial in their local parish church.[109] When the burial choices of women have been specifically examined, the findings in English studies have shown that, although scholars generally have assumed that women would prefer to be buried in women's monastic houses than in male monasteries, there is not much evidence to support this in local studies.[110] Women in medieval England were generally excluded from the choir of the male monasteries in death as well as in life, with burial of female benefactors restricted to the nave of the church, cemeteries and occasionally cloister walks.[111]

Choice of burial place was also determined by social status, with burial in cathedrals or religious institutions to which the testator had given substantial patronage being a signal of considerable prestige.[112] Among those who chose

105 *Cal. Christ Church deeds*, no. 380. **106** Hand, "The Psalter of Christ Church", pp 316–17. **107** Dinn, "Monuments answerable to men's worth", p. 238. **108** Harding, "Burial choice", pp 119–35. **109** Mac Donald, "Women and the monastic life in late medieval Yorkshire", p. 84. **110** Gilchrist, *Gender and material culture*, p. 58. **111** Gilchrist, "Community and self", p. 61. **112** This has been reinforced by archaeological excavations of parish churches; see for

burial in their parish, the elite would usually choose burial inside the church, placing their bodies in physical proximity to the most holy places and also to the daily round of prayers. These positions were usually taken by the wealthy of the community along with significant patrons.[113] The less well-off asked to be buried in the cemeteries of their local parish churches, with the most coveted positions being nearest to the altar.[114] This has been demonstrated in Ireland by both written records and archaeological finds of burials in and around different churches.[115]

For many women in Ireland, the choice of burial place would have been made in accordance with the burial practices of either their husbands' families or less frequently their own birth families. This accords with evidence from England where loyalty to family burial plots in family-patronised monasteries and parish churches was usual.[116] Evidence from archaeological sites suggests that some women were buried in genetically related family groups, possibly their birth families.[117] If the birth family of the woman was prominent, then the choice of her burial and possibly her husband's was in her family's burial place. The Franciscan friary of Ennis, an Ó Briain foundation, was the chosen burial place of the powerful Ó Briain, lords of Thomond.[118] The beautiful Creagh tomb in the friary was built by Mór Ní Bhriain for herself and her husband in 1479.[119] The abbess of Killone, Renalda Ní Bhriain, who died in 1510, requested burial, not in the graveyard of her nunnery but in the friary of Ennis, indicating that she felt a high degree of allegiance to the family.[120]

The majority of women's burial choices were for burial with their husbands, clearly indicating both a sense of loyalty to their partners and combined spiritual and material resources. This is made explicit in the obituary for Gormlaith, wife of Aed Ó Néill son of Con, who died the same year as her husband in 1524. The couple were described as having:

> afforded a kindly and honourable companionship to one another in the world to the time of the death, so may their souls give to one another a cherishing and a companionship of glory in the presence of the Lord.[121]

Choices of burial place for married couples were usually based on paternal family burial places, which may have extended over many generations. In 1353 Gormlaygh, daughter of Ó Domhnaill, wife of Domhnaill Ó Néill, was buried in the friary at Armagh, which was patronised by her husband's family.[122] When

example Milne, *St Bride's church London*. **113** Dinn, "Monuments answerable to men's worth", pp 244–5. **114** Murphy, "The high cost of dying", p. 113. **115** Power, "A demographic study of human skeletal remains", p. 96, and Fry, *Burial in medieval Ireland*. **116** Fry, *Burial in medieval Ireland*, pp 171–80; Golding, "Burials and Benefactions", pp 74–5. **117** One cluster of four female skeletons was recovered from one burial stack at St Peter's church, Waterford. Two of these women had the same genetic malformations in their bones while the other two had another, suggesting that they were a family group. Power, "A demographic study of human skeletal remains", pp 112, 115. **118** *AFM* 1247. **119** Hunt, *Irish medieval figure sculpture*, I, p. 121. Westropp, "Ennis abbey", pp 135–54. **120** NLI MS D 1978. **121** *AConn.* 1524. **122** "The annals of Nenagh", p. 161

Siobhán, daughter of Conn Mac Énrí Mac Eóghain Ó Néill, died in 1535 she was buried in the friary of Donegal which had been founded in 1474 by her husband's family of Ó Domhnaill.[123] At Jerpoint abbey, there are many examples of the patronage of the Butler family, with the grave slabs of Peter son of James Butler of Orchyl and Isabella Blanchfeld his wife who died in 1493 as well as Edmund Walsh and his wife Johanna Butler.[124] A number of members of another branch of the Butler family were buried in the church of St Mary's, Gowran, Kilkenny, indicating a strong family connection there.[125] However, by the sixteenth century one branch of the family had higher aspirations and these are reflected in their burial places. The very fine tomb of Margaret Fitzgerald and her husband Piers Butler, earl of Ormond, is in St Canice's cathedral, Kilkenny, representing their desire in death to be present in the most important of the churches in their area of influence, as might be expected from the ambitious Piers.[126]

For poorer people, it appears that their pious bequests were to the church in which they chose to be buried, usually their parish church. Thus in 1472 Agnes Bourke, wife of Thomas Hassard of Balscadden, wished to be buried in the church of St Mary, Balscadden, and her donations were 12*d.* each to the vicar and to the church itself.[127] Some women were very precise in their instructions about their burial place, such as Margaret Nugent, widow of Sir Thomas Newberry, who wished to be buried in the chapel of St Mary in the parish church of St Michan, and left all her moveables not needed to pay for debts to that chapel.[128] Her request signalled a particular devotion to the Virgin, as well as suggesting that she was childless.

Burial expenses were often specified in medieval wills. Such expenses could be heavy and represented considerable expenditure on both the social display of the funeral and the spiritual benefits which occurred at such a significant time in the journey of the soul. These expenses did not pay only for the display of the funeral, but were a considerable source of charity, any funds remaining from the funeral being distributed to the poor of the parish as well as specific alms for distribution after the funeral. In one case from Limerick, the church of the Friars Minor were required to spend 32*s.* on the burial of John Maunsel, which they expected to be reimbursed from his estate. To do this they had to pledge a cup to borrow the money.[129] Margaret Browneusyn of Killadoon, whose husband and son survived her, left a detailed list of funeral expenses for her burial in the church of St James, Killadoon. There was to be 2*s.* 4*d.* for the burial, 2*s.* for wax, 8*s.* for bread, 8*s.* for ale, 10*s.* for meat and 7*s.* 8*d.* for the principal.[130] Margaret was not necessarily a very wealthy woman, and in common with other poorer testators, she left very precise amounts to be spent from her estate.[131] The

and Lynn, "Excavation in the Franciscan Friary church, Armagh", pp 63 and 78. **123** *AConn.* 1535. **124** Langrishe, "Notes on Jerpoint Abbey," p. 190. **125** Hunt, *Irish medieval figure sculpture*, I, p. 168, and Roe, "Funerary monuments of south-east Ireland", p. 216. **126** Hunt, *Irish medieval figure sculpture*, I, p. 186 ff. **127** *Register of wills*, ed. Berry, pp 45–7. **128** *Register of wills*, ed. Berry, pp 78–81. **129** Transcript of plea roll no. 116, (NAI KB 2/9), pp 72–3. **130** *Register of wills*, ed. Berry, pp 3–5. **131** Murphy, "High cost of dying", pp 114–15.

amounts for food would have been shared between the mourners, the celebrants of the funeral mass and the poor of the parish. Alice Andrews, wife of Patrick Rosell, and Joan Usbern also left instructions specifically for wax for use at their funerals.[132] If any funeral expenses were noted, it was invariably for wax for candles. A fine display of lights was considered an appropriate way of honouring the dead and ensuring their spiritual health. The wax from these lights was then given to the parish church, and usually proved to be a welcome donation.[133]

Apart from the funeral, there were also other provisions for the souls of the departed. Expenses were varied but included donations for the building programmes of both the burial church and other churches, bequests of liturgical items, as well as pious donations to mendicants and the poor.[134] Some of the wealthier women included specific donations apart from those for their parish church and funeral expenses. Agnes Laweles bequeathed money for the works of the parish church where she requested burial, as well as for the works of three other churches, the White friars of Dublin and the Franciscans.[135] Why these churches were remembered is not made clear in the will, although it does indicate that Agnes was familiar with churches all around Dublin. Not surprisingly, women were also more likely than men to leave moveable goods for the good of their souls. Joan White left wheat, malt, a cow and wax for her funeral and then, as mentioned earlier, left some items for the use of her neighbours for the good of her soul and those of her ancestors.[136] There were also some disputes over the bequests of women, although generally it appears that the church went to some lengths to ensure that their wishes were carried out. In the late thirteenth century Eleanor Purcell bequeathed the tenth part of produce from her manor of Maylen to St Mary's priory, Rathkeale, in Co. Limerick. After her death her son Hugh contested her right to alienate the produce. The matter was settled with a compromise, however the intention of the donation was carried out.[137]

Possibly reflecting their decreased ability to control property, the women whose wills survive do not generally leave large amounts of cash to charitable causes. Cecily Langan, for example, left the church of St Mary of Grace Dieu a cow and a gratuity in the town for her soul.[138] Since the majority of these women predeceased their husbands it could be that any major pious donations which had been arranged from their matrimonial estate would be detailed in their husbands' wills. It could also be that because the bulk of the matrimonial property was still intact and in the control of their husbands they had very little disposable income of their own to donate and bequeath. This is not necessarily a situation that indicates that the spiritual needs of these women were not being met. Sometimes the life use of a valuable piece of moveable property was bequeathed to

132 *Register of wills*, ed. Berry, pp 75–6, 125–6. **133** Burgess, "A service for the dead", p. 188. **134** Murphy, "High cost of dying", pp 116–17. **135** *Register of wills*, ed. Berry, pp 133–5. **136** *Register of wills*, ed. Berry, pp 47–8. **137** Westropp, "A survey of the ancient churches of the county of Limerick", p. 391. **138** *Register of wills*, ed. Berry, pp 65–6.

a female relative and after her death it was to go to a religious institution. This was the case with a cup called "Grobbe" owned by Robert, son of John Passavaunt, and bequeathed to his mother for life and after her death to the high altar of St John's for a chalice.[139] There is no way to tell from the will itself what this arrangement signifies; it may mean that the final resting place of the cup was an agreement between mother and son; it may mean that the cup had been inherited by Robert and it had always been destined for the church at some point, or it may mean that this arrangement was of Robert's choosing and indicated his own pious intentions. This particular testator left almost all his real property to his mother for life, then to a relative for life and then to Christ Church cathedral.

In the wills of some widows it is possible to see what may have been joint marital decisions. Joan Stevyn, widow, left a cup of silver overgilt with a band in her son's possession for the health of her soul and that of her husband to the abbot and monastery of St Mary's in Dublin.[140] Although there is every likelihood that this may indicate the pious wish of Joan herself, it may also represent an agreement between the couple as to how to manage their resources for their spiritual health. It is unfortunate that there are so very few wills of married couples in which the intentions of the couple for the disposal of their marital estate can be judged.

In life and death, lay women in Ireland expressed their personal religious feelings and piety within the spaces in which they lived. There is evidence for personal charity and piety in the homes of women who had personal altars, private confessors and priests, as well as those women who gave alms to the needy. Gaelic Irishwomen were praised for these personal attributes emphasising piety and generosity. Women participated in the rituals offered by their parish churches and priests, they went to mass, had the last rites on their deathbeds, contributed to the upkeep of their parish churches and family monasteries, built tombs and chose to be buried where their loyalties were strongest. When able they also went to considerable trouble and expense to go on pilgrimage both to holy places within Ireland and abroad to Compostela, Rome and the Holy Land. The evidence for their religious activities is scattered, reflecting the fact that lay women lived in the wider community. They were present throughout the landscapes of medieval Ireland and so were the signs of their piety and interactions with the church.

139 *Cal. Christ Church deeds*, no. 290. **140** *Register of wills*, ed. Berry, pp 159–62.

CHAPTER 2

Women's patronage of religious institutions

In Ireland, as elsewhere in medieval Europe, expressing personal and familial piety included patronage of religious institutions. The form of these donations was varied, but the most enduring and most expensive were the donations of land. Evidence for donations of land have survived better than evidence of more ephemeral piety such as prayers, mass attendance and personal religious devotions. Although the reasons for donation to monastic institutions and churches no doubt were varied, few reasons were recorded in the formulaic language of the land charters and deeds of transfer. Personal religious feelings, and the desire to ensure the spiritual well-being of family members in a culture that placed a high value on prayers for the dead, were the overt reasons for patronage of monasteries which provided the services of monks and nuns to pray for lay supporters. In many donations these were the main reasons for patronage. Other more secular concerns were also present for some donors, although teasing out different motivations is difficult. In order to probe beneath the bare facts of lay support for religious houses, patterns of donations need to be analysed in order to investigate why wealthy lay women transferred property to the monasteries.

Although precise calculations and comparisons are not possible given the state of the records, there is no evidence to suggest that women were more or less likely to patronise women's houses than male houses. Contemporary views may have been that women were particularly pious for supporting nuns, or that the support of nuns was particularly appropriate for wealthy women, but the evidence is so slight that no firm conclusions can be drawn. In the mid-fifteenth century, Órlaidh daughter of Muircheartach Ó Ceallaigh was praised for many acts of generosity and piety, among them: "Tis a noble deed to maintain the ladies who have chosen virginity; their expense is borne by the princess of the Bóinn, the white branch of the royal stock."[1] The poetic conceits which were commonly employed in praise poetry mean that widespread attitudes to women supporting convents or individual religious women cannot be gauged from this description. Órlaidh's piety and nobility were enhanced by her support for nuns and this is unlikely to have been an isolated instance of such an opinion.

The other factor which may have swayed wealthy women in their choice of monastic houses to support was that there were many more monastic houses for

1 *Aithdioghluim dána*, vol. 37, p. 42; vol. 40, p. 26.

men and local houses were more likely to attract support than far-flung establishments. Women were likely to have found that channelling their expendable resources towards monastic institutions that were favoured by their husband's family or were closer geographically made more sense than seeking out a far-flung convent for women, perhaps in hostile territory.

There were differences between Anglo-Irish and Gaelic Irish women's patronage of religious institutions. These were based on differences in legal abilities to own, sell and donate land. In Gaelic Ireland, legal ownership of land was generally restricted so that major donors of land to religious institutions were almost always male heads of families. The Gaelic legal tracts specified that land could not be alienated by women, and though they might have a life interest in land after the death of their husbands or fathers, they could not bequeath it.[2] There is evidence that Gaelic Irishwomen could inherit land, in pledge for their dowry or marriage portions, that would be redeemed on payment of cash or kind.[3] Notwithstanding these restrictions there are instances where women did donate land, though this would have been with the consent of their male relatives. Derboghyll daughter of Diarmait Mac Murchada was a major patron of Cistercian abbey of St Mary's in Dublin, donating large tracts of land with her husband and alone in the 1190s.[4] Lasarina, daughter of Cathal Crobderg Ó Conchobair, wife of Ó Domhnaill, gave a half townland of her marriage dowry, Rosbirn, to the monastery of Loch Cé in 1239. This land was in an area controlled by Ó Domhnaill at this time, so presumably the land had been given to Lasarina by her husband.[5] It was more usual for the wives of Gaelic Irish chiefs to control considerable moveable wealth that they were expected to use to enhance their position.[6] In 1157, for example, among the many prominent donations to the newly founded monastery of Mellifont was the gift of three ounces of gold as well as a gold chalice for the altar of Mary and cloth for nine other altars by Derbforgaill, daughter of Murchad Ua Maíl Sechnaill and wife of Tigernán Ua Ruairc.[7] These types of donations are more usual for Gaelic Irish women, while records of donations of land to monasteries by Gaelic Irish women are not as common.[8]

When the Anglo-Normans arrived they brought with them land ownership customs that meant women had access to land in different ways to Gaelic Irish women. The main ways that women acquired land under these laws was through dower rights as widows or inheritance. Under English common law, married women had only minimal authority to control property. Any property a woman

2 Simms, "The legal position of Irishwomen", pp 105–6 and for the later period see O'Dowd, "Women and the law in early modern Ireland", pp 96ff. **3** Nicholls, *Gaelic and Gaelicised Ireland*, pp 76–7. **4** *Chart. St Mary's Dublin*, I, pp 31–4. **5** *AFM* 1239, and see note by the editor, p. 298. **6** See among others McKenna, "The gift of a lady", pp 87–9 and Hall, "Women and religion", pp 34–6. **7** *AFM* and also see Watt, *Church in medieval Ireland*, p. 43. **8** For a discussion of secular and religious patronage patterns among Gaelic Irishwomen see McKenna, "The gift of a lady", pp 84–94.

did own was assumed under the legal ownership of her husband on their marriage and he could alienate it if he chose, although there was the safeguard that if he did so without the consent of his wife these transactions would only be valid for the duration of the marriage, because of the need to protect the dower of the wife.[9] English common law allowed widows a dower of the life interest in one third of their husbands' property if there were children and one half if there were not.[10] The laws of dower were specifically transferred to Ireland in 1216, and women were allowed to bequeath the profits of their dower as they wished, as long as the normal services were reserved to the lord of the fee.[11] The woman could not, however, do so during the life of her husband. There were checks to the disposal of marital property to the detriment of a woman's dower and, by the thirteenth century, royal judges in England were refusing to accept consent of a wife during marriage to the alienation of dower land as a bar to the widow later claiming dower of a third of all the lands which her husband had held during his life.[12] Under English law as it operated in Ireland, women also could inherit in the absence of legitimate male heirs, although the inheritance was then deemed to be partible, or divided equally between all the female heirs.[13] Overall, these laws meant that women who lived under English law could inherit land from their male relatives, although while they were married this land was legally controlled by their husbands. As widows, these women also had control over their dower, which included donating profits from any land that after their deaths reverted to their husbands' heirs.

Many women chose to use their property to express their piety and patronise religious institutions with either land or rents from property. The charters and chartularies where donations were recorded, however, frequently conceal or obscure the intentions or even the existence of women donors. As Penelope Gold has noted, women occupied the margins of recorded property transactions and moved to centre stage only under quite specific circumstances.[14] Only the person who had legal control of the property could donate or sell it and women had unlimited legal control of land only in specific circumstances. Nevertheless, charters reveal that women were significant partners in management and disposal of family lands for the mutual benefit of all members of the family.[15] It is thus important to look for women's activities not just in their donations but also in other transactions that represented decisions of whole families.

9 Smith, "Women's property rights", p. 167. **10** Simms, "Women in Norman Ireland", p. 15 and Biancalana, "Widows at common law", pp 255–329. **11** *Statutes of Ireland, King John-Henry V*, p. 9; and the "Provisions of Merton" promulgated in 1236, p. 27. For a discussion of dower rights earlier than this in the case of Aoife, widow of Strongbow, see Flanagan, *Irish society*, p. 125. **12** Biancalana, "Widows at common law", pp 305 ff. **13** *Statutes of Ireland, King John-Henry V*, p. 30. **14** Gold, *The lady and the Virgin*, pp 116–17. **15** Johns, "The wives and widows of the earls of Chester", pp 117–32.

WOMEN'S PATRONAGE PATTERNS

Lay patronage of monastic houses is relatively easy to access given the archival survival of cartularies where charter information was transferred for ease of use. The surviving cartularies of six monastic houses were examined: St Mary's, Dublin; St Thomas the Martyr, Dublin; St John the Baptist outside the Newgate, Dublin; All Saints, also in Dublin; and two outside the city of Dublin – the dependent cells of Llanthony Prima and Secunda at Colp and Duleek (Co. Meath) and the priory of Tristernagh (Co. Westmeath). These six monasteries are a good sample of the monastic houses in the colony of Ireland. The Cistercian monastery of St Mary and the Victorine monastery of St Thomas were the largest and wealthiest monasteries in the colony, the Augustinian priory of All Saints was a smaller urban priory and the hospital of St John under the order of Fratres Cruciferi was probably the largest and wealthiest of the hospitals which were established in the Anglo-Norman colony.[16] The holdings of the cells of the English monasteries of Llanthony in Meath and the priory of Tristernagh are examples of the rural monastic houses which attracted support mostly from local wealthy families.[17]

The sampled cartularies record charters made between the beginning of Anglo-Norman settlement and the sixteenth century, with most donations occurring in the late twelfth and early thirteenth centuries after the initial settlement and before the Statute of Mortmain was promulgated in Ireland in the late thirteenth century.[18] There are 1,034 records of donations in these cartularies and of these there are 297 charters (29 per cent) in which women were involved in the donation in some way.

It is not always possible to distinguish the difference between deeds of donation and deeds of leasing or sale, especially after the introduction of the Statute of Mortmain, and although I have excluded obvious examples of leases, it is possible that some of the charters which appear to be donations were in fact sale or leasing agreements.[19] Another category which presents some difficulties is confirmation charters sought by monastic houses from heirs of earlier grants to ensure secure possession of title. These deeds are also not always distinguishable from original donor charters, and even when they are confirmation deeds they have been included because they generally represent continued active patronage and usually include pious wishes of the confirming donor.

16 See the introductions by Gilbert to his editions of the cartularies of St Mary's and St Thomas'; there have also been several particular studies on these monasteries and their land holdings; Ó Conbhuí, "The lands of St Mary's Abbey", pp 21–86; Gwynn, "The early history of St Thomas' abbey," pp 1–35. The priory of St John the Baptist has been examined by Hennessy, "The priory and hospital of New Gate", pp 41–54. **17** For specific studies on the property of Llanthony see Brooks, "Fourteenth century monastic estates in Meath", pp 140–9, and Simms, "The geography of Irish manors", pp 291–326. For Tristernagh priory see Eager, "Tristernagh priory", pp 25–36. **18** Brand, "The licensing of mortmain alienations", pp 125–44, and "King, church and property", pp 481–502. **19** Scrase, "Working with British

Table 1. Donor charters in the sample

Percentages are rounded to the nearest whole number.

House	*Total number*	*Percent with women*
All Saints	52	23
St John	298	102
Llanthony	93	23
St Mary	208	51
St Thomas	292	55
Tristernagh	91	27
Total	1034	281

It is not easy to assess women's intentions concerning donations of property when their control of property was usually subject to their husbands' and families' legal authority. The charters showing women as leading donor reveal only some of the donations instigated by or involving women. This means that many charters that do not mention women at all may be the end result of family consultation about the expenditure of joint resources for mutual spiritual welfare. Some evidence of this occasionally emerges in the sample documents. In 1302, Richard le Noble assigned his rights in his lands in Jordanston to the Hospital of St John, then in 1318 his widow, Mathie, confirmed the donation.[20] Since Richard did not mention his wife in his original charter, there would have been no way of knowing that she was or would be involved in this transaction if not for the subsequent charter. Another example is when Reginald de Turbeville donated land to St Thomas's and did not mention his wife in any other way except to indicate that the lands in question had been her marriage portion. This could suggest that she was now dead or that she may have been involved in the transaction, but the language almost totally excludes her.[21] There are a number of remaining charters which do show women in an active role. The women who appear in the sample cartularies appear in one or more of five categories – alienor; joint alienor; consentor; spiritual beneficiary; and witness.[22] Almost all the women are also defined within the cartularies by their relationships to their families, so women appear as wives, mothers, daughters, sisters. They also occasionally appear defined by other relationships, such as feudal overlord.

property records," p. 24. **20** *Reg. St John Dublin*, pp 138–9. **21** *Reg. St Thomas, Dublin*, p. 33. **22** Similar categories have been used in other studies of women through charters; see John, "The wives and widows of the earls of Chester", p. 188.

Table 2. Categories of women participating in donor charters

The percentage figures refer to the category figure as a percent of the total number of charters referring to women in that house. Some women are mentioned in two or more roles.

House	*Percent*				
[total number of women's charters]	*Alienor*	*Joint alienor*	*Consentor*	*Spiritual beneficiary*	*Witness*
All Saints [23]	39	13	22	26	4
St John [102]	47	10	16	25	3
Llanthony [23]	43	13	17	22	4
St Mary [50]	24	20	24	30	8
St Thomas [55]	29	9	15	38	16
Tristernagh [27]	26	0	7	60	3

CATEGORIES OF PARTICIPATION

Sole alienor

The first category of charters to be analysed are those where the sole donor or alienor of the land or rent from land is a woman. These are easily identified in the cartularies and make up a significant minority of women's charter involvement. In Gold's study of eleventh- and twelfth-century Angevin donor charters, she finds that 11.9 per cent of donations and sales to monasteries were made by women. In other studies of women's charter participation on the continent the range is similar.[23] Herlihy gives percentages for women appearing as principal alienors of land in charters for the twelfth century in five regions of Europe: Italy 9 per cent; Spain 18 per cent; S. France 9 per cent; N. France 9 per cent; and Germany 12 per cent.[24] In Cownie's survey of 143 early Anglo-Norman donor charters, she finds that 14.68 per cent were from female donors.[25] Within the present sample study there are 102 charters where a woman is the sole alienor, or 9.8 per cent of the total charters, a figure which is similar to the figures obtained for other parts of Europe. As expected, the women who were sole donors of land or assets are defined as widows in a majority of charters, although there are a number who are not defined at all. Of the 102 charters, thirty-six were from women defined as widows, and a further fourteen were women defined as widowed daughters, making a total of fifty women who were able to alienate property because of the legal abilities afforded by their

23 Gold, *The lady and the Virgin*, pp 121–2. **24** Herlihy, "Land, family and women", pp 108–9, particularly table 3 and graph 3. **25** Cownie, *Religious patronage*, pp 153–5. In this sample she is actually examining the types of *pro anima* requests rather than the status of the donor.

widowhood. This is to be expected considering that widows were the largest group of women under English common law to control property. There are also a further fourteen charters where the status of the woman alienor is not stated, and these women most were probably widows. Single women were also able to alienate property, and women defined only as daughters donated property in twenty-seven (26 per cent) of the women's charters. Some of these women may also have been widowed at the time of the donation, their designation as daughter serving to indicate that the property almost certainly originated with their own family. Few charters explicitly state where the women's assets originated. One example is the charter where Leuki donated ecclesiastical rights to lands in Cork to the abbey of St Thomas and she stated in her charter that these had been part of her dower, a third of the land her husband Luke of London had conquered.[26] Among these raw numbers are several where the same woman donates several pieces of property in different charters.

Women who were married could not alienate land without their husbands' explicit consent. The one exception to this in the sample was in the 1190s, when Basilia, the sister of Earl Richard Fitz Gilbert known as Strongbow, and wife first of Raymond le Gros and then Galfrid Fitz Robert, was an important patron of the newly established royal monastery of St Thomas.[27] In some of these grants she is acting with one of her husbands, and in others she is acting alone.[28] In two deeds where she is acting alone, she is probably married to Raymond as she donates the land for the souls of "my father, Gilbert, and my brother, Earl Richard and my lord, Raymond".[29] This certainly indicates that the land she is donating is in her control and that she is exercising that control on her own. Since three of the charters in the sample where the woman's status is defined as daughter alone were from Basilia when she was married, it is possible that a few of the other daughters' charters were from women who were also married. There is evidence from twelfth-century Anglo-Norman England that aristocratic married women could exercise considerable control over some parts of their property, particularly if this property was their inheritance. For example, Hawise, countess of Gloucester, issued her own charters alienating lands from her marriage portion during her husband's lifetime in late twelfth-century England.[30] Another married woman who probably donated land while her husband was alive was Alicia, daughter of William Brun and wife of Gilbert Lyvet, who gave property to St Thomas' monastery in Dublin.[31] Other women besides the celebrated Basilia donated their own land for pious purposes, with their husband's consent. Elicia, daughter of Adelem the brother of Hamund of Bristol, donated lands to

26 *Reg. St Thomas, Dublin*, pp 207–8. **27** Basilia married Raymond le Gros in 1174. See Orpen, *Ireland under the Normans*, I, p. 336. **28** With Raymond le Gros, her first husband, Basilia gave the advowsons of the church of Radsilan with surrounding lands, and rents. *Reg. St Thomas Dublin*, pp 113–14. With her second husband, Galfrid, she confirms this grant and adds land to it, pp 112–13. **29** *Reg. St Thomas Dublin*, pp 110–11. **30** Johns, "Wives and widows of the earls of Chester," pp 129–30. **31** *Reg. St Thomas Dublin*, pp 374–5.

the abbey of St Mary's, with the consent of her husband Stephen de Meisintun in the later twelfth century.[32]

Joint alienor

The next category to be discussed is that of joint alienor, when women make donations together with another person, almost always their husband. The usual language used here is significant:

> Let it be known to all here present and in the future, that I, Reginald Camera and Roes my wife give and concede and with this charter we confirm to God and the Church of St John the Baptist at Llanthony prima and the canons serving God therein ...[33]

The verbs used in such deeds are first person plural and the cartularies often mention that both husband and wife have affixed their separate or joint seals to the charter. As Johns has noted, in her study of the charters involving the wives of the earls of Chester, joint charters convey no sense of female dependency, suggesting rather that the husband and wife are acting together.[34]

In the charters in this sample, thirty-one refer to women as joint alienors. Four charters in this category give the woman's status as married daughter, which almost certainly means that the land originally belonged to their fathers. In many cases the charters refer to land which belongs to the woman, either as her marriage portion, dower or inheritance. One example of this is when, in about 1280, Thomas Blund and his wife Elena de Lyvet donated the rents of land originally owned by Galfrid de Lyvet, her father, to the Hospital of St John the Baptist, Dublin.[35] Although many of the joint charters do not indicate where the common land or assets originated, for many it is probably reasonable to assume that when the father of the woman is named, the assets were originally hers. Under English law, the property of the wife was controlled by her husband, yet during the twelfth and particularly the thirteenth centuries there is increasing evidence that women's own property, particularly dower, was regarded as outside that control as far as permanent alienation. This began to mean that in order for charters to be upheld after a husband's death, his widow had to be shown to have consented to the original deed and usually also that some other property had been substituted for her dower.[36]

Since women could acquire property jointly with their husbands, transactions that to some extent protected them from dower disputes, they could also jointly alienate such property.[37] This is difficult to trace in the charters of the monastic

32 *Chart. St Mary's Dublin*, I, p. 325. Dates are approximate. **33** *Ir. chart. Llanthony*, p. 98. **34** Johns, "Wives and widows of the earls of Chester", p. 122. **35** *Reg. St John Dublin*, p. 159. **36** Biancalana, "Widows at common law", pp 306, 312–13; See also Smith, "Women's property rights", p. 167. **37** Biancalana, "Widows at common law", p. 284, points out that widows if put out of property jointly acquired with their husbands could claim entry under writ of *novel*

houses because only some of the preceding secular charters are included in the records. However, in a brief survey of surviving secular charters, there are many where husbands and wives acquired and disposed of land jointly. In 1324, Sarra de Thobir conceded to John de Kynnegth and Margaret, his wife, land with buildings in the suburb of Dublin. In the next year John and Margaret granted the land to Nicholas de Eteley.[38] Some joint donations of land to monastic houses then undoubtedly indicate joint acquisitions of the couple and not the dower or inheritance of the woman. These donations may indicate deliberate policies of acquiring land outside of the family assets with the intention of providing for the spiritual welfare of the family.

Consentors

The category of consentor has been distinguished in this study from that of joint alienor, although other scholars such as Gold do not find significant differences between joint (co) alienor and consentor.[39] The practice of obtaining the consent from relatives was common in the early development of land transfers until the mid-thirteenth century.[40] Many consentors may have been women whose dower was potentially involved in the transaction rather than joint alienors where the property was the woman's marriage portion or inheritance. The other explanation is that joint alienors were more likely to be women who were the main instigators of the donation, although they needed to be linked with their husband's in the charter. Consentors then may have been women who agreed with their husband's or relative's donation but may not have been the driving force behind it.

Since there are very small numbers involved in the sample and there is little other information to consider, it would be pushing the evidence too far to insist on definite differences in these categories. There are also significant exceptions, where the term consentor probably has more in common with the category of joint alienor. This can be seen particularly in earlier examples, such as when Basilia wife of Raymond le Gros and sister of Strongbow both consented and witnessed a charter by her husband.[41] Consentors were also not always wives, whereas joint alienors were almost exclusively wives. This may again indicate different relationships to the assets being donated. In the sample there are forty-nine charters where women were included as consentors. Of these forty-nine women, forty consented to charters of their husbands.

Witnesses

Gold found in her study of monastic charters in France that there were very few women witnesses, and these women were not interested parties to the transactions.[42] Conversely Postles, in his study of the witnesses of twelfth-century

disseisn. **38** *Reg. St John Dublin*, pp 121–2. **39** Gold, *The lady and the Virgin*, p. 120. **40** Hymans, "The charter as a source of the early common law", p. 183. **41** "An unpublished charter of Raymond le Gros", pp 167–9. **42** Gold, *The lady and the Virgin*, p. 120, n. 10.

English charters, finds that when women were included as witnesses they were usually described as wives and implicitly therefore renouncing rights of dower.[43] This is confirmed in Johns' study of the charters of the wives of the earls of Chester, where she notes that the act of witnessing charters indicates that the witnesses were present while the charter was drawn up and that the women witnesses were clearly participating in the transfer of land signified by the charter.[44]

In the charters in this sample there are sixteen charters with women witnesses. Although the numbers are small they do merit some consideration. Some women witnesses were the daughters and wives of the first Anglo-Normans to arrive in Ireland. In this category is Basilia, sister of Strongbow, and Amabilia, sister of Meiler FitzHenry justiciar of Ireland between 1199 and 1208, and married to Walter de Riddlesford, one of Strongbow's followers.[45] There were some charters where the women witnesses may have been disinterested in a similar way to those involved in the charters studied by Johnson. Lady Basilia, sister of Strongbow, for example, witnessed some charters as an apparently disinterested party, being signatory to two charters in the Register of the Hospital of St John and one in the Register of St Thomas.[46] There are also five women whose status was not defined. They were possibly disinterested parties, included because they were important land owners in the area. One of these women was Margery de Lacy, wife of Hugh de Lacy, who was witness to the grant of a mill by John Tyrel to the priory of Tristernagh in about 1250.[47]

Thirteen of the female witnesses in the donation charters are defined as wives of the donors. When Amabilia signed two charters issued by her husband Walter de Riddlesford in about 1200, she was also defined as a consentor, signalling her active involvement in the donation. In another charter she is defined also as the daughter of Henry, and as well as witnessing the donation she also consents.[48] There are also three charters where the female witness is included in the list of spiritual beneficiaries of the pious donation.[49] In the charter where Osbert de Coleshulla gave to the abbey of St Thomas the tithes of his territory in Uriel, both his wife Agatha and his son Alexander sign, after the chaplains and before the clerks, signifying the family's support for Osbert's donation.[50] These examples support the findings of studies of women witnesses in English charters, rather than those of the northern French samples examined by Gold. Although there were some exceptions, clustered towards the earliest years of the Anglo-Norman colony in Ireland, women who were included as witnesses in the charter information were all involved in some way in the transfer of land and probably signalling their consent by witnessing the deeds.

43 Postles, "Choosing witnesses in twelfth-century England", pp 340–1. **44** Johns, "The wives and widows of the earls of Chester", p. 124. **45** Brooks, "The de Ridelisfords", p. 129. **46** *Reg. St John Dublin*, p. 269 and pp 263–4. *Reg. St Thomas Dublin*, pp 106–7. **47** *Reg. Trist.*, p. 32. **48** *Chart. St Mary's Dublin*, I, p. 30; *Reg. St Thomas Dublin*, p. 369. **49** Claricia wife of John, son of Dermic, *Reg. All Saints*, p. 23; Amabilia wife of Robert de Mandeville, *Reg. St Thomas Dublin*, p. 28; Mabilia wife of Robert Taillefer *Reg. St Thomas*, p. 30. **50** *Reg. St Thomas Dublin*, p. 49.

Spiritual benefits

The final category to be examined is what I have termed spiritual beneficiaries. These are the women who were named in the list of "pro anima" recipients. In almost all donation charters there is a list of those whose souls the donor wishes the donation to benefit. Many men and women when donating property to the monasteries included the formula that the donations were for the benefit of their own souls and other relatives such as their wives, descendants and parents. In 1230, for example, Galfrid de Kiweshac promised an annual donation to God, St Mary and the Hospital of St John the Baptist of Dublin:

> for the salvation of my soul, and M. my wife and my heirs and for the souls of my father and my mother and for the souls of our ancestors and descendants.[51]

Another common and very general dedication was for "the souls of all the departed faithful". The language used is formulaic and cannot be relied upon to depict wholly the intentions of the donors, yet donors chose to include different people as benefactors of the spiritual benefits accruing from their own donations and it was not universal that the health of the souls of the relatives would be included.[52] They were also not always viewed by the law as meaninglessly formulaic: in England in the earlier twelfth century it appears that when a woman was believed to have received some spiritual benefit in return for her husband's gift of her dower her own rights to this land were revoked.[53]

Women who were named in "pro anima" clauses have been included in this sample because the women mentioned probably had a particular interest in the donation, which may have included some control over the form or destination of the donation. Women's active involvement is not usually evident when they are named in this category, although there are exceptions. When in 1240 Raymond Lamboc gave the canons of All Saints priory the use of peat on his land near Fynglas the spiritual beneficiaries he named were his wife Alice Bret, and his mother and father. Although he appears as the sole alienor, the gift is referred to as "our donation" and the seal used is "our seal", indicating that the gift was probably a joint one, even though Alice Bret did not appear as a joint alienor or consentor to the deed.[54] Generally, however, the women mentioned as spiritual beneficiaries in charters do not appear in any other capacity in the deed, making this category the most speculative chosen for this sample and more open to both clerical formulae and the loving wishes of men without the involvement of their female relatives. The names may also have survived due to accidents of scribal activity. That is, there may have been many more names in the original charters that later were compressed by scribes in the cartularies.

In the sample there are eighty-nine charters that mention women as spiritual beneficiaries. This only includes women who are named specifically; there are many more charters where a male donor made a donation with spiritual

51 *Reg. St John Dublin*, p. 232. **52** For discussion see Cownie, *Religious patronage*, pp 153–8. **53** This was included in the Leges Henrici Primi. Biancalana, "Widow at common law", p. 306. **54** *Reg. All Saints*, p. 55.

provision for his female relatives but does not name them. Like the other categories, most of the women mentioned in this capacity are the wives of the donors, with seventy-eight defined as wives; eight as mothers; one sister; two aunts; and in only one instance the woman's status is not defined; here she may have been the relative of the feudal lord of the land.[55] There are also two where the women were probably the feudal lord or his wife. Rohesia wife of Hugh de Lacy is mentioned in a list of spiritual beneficiaries of a donation by William Clut to St Thomas, Dublin, where Hugh was the feudal lord of the land in question.[56]

This is the category where mothers are mentioned more frequently. It is most likely that this was for genuinely pious reasons. It may also be that the land in question had belonged to the mother of the donor or it had been her dower and that she wished this land to be donated for a pious cause. As dower land was inalienable during a widow's lifetime, one way to donate the land to a monastery was for her son to do so after his widowed mother's death. There is often no way of recognising this scenario in the surviving cartularies, but one where this may have been the case is when Robert de Mandeville gave lands which had been occupied by his mother Isabelle to the abbey of St Thomas.[57]

The pattern of requests for spiritual beneficiaries reveals some interesting insights into the ways that Anglo-Irish families saw their obligations. Frame has noted that direction of spiritual benefits to paternal kin seem to be favoured in donations to monasteries.[58] This holds true for many of the donor charters in this survey. While there are many directions of spiritual benefits to parents of the male donor, there are fewer to parents of the female joint alienor or consentor in the charters and even fewer are named specifically. A common donation formula names the parents of the male donor and then mentions the parents of the female consentor or joint alienor, as when Thomas Blund gave land in Dublin to the Hospital of St John, with the consent of his wife Eva, for both their souls, the souls of his father Thomas, his mother Agnes and his wife's parents, unnamed.[59] It is also uncommon for women to mention maternal kin. An exception is the donation by Elena, widow of Adam Norren, who donated a pound of cumin annually for her own soul and that of her mother's sister, Margaret, wife of Robert Stirop.[60] The preference for naming paternal relatives as spiritual beneficiaries suggests that sons may have felt a particular obligation to ensure specific spiritual benefits to their parents. There are other possibilities, including sons who were more likely to be the primary donor and owner of land and so chose spiritual beneficiaries they most wished to honour – usually their wives and parents. Spiritual obligations may also have been considered to accompany the land, so that if land was donated to the church, the previous owners of the land would normally be particularly honoured by the donation. The women who married these sons did not usually include their own parents directly, perhaps because their parents' spiritual health was being cared for by

55 *Reg. St Thomas Dublin*, p. 33. **56** *Reg. St Thomas Dublin*, p. 45. **57** *Reg. St Thomas Dublin*, p. 28. **58** Frame, *English lordship in Ireland*, p. 30. **59** *Reg. St John Dublin*, p. 25. **60** *Chart. St*

their brothers. When there are exceptions it is often because a woman inherited the land from her parents, so that perhaps any spiritual benefits were again perceived as being tied with the land itself or with their heirs, whether they were sons or daughters.

The women who patronized these male monasteries did so for different reasons and in different ways. Since only a minority of women had sole legal control of land it is not surprising that only a small number were sole donors. Careful scrutiny of the surviving chartularies suggests that women were actively involved in many more donations than this small number, through joint donations with their families and through the "pro anima" clauses that were designed to ensure that the spiritual benefits of donating assets would be spread throughout the patron's family. Given this broad picture of the ways in which women could participate in the donations to monastic houses in Anglo-Irish Ireland, the next question is whether it is possible to detect any gender differences in the destinations of donations. There has been an expectation among modern scholars that women would tend to support women's monastic houses or causes which favoured women in some way, and there is some evidence to support this in studies of donor patterns from other places in Europe. Berman, for example, finds that women used their powers of patronage to support women's foundations, where they could, in twelfth-century southern France.[61] In the context of medieval Ireland, the quality of the surviving evidence does not make it possible to judge with certainty which religious institutions women preferred to support. The wills which survive show almost no support of women's monastic houses, though there are too few surviving wills to make any firm generalizations. From the surviving evidence it seems unlikely that women chose to support monasteries solely on basis of the gender of the inhabitants.

In a study of the charitable activities of women in York for the later medieval period, it appears that women may have been more likely than men to devote their charitable impulses to the care of the sick.[62] In Dublin, and other regions within the Anglo-Irish region, there is evidence that some women did extend themselves considerably to support sick people. In about 1317, Agnes of Wexford tried to donate a stone house to the infirmary of St John's priory in Waterford.[63] St Stephen's leper hospital was established with a sizeable donation from Geoffrey Tyrell and his wife Sara, from land that belonged to her father.[64] There were several important women patrons of this hospital including Katherine, wife of John le Gort, and a descendant of Geoffrey and Sara Tyrel, Elena Morton, who gave an important donation in 1378 stabilising the hospital's financial viability.[65]

Mary's Dublin, I, pp 444–5. **61** Berman, "Women as donors", pp 54–5ff. **62** Cullum, "And hir name was charité", p. 193. Cullum studied wills, not donations to monasteries made during life. **63** "Extracts from the pipe rolls" (NLI, MS 760) p. 346. She contravened the relatively new statute of Mortmain and the property was confiscated. **64** Mills, "The Norman settlement in Leinster", p. 161; Ronan, "Lazar houses", pp 480–9. **65** Ronan, "Lazar houses", p. 484 and Lee, *Leper hospitals*, p. 47.

The Hospital of St John the Baptist in Dublin was a popular recipient of small and large donations from women, particularly rents from land held in dower, as Mark Hennessy has noted in his study of the house.[66] Women were represented in about 34 per cent of the total charters surviving from St John's and in half of these women appear as sole alienors. A large number of these donations were rent from dower lands rather than donations of land outright. St John's was the only hospital in the sample, admitting both men and women as inmates and carers living under the Augustinian monastic rule, and may have attracted women's donations on the strength of its charitable work for the poor and sick.[67] It is difficult to detect whether women patrons of St John's had a particular affinity with its role as a hospital. There are differences recorded between the designation of the charters: some are directed to the prior and brethren, some to the prior, brethren and sisters, and others to the sick themselves. There is no indication that women mentioned women or the sick particularly in the charters. In a majority of the charters (118), the sick are mentioned specifically, and of these there are fourteen with women as sole alienors and six with married couples as joint alienors. Yet of these it is clear that individual women did contribute specifically for the care of the infirm and sick. Elena Lyvet was one woman who seems to have been particularly concerned with the sick in her donations. A wealthy heiress, she, both together with her husband, Thomas Blund, and later alone, donated a series of properties and rents to St John's for their work in the care of the sick in about 1280.[68] In one deed, she indicates that as she is now alone in the world, without her husband and father, she will give to the sick and poor of St John's.[69]

There does not seem to be a significant difference in the number of men and women who mentioned the sisters serving at St John's in their charters. Of the thirty-three charters that do mention the sisters, three are from women sole alienors. The decision to include the sisters in charter language may indicate scribal practice rather than any indication on the part of the donors that they acknowledged or particularly wanted to include the women who did serve in the hospital. It is not certain whether women continued as carers at the hospital throughout the history of the hospital. Although the sisters were noted in the deeds drawn up by the hospital until the end of the thirteenth century, there were no women listed for pensions at the dissolution. It is nevertheless possible that women may have particularly desired to support an institution where there were opportunities for women to be both cared for and to work as carers.

Another reason for the large percentage of women donating small sums to the hospital of St John was that women may have been alienating their property or the income from property in return for subsidised accommodation or care in old age, infirmity or widowhood. The care may not have been within the hospital itself:

66 Hennessy, "The priory and hospital of New Gate", p. 46. **67** McNeill, "Hospital of St John without the New Gate", pp 58 ff. **68** *Reg. St John Dublin*, pp 18, 25, 42, 56, 57, 66, 80, 84, 159. **69** *Reg. St John Dublin*, p. 56.

poor or widowed women may have been given preference in subsidised leases in hospital property. Care of this sort seems to have been offered to widows in some of the larger hospitals in London, such as St Bartholomew's.[70]

Another house that attracted considerable female patronage is the priory of All Saints in Dublin. Women were involved in 44 per cent of the total surviving charters from All Saints, and in 39 per cent of these women were sole alienors. Although these percentages are comparable to those for St John's, it must be remembered that they represent only small actual numbers of charters; only nine charters from All Saints were from female sole alienors. The reason for women appearing to be more inclined to support the smaller urban priories such as All Saints may have been that these houses were interested in receiving relatively small donations of partial rents or small urban properties, and so were open to support from other than the major land holders who supported the Cistercian abbey of St Mary and the royal foundation of St Thomas.[71]

The lower numbers of charters from female alienors for the monasteries of St Thomas and St Mary can also be understood by considering the differences in the foundation of these houses. St Thomas' was an Anglo-Norman royal foundation that from the beginning was a bastion of English power and prestige. St Mary's, although of Gaelic Irish foundation, was quickly appropriated by the Anglo-Normans and became a major recipient of donations from the first generations of Anglo-Normans. Both received donations from the crown and tenants-in-chief in the beginnings of the Anglo-Norman advance into Ireland.[72] Many of the donations made in the last years of the twelfth century represented both land and spiritual revenues from recently conquered lands.[73] The feudal lords who were granted the first knight fees by the king at the start of the English lordship were major donors to these two abbeys, giving both land and the spiritual revenues.[74] This was a similar pattern as had been experienced in the first generation after the Norman conquest of England, when the richest men in the kingdom donated lands and property, then in following generations the donations become smaller and from lower down the social scale.[75] This means that few of the first generation of donors could be women, who were not granted conquered land to hold in knight's service. It is only when the first generation of arrivals died and left heirs, some of whom where women, or when they married off their daughters with marriage portions, that there started to be significant numbers of donations from women alienors. One example of this is in the charter of Elicia, daughter of Adelem. She donated lands outside Dublin to St Mary's in the later part of the twelfth century and included in her charter the charter whereby Henry II had granted the lands to her father in 1172.[76]

70 Steuer, "Financial planning and the urban widow". **71** Graham, "The high middle ages", p. 77, discussing the pattern of patronage in Anglo-Norman Ireland, notes that only tenants-in-chief could afford to patronise the Cistercians. **72** *Chart. St Mary's Dublin*, I, p. xxiv. **73** For comparison with England see Mason, "Timeo Barones", pp 70–1. **74** Empey, "The sacred and the secular", pp 138–9. **75** Cownie, *Religious patronage*, pp 168–9. Thompson, "Monasteries and their patrons", pp 105–6. For comparison with monasteries in Wales see Butler, "The archaeology of rural monasteries", pp 2–3. **76** *Chart. St Mary's Dublin*, pp 140, 325.

Figure 1. Total sole donations by women

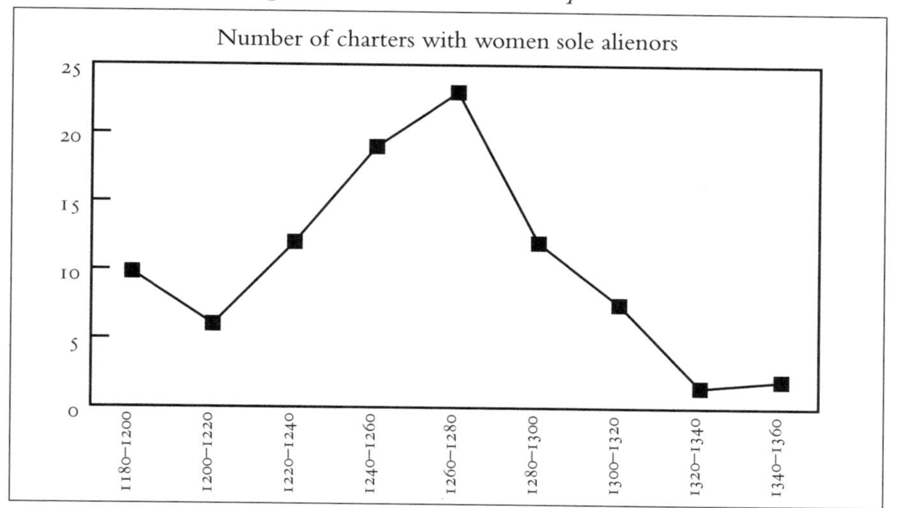

There is a marked surge of donations around the mid-to late thirteenth century. (See Figure 1.) This also appears for the other categories of joint alienor, consentor and spiritual beneficiary.[77] It is in this period that more women would have come into control of property after the first generations of original settlers had died out.

When female donors or women's participation in donations were part of a series of donor charters it is sometimes possible to determine patterns of patronage and thus to detect the negotiations within families which went on behind the bland language of the charters. In a series of charters from about 1281 Adam de Helmiswell and his wife Mabilla accumulated all the shares of a large rental that were apparently the inheritance of Mabilla and her two sisters, Isabelle and Anastase. Adam and Mabilla then donated the parcel to the canons of Christ Church cathedral.[78] This donation may have been a family concern, however it is also possible that Adam and Mabilla were the instigators of the donation and negotiated to organise a bigger donation rather than just Mabilla's share. Some entries in the chartularies provide extra information, for example when Beatrice Walter gave her marriage portion to the abbey of St Thomas in a memorable ceremony at the grave of her husband, Thomas de Hereford.[79] She was the daughter of Theobald Walter, Butler of Ireland, who had came to Ireland with Prince John in 1185, and both her husband and her father had been generous benefactors of the abbey. Here Beatrice was continuing to support the family's choice of monastic house, no doubt for social and political as well as

77 Hall, "Women and religion", p. 66. **78** *Cal. Christ Church deeds*, no. 114–16. **79** *Reg. St Thomas Dublin*, pp 194–8. For Theobald Walter see Orpen, *Ireland under the Normans*, II, pp 94–5.

religious reasons. It was not the only monastery supported by her father: he also established Cistercian monks at Abington, where he was buried.[80] Beatrice was evidently choosing St Thomas's for her donation because of her own and probably her husband's associations with it. As has been noted with respect to English women land-holders, husbands and wives usually acted in concert to preserve, extend and dispose of their joint assets as they were able.[81]

There are many examples in the sample of women who gave generously to monasteries as part of planned family donations. Roesia de Capella was daughter of Robert de Capella, lord of Straphan. Robert donated lands to St John's in about 1250, his daughter and her husband Thomas Fanyn continued to donate lands and tithes and after Thomas's death Roesia continued her support. Her son John then maintained these donations to the hospital.[82] Here the patronage patterns are followed from maternal grandfather rather than through the paternal families, which was more common.[83] This may indicate Roesia's own preferences or it may be that the patronage patterns went with the lands Roesia inherited. Donations and patronage were often designed as much for prestige and furthering temporal interests as for religious motivations, and continuing the patronage patterns of the father of an heiress could have been from secular rather than religious motives.[84]

Some women influenced the course of their families' pious patronage patterns to fit their own personal preferences. A woman's personal piety is particularly notable when the daughter's patronage habits are different from her father's or husband's family. In Dublin, Alicia daughter of William Brun and her husband Gilbert de Livet, a prominent citizen and one time mayor, were patrons of St Thomas's in the 1220s and 1230s.[85] After Alicia's death, her husband continued patronising St Thomas's with his second wife. His grand-daughter Elena de Livet, daughter of Galfrid and wife of Thomas Blund, donated much of the land and tenements which she had inherited to St John's in the 1270s.[86] This change in the favoured monastic house for this family may reflect changes in fashion, away from the large royal foundations of the early Anglo-Norman arrivals to smaller houses which were more attuned to the local needs of the urban population. The change may also indicate Elena's personal preferences.

Other women gave donations in return for care and accommodation. These corrodories almost certainly existed in most of the monastic houses, but there are not many traces of the people who lived as pensioners of the monasteries during their old age. That this was an option for women in Anglo-Norman Dublin is confirmed by several charters from outside the sample. In about 1283,

80 *Med. rel. houses Ire.*, pp 126–7. **81** Archer, "How ladies ... who live on their manors", pp 150ff. **82** *Reg. St John Dublin*, pp 214–20. **83** The names of paternal relatives are many times more common in lists of spiritual beneficiaries across the sample. This has also been noted for pious donations outside of the sample. See Frame, *English lordship in Ireland*, p. 30. **84** Mason, "Timeo Barones", p. 61, for discussion of this in the English context. **85** *Reg. St Thomas Dublin*, pp 347–6. Dates based on charters in *Reg. St John Dublin*, p. 47. **86** *Reg. St John Dublin*,

Scholastica, a daughter of Vincent Coupun, granted to Christ Church cathedral land and a house in St Nicholas Street in Dublin. In return, the priory of the cathedral granted Scholastica and her maid food and drink from the priory cellars as well as accommodation in the house for her life.[87] Robert Barrett, his wife Alicia and a female servant were granted a corrodory in the Templar house at Clonoulty (Co. Tipperary) in 1339.[88] There is more evidence for the establishment of corrodories at the priory of the Hospitallers at Kilmainham.[89] For example, Alice le Reue and her daughter Matilda were granted a corrodory at Kilmainham during 1326–50.[90] These women are unusual as they appear to have been accepted as charity corrodarians. Since the records from Kilmainham are not complete, it is not known for certain how many such women lived there over its history.[91]

WOMEN AS FOUNDERS OF MONASTIC HOUSES

As well as patronizing established monasteries, women were also involved in the foundation of new religious establishments. From the twelfth to the fourteenth centuries in Ireland, both Anglo-Norman and Gaelic Irish lay founders were drawn to the Augustinian order, both for founding new houses and re-founding older ones. Although there continued to be a significant Cistercian presence in medieval Ireland as well as a smaller number of Benedictine houses, the Augustinians were by far the most popular of the regular religious orders with both lay patrons and religious men and women. As the appeal of the older orders of Benedictine, Cistercian and Augustinian faded in the fifteenth century, there were moves in Ireland, as in England and the continent, to found religious houses better able to cater for the spiritual needs of lay communities. In Ireland mendicant orders were particularly strong in the Gaelic communities, with the Observant Franciscans, Dominicans and Augustinian friaries spreading widely throughout Gaelic Ireland with the active support of many wealthy lay patrons. The laity in the Anglo-Irish communities supported fraternities and chantries more strongly and founded many in the later fifteenth and early sixteenth centuries.[92]

Women were involved in all these enterprises in similar numbers to women patrons of the older established houses surveyed above, that is, they were a significant minority who directed their resources into new ecclesiastical avenues. Although there is evidence from England and the continent that some wealthy women particularly favoured female monastic houses, and supported them actively with generous donations, correlation between the gender of the founder and the gender of the occupants of the house is not straightforward. In her study of Cistercian houses in the south of France, Berman suggests that women found

pp 56–5, 58, 66, 80, 84. **87** *Cal. Christ Church deeds*, nos. 133 and 134. **88** Archdall (1786) p. 652 citing King, p. 83. **89** McNeill, "The Hospitallers of Kilmainham", pp 15–39. **90** *Reg. Kilmainham*, pp 90–1. **91** Massey, *Prior Roger Outlaw*, p. 17. **92** Dobson, "Citizens

adequate outlet for their spiritual aspirations by patronising male houses, perhaps because there were fewer opportunities for supporting female houses, but also because the male houses may have been viewed as more successful and so more worthy of support.[93] The foundation of female monastic houses will be discussed in detail in chapter 3, but it is worth noting here that women founders of women's houses were a minority in Ireland. The most notable exceptions are the convent of the Holy Trinity of Lismullin (Co. Meath) that was a joint foundation of a brother and sister, Richard and Avice de la Corner, and the obscure convent of St John the Baptist in Cork, founded by the Barry family at the instigation of the hermit Agnes de Hareford. Some convents may have been established specifically for women who were possibly the driving force behind the foundation, and these may be seen in houses where the first prioress was a member of the founder's family. These include Timolin (Co. Kildare), whose first prioress was Leclina, a member of the family of the founder Richard of Norragh, and the small Franciscan house in Galway founded by Walter Lynch for his daughter in 1511. Other convents were founded by leading Gaelic families and staffed by female members of these families. The most important of these Gaelic Irish convents were Kilcreevanty, Co. Galway, founded and staffed by Uí Chonchobair; Killone, Co. Clare, founded and staffed by Uí Briain; and Clonard, initially founded by Ua Máel Sechlainn and whose first abbess was his granddaughter Agnes.[94] The impetus behind these foundations is impossible to gauge from the surviving records, although it is entirely possible that the women themselves urged their families for the foundation.

The spiritual benefits which were believed to flow to founders and donors of religious houses is effectively symbolised by the probable seal for the Dominican priory of Trim, founded in 1263 by Geoffrey de Joinville and his wife Maud de Lacy. Geoffrey entered the priory in his old age in 1308, after the death of his wife in 1302. He himself died in 1314.[95] The seal shows the Joinville arms below a depiction of a woman and a man reaching up to the Virgin Mary, who is handing out wreaths to the couple. The woman has reached hers while the man's hand has not quite touched his. This has been interpreted as meaning that the seal was used during the residence of Geoffrey at Trim, after his wife's death and before his own. The symbolism clearly indicates that the couple were operating as a team in founding the priory and their joint enterprise was commemorated in the corporate seal of the priory. It is also an example of the most common way that women participated in founding monastic houses in Ireland, that is in concert with their husbands, united to provide for the spiritual health of their families.

Founding monasteries was not only for the spiritual benefit of the founders. The political and social considerations in establishing such a permanent feature in the physical and cultural landscape were also very important. John de Courcy,

and chantries in late medieval York", pp 311–32. **93** Berman, "Women as donors and patrons", p. 54. **94** These foundations will be discussed in the next chapter. **95** Fenning, "The Dominicans of Trim", pp 15–23 and Conwell, *A ramble around Trim*, p. 30.

whose conquest of Ulster in 1177 brought him vast estates, was also active in establishing his ecclesiastic credentials, incorporating new monastic houses with reform of existing houses, to alter permanently the spiritual landscape of his territories. His wife Affrica, daughter of the king of the strategically important Isle of Man, founded Grey Abbey (Co. Down), which was culturally and politically connected with both the Isle of Man and de Courcey's Cumbria, and, Duffy argues, was part of a long-term and well-thought-out strategy by de Courcey in his plans of conquest.[96]

Although many couples used their assets to jointly establish monasteries for their mutual spiritual benefit, there were instances where couples disagreed. In 1252 Basilia, daughter of Miler de Bermingham and wife of Jordan de Exeter, insisted that the new friary being founded by her husband be of the Dominican order, not the Franciscans as planned. She reportedly refused to eat or drink until her wishes were granted.[97] Although this is a well celebrated and dramatic account of the ways that women could influence monastic foundations, there were probably many others where consensus was achieved through less dramatic and therefore undocumented means. Given the late date of the source for this story, it also very possible that it was a later justification for the order being changed at short notice and may reflect more about monastic misogyny than the methods used by Basilia to direct the foundation.

It was common for women to participate in, rather than initiate, the foundation of monasteries. This may have involved the donation of some land and may also have included money and other resources required to build the conventual buildings. The wave of religious zeal and reform which swept Gaelic Ireland in the late fifteenth century included women with the resources to encourage the spread of the Observant Franciscans.[98] Although the foundation in 1474 of the famous Franciscan friary of Donegal was accomplished by Aodh Rua Ó Domhnall, the records are quite definite about the encouragement and influence of both his wife, Nuala Ní Bhriain, and his mother, Finola Ní Chonchobair, who argued at the Franciscan chapter for its establishment.[99] Nuala's sister Margaret, wife of Eoghan Ó Ruairc, founded a friary of Observant Franciscans at Dromahair in Co. Leitrim in 1508.[100] Ruaidhrí Mac Suibhne and his wife Máire, daughter of Eoghan Ó Máille, founded the Carmelite friary at Rathmullan in Donegal after the death of their eldest son at Rathmullan in 1516. The Leabhar Chlainne Suibhne credits Máire with erecting the monastery itself, as well as numerous other churches in Ulster and Connaught and the great hall for the Friars Minor in Donegal.[101] This suggests that Máire contributed the raw materials or money to purchase them rather than the lands which were needed

96 Duffy, "The first Ulster plantation", pp 24–6ff. **97** *Med. rel. houses Ire.*, p. 230. **98** For the history of the Franciscans prior to the emergence of the Observant movement see Cotter, *The Friars Minor in Ireland*, for the reform of the Augustinians see Martin, "The Irish Augustinian reform", pp 230–64. **99** *AFM* 1474 and "Brussels MS 3947", pp 38–9. **100** *Med. rel. houses Ire.*, p. 248. **101** *Leabhar Chlainne Suibhne,* pp 66–9, 51, 86.

to maintain the friary. This fits well with the known property rights of chiefs' wives in later medieval Ireland.

The analysis of a sample of donor charters for monasteries in the Anglo-Norman colony of Ireland in this chapter has shown that women from the landholding class were a significant minority of donors and patrons. When the scope of inquiry is broadened to examine patterns of foundation of monasteries by women throughout medieval Ireland, similar patterns emerge. Women were involved in donations to religious institutions in a variety of ways that are not always transparent. Although the most obvious involvement occurred when women donated land or assets in their own right, women were also involved in the joint decisions with their husbands in how best to use the marital assets for the spiritual well-being of the family. There is evidence that women may have favoured monastic houses which were involved in the care of the sick and poor. While some women favoured supporting hospitals, others continued the patterns of pious donating which operated either in their birth or their marital families, giving to the monks who kept up the rounds of prayer considered so important to medieval society.

Estates donated by the laity created a visible presence for monastic houses in the landscape. The boundaries of these monastic lands thus became the divide between lay and church property. Creating these estates usually required the donations of many lay people keen to support the church in practical, visible ways which were known and appreciated by their families and neighbours. Although the legal practicalities and the formulaic language used to record land transfers tends to obscure and marginalize women's participation in these donations, close examination of the varied sources for medieval Ireland reveal that women played significant if minor roles in arranging and managing donations to ecclesiastical institutions as individuals and more commonly as members of families who used their collective resources to ensure their spiritual welfare.

CHAPTER 3

Foundation of nunneries in medieval Ireland

As well as the stone towers and large estates of monastic houses for men that dotted the landscape of medieval Ireland, there were also convents where women spent their lives in prayer and the work of God. The women who lived within convent walls were marked apart by their withdrawal from families and their communal life under religious vows, and were usually symbolised by their distinctive dress. Like others throughout medieval Europe these women entered religious life for different reasons – some through intense personal religious feeling, others because of family pressures or lack of alternatives. Medieval convents were usually founded to provide quiet havens of prayer for women, separate from the cares and concerns of the secular world. To maintain this separation from the world, convents needed sufficient resources to support themselves – land for growing food, domestic buildings and churches for prayer. These resources were given to religious women by founders who hoped to ensure safe, secure environments for the women in perpetuity.

In broad terms, there were four waves of foundation of nunneries in later medieval Ireland. The first rightly belongs with the early medieval period and includes those nunneries that survived the upheavals of the tenth and eleventh centuries and continued in some form until the later period. These nunneries do not have many common characteristics, although most probably adopted the Augustinian or Arroasian Rule by the late twelfth century. The second wave involves the foundations that occurred as a result of native twelfth-century reform. These houses were founded by Gaelic kings and planned as part of large-scale reorganisation of Irish monasticism. The third wave occurred when the first generations of Anglo-Normans altered the course of native reform, hastened changes to diocesan and parochial structures and redistributed conquered lands. The main characteristic of this wave was more individual Augustinian, Benedictine and Cistercian houses, founded most commonly by the second tier in the hierarchy of Anglo-Norman settlers. These foundations of convents, though fewer in number than the associated wave of male foundations, demonstrate that convents were an important factor in the colonisation of Ireland. The fourth and much smaller of the foundation waves involved the houses for women that were founded during the fifteenth-century reform movement that swept Gaelic Ireland and predominantly involved the mendicant orders.[1]

1 For full details of all convents, their affiliations, dates of foundation and dissolution, see

The chronology of these foundations (see Figure 2) shows important parallels with the foundation of nunneries in parts of England and France and is worth considering in detail. They also indicate significant levels of lay involvement in the affairs of the nunneries from their inception.

Figure 2. Rates of new convent foundations in Ireland, c.1100–1500

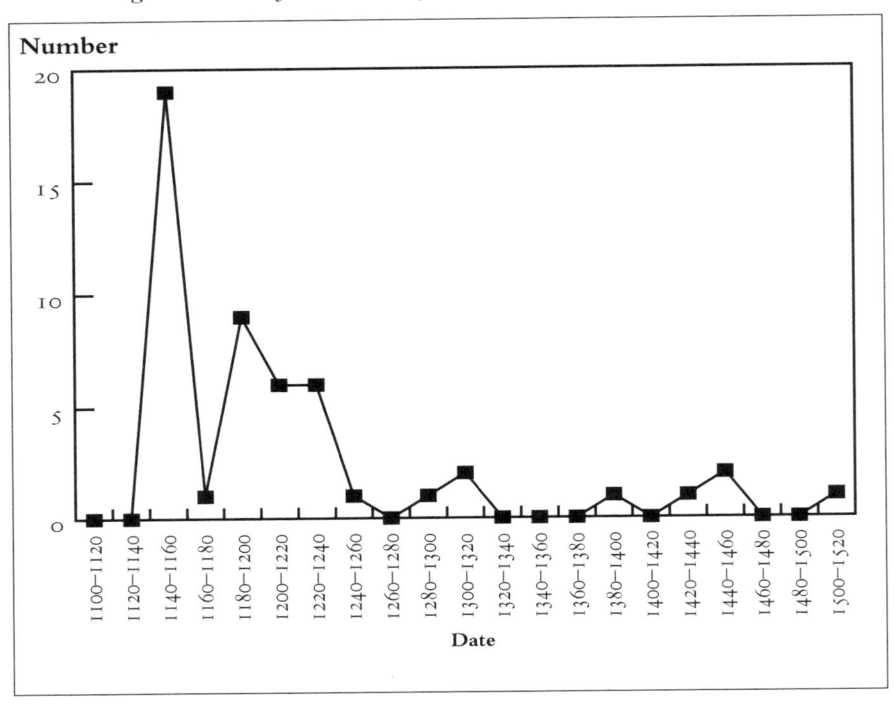

SURVIVAL OF EARLY CELTIC FOUNDATIONS

Women's monasticism prior to the twelfth century has left relatively few traces on either the landscape or the archival memory in Ireland. This does not necessarily mean there were few religious women, although it is probable that, as on the continent, there was a decline in monastic opportunities for women around the ninth and tenth centuries.[2] Women's monasticism only rarely surfaces in the earlier records in Ireland, and usually nuns are noted in passing in the records of other events. Although this could mean that they were few in number, it is also possible that nuns were obvious features of the mental and physical landscape of early medieval Ireland and not specifically discussed because they were not considered important to the concerns of the male monastic annalists and poets.[3]

Appendix 1. **2** Schulenburg, "Women's monastic communities, 500–1100", pp 261–92. **3** Bitel, *Land of women*, pp 169–75ff.

Some of these early nunneries have well-established histories, such as Kileedy (Co. Limerick) founded by St Ité, whereas others are believed to be early through local or antiquarian tradition. There are also references to early medieval nunneries that cannot now be confirmed.[4] Again, this does not mean that they did not exist; merely that the records are particularly disappointing. Hagiography is a rich source for early church history in Ireland and there are records of nunneries in the hagiographical sources for which no other evidence exists.[5] Some of these early nunneries have left their only traces in place names; generally names that include a component of *calliagh/callech* (nun/old woman) were associated with religious women.[6] Although the dating of these place names is not completely reliable, in the anglicized areas of medieval Ireland place names that included *calliagh* were usually the property of nuns prior to the arrival of the Anglo-Normans.

There were several of the older Celtic nunneries in existence at the beginning of the twelfth century. One of the most significant was Kildare, founded by St Brigit in the fifth century. Its importance in the twelfth century is attested by the rather scandalised report of John Paparo, papal legate to Ireland in 1152, who decreed at the council of Kells that the abbesses of Kildare should no longer "take precedence over the bishops in public assemblies, for they had been accustomed to sit at the bishop's feet".[7] Kildare was also of political importance, with Diarmait Mac Murchadha, king of Leinster, attacking the abbey in 1132/5, abducting and raping the abbess and then replacing her with a relative.[8] After the conquest of the area by the Anglo-Normans, the abbey continued in reduced circumstances with Anglo-Norman nuns.

Other nunneries surviving to the twelfth century were smaller and have rated fewer mentions in the records. Not surprisingly, most of them were in areas that were settled least or not at all by Anglo-Normans. In Armagh the ancient nunneries of Temple Breed and Temple-na-Ferta, founded by St Patrick, continued quietly through the reform period until after the dissolution in the late sixteenth century.[9] Another important nunnery in Ulster was Killeevy (Co. Armagh) founded by St Monenna in the sixth century, where nuns continued until they surrendered the abbey at the general dissolution in 1542.[10] Killaraght (Co. Sligo) a convent founded in the early Christian period by St Attracta continued until the dissolution, leaving virtually no trace in the surviving archives.[11] Some later nunneries whose origins are obscure may have been re-established on older abandoned sites. Dedication to Brigit is probably a sign of

4 *Med. rel. houses Ire.*, pp 370–409, lists 41 sites of nunneries which faded before the eleventh century. 5 For example, the convent of nuns at Cloonburren, Co. Roscommon, see *Med. rel. houses Ire.*, p. 315. 6 The derivation and range of meaning of *calliagh/caíllech* are explored in Ní Dhonnchadha, "Caillech", pp 71–96. 7 John of Salisbury, *Historia Pontificalis*, p. 72. 8 *ALC* 1132 and *AClon.* 1135. The deposed abbess was one of the Uí Failge. 9 Reeves, "The ancient churches of Armagh", pp 201–2. For summary see *Med. rel. houses Ire.*, p. 312. 10 Reade, "Cill-Sleibhe-Cuillinn", pp 93–102. 11 *Med. rel. houses Ire.*, pp 320–1 gives a summary; see also Knox, *History of Tuam*, pp 273, 388.

early foundation, as nunneries were usually dedicated to the Virgin Mary after the twelfth century. The nunnery of St Brigit at Molough (Co. Tipperary) was founded in the early Christian period, when it was called Mainister Brighde, Molacha Brighde, or Mag Laca.[12] The surviving buildings date from the twelfth or thirteenth centuries with textual references from the thirteenth century, so it may have continued throughout the intervening years or the nunnery may have been re-established on the old site.[13] Analysis of place-names has led historians to posit that the large and important nunnery of Kilcreevanty (Co. Galway) was probably established on the site of an earlier nunnery about 1200.[14]

There were also documented nunneries that survived the crises of the tenth-century disturbances but did not continue past the twelfth century. An important one was the nunnery of Clonbroney, founded by St Patrick and the eighth-century home of the reforming St Samthann whose vita is one of the few examples of hagiography of female saints which survive from medieval Ireland.[15] The last abbess of Clonbroney mentioned is Caillechdomhnaill, daughter of Naonaenaigh, who died in 1163.[16] This convent seems to have been under this family's patronage as the annals record the death in 1108 of another abbess of that family, Cocrich.[17] The abbey's position in the borderlands around the early lordship of Meath, which were being subinfeudated and incastellated by Hugh de Lacy and his tenants, may have meant that it was no longer viable after the arrival of the Anglo-Normans. It evidently failed to secure the patronage of any of the new settlers and there is no evidence that it was involved in the spread of the reformed Arroasian observance.

The places where women could practise a regular religious life under recognised vows were few in the early twelfth century. It is likely that some women lived quietly and anonymously as hermits on their families' estates or in their own homes, while a small number lived communally as nuns in recognized convents. This has parallels to the situation that Elkins has found in early twelfth-century England, where there were few nunneries available for women.[18]

THE TWELFTH-CENTURY REFORM

For women's monasticism in Ireland, as in other parts of medieval Europe, the twelfth century was a watershed marking an upsurge in women's participation in an invigorated monastic world. The twelfth-century reform movement saw great change generally in the physical and ideological landscape of the Irish church, with the reorganisation of dioceses and monasteries as well as concerted efforts to bring the aberrant practices of clerical marriage and lay patronage in

12 "Life of St Declan of Ardmore", pp 62–3. *The Martyrology of Donegal*, p. 257, notes that the daughters of Cainnech established the house of Mag Lacha. **13** Power, *Waterford and Lismore*, pp 231–2. **14** Knox, *History of Tuam*, p. 280, as Craebhnata, the name element is a woman's name. **15** "Vita St Samthann", in *Vitae Sanctorum Hiberniae* II, p. 258. **16** *Med. rel. houses Ire.*, p. 314. **17** *AFM* 1108. **18** Elkins, *Holy women*, p. xiii.

line with those of the continent.[19] Concurrent with the native reforming synods was the introduction of new monastic orders – Cistercian, Benedictine and Augustinian – under the influence and patronage of kings such as Diarmait Mac Murchadha and Tairdelbach Ua Conchobair, and churchmen, Malachy of Down (Máel Máedóc Ua Morgair), Áed Ua Cáellaide and Lorcán Ua Tuathail.[20] By the mid-twelfth century, when Malachy of Down returned from his travels in Europe fired with zeal to rejuvenate religious life in Ireland after the example of the monastery of Arrouaise, there were enough willing women for him and others to introduce the Arroasian rule to about nineteen nunneries.[21]

The Arroasian observance was a stricter and more contemplative version of the Augustinian rule, heavily influenced by Cistercian thought and practice and popular in the mid-twelfth century in England and northern France.[22] It proved very attractive to Irish religious men and women and their patrons. This may be partly fortuitous in that the Arroasian rule attracted the obviously charismatic Malachy and he supported it strongly both personally and through his relatives and allies.[23] It may also have been because of the differences between the Augustinian and the alternative rules – principally Cistercian and Benedictine. The Cistercians were forbidden from taking donations in spiritual revenues, or rents, and so needed large tracts of land in outright donations, meaning they were expensive houses to found.[24] Historians have identified several factors in the appeal of the Arroasian Rule for Irish patrons. Donations of rents and tithes rather than large tracts of land were more attractive since these did not diminish family estates, which under brehon law were difficult for any except the head of the fine to alienate. The Augustinians may also have appeared well-placed to take up the mantle of parochial duties in the newly reorganised dioceses and emerging parishes, although there are now doubts about the extent of their involvement in parish duties.[25] The relative independence of the Arroasians may also have appealed. Since they were only ever loosely connected to continental motherhouses or to the chapters of the order, they were more suited to the complex dynamics of local lay politics than monasteries that were more strongly connected to the continent.[26] Other factors of the Augustinian order which emphasised their independence, such as flexibility in the choice of site and no

19 See the series of articles by Gwynn, *The Irish church in the eleventh and twelfth centuries.* **20** *Med. rel. houses Ire.*, pp 114–20; 146–52; Dunning, "The Arroasian order in medieval Ireland", pp 297–315. **21** He is credited with establishing 54 congregations of monks, canons and nuns. See *Visio Tnugdali*, p. 155. Whether Malachy personally established or influenced this number of monasteries is not totally clear. See Preston, "The canons regular of St Augustine", pp 19–34. **22** For England specifically see Dickenson, "English regular canons", pp 71–90; Thompson, *Women religious*, p. 145, discusses the Arroasian observance in the context of English nunneries. For the Augustinians and Arroasians in Ireland see Dunning, "The Arroasian order in medieval Ireland", pp 297–315. **23** Flanagan, "St Mary's Abbey, Louth", pp 233–4. **24** Hennessy, "The priory and hospital of New Gate", p. 42 and Empey, "The sacred and the secular", pp 137–9. **25** Preston, "The canons regular of St Augustine", pp 175–9. **26** For discussion of this rather vexed issue, see Dunning, "The Arroasian order in medieval Ireland", p. 315, and Milis, *L'ordre des chanoines règuliers d'Arrouaise*, pp 338–77, esp. pp

requirement for a minimum number of religious, meant that relatively small endowments were acceptable.[27] It is also possible that the Anglo-Norman or at least the foreign connections of the Cistercians and the Benedictines made them unpopular with the Gaelic Irish.[28] Simms has recently argued, however, that the alignment of the Augustinians with the native reform movement was more important for the church in medieval Ireland than any direct split between Gaelic and English.[29] It is likely that while the reasons for choosing the Augustinian rule were complex and multi-layered, the potential for a meaningful role for the lay founders and their families was probably an important factor in the establishment of Augustinian houses.

Irish women seem to have entered the newly established convents enthusiastically in these heady years of reform. An obscure reference to the synod of Clonfert in 1179 indicates that there were women who were defying family opinion by joining nunneries. The obviously corrupt reference is: "no portion Canons should be sought of women their husbands still living".[30] Gwynn has interpreted this to mean that no woman should be admitted as a canoness while her husband was still living.[31] This implies that at the height of the reform enthusiasm there were women wishing to join religious institutions who did not have their families' approval.[32]

The increased numbers of foundations for women at this time are also seen in other parts of Europe, where a similar upswing has been noted by Vernarde in his study of nunnery foundations in France and England, and by Elkin and Gilchrist in their studies of English nunneries.[33] Venarde has argued that the increase in women's monastic houses was associated with the great charismatic preachers and hermits who inspired hundreds of women and men to join religious institutions or to found houses where others might live the coenobitic life.[34] This situation has obvious parallels in Ireland with the influence of Malachy of Down in inspiring patrons and religious men and women to embrace the reform of monasticism.

One of the paradoxes of the rise in foundations of nunneries in the period is that it was a time of political and social uncertainty in both England and France. Venarde argues that it was this uncertainty that seems to have proved a fertile background for laity of the lesser nobility to express their piety by founding

360ff; Empey, "The sacred and the secular", p. 139, and Barry, *Archaeology of medieval Ireland*, pp 157–8. **27** Robinson, *Geography of Augustinian settlement*, I, p. 45. **28** This is the reason suggested by Gilchrist, *Gender and material culture*, p. 110. **29** Simms, "Frontiers in the Irish church", pp 178, 190–1. **30** *AClon.* 1179. **31** Gwynn, *The Irish church in the eleventh and twelfth centuries*, p. 138. See also Gwynn, "St Lawrence O'Toole", pp 230–1. **32** The term canoness had specific meanings in convents in Europe, especially Germany, see McNamara, *Sisters in arms*, pp 195–201, however women following the Augustinian and Arroasian rules in England and Ireland were usually referred to in contemporary documents as "moniales" or "sorers", see Thompson, *Women religious*, pp 145–56. **33** Venarde, *Women's monasticism*, see figure 6, p. 56, figure 9, p. 180, for the situation in England and for general discussion see pp 82–8; Elkins, Holy women, pp 45–104; Gilchrist, *Gender and material culture*, pp 36–62. **34** Venarde, *Women's monasticism*, p. 79.

monastic houses for women. He suggests that there was an element of perceived social advantage to making such pious gestures, a way of allowing a family on their way up the social ladder to make their mark both upon the physical landscape and in the minds of their contemporaries.[35] In contrast, when political stability returned in the thirteenth and fourteenth centuries, the increased economic security and political harmony felt by communities made it paradoxically harder for nunneries to establish a toehold in the landed structures. Such broad analyses are by no means certain and Elkins suggests that it was the increased population and prosperity of the twelfth century in England that influenced the growth of monasticism in such a profound way.[36]

Significant differences have been observed in the timing of foundation of houses for men and women during the twelfth century. Men's houses were usually established first. In England there was a wave of foundations lasting from about 1080 to 1110 for Benedictines and from 1130 to 1140 for Augustinian foundations.[37] Houses for women were founded about a generation or two later in both orders, with Benedictine houses for women founded in a peak around 1160 and for Augustinian around 1180.[38] The founders of nunneries in both England and France in this period tended to be lay and of the lower nobility.[39] This is also borne out by the backgrounds of the nuns themselves, both at this time and for later centuries.[40]

In Ireland, the pattern of foundations was influenced by similar factors, as Venarde has found for England and France, although with particular differences unique to the Irish context. The twelfth century in Ireland was both a period of social and political upheaval and a time of centralization of power and reform within the church. Even before the political changes associated with the invasion of the Anglo-Normans in the late twelfth century, there were disruptive power struggles between warring Gaelic kings. Although there were some attempts at centralisation, the twelfth century was a time when alliances were shifting and political overlordship was not realized.[41] It is in this context that Ireland experienced the influence of charismatic religious reformers, so that the will for ecclesiastical change was joined with a relatively fluid political landscape. Foundation of monasteries and convents was often associated with attempts to solidify political claims to land and territory. The later shift of resources from the

35 Venarde, *Women's monasticism*, pp 112–14. **36** Elkins, *Holy women*, pp xix, xx. **37** Robinson, *Geography of Augustinian settlement*, I, p. 24 for chart showing dates of foundation of male Augustinian houses in England, the peak is between about 1120 and 1140 with very few established after 1225. **38** Gilchrist, *Gender and material culture*, pp 40–1. See also the tables p. 37 and the tables listing date of foundation, filiation and rank of founder. The graphs in Venarde, *Women's monasticism*, pp 8, 12 and 180, show the rates of foundation of nunneries in England and France very clearly. **39** Elkins, *Holy women*, pp 61–2 and 94–7, has analysed the ranks of the founders of nunneries in the south and the north of England, whereas Venarde has looked at the ranks of the founders of twelfth-century nunneries in France. *Women's monasticism*, pp 128–9. **40** Oliva, *Convent and community*, pp 52–61; 221–9. Harris, "A new look at the reformation: Aristocratic women and nunneries", pp 89–113. **41** The literature on the political situation of Ireland just prior to and after the arrival of the Anglo-

kings of Gaelic Ireland to the new Anglo-Norman lords meant that large tracts of land changed hands and were then available for donation to religious institutions perceived to meet the needs of new lay landowners. These political and social upheavals show more in common with the strife-torn landscapes in England during the period known as the "anarchy", in which a surprisingly large number of nunneries were successfully founded.[42]

The Clonard group: the first Arroasian network of nunneries

At the end of the twelfth century there was a recognisable network of nunneries dependent on the convent of St Mary's, Clonard (Co. Meath), made up of three separate groups of nunneries founded since 1144. These groups were the Leinster group, the Clonard group and the Clonmacnoise group.

The reforming bishop of Airgialla, Áed Ua Cáellaide, was instrumental in introducing the Arroasian observance into the priory of Louth. He did this with the collaboration of the king of the area, Donnchad Ua Cearbaill, whose reform agenda included introducing the new religious orders into other monasteries in his territories.[43] As well as being one of the patrons of the new Cistercian monastery at Mellifont, Donnchad Ua Cerbaill founded an abbey for Arroasian canons at Knock and the monasteries for nuns and canons at Termonfeckin in 1142.[44] All these monasteries were then placed under the motherhouse of Louth.[45] Áed Ua Cáellaide also influenced Diarmait Mac Murchadha, king of Leinster, in the choice of rule for his monastic foundations. A group of nunneries under the Arroasian observance was founded in Leinster by Mac Murchadha between 1146 and 1151, including Kilculliheen, near Waterford, St Mary del Hogges outside the walls of Dublin, and the small nunneries of Aghade (Co. Carlow), Taghmon (Co. Wexford) and Lusk (Co. Dublin).[46] Together with the nunnery at Termonfeckin these were among the earliest to follow the Arroasian observance and may have been instrumental in ensuring the further spread of the order.[47] Certainly, the early foundations of the nunneries of St Mary del Hogges, Kilculliheen and Aghade indicate an unmet need for nunneries in the Dublin and Waterford areas. Lands once belonging to older abandoned nunneries were probably included in this reorganisation of women's convents in Diarmait's area of influence. Calliaghstown, included in the estates of St Mary del Hogges,

Normans is extensive. For a useful summary of the historiography of the period see Duffy, *Ireland in the middle ages*, pp 1–6. For the political alliances leading up to the twelfth century see Ó Cróinín, *Early medieval Ireland*, pp 272–92. **42** Venarde, *Women's monasticism*, p. 127. **43** Smith, *Colonisation and conquest*, pp 16–18ff. **44** Donnchad Ua Cerbaill's foundation of Termonfeckin and his patronage of Mellifont are described in his obit preserved in an antiphonary of Armagh Cathedral, T.C.D. MS 77, f. 48v. For translation and discussion see Lawlor, "The genesis of the diocese of Clogher", pp 138–9. **45** Flanagan, "St Mary's abbey, Louth", pp 228–30 and Preston, "The canons regular of St Augustine", pp 88–90 for discussion of this argument. **46** *Med. rel. houses Ire.*, p. 325, for Tagmon. For the foundation of the house of Lusk see *Alen's reg.*, p. 49. For the foundation of Aghade see *Alen's reg.*, p. 293 and Flanagan, *Irish society*, pp 102, 125. **47** Flanagan, "St Mary's abbey, Louth", p. 233.

was originally the site of a nunnery. While the place name suggests nuns, there is no firm evidence of any later medieval nunnery, so it is probable that Diarmait annexed lands formerly used by nuns to his new foundation. If there were any nuns still living there at this time, they may have been transferred to Dublin. In 1837, Eugene Curry reported that "cartloads" of bones had been carried away from a field known as "chapel field" in this townland. He also discovered an old font being used as a water trough. He surmised from these finds that this was the site of the nunnery dependent on Hogges, though it is more likely that the church was used as a medieval parish church, as there are no other records of nuns at this site.[48]

A further group of Arroasian monasteries for nuns and canons in the Meath area was established around 1144 when Malachy visited the area. The first of these was probably St Mary's, Clonard. It was founded under the patronage of Ua Maél Sechlainn, king of Meath, in association with Malachy, and in turn was probably made dependent on the Arroasian community of canons at Louth.[49]

In 1195 St Mary's, Clonard, received papal confirmation of its possessions and this document makes clear that there was a group of thirteen nunneries dependent on Clonard at that time.[50] Since the nunneries of St Mary's Hogges and Lusk established by Diarmait MacMurchada and the nunnery of Termonfeckin are included in the 1195 Clonard document it is clear that at some point Clonard became the head house for this filiation of the Arroasian nunneries in the east of Ireland. Some of the nunneries were at older monastic sites, such as Kells, Trim, Durrow and Clonard itself. At Clonard the reformed Augustinian monasteries established in the 1140s were separate from the older monastic house and were dedicated to universal saints of the church – St Mary and St Peter.[51] The houses at the other sites may also have been established in parallel with older houses, rather than replacing them. Although most of these nunneries are in the Meath and Dublin areas, there were also some included from further afield: Annaghdown (Co. Galway); Drumalgagh (Co. Roscommon); Clonmacnoise and Durrow (Co. Offaly). Annaghdown was traditionally the site of a nunnery given to Briga, the sister of St Brendan. There are no surviving records of the convent of Annaghdown between the sixth century and 1195, so it is not clear whether it had survived in some form or was a new establishment on the old site.[52] These convents may have been small houses affiliated to Clonmacnoise at the time of Malachy's reforms,

48 Ordnance Survey Letters, Co. Dublin, NLI Typescript, pp 40–1, also see Otway-Ruthven, "The medieval church lands of County Dublin", pp 69–70, for details of the extent of the medieval parish of Calliaghstown. **49** For the affiliation with Louth see Flanagan, "St Mary's abbey, Louth", pp 231–2. **50** Brady, "The nunnery of Clonard", p. 6, for his identification of the place named in the confirmation as dependent nunneries. *Med. rel. houses Ire.*, pp 310–25 mentions other communications with Brady in their identification of the fate of these dependencies. The bull confirming the possessions of Clonard, in *Pont. Hib., I,* pp 83–6. **51** Hadcock, "The origin of the Augustinian order in Meath", pp 125–7 and Hickey, *Clonard*, pp 36–9. **52** Goaley, *Monastic ruins at Annaghdown*, pp 8–11. Wilde, *Lough Corrib*, p. 70, considered the ruins of the nunnery to be the oldest in the site of Annaghdown.

or established on land originally belonging to Clonmacnoise. The Ua Máel Sechlainn kings were long-standing patrons of Clonmacnoise and, along with the Ua Conchobair kings of Connacht, had been granted burial rights there in the early medieval period.[53] The earliest mention of the nuns at Clonmacnoise is in 1026, when a pavement was built from the abbess's garden.[54] There were also personal ties with St Mary's, Clonmacnoise, where Derbforgaill was a major patron. She was also granddaughter of Murchad Ua Maél Sechlainns founder of St Mary's, Clonard, and sister of Agnes, Clonard's first abbess.[55] Ua Maél Sechlainn was consolidating his position in the diocese of Clonmacnoise at this time, and it is likely that the inclusion of St Mary's Clonmacnoise and smaller dependent nunneries (see figure 3) in the affiliation with his foundation at Clonard was part of these ambitions.[56] The nunnery at Durrow was probably associated with the male house of Canons at Durrow, where their founder Murchad Ua Maél Sechlainn and his wife chose to be buried. This would indicate that the nunnery at Durrow and then Killeigh remained dependent on Clonard.[57] The grouping of these nunneries in one affiliation may, however, have been predicated solely on the choice of rule and a desire to bring them closer together in a similar way to the affiliations in France at the time.

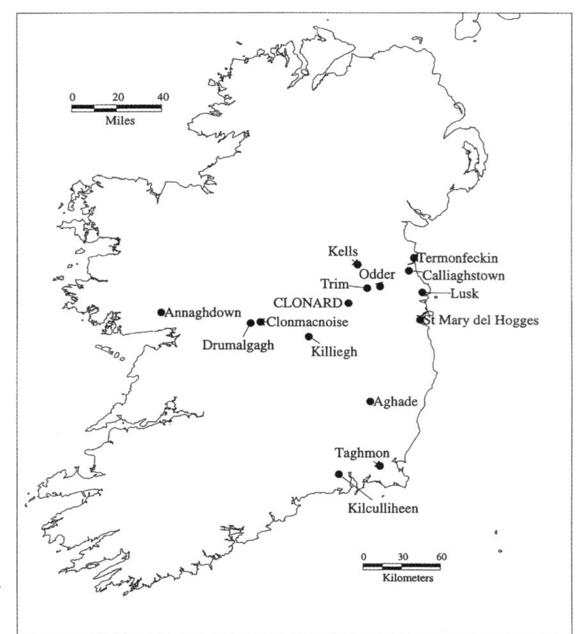

Figure 3. Clonard's dependencies in c.1185

53 Kehnel, "The lands of St Ciarán", p. 13. **54** *AClon.* 1026. **55** The church in the nuns' graveyard was burnt in 1082 and it was 1180 when Derbforgaill rebuilt the nuns' church at Clonmacnoise, *AClon.* **56** Ó Corráin, *Ireland before the Normans*, pp 153, 158–67, details Ua Maél Sechlainn's place in the manoeverings for power at this time. **57** For the death of

A feature of these convents' distinctive nature, their conscious break with the older Celtic monasticism and the way they embraced new reforms, was their dedications to St Mary. The introduction of dedications to the Virgin at this time was part of the wider upswing in devotion to Mary and is a good indicator of the foundation date of the convents, as it is extremely rare for churches or monasteries before the twelfth century in Ireland to be dedicated to any but native saints.[58] There is a poem to Colum Cille, which has been tentatively dated to the twelfth century and mentions the connection between virgins living in communities associated with Mary: "Mary exhorts them, Mary instructs them, she desires that her Son should have large communities."[59] It is possible that this refers to the numerous new communities that were emerging at this time and that must have appeared to have been filled with enthusiastic nuns dedicated to Mary.

Most of the Arroasian monasteries established in Ireland under the influence of the ecclesiastical reform were houses of nuns and canons living in proximity and sharing a church, a feature of the early years of Abbot Gervase of Arrouaise. When the observance spread outside France, the double structure was also incorporated in the early foundations in England.[60] Although traditionally double monasteries have been seen as something of an anomaly, practised on the Celtic fringes of Christian Europe and not tolerated for long within the mainstream of European monasticism, recently scholars such as Elkins and Gilchrist have argued that men and women living in proximity were a significant feature of twelfth-century monasticism generally in England and France and were not, as previously believed, influenced by the Celtic fringe. They argue that these double houses were a mainstream response to the reforms and enthusiasms of this period, with nearly 25 percent of nunneries founded at this time being also in some way double houses.[61] This means that the double houses established in Ireland were at the forefront of ecclesiastical reform, although the resonances with older Celtic monasticism and its embrace of religious women and men living in proximity no doubt meant it was not a startling innovation. They were not without their critics, however, with that acerbic reporter Gerald of Wales describing the double houses of Irish Augustinians as scandalous.[62]

How the relationships between the different Augustinian and Arroasian houses worked in practice in Ireland is obscure. Certainly the Arroasians in Ireland, as in England, seem fairly early to have relinquished ties with the mother house in Arrouaise, since before 1200 there were unheeded calls for the Irish to attend the general chapter of the order.[63] This does not necessarily mean that the observances were no longer followed, although Milis argues that the Irish probably dropped the separate observances of Arrouaise sometime in the

Murchad's wife see *AClon* 1137 and for Murchad see *AFM* 1153 and see Fitzpatrick and O'Brien, *The medieval churches of County Offaly*, pp 98–9. **58** O'Dwyer, *Mary*, p. 73. **59** "Día mór dom imdeghail", cited in O'Dwyer, *Mary*, p. 74. **60** Dickenson, "English regular canons", pp 81–3, and Thompson, *Women religious*, p. 56. **61** Elkins, *Holy women*, pp xvii–i and 55–60, and Gilchrist, *Gender and material culture*, pp 38–9. Johnson, *Equal in monastic profession*, p. 7. **62** Giraldus Cambrensis, *Opera*, IV, p. 183. **63** Milis, *L'ordre des chaniones*

fourteenth century.[64] Within Ireland, the ties between the daughter houses of Clonard probably continued to be active, although the evidence is scanty. At the death of Finola ny Melaghlen, abbess of Clonard, in 1286, she was described as "arch-abbess of Meath", indicating that Clonard was still viewed as the motherhouse.[65] Canons from Durrow, Trim and St Peter's, Clonard, all associated with St Mary's, Clonard, as dependencies in the 1195 bull, represented the business interests of nuns of Clonard several times between 1282 and 1310, perhaps suggesting that there were still nuns in these houses then.[66] The links between the Clonard group and the prior of the Arroasian monastery of Louth were preserved for many years, because he claimed first right of presentation in the election of the prioress of one of the daughter houses, Termonfeckin, in 1418, and at the dissolution also held land and the rights to the vicarage at Termonfeckin.[67] However, when an election of the prioress of Termonfeckin occurred in 1535, the abbess of Clonard and Odder claimed the right of presentation, and presented in turn nuns from St Mary del Hogges in Dublin and Odder for the post.[68] This suggests that the links between the nunneries created in the twelfth century were still active in some way in the sixteenth century. Whether the links were used in any other ways except in the presentation of abbesses and prioresses is not known, although there is no evidence to suggest that they were completely redundant.

Killone and its daughter houses

Reforming Gaelic rulers also established the nunnery of St John's or Killone (Co. Clare) and probably the dependent small nunnery of St Peter's in Limerick. A fifteenth-century document that purports to be a copy of an earlier charter lists the possessions of the abbey of St Peter and St Paul at Clare Abbey, including Killone, and appears to represent the foundation of a network of Augustinian houses in the Thomond area under Domnall Mór Ua Briain in the latter years of the twelfth century.[69] Recent analysis by Marie Therese Flanagan has established that it is not a copy of a lost twelfth-century charter but a fifteenth-century constructed narrative of the foundation of Clare Abbey and its network of monasteries. The lands and resources mentioned in the 'foundation' charter were more probably those associated with the monasteries in the fifteenth rather than the twelfth

règuliers d'Arrouaise, pp 367–70 and see Preston, "The canons regular of St Augustine", pp 81–3. **64** Milis, *L'ordre des chanoines règuliers d'Arrouaise*, p. 370. **65** *AClon.* 1286. She is identified as the abbess of Clonard by Brady, "Nunnery of Clonard", p. 4. See also *Cal. doc. Ire., 1252–1284*, p. 511. **66** 1282: Brother Walter, canon of the church of St Mary, Durrow *Cal. doc. Ire., 1252–84*, p. 436; 1286: Brother William, canon of St Mary's Trim, *Cal. doc. Ire., 1285–92*, p. 109; 1288: Brother John, canon of the house of St Peter's Clonard, *Cal. doc. Ire., 1285–92*, p. 177; 1295: Brother William, canon of the house of St Mary's, Trim, *Cal. doc. Ire., 1293–1301*, p. 117; 1310: Brother Hugh, canon of St Mary's, Trim, *Cal. pat. rolls, 1307–13*, pp 290–1. Brother Robert from the house of Navan was also used as a messenger in 1288, see *Cal. doc. Ire., 1285–92*, p. 184. The suggestion that there were still nuns at the houses of Trim and Durrow at this time has been made by Brady and cited in *Med. rel. houses Ire.*, p. 318. **67** NLI MS 13, f. 292. For the rights to the vicarage see Flanagan, "St Mary's abbey, Louth", pp 226–30. It is probable that the land and the vicarage were the property of the long-disbanded canons of Termonfeckin. **68** "Reg. Cromer", *Louth Arch. Soc. Jn.* 10 (1941–4) pp 177–8. **69** Westropp,

century, and may indicate that the estates were substantially augmented around this time.

Leask dated surviving buildings at both Clare Abbey and Killone to the first third of the thirteenth century.[70] Since the charter claiming foundation by Domnall Mór is not authentic, it makes more sense to credit Donnchad Cairprech Ua Briain rather than Domnall Mór with the foundation of both Clare Abbey and Killone.[71] The inclusion of houses for nuns in this organisation of the spiritual resources of Thomond in both the early thirteenth century and later in the fifteenth, indicates that the Ó Briain family considered nunneries to be an essential feature of the landscape. Although there is no other direct evidence of connections between the monasteries, it is probable that the monks of neighbouring Clare Abbey provided spiritual support for the nuns of Killone and probably the staff for the parishes that were impropriated to it.[72] It is also likely that the small nunnery of Ballynagallagh in Small County (Co. Limerick) was added to this group in the fifteenth century, when the area around it was overrun by Tadhg Ó Briain.[73]

Kilcreevanty and its daughter houses

Another royal foundation was the nunnery of St Mary of Castasilva at Kilcreevanty (Co. Galway), founded by Cathal Crobderg Ua Conchobair, king of Connacht, in about 1200, initially under the Benedictine rule.[74] The records of its foundation give tantalising extra details on the choice of rule and the relationships between lay founder, episcopal overseer and the nuns. It is likely that members of Cathal Crobderg's family were nuns at Kilcreevanty. Not only was this accepted practice throughout Gaelic Ireland at the time but also all the nuns of Kilcreevanty whose names are known were surnamed Ó Conchobair. It is necessary to remain cautious of assuming that members of the same family would automatically render support to each other, especially in the milieu of the Ui Chonchobair struggles for the kingship of Connacht. Certainly, it is probable that they did support their founder and kinsman, but they may not always have done so. The family name of the abbess at the time, Orata, is not mentioned, but the death of Duibhessa, daughter of Ruaidrí Ua Conchobair and wife of Cathal Mac Diarmada, was recorded in 1230, and she was described as "a black nun". It is possible that she had retired to Kilcreevanty.[75]

The first surviving significant record of the convent is when the nuns changed their rule, first to Arroasian then to Cistercian, apparently causing a dispute with the archbishop of Tuam sometime between 1216 and 1223.[76] It is the resolution of this dispute, negotiated by Domnhall Ó hÉanna, bishop of Killaloe and papal legate in 1223, that has been recorded. The resolution

"Foundation charter of Forgy Abbey", pp 78–9. **70** Leask, *Irish churches and monastic buildings*, II, p. 63. **71** My thanks to Marie Therese Flanagan for discussing her dating and analysis of this charter with me. **72** Westropp, "Augustinian houses of Co. Clare", p. 127. **73** This scenario is argued by Ó Dálaigh, "Mistress, mother and abbess", p. 61. **74** For the bull confirming the possessions of Kilcreevanty see *Pont. Hib.*, I, pp 239–43. Ware gives the founder in *Whole Works*, II, p. 110. **75** *ALC*, 1230; *AConn*. 1229. **76** The changes are referred

involved the exemption of the nuns from the supervision of the archbishop of Tuam except for a triennial visit by him and the abbot of Cong, and the nuns agreed to return to the Arroasian observance.[77] The reason for the proposed change of order and the dispute between the nuns and archbishop of Tuam is not clear from the surviving documentation, although the complexities of the relationships between the Uí Chonchobair, the archbishops of Tuam, and the reforms in the church in Connacht are probably at the heart of the dispute with Kilcreevanty.

The nuns themselves may have wished to change their order. The Cistercians were popular with women in other countries and there were nunneries in England that followed the rule while never being admitted formally as members of the Cistercian affiliation.[78] Part of the problem with Kilcreevanty following the Cistercian rule may have been the contemporary disapproval from the Cistercian general council towards admitting convents of nuns to the order.[79] Cathal Crobderg himself was a supporter of the Cistercians, having founded the Cistercian monastery of Knockmoy in 1190, and retired there to die in the habit of the order in 1224, so it may have been his wish that the nuns of Kilcreevanty follow that order.[80]

The other difficulty in following the Cistercian order was that these monasteries were exempt from local episcopal authority, including the levying of procurations and fees to episcopal funds. The reforming Augustinian prior of Saul, Felix Ua Ruanada, was consecrated as archbishop of Tuam in 1202 and did not resign until 1235. He was captured by a hostile member of the Uí Chonchobair, Máel Ísa, in 1216, however, and may not have fully retained control over the diocese from that time on. Felix Ua Ruanada, although originally Augustinian, ended his life in the Cistercian habit, and was also a well-travelled man and would have been aware of the developments within the Cistercian order outside Ireland.[81] It may then have been his opposition to the plan that led to the dispute.

Felix was removed from the archbishopric and a rival set up in his place around the time the nuns successfully petitioned the pope to change to the Cistercian order.[82] This rival, likely to have been an uncle of Ruaidrí Ó Conchobair, was then possibly archbishop at the time of the dispute with Kilcreevanty.[83] The problems with the different factions within the diocese of Tuam were complex and revolved

to in a later dispute with the archbishop of Tuam. See *Cal. justic. rolls Ire., 1307–13*, p. 113–4. **77** *Cal. papal letters, 1396–1400*, pp 335–7. The abbey of Cong was Arroasian, and other witnesses to this agreement are canons from Cong and Tuam, also Arroasian. Dunning, "The Arroasian order in medieval Ireland", p. 306. **78** Degler-Spengler, "The incorporation of Cistercian nuns", pp 99–101. **79** Although the Council passed legislation dealing with nuns in a manner suggesting their long-standing inclusion in the order in 1213, by 1220 decrees were passed forbidding more convents of women being accepted into the order. For general discussion of this see Thompson, *Women religious*, pp 94–5. **80** See *AConn.* 1224. **81** Gwynn, *The Irish church in the eleventh and twelfth centuries*, p. 266, where he notes that Felix was present at the Fourth Lateran Council in Rome. **82** The actual petition does not survive, only an exemplification of it dated 1400. See *Cal. papal letters, 1396–1404*, pp 335–7. **83** Felix Ua Ruanada, who was consecrated in 1202, was captured and made a prisoner by Máel Ísa Ó Conchobair, coarb of Roscommon in 1216. See *ALC* 1216 and Gwynn, *The Irish*

around attempts by the papal legate, with probable support of Cathal Crobderg, to usurp the power of the family of Uí Dhubhthaigh who traditionally held the bishopric.[84] It is also possible that once Felix was deposed Cathal Crobderg himself changed sides and eventually supported the rival archbishop rather than Felix.[85] It may also have been Cathal Crobderg who decided that the Arroasian rule was better for Kilcreevanty, as this would make it the mother house for the order in Connacht, affiliated with a significant number of smaller nunneries throughout the territory that Cathal controlled and wished to secure.[86] The abbots of the Arroasian monasteries of Cong and Tuam, who were also involved in the resolution, may have been unwilling to allow such a wealthy house as Kilcreevanty to pass to the Cistercian order and out of their orbit of influence.[87] Convents needed chaplains and other administrative personnel who were routinely supplied by the nearest monastery of the same order. In this case the nearest Cistercian house would have been the Uí Chonchobair-patronized house at Boyle, while both Cong and Tuam were much closer.

How the dispute arose is therefore not totally clear from the surviving evidence. The interests of powerful secular and ecclesiastical people were involved, however, putting Kilcreevanty on a course that it would probably follow for the rest of its history. Wherever the impetus for the change of rule originated, it resulted in a dispute with the archbishop which was obviously important enough for the papal legate to be involved and for there to be several communications with Rome over the matter. Despite the lack of a final explanation, the vivid and enduring connections between the convent, the founder and the wider ecclesiastical communities emerge as paramount.

Most of the nunneries affiliated with Kilcreevanty in the 1223 agreement were probably in existence in the twelfth century, some having been founded by Tairdelbach Ua Conchobair, possibly with the support or influence of Malachy in the 1140s.[88] From the 1223 agreement it is clear that some of Clonard's dependencies had been transferred to Kilcreevanty. The convents were those at Annaghdown, Clonmacnoise and Drumalgagh, all in or near the archdiocese of Tuam. The transfer possibly occurred because of the changes to the political

church in the eleventh and twelfth centuries, pp 268–9 and also *NHI, IX*, p. 30, note 3. The exemplification of the agreement between the Archbishop and Kilcreevanty mentions that it occurred in the fifth year of the archbishop's consecration, which would suggest a date of 1216/17. See *Cal. papal letters, 1396–1404*, p. 337. This is either an error, or proof that the archbishop was not Felix but a rival, whose name has not been recorded. He is named as Florence in papal order to visit Kilcreevanty issued in 1321. See *Cal. papal letters, 1305–42*, p. 212, however all other references to him are as F. **84** Simms, "Frontiers in the Irish church", p. 195, and Gwynn, *The Irish church in the eleventh and twelfth centuries*, pp 230–1. **85** Simms, "Frontiers in the Irish church", p. 195, suggests that Cathal Crobderg may have changed sides by 1216. **86** For a summary of Cathal Crobderg's ambitions and the steps he took to secure his territories in Connacht, see *NHI*, II, p. 161. **87** They are witnesses to the agreement. See *Cal. papal letters, 1396–1404*, p. 335. **88** The convents at Ardcarn, Clonfert, Derrane, were probably originally joint foundations of men and women founded by Toirrdelbach Ó Conchobair in the 1140s. See *Med. rel. houses Ire.*, pp 312 and 315, for suggestions that Malachy

landscape after the arrival of the Anglo-Normans, or possibly because of realignments of territory between the archbishops of Tuam and Armagh.[89] The nunnery of Inishmaine is not mentioned in the 1223 document. Its lands, however, were included in the post-dissolution surveys, confirming that it was a part of the Kilcreevanty network.[90] There was an early medieval house of monks at Inishmaine, but there are no mentions of monks at this convent after the twelfth century, when the main portions of the surviving ruins were built, incorporating earlier structures.[91] It is possible that the nuns from the convent at Annaghdown, which is not mentioned after the early thirteenth century, were transferred to a new foundation at Inishmaine soon after 1223, retaining their affiliation with Kilcreevanty.[92]

The nunneries that were transferred to Kilcreevanty from Clonard were probably those originally affiliated with Clonmacnoise. While the kings of Meath were trying to gain ascendancy, these were affiliated with Clonard. After 1220, when the fortunes of the Ua Máel Sechlainn dynasty were rocked by the incursions of Anglo-Norman settlers, the Ui Chonchobair seem to have claimed them for Connacht. Other convents not mentioned in connection with Clonard were included in the Kilcreevanty filiation (see figure 4). Some of these convents, such as Cloonoghill, may also have been originally a dependency of Clonmacnoise.[93] Small nunneries founded later in the medieval period were also made dependent on Kilcreevanty, indicating that it continued to be recognised as the head of the Arroasian nuns in Gaelic Ireland. It is probable, for example, that when Walter de Burgo founded the small house of Annagh in the fifteenth century it was made dependent on Kilcreevanty.[94] The relationships between these daughter houses and the mother house are not made clear in any of the surviving documentation. In general, dependent houses were financially and administratively under the control of the mother house. There is, however, little evidence of how this worked in practice for the convents of Ireland. Since the lands and revenues associated with the daughter convents were listed as part of Kilcreevanty's estates in the sixteenth century, there were almost certainly some sort of administrative and financial ties that endured throughout the medieval period.[95]

was influential in these foundations. **89** Flanagan, "St Mary's abbey, Louth", p. 232. **90** Knox, *History of Tuam*, p. 284. **91** Healy, "Two royal abbeys", pp 3–9. The suggestion that the male house continued into the thirteenth century is based on an obituary for Mailisa Ó Conchobair, whom *AFM* described as being Prior of Inishmaine. For explanation of the error of the Four Masters in this and proof that Mailisa was prior of Roscommon see Nicholls in "A list of the monasteries in Connacht, 1577", p. 39, n. 107, and pp 41–3. **92** This is the view expressed in *Med. rel. houses Ire.*, p. 318, and Goaley, *Monastic ruins at Annaghdown*, p. 11. Goaley also suggests that the buildings of the nunnery at Annaghdown were converted for use by the Premonstarian canons. Kilcreevanty retained some land at Annaghdown; see Knox, *History of Tuam*, p. 281. **93** Moore, "The cell of the canonesses regular of St Augustine at Clonoghill", pp 15–16. **94** *Med. rel. houses Ire.*, p. 312. When Kilcreevanty was dissolved in 1543, its possessions included 80 acres in "Annaghe of the Nuns", Archdall (1786), p. 799. **95** Preston, "The canons regular of St Augustine", pp 91–2, discusses the dependencies of Augustinian

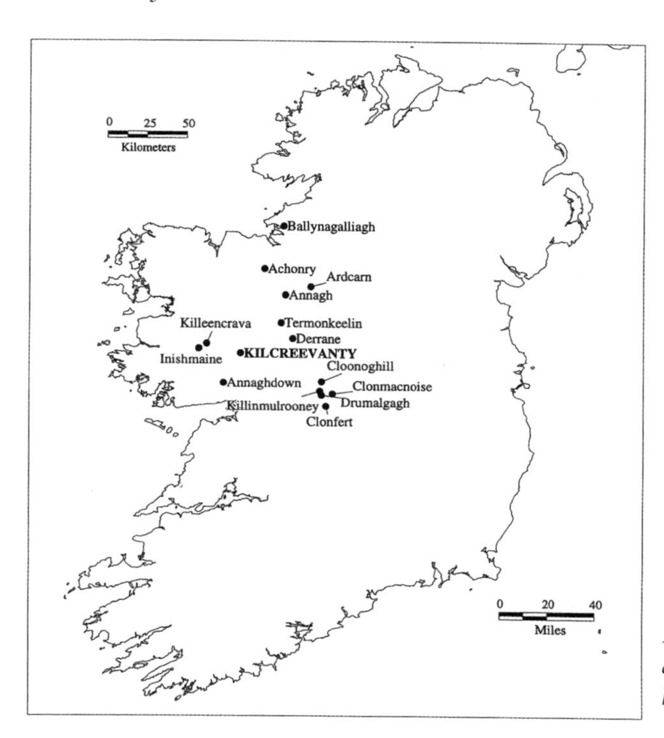

Figure 4. Kilcreevanty and its daughter houses, c.1223

Cistercian nuns in Gaelic Ireland

Malachy also introduced the Cistercians to Ireland and created a thriving network of Cistercian monasteries, many of which were dependent on Mellifont (Co. Louth). Some of these early foundations also included women. One of the patrons of Mellifont was Derbforgaill, granddaughter of its patron, Ua Maél Sechlainn, and she chose to retire to Mellifont dying there at the age of eighty-five.[96] Although this is not direct evidence for a nunnery at Mellifont, her residence there certainly proves that women were admitted in some capacity, even if only as noble lodgers. Further suggestion of the presence of nuns occurs in the early thirteenth century, when Irish Cistercian houses incurred the reforming ire of Stephen of Lexington.[97] He objected strongly to the admission of nuns into any of the Cistercian houses in Ireland, and strictly forbade the practice.[98]

In 1228, the prior of Inishlauaght in Co. Tipperary launched his ambush against Stephen's representative from behind a hedge of the nuns' house adjoining the abbey.[99] Although Stephen did not mention any nuns here particularly, he did order the sale of the abbot's house "in the courtyard of the nuns at Mellifont". At

canons. **96** *AFM* 1193. **97** For the history of the revolt at the Cistercian house of Mellifont see O'Dwyer, *The conspiracy of Mellifont*. **98** Stephen of Lexington, *Letters*, p. 211. **99** Stephen of Lexington, *Letters*, p. 163, for the complaint about Jerpoint; p. 185 for the attack

Jerpoint he was more specific, ordering the removal of "the nuns' monastery", which was adjacent to Jerpoint, and that the nuns be suitably rehoused, ostensibly because of the complaints of Count Marshall and others. These rather laconic references certainly establish the presence of women at these Cistercian houses. They may have simply been houses where noble patrons could retire and die in the religious habit, or they may have housed women who had taken more formal vows. The mention of Count Marshall in the complaints against Jerpoint is interesting, suggesting that there was disquiet among Anglo-Irish patrons about the close proximity of nuns and monks.

NUNNERIES IN ANGLO-IRISH COMMUNITIES

The arrival of the Anglo-Normans and the resulting changes in secular property holdings and ecclesiastical structures affected the patterns of foundation and affiliation of nunneries in the later twelfth and early thirteenth centuries. It is easy to overestimate this effect because, as Simms and others have pointed out, the process of reform among the Gaelic Irish – which had been started in the twelfth century – had long-lasting consequences which were not fully realised by the end of the twelfth century.[100] Within the ambit of the newly arrived Anglo-Normans, the ecclesiastical landscape was substantially reshaped. Parishes were established to fit the changed political landscape and to advance Anglo-Norman settlement. Another change in areas settled by Anglo-Normans was a shift in patrons and founders of religious houses generally. Many existing women's houses were received well by the new lords of their districts, particularly those under the patronage of Mac Murchada, whose alliances with the incoming Anglo-Normans must have smoothed the path of acceptance for the nunneries formally under his protection. St Mary del Hogges in Dublin was made effectively independent of Clonard sometime after 1195, had its possessions confirmed and was the recipient of further grants of lands and rents from the Anglo-Normans. This is reputed to have occurred after the nuns proved their loyalty to the new regime by hiding Englishmen from the Irish during the reign of Henry II, with the result that they were rewarded by King John with the confirmation of their property and new grants.[101] St Mary del Hogges was always well supported by the archbishops of Dublin, including Lorcán Ua Tuathail, the archbishop at the time of the arrival of the Anglo-Normans. This association may have meant that members of his family became nuns there.[102]

by the prior of Inishlounaght (Suir) p. 185. **100** Simms, "Frontiers in the Irish church", pp 194–6ff. **101** BL Add. MS 4813, pp 51–2. **102** Ware reports that that Laurence's sister, Mór, was "grossly ill-used" by her husband, Diarmait Mac Murchada, and found refuge in the abbey. She gave all her husband's wealth to the nunnery and hid there for seven years after she left him, only emerging for the funeral of her brother Laurence, when she was recognised. No reference to this story is found in the vitae of Lorcán Ua Tuahail, and I have found no

Another nunnery founded by Diarmait Mac Murchada, Kilculliheen, received generous grants and confirmation of its holdings from King John, when Lord of Ireland, and was made independent of Clonard sometime between 1185 and 1195. The inspeximus of its original charter refers to A. abbess of all Ireland, almost certainly Agnes of Clonard. Therefore, at the time of John's grant, around 1185, Kilculliheen was filiated with or dependent on Clonard. However, it was not included in the dependencies of Clonard made in 1195 and certainly by 1239, when the inspeximus was made, Kilculliheen is referred to as an abbey in its own right.[103] Requesting the inspeximus itself probably signals a substantial change in lay patronage, and it includes substantial grants from David FitzMilo made in or before 1239. David FitzMilo also granted land known as Addrigoole to Kilculliheen at this time. There are no references to the nuns of Addrigoole after this date, although the land was still in the possession of Kilculliheen at the dissolution.[104] This may mean that the nuns of Addrigoole transferred to Kilculliheen at the time of the grant or that they had died out sometime earlier. Carrigan suggests that FitzMilo's donation of the remote area of land at Addrigoole indicates it was an ancient nunnery.[105]

There were also new foundations of nunneries made by the Anglo-Normans. The foundation of monasteries has been associated by historians with the colonisation process, and these monasteries have been assumed to have been fortified and willing to defend their lands and interests from resisting Gaelic Irish.[106] Mapping foundations of Augustinian canons along with Anglo-Norman mottes shows that the spread of the Augustinian was contiguous with the spread of English settlers.[107] Nunneries are not usually considered in this process, but there were several significant convents established by the first generations of tenants-in-chief, which suggests that they were considered to have a place in the conquest of Ireland, probably more in cultural reorganisation of resources than in defence of lands.

These nunneries were founded relatively soon after the arrival of the Anglo-Normans, generally around 1200, at the end of the lives of the first generation of arrivals. This suggests that estates and manors needed to be organised and secured before nunneries could be considered. While the numbers of nunneries founded at this time are small compared with the number of men's houses, two of the larger Anglo-Norman land holders did choose to found and build nunneries as their major contribution to new monastic foundations. These two nunneries were founded in Co. Kildare at Timolin and Graney, and both were situated close to the castles of their founders, suggesting that this proximity compensated for their relative inability, as religious women, physically to defend their houses.

medieval references to it. It has a romantic quality which makes it suspect, however Ware must have had older sources than now survive, so perhaps it has a medieval origin. BL Add. MS 4813 pp 51–2. For Mór's marriage see Flanagan, *Irish society*, pp 101–4. **103** *Cal. doc. Ire., 1171–1231*, p. 370. **104** *Extents Ir. mon. possessions*, p. 204. **105** *Med. rel. houses Ire.*, p. 312, and see Carrigan, *History and antiquities of Ossory*, II, pp 234–5. **106** "Introduction", *Reg. Trist.*, p. xxx. **107** Duffy ed., *Atlas of Irish history*, p. 39.

The nunnery of St Mary at Timolin was founded about 1191 by Robert son of Richard Norragh, Lord of Norragh, who placed his granddaughter, Lecelina, as first prioress.[108] Robert had been granted the district thereafter known as the "Norrath" by Hugh de Lacy in his original sub-infeudation of Leinster.[109] His foundation of the nunnery at Timolin followed a familiar pattern of monastic foundations by the early Anglo-Normans which were typically Augustinian and situated close to the founder's castle.[110] It is possible that there were women living as religious in the area who were transferred to the new nunnery. The name, Timolin, or Teach Moling, house of St Moling, and often distinguished from the monastery of St Mullins as Techmolinbeg or the small house of St Moling, suggests an earlier Celtic foundation for at least the church.[111] On this evidence, there may have been a house of nuns here, or it may have been ecclesiastical land. There is a slight corroboration of the existence of nuns at Timolin prior to the foundation by Robert, son of Richard Norragh. The archbishop Alen, in his sixteenth-century survey of the diocese of Dublin, noted that the nuns of Timolin, like those of Grace Dieu, were originally without a recognised rule.[112] This may indicate nothing more than Alen's disapproval of nuns, although it is also possible that the Augustinian rule was adopted at the request of Robert of Norragh, and that before that time the nuns' community was considered by the episcopacy to be a more informal institution.

The priory of Timolin was close to the founder's castle and endowed with the rectories of the churches on his lands.[113] Timolin was also supported by Hugh Dullard, probably one of Robert's tenants, with donations of the rectories of his land.[114] Timolin acquired substantial estates with many rectories in its holdings, suggesting that it was the favoured monastic destination for the spiritualities from the lands of several of the Anglo-Norman settlers in this area. A number of these rectories were in the Wicklow area, never heavily settled by the Anglo-Normans and quick to return to control of the Gaelic Irish. This meant that they were later more liabilities to Timolin than assets. The donation of rectories in areas that were not completely settled indicates that, like monasteries, the new settlers conceived convents as part of the colonisation process.

St Mary's at Graney was founded by Walter de Riddlesford I sometime before 1200, with significant estates of land and churches donated by both Walter and his tenants and spread over the dioceses of Dublin, Leighlin, Ferns and Cork.[115] Walter de Riddlesford I was one of the original arrivals with Strongbow and the

108 *Med. rel. houses Ire.*, p. 325, "Rep. Viride, Alen", p. 212. **109** *Song of Dermot*, lines 3122–5, and see Orpen, *Ireland under the Normans*, I, p. 383, and Fitzgerald, "Narraghmore and the Barons of Norragh", p. 243. **110** Carville, *The occupation of Celtic sites*, p. 57. Robert's castle had been built for him by de Lacy in 1185. Orpen, *Ireland under the Normans*, I, p. 356. **111** Joyce, *Irish place names*, p. 116. **112** *Alen's reg.*, p. 179. **113** Lewis, *Topographical dictionary of Ireland*, II, p. 626. **114** Archdall (1786), pp 343–4. **115** Brooks has argued that it was the first Walter de Riddlesford who founded Graney, as opposed to his son of the same name. Brooks, "de Ridelisfords", p. 117. The confirmation of the original charter of Walter de

tenant-in-chief of a large area around Bray.[116] He donated not only significant amounts of land close to his own castle, but also a large proportion of the spiritual revenues of his holdings including the tithes of the mills from his holdings in Bray.[117] One of his castles was near Graney, possibly near the church of Kilkea, which was itself appropriated to the nuns of Graney.[118] Other major landholders in the area also donated lands to Graney, including William de Carew, who was enfeoffed with Idrone by Strongbow. William's nephew, another William, donated the advowson of the caput of his holding, Dunlecney, to Graney before 1207, along with lands there and in St Mullins.[119] Graney was obviously the most important monastic establishment patronised by Walter. He organized his tenants to donate lands and rectories from their holdings and Graney remained the only monastic house on his estate during his lifetime. He or members of his family may have been buried at the convent. There survives one Norman grave slab from the convent and there were reports of other medieval slabs.[120] Although Graney was the most important monastery founded by de Riddlesford, he, like so many of the early generation of Anglo-Normans, also donated lands and rents to St Thomas', Dublin, and St Mary's, Dublin, while he and his wife founded the hospital of St John the Baptist in Castledermot.[121] This pattern was in keeping with the first generation of Anglo-Normans who established monastic institutions to provide different services for the nascent communities being fostered by the settlers.

A number of rectories in Cork were donated to Graney.[122] The donation of rectories so far from the convent is surprising, though not unprecedented, and may be explained by the family connections of Walter de Riddlesford. One of his daughters, Basilida, married Richard de Cogan before 1213 and the de Cogans had been granted substantial lands in Co. Cork.[123] They also held lands around Castledermot, possibly dating from this time.[124] The de Carew family

Riddlesford, *Pont. Hib.*, pp 137–9. Geraldine Carville discusses the site and history of Graney in "Graney Convent," *Hallel* 27(2002) 13–31. **116** *Song of Dermot*, lines 3094–9; and Orpen, *Ireland under the Normans* I, pp 226, 369, 386. **117** The charter is examined in detail by Brooks, "de Ridelisfords". **118** Orpen, "Mottes", p. 248. Kilkea is one of the churches which was listed at the Dissolution commissioners belonging to Graney. *Extents Ir. mon. possessions* p. 24. **119** *Knights' fees*, pp 60–1. **120** Harbison, "A medieval tombstone from Graney", pp 216–17; FitzGerald, "The priory and nunnery of Graney" p. 380, reports the destruction of a tomb slab in 1875 which had been used to cover the well of the Convent, known locally as Mary's well. **121** "Rep. Viride Alen", p. 206. *Chart. St Mary's Dublin*, I, pp 29–30; Reg. *St Thomas Dublin*, pp 170–1. **122** *Fiants Ire., Hen. VIII-Eliz., I,* p. 35, lists five rectories in Cork which were part of the property of Graney. Also see Smith, *Ancient and present state of Cork*, pp 66, 67, 69, 71. The foundation charter of Bridgetown Priory (Co. Cork) mentions lands of the nuns of Graney adjacent to its newly donated lands around Fermoy. The charter is dated before 1216. See O'Keeffe, *An Anglo-Norman monastery: Bridgetown priory*, p. 34. For full details of the landholdings of Graney and other nunneries see, Hall, "Women and religion", pp 357–83. **123** Brooks, "de Rideliesfords", p. 131; *Chart. St Mary's Dublin*, II, p. 15 for Basilida's marriage and Orpen, *Ireland under the Normans*, II, 45–46. **124** Brooks, "de

also patronised Graney and held lands in Cork.[125] These connections suggest that it was through either personal connections with the de Cogans or Carews or through patronage from Walter de Riddlesford's daughter that Graney acquired the rectories in Cork. As with the donations to Timolin, Graney's administration of these rectories represents part of the cultural colonisation of the newly conquered lands of the Anglo-Norman settlers.

Another of the major Anglo-Norman settlers to establish a convent on his lands was Walter de Lacy, who founded the Cistercian nunnery of Loughsewdy or Plary in 1218.[126] Like the other nunneries founded by Anglo-Normans in the first generation or two, such as Timolin and Graney, this nunnery was established in close proximity to an important castle in the patron's holdings, in this case the castle of Ballymore. Walter de Lacy was a son of Hugh de Lacy, who had been granted the lordship of Meath in 1186. The adoption of the Cistercian rule for this nunnery is interesting, since there was an Augustinian male house, probably dependent on Tristernagh, about half a mile from the nunnery, and it would have been logical for the nunnery to follow the same rule. Indeed, it appears that the monks of the monastery undertook the pastoral and administrative care of the nuns.[127] The Cistercian rule may have been the choice of the nuns themselves, although in the absence of direct evidence of the first nuns this can only be speculation. The patronage of Cistercian houses seems to have been popular with the de Lacy family. There was a Cistercian monastery on the family holdings in England, and Carville has speculated that the name Plary, which was an alternative name for the nunnery, may be a corruption of the English name of this monastery – Plarton.[128] The de Lacys were also not among the donors to St Mary's Cistercian abbey in Dublin, preferring to patronise the Victorine abbey of St Thomas.[129] However, this does not mean that de Lacy would not choose the Cistercian order when founding a nunnery on his own land. Whatever the reasons for the choice of rule, the de Lacy family founded the nunnery and continued to support it over a number of generations.

The process of colonisation occurred later in the west of Ireland than in the east, and as part of that process a similar pattern of monastic foundations occurred there, again involving small numbers of nunneries. In Co. Limerick, on lands which were wrested from Gaelic control later than in the east, the rather obscure nunnery of St Catherine d'Conyl was founded in the first half of the thirteenth century by ancestors of the earls of Desmond. Although the cult of St Catherine became popular in Ireland this is the only church in medieval

Ridelisfords", p. 132, note 86. **125** McCotter, "The sub-infeudation and descent of the Fitzstephen/Carew moiety, I", p. 68. **126** Carville, "Cistercian nuns in Ireland", p. 68. **127** The nuns of Loughswedy and the monks of Tristernagh are mentioned as sharing the presentation of a benefice in 1395 and 1397. *Cal. papal letters, 1362–1404*, p. 513, and *Cal. papal letters, 1396–1404*, p. 80. The lands of the nuns of Loughswedy were absorbed into the estates of the monks by the dissolution, probably indicating that the nuns were no longer in residence. See *Extents Ir. mon. possessions*, pp 284–5. **128** Carville, "Cistercian nuns in Ireland", p. 67. **129** *Reg. St Thomas Dublin*, pp 11–12.

Limerick known by this name, so its dedication may represent a personal choice of the founder.[130] The earliest definite mention of the convent is in 1298, when in a survey made of the manor of Shanid belonging to Thomas FitzMaurice there is mention of land which Thomas's grandfather had granted to the nuns of "Okonyl".[131] There is also an obscure reference to a Beatrice, prioress of St Catherine "de Balyelan", bringing to warrant Thomas Fitz Maurice in a dispute over eighty acres of land in Limerick in 1291.[132] Although it is possible that Beatrice was from the small convent founded at Ballynagallagh, it is likely that the prioress would call on the patron to give warranty in any dispute. As Thomas FitzMaurice was the patron of St Catherine and not Ballynagalliagh, it is probable that the priory mentioned is St Catherine d'Conyl. The cantred of Shanid had been granted in about 1215 to Thomas, son of Maurice FitzGerald, and was considered the "most ancient house" of the Desmond earls.[133] It was probably this Thomas's son, John, who founded the abbey.[134] The lands of St Catherine were all within the boundary of the FitzMaurice cantred of Shanid and the nunnery itself was built close to the Desmond castle at Shanid.[135] The founder's family remained patrons of the abbey and it was James FitzMaurice, earl of Desmond, who claimed the right as patron to inform the papacy of the scandalous living arrangements of the nuns in 1432 and probably had the nunnery suppressed.[136]

St Catherine d'Conyl, then, follows the pattern of foundation of nunneries in other parts of Anglo-Irish Ireland: they were established towards the end of the first generation after conquest and they were not usually the first monastic houses to be established. These nunneries were situated close to the founders' castles and were supported by grants of land and resources from throughout the holdings of the founder. This indicates that the nunneries were a significant part of the reorganisation of land and ecclesiastical resources of the new Anglo-Norman settlers, and that their relative inability to directly defend their lands, as male monastics may have been able, was not seen as a definitive disability in their foundation. They were obviously considered to be a part of the cultural colonisation of the land that accompanied the spread of the newly founded monasteries throughout Anglo-Norman Ireland.

130 Westropp, "A survey of the ancient churches in the county of Limerick", p. 469. **131** *Cal. doc. Ire., 1285–92*, p. 259. **132** Calendar of common bench roll, no. 16, 19 Ed I (NAI RC 7/3), pp 26, 195. The convent dedication is given as St Mary on p. 26. The lands are named in the calendar, however they are not immediately recognisable as lands which later belonged to St Catherine d'Conyl. **133** Orpen, *Ireland under the Normans*, II, p. 164. For further discussion of the sub-infeudation of Shanid and its acquisition by the FitzThomases see McCotter, "The sub-infeudation and descent of the Fitzstephen/Carew moiety, II", pp 97–8. **134** John died at the battle of Callan in 1261. Lydon, "Land of war", *NHI*, II, p. 252. **135** The later barony of Shanid was probably similar in boundaries to the old cantred. Wardell, "The history and antiquities of St Catherine's Old Abbey", p. 41. **136** *Cal. papal letters, 1427–47*, p. 400. The nunnery is referred as suppressed in 1428, see "Obligationes annatis pro diocesis Limiricensis", p. 111. Although this may not represent the final suppression of the convent, there are no references to the nuns after this date.

Bishops were involved in the foundation of two nunneries in the heartland of English settlement and were part of episcopal plans to reorganize spiritual resources and revenues within their dioceses. Archbishop John Cumin of Dublin, the first English archbishop of Dublin, founded Grace Dieu (Co. Dublin) in 1195. The priory of Grace Dieu was probably founded on lands donated by Cumin from church lands and staffed with nuns transferred from nearby Lusk, one of the dependencies of Clonard. It is possible that the nuns of Lusk came under episcopal disapproval for lapses in their observance of their rule or that they were not following a recognised rule at all, as there is a late reference to the fact that these nuns, like the nuns of Timolin, were "originally claustral without a cloister and regulars without a rule".[137] The church at Lusk itself was later appropriated to All Saints Priory in Dublin. Once the nuns had transferred to Grace Dieu, they were no longer dependent on Clonard. Cumin conferred several other churches on the nuns of Grace Dieu, including the valuable church of St Audoen inside the walls of Dublin. This, however, was taken away from the nuns by the next archbishop, Henry of London, and reallocated to the chapter of St Patrick's cathedral, while the nuns received the church of Ballymadon in return.[138] This may have been in line with Henry of London's reforming agenda and his desire to enrich St Patrick's cathedral.[139]

The nunnery of the Holy Trinity at Lismullin (Co. Meath) was another important nunnery founded by an Anglo-Irish bishop. The history of its foundation is slightly different from that of Grace Dieu because it was founded about fifty years later, after the ecclesiastical resources of the area had been reallocated. The site of Lismullin itself was probably already church property before the arrival of the Anglo-Normans, as land at Lismullin was included in lands confirmed to the nunnery of Clonard.[140] By 1242, Richard de la Corner, bishop of Meath, had enfeoffed it to Avicia de la Corner, and she then used it to found the priory of the Holy Trinity at Lismullin.[141] Since there are no further notices of the nuns at St Mary's Skreen after 1195 it is possible that nuns who may still have been at this nunnery were incorporated into the new house at Lismullin. Richard de la Corner also gave other lands in Meath and Dublin that formed the nucleus of the priory's holdings. He had arranged the transfer of some of these lands from other monastic institutions in the area. For example the lands of Dunsink were originally held from Hugh Tirrell by the priory of Little Malvern in England. A prior in the early thirteenth century enfeoffed the priory of St Peter's Trim with these lands and Bishop Richard then acquired them for Lismullin.[142] There was at least one lay donor at the foundation, and probably more because in a fourteenth-century

137 *Alen's reg.* p. 179. **138** "Rep. Viride, Alen", p. 194; *Alen's reg.* p. 49, where Alen records that this action still rankled with the nuns of Grace Dieu three centuries later. "Liber Niger and Liber Albus of Christ Church, Dublin", p. 315. **139** Murphy, "Balancing the concerns of church and state", pp 41–56. **140** *Pont. Hib.*, 1, 84, and see Hickey, *Skryne and the early Normans*, p. 111. **141** The earliest charters of Lismullin survive in London PRO C 66/277–2 and edited in "Unpublished medieval notitiae" pp 8–11. **142** "Calendar of common bench roll, no. 37", (NAI RC 7/5) pp 355–8. See Hall, "The nuns of Lismullin", p. 59.

confirmation of the nunnery's holdings Richard Fitz John is also described as donating land in Powderlough (Co. Meath) at the foundation of the nunnery.[143]

The foundation of Lismullin may have been part of Bishop Richard's ambition to tighten his episcopal control over the spiritualities of his diocese that had been previously granted to other monastic houses, principally the Cistercian abbey of St Mary's Dublin.[144] That there was disagreement over these arrangements is suggested by the compensation that was arranged for lost tithes and revenues to the abbey of St Mary's when Lismullin was established. A papal indult was obtained which exempted the nuns of Lismullin from "setting aside any portion of the offerings made to their church when the founders have shown to the diocesan a fair exchange for the mother church, which the abbot and convent of St Mary's Dublin hold to their uses".[145] Lismullin's position in the Anglo-Irish heartland of Meath with substantial estates helped to make it ultimately one of the most successful of the nunneries in the medieval colony of Ireland.

Convents in towns

Anglo-Irish families were also responsible for establishing nunneries in towns and villages. A Cistercian nunnery was founded in Down in the late twelfth century by the Bagnal family, probably on the site of the Celtic nunnery of St Brigid.[146] It may have later changed rule, as Anne Mandeville is recorded as the Benedictine prioress of Down in 1353.[147] Although little is known about this convent, it did continue until the early sixteenth century and the names of several of the nuns from the fourteenth and fifteenth centuries are known.[148] The convent of St Mary's in Derry may also have been re-founded on the site of an earlier Celtic nunnery, as there are references to both a "lady erenegh" in 1128 and then to the foundation of the convent in 1218.[149] The nunnery was described as Cistercian in the early sixteenth century with lands in and around the city of Derry.[150] Another small nunnery founded by an Anglo-Irish family was the convent at Killeigh (Co. Offaly). Alemand says that the family were the Warrens, while Ware only says that it was Augustinian.[151] As the canons of the Augustinian house of Killeigh were dependent on Durrow, it is possible that the nuns of Durrow relocated there at this time.[152] The nunnery was on the north side of the village, and was one of three religious houses that owned most of the land in the area between them.[153]

Religious women who wanted to form a recognized monastic institution in the city of Cork in the last years of the thirteenth century had apparently

143 *Calendar of inquisitions miscellaneous (chancery), 1348–77*, p. 236. **144** See Hickey, "St Mary's abbey and the church at Skryne", p. 149. **145** Theiner, *Vetera mon.*, p. 86; *Pont. Hib.*, II, p. 317. **146** St Brigit's Down mentioned AU 1006. **147** *Cal. papal letters, 1342–62*, p. 509. **148** Its lands were incorporated into the cathedral of Down in 1513. Bradshaw, *Dissolution*, p. 37. **149** *AFM* 1134. Ware refers to its foundation in 1218; see *Chart. St Mary's Dublin*, II, p. 234. **150** Colby, *Ordnance survey memoir of Londonderry*, pp 25, 208, 212–13, citing an inquisition of 1609 for the position of the lands of this nunnery. **151** *Med. rel. houses Ire.*, p. 321. **152** *Med. rel. houses Ire.*, pp 183 and 321. **153** Fitzpatrick and O'Brien, *The medieval churches of County*

gathered around a recluse, Agnes de Hareford. This indicates a rather informal arrangement that was common in Europe at the time, when women wishing to live a religious life would become inspired by one charismatic person, often a recluse or anchorite, and would then form themselves into a community. At some point they often either sought official recognition or were pushed into doing so by church officials who believed that women in particular needed the security and discipline of one of the recognised monastic rules and the official guidance of a bishop or neighbouring abbot.[154] The official notices of Agnes de Hareford's proposed foundation of the convent of St John the Baptist were obviously the end result of a period of negotiation with the local land-holders for donations of land and income to support the new convent. It is probable that the nuns had already been living together for some time before 1297 when the first inquiry was ordered into the grants of land for the convent in preparation for the necessary license from the crown. The petition filed with the inquisition makes clear that the nunnery was not yet securely founded and did not have the resources to purchase lands.[155] The first inquiry found that the lands should not be granted as such a grant would be prejudicial to the crown's interests. The second inquiry, however, allowed the grants, noting that the lands were all "waste" – perhaps literally destroyed, no longer tenanted or merely given over to pasture – and the nuns and their patrons were expected to make sure that tenants made the land profitable or at least defensible. How far this was able to be accomplished is not certain because there are very few further references to the nuns of St John.

In the two inquiries, which mention slightly different lists of donors, the nuns were to be granted land and incomes of churches predominantly from the important Barry family of Cork.[156] Since Agnes's name is prominent in all the documents it is probable that Agnes was decisive in the impetus for the foundation. One of the donors was probably a relative of hers. John FitzGilbert, who donated a half carucate of land and the advowsons of two churches, was also known as de Hereford and it is possible that Agnes involved her relative and other contacts in order to acquire the land necessary to firmly establish her nunnery.[157] There were probably further grants to the nunnery, although the only surviving reference is to the almost certainly exaggerated tale of an "Armorican" who came to visit the nuns with a "lecherous design" and was constrained to give the convent £40 per year for ever.[158] Since this is a huge

Offaly, pp 85–8, and see the aerial view with sites marked, pl. 13; and the plan p. 82, and Kearney, *Killeigh and Geashill*. **154** See, for example, Thompson, *Women religious*, pp 16–17ff. **155** PRO London, c 143/36 no. 10, cited by Brand, "The licensing of mortmain alienations", p. 126, n. 11. **156** The Barrys were descendants of the Philip de Barry, brother of Gerald of Wales the chronicler, who participated in the original conquest of Cork in the train of Robert Fitz Stephen. Orpen, *Ireland under the Normans*, II, pp 41, 43; III, 119–20. **157** McCotter, "The sub-infeudation and descent of the Fitzstephen/Carew moiety, I", p. 75, who notes that John Fitz Gilbert de Hereford held his lands from Gerald de Prendergast and Maurice de Carreu. **158** BL MS Egerton, 1774, p. 74. There is no medieval source mentioned for this episode, only a reference to a *Mon. Hib.* by Thomas, which I have been unable to trace.

sum, the story is probably apocryphal. However, it may be a memory of some sort of attack on the nuns.

THE LAST WAVE OF FOUNDATIONS

There were other small nunneries founded throughout Ireland during the later medieval period. Most of these have left very few traces on the records or the landscape and may not have lasted long, but this is difficult to establish with any accuracy. Antiquarian scholars attribute Matilda de Lacy with founding a nunnery at Gageborough (Co. Offaly) in the thirteenth century. There are no other references to this nunnery, so it may have been a very small and short-lived house or it may have been the house of a hermit or anchorite.[159] A Fitzgibbon founded the small house of Ballynagallagh or Monasternicalliagh near Lough Gur in Co. Limerick in 1283. The portion of surviving structure indicates that it was always small.[160] The area in which it was situated was taken over by Tadhg Ó Briain in the fifteenth century and Ballynagallagh was made dependent on the Ó Briain foundation of Killone; however, it probably retained connections with the monastery of Adare, another Fitzgibbon foundation. One of the Ó Briain abbesses may have lived there or had some connections with the nunnery in the late fifteenth century, as Renalda Ní Bhriain, abbess of Killone who died in 1510, owed money to the convent when she died, which was then administered by the monastery of Adare.[161]

There were also nunneries that were possibly founded at the instigation of women desiring to live pious and regular lives and inspired by the religious revival of the fifteenth century. The small house of Ballymacadane in Co. Cork is recorded as being founded by Cormac Láidir Mac Carthaigh, Lord of Muskerry, in 1450 or possibly 1472 for his relative Honor.[162] With this sort of foundation it is often very difficult to interpret the evidence to ascertain where the impetus for a foundation originated. As Cormac Láidir also founded the Observant Franciscan house at nearby Kilcrea, this foundation is similar in pattern to other foundations by Gaelic Irish lords, who often founded several religious houses in their careers.[163] Ballymacadane may have been on the site of an earlier monastery that has vanished without any archival record. One commentator

159 Lewis, *Topographical dictionary of Ireland*, I, 56 and see *Med. rel. houses Ire.*, p. 317. **160** Westropp, "A survey of the ancient churches in the county of Limerick", p. 449, describes it as being a "very small building". **161** Her will is in NLI D 1978. The identification of the Inis Patraic, to which Renalda owed 20 marks, as Ballynagallagh is made by Ó Dálaigh, "Wife, mother and abbess", p. 61. **162** As with many of the small and poorly documented foundations there is some uncertainty about much of the history of Ballymacadane. Smith, *The ancient and present state of Cork*, p. 171, gives the date as 1450, whereas Hayes, "Ballymacadane Abbey", pp 141–3, citing "a roll in the British Museum" gives the date 1472. Both may be correct in that the second date possibly refers to enlargement or completion of significant buildings. **163** Smith, *The ancient and present state of Cork*, p. 166.

believes the surviving ruins may be of an older date than fifteenth century.[164] However, since no archaeological work has been done on the site, it is not possible to be certain of the architectural evidence at this time.

Abandoned church buildings and lands were sometimes used for pious purposes, and some of these were for women who may not have founded lasting communities, but rather small places used for hospices or places of prayer. One woman who seems to have done this is Sawe ingen Oconnolen, who petitioned the archbishop of Armagh in 1456 for permission to live continently and to keep a hospice in the church lands of Donoghmore.[165] No more is heard of this hospice and it is probable that it lasted only during the life of Sawe. Founders seem to have often wanted to establish nunneries for specific members of their families, or in one case as a sort of contingency plan, in the event that a female relative wanted to enter the monastic life. When the land was given to Cong abbey to establish a nunnery at Annagh by Walter de Burgo Mac William Oughter, the stipulation accompanying the donation was that any female member of his family who wished to enter the religious life could do so in this convent.[166] Walter must have felt some special spiritual affinity with the convent he founded, as he chose to be buried there in 1440.[167]

The history of Franciscan nuns in medieval Ireland is very obscure. In 1316, six houses for Franciscan nuns in Ireland were reported to the chapter at Naples; however, in a list drawn up in 1384–5 there were only three mentioned.[168] These three have been identified as at Carrick-on-Suir, Youghal and Fooran. Of these the identification of Franciscan nuns at a house at Carrick-on-Suir rests on a tradition that the Elizabethan house of Thomas, earl of Ormond, at Carrick-on-Suir was built on the site of a nunnery of Poor Clares.[169] The history of the convent at Fooran (Co. Westmeath) is also extremely poorly documented. An inquisition in 1605 found that there were walls still standing of a house of nuns at "Farron McNeighon", together with certain lands that had belonged to it.[170] As these lands were described as a parcel of the lands of the Franciscan friars of Athlone it has been assumed that the nuns were Franciscan as well.[171]

The house of nuns at Youghal has a slightly better documented history, even if it is more legendary than factual. The traditional history of the nunnery of St Anne's starts with the Anglo-Norman foundation of the town, when a lighthouse was built and donated to nuns on the condition that they maintain the light. This supposedly was to deter attack on the nuns and the lighthouse by the

164 MacCarthy, "Ballymacadane Abbey", p. 13. **165** *Registrum Iohannis Mey*, pp 336–7. This is possibly the lands which were in the hands of the Culdees of Armagh until the sixteenth century and the site of an early monastery. **166** Archdall (1786), p. 500. **167** Lewis, *Topographical dictionary of Ireland*, I, 29. **168** *Med. rel. houses Ire.*, p. 309. **169** *Materials for the history of the Franciscan province of Ireland*, p. 163, lists the rather thin evidence for this. **170** Archdall (1786), p. 710. The full transcription is given in BL Egerton MS 1774, ff. 249–51. The land and the abbey were later granted to Francis Blundell, *Cal. pat. rolls Ire., Jas. I*, p. 244. **171** *Med. rel. houses Ire.*, p. 317. This is not definite of course, but in the absence of any other evidence it is reasonable to assume that the nuns were Franciscan.

Gaelic Irish.[172] A French traveller in 1644 described the convent by the sea and the remains of the tower from which the lights were shone.[173] When the old lighthouse was finally demolished in 1848, there was a small cottage connected to it on the land side, which was possibly a remnant of the nunnery or built from its ruins. Although it could not have been Franciscan from foundation, it is assumed to have been Franciscan at the dissolution as it was dissolved with the Franciscan friary in 1542.[174] The only other contender for inclusion in the meagre list of houses of Poor Clares is in Galway, where in 1511 Walter Lynch, one of its prominent citizens, gave his daughter a house near the church of St Nicholas which was afterwards known as the house of the poor nuns of the Order of St Francis.[175]

LOCATION OF CONVENTS

The position of nunneries and their lands could have a significant impact on their later ability to manage their property and attract patronage. Characteristics of nunnery positioning that may have affected their long-term survival included the position relative to the founder's or patron's holdings, and the distance to water, mountains, roadways and other monastic houses. Like monasteries, rural nunneries in Ireland were almost all situated near water, although how this water was managed with mill streams and construction to facilitate water flows has not been fully investigated for nunneries, as it has for some monastic houses. Nevertheless the distance to water, whatever the means of water management, must have been a significant factor in the maintenance and long-term survival of nunneries.[176] The existence of mills, dependent on water flow and essential for grinding of grain for domestic use by the nunneries and their tenants, was also essential to the good management of monastic estates, and there is evidence of mills at many of the nunneries. Founders seemed to have been anxious to ensure that nunnery estates were equipped with all the facilities needed for good monastic and manorial management.

As with the monasteries, nunneries in Ireland were concentrated in areas of higher population, avoiding boglands and mountains that held potential dangers and difficulties. Although nunneries were probably in relatively secluded positions, these positions were usually within the reach of populous areas, suggesting that it was in these areas that the need for nuns and their services was

172 Hayman, *Notes and records of the ancient religious foundations at Youghal*, pp 40–1. **173** Cited in "Notes to Archdall", *IER* 8 (1872) p. 137. **174** Hayman, *Notes and records of the ancient religious foundation at Youghal*, pp 41–2. In 1597, the lands of the Franciscans of Youghal included the site of the chapel of St Anne, "near the same town" see *Fiants Ire., Hen. VIII-Eliz, III*, p. 295. **175** Hardiman, *History of the town and county of the town of Galway*, p. 274. Mooney, "Franciscans in Ireland", *Terminus* 11 (1955) p. 131. **176** Carville, *Occupation of Celtic sites*, p. 29. See also Stalley, *The Cistercian monasteries of Ireland*, pp 33–5, for the importance of water for the siting of Cistercian monasteries.

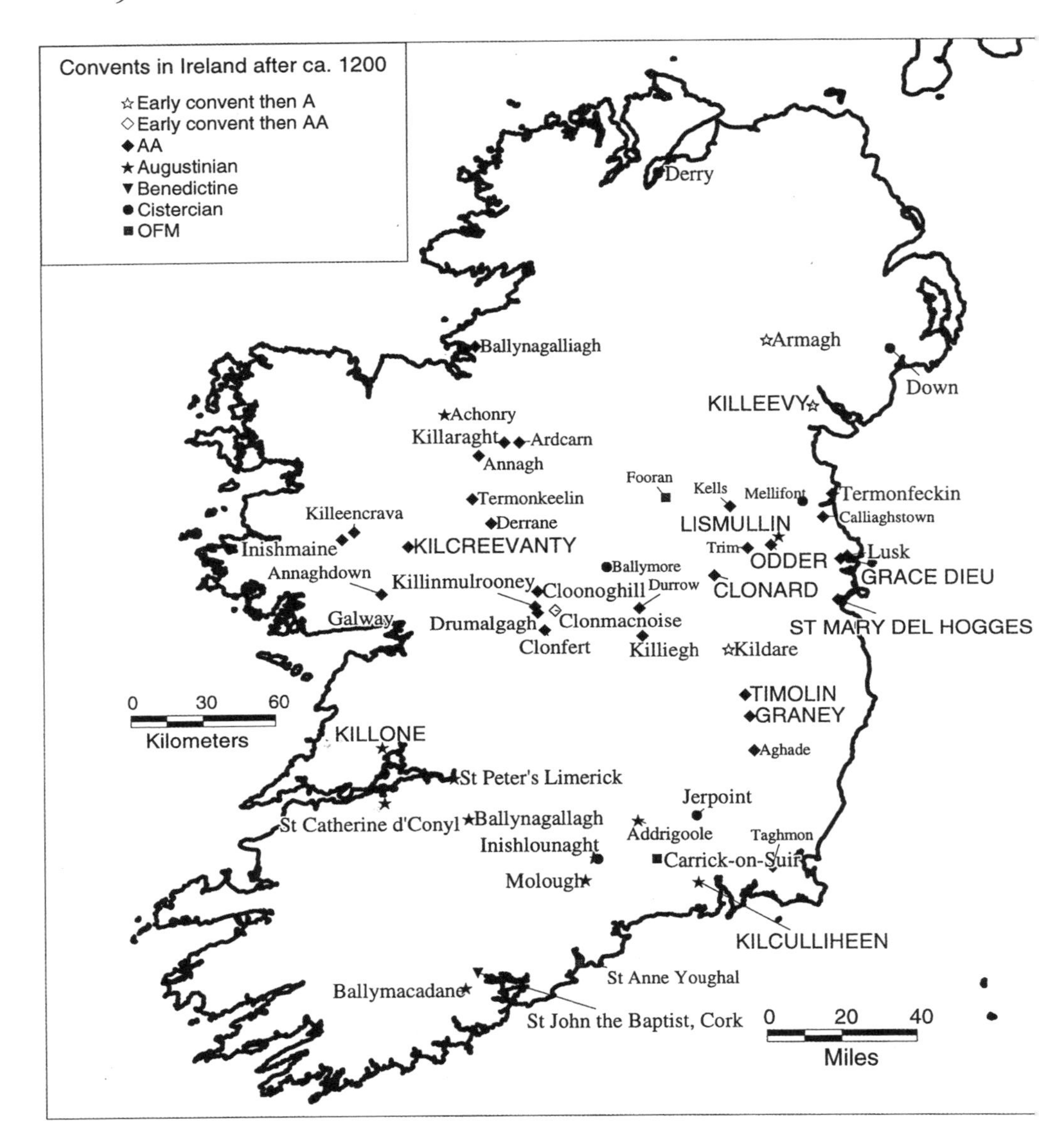

Figure 5. Map showing all convents known after c.1200

felt and that resources were sufficient to support nunneries. Defining populous areas within medieval Ireland is usually based on patterns survival of mottes for the Anglo-Norman settler population and the distribution of raths for the pre-Norman and remnant Gaelic areas. Another indicator of population distribution is the ancient roadways that traversed Ireland and followed geographically favourable paths between mountains and boglands. When a map of the nunneries is compared with maps of mottes, raths and roadways, it is clear that nunneries, like most of the medieval monasteries, were founded within areas where conditions were conducive to settled communities.[177] The relative seclusion of both rural and urban nunneries, within populated areas, enhanced the ideology of claustration that was meant both to protect and contain nuns from the wider communities.

Examining the map of later medieval nunneries, it is clear that nunneries were not evenly distributed throughout Ireland. There are few nunneries in Ulster or the south-west of Cork and Kerry. Given the state of the surviving written records from these areas, some smaller communities may have escaped historical notice altogether. However, to some extent this pattern of convent foundations follows earlier church and monastic settlement patterns which avoided bogland or mountainous terrain and tended to follow secular settlement and communication routes. The topographically difficult areas of Kerry and Donegal, for example, did not support many Celtic monasteries, nor were monasteries attracted there after the twelfth-century reform.[178] It is not surprising, then, to find no nunneries in these areas. Nunneries in Ireland were built within reach of population centres and male monasteries, both of which provided personnel and support needed by groups of women living communally. Women in isolated parts of the west and north who wished to live religious lives would not have had the same opportunities for entering convents as women in more heavily populated areas of Connacht, Thomond and the Anglo-Irish areas of the east. Some would have lived under private religious vows and have escaped notice in the records. For others there would have been no other option but to marry and raise children as devout lay women.

Urban nunneries were also located in relatively secluded positions, in a similar way to nunneries in urban centres in England.[179] The convents in the towns of Dublin, Derry, Limerick, Armagh, Cork, Youghal, Waterford and Galway were all close to the walls or within them, but usually in a quieter part of the settlement. Kilculliheen, although close to Waterford, was across the mouth of the Barrow river from the town itself. In Dublin, St Mary del Hogges was built outside the walls in an area which has recently been described as having a "recreational" function within Dublin, set back from a major road and in a position dominated

177 For a map of medieval raths with male Augustinian and Cistercian houses superimposed see Carville, *Occupation of Celtic sites*, p. 20. For a map of ancient roadways see ibid, p. 24, map 10. **178** See maps of Celtic monastic sites, boglands, and communication routes in Carville, *Occupation of Celtic sites*, pp 17–24. Also *Map of monastic Ireland*. **179** Butler, "Medieval urban religious houses", pp 168–9.

by this convent, the priory of All Hallows and open land called Hoggen Green.[180] The Green had been an open area within the Viking settlement of Dublin and was where their open-air gatherings took place. The founder of Hogges, Diarmait Mac Murchada, may have chosen to site the nunnery and monastery here because of the existing open spaces and relative seclusion. The small nunnery of St Peter's in Limerick was located inside the boundary of the city, adjoining the wall itself, although the wall was probably built after the nunnery, so a deliberate decision was made to include the nunnery within the walls.[181] The siting of the nunneries in Cork and Limerick within the walls of the cities may have been for practical defensive reasons, or it may have reflected their function in serving their local communities.

Nunneries were established in a variety of rural and urban situations throughout medieval Ireland. There were a handful which survived from Celtic times in areas that were not heavily colonised by the Anglo-Irish, but the majority of Gaelic Irish nunneries which operated through the medieval period had been established or re-established under the auspices of the reforming kings and bishops of the mid-and late twelfth century. These convents were established according to reform agendas that included male houses, and were formed into affiliations and dependencies by their founders. The twelfth and early thirteenth centuries saw the foundation of the Mac Murchad group of nunneries in his territories of Leinster which were eventually affiliated with the Clonard group of nunneries in Meath under the auspices of Ua Maél Sechlainn. The daughter houses of Clonard in Connacht changed affiliation in 1223, when they were made dependent on the Ui Chonchobair nunnery of Kilcreevanty along with numerous other smaller Arroasian houses throughout the Ui Chonchobair territories. In Thomond, a group of Augustinian monasteries were established in the late twelfth century that included the nunneries of Killone, Co. Clare, and St Peter's, Limerick. All these nunneries were founded by Gaelic kings and bishops under the reformed rule of Arrouaise or Augustine, their territories and dependencies were within the territories of their founders and they were obviously considered necessary ingredients to the vibrant reform of monastic culture, land and resources which occurred after the synod of Kells in 1152.

The Anglo-Norman advance, from the late twelfth and early thirteenth centuries, included foundation of convents and monasteries to hold the spiritual resources of the conquered land and to advance the English cultural colonisation. Although nunneries have not usually been considered by historians as having a part in this agenda, their foundation by several of the first generation of tenants-in-chief, and the transfer of considerable amounts of land and spiritual resources to their care, indicates that a healthy network of convents was a feature which the Anglo-Normans considered necessary in their new lands. Nunneries were

180 For a modern reconstruction of medieval Dublin see, Clarke and Simms, "Medieval Dublin", *NHI,* IX, p. 37. Clarke has argued that this section of suburban Dublin was "recreational". See "Urbs et suburbium", p. 55. **181** *Civil Survey, Co. Limerick*, p. 441.

established close to significant castles of Walter de Riddlesford and Richard, lord of Norragh, in Co. Kildare, and FitzThomas, in Shanid in Co. Limerick. The first generations of Anglo-Irish bishops in Meath and Dublin also sought to establish well-resourced nunneries in their dioceses with the foundation of Lismullin, Co. Meath, and Grace Dieu in northern Co. Dublin. These, combined with the older Gaelic foundations of Kilculliheen, Co. Kilkenny, and St Mary del Hogges in Dublin, received substantial grants of lands and privileges of the new local lords, which mean that there was a string of well-endowed and substantial nunneries in the Anglo-Irish areas by the middle of the thirteenth century.

The upsurge in foundations and interests in monastic life in the twelfth and thirteenth centuries in Ireland mirrored a pattern occurring in England and France. In these three areas this was followed by a decline of both the economic and religious will to establish further monastic houses for men and women. In Ireland the religious boundaries once drawn by native Irish reform and Anglo-Norman political reorganisation were not easy to alter and there were few foundations later than the mid-thirteenth century. Another factor likely to influence the rate of new foundations was a decline in both economic support for nuns and the numbers of women willing or able to join nunneries. The ability of nuns to manage their estates under these changed conditions was dependent on the support which they could muster among the local lay communities, both as patrons of the convents themselves and as tenants for conventual lands. The next part of this book will analyse in detail the ways in which religious women managed their estates and the environments in which they found themselves during the troubled centuries of the later medieval period.

CHAPTER 4

Convent buildings and estates

The most obvious reminders of medieval nuns in the modern landscape are the surviving buildings. The presence of nuns in the landscape was clearly visible in the buildings of their convents and the spires of their churches. Looming stone buildings, solid cloister ranges and bell towers dominated the physical landscape for many miles around, just as the presence of the nuns in the parish church and as land-holders did in the daily lives of their lay neighbours. These buildings also functioned as powerful markers of the divide between religious space and that shared with the laity. Some churches were shared with the local parish, some lay people worked within the cloister, while members of the elite were able to enter many other parts of the conventual spaces, but the cloister and its buildings were otherwise marked apart, separate from the concerns of the laity and only open to those vowed to God.[1] These physical boundaries were reinforced with the ideology of claustration, that nuns were enclosed behind the cloister walls forever once their vows were taken, set apart from worldly concerns, protected from worldly dangers and able to concentrate on their devotional work. The walls of the cloister marked out the nunnery buildings as a separate space, differentiated from the surrounding landscape by its standard design and meant to ensure that the women within remained separate from the world outside.

Monasteries and nunneries were built with patrons' money, the support of ecclesiastical officials and the labour and skill of artisans, so the resulting buildings show a mixture of all these influences.[2] Surviving structures indicate something of the aspirations of the founders and, perhaps, whether these aspirations came to fruition over the centuries.[3] The size of the churches and cloisters is, for example, one indicator of the scope of the planned convents. There would be little point in investing in large stone buildings and churches if founders and patrons anticipated that nunneries would be short-lived and therefore unable to provide prayers for the founders' souls over many generations.

The structures of surviving medieval nunnery buildings in Europe have not been studied in detail until relatively recently, and there have been no recent

1 I have drawn on the ideas of Gilchrist, particularly in "Community and self", pp 55–64, in formulating these ideas of the religious landscape. 2 Greene, *Medieval monasteries*, p. 68. 3 For a discussion of the influence of founders on Irish church design see Stalley, "Irish Gothic and English fashion", pp 67–8, and more generally see Gilchrist, *Gender and material culture*,

archaeological surveys, excavations or analysis conducted on nunnery remains in Ireland.[4] In the absence of archaeological surveys and excavation, significant information is available from the plans and reports of the surviving ruins of medieval nunneries in Ireland. Full-scale analysis of the extant conventual buildings, development phases and remains of surrounding structures must wait until archaeological excavations of nunnery churches, cloisters, domestic buildings and granges are made. The nunnery ruins I have chosen as examples for discussion are those with either substantial post-twelfth-century structures or documented histories. I have analyzed this information and compared it with the findings of scholars such as Gilchrist on English nunneries, and have found that medieval nunnery buildings in Ireland were conceived and built to patterns that would have been familiar to visitors from outside Ireland, although there were specific local variations.

THE CONVENT BUILDINGS

The familiar square stone-built cloister with surrounding church and domestic buildings was imported into Ireland with the Cistercians in the 1140s, and symbolized the start of the new reformed orders that had such a profound effect from the twelfth century.[5] Earlier monastic buildings were built on a more circular model, and some later monastic buildings in the Gaelic areas of Ireland, particularly in the west, continued this pattern.[6] Scholars of English medieval monastic geography have used architectural measurements such as cloister, nave and chancel lengths as indicators of monastic status and wealth.[7] Robinson compiled measurements of over fifty English Augustinian churches and compared these measurements with the final dissolution valuations, and found that there was a close relationship between the dimensions of the buildings and the wealth of the houses.[8] Gilchrist's analysis suggests that English nunnery churches were similar in length to the smaller Augustinian canons' churches, although some nunneries were particularly small. She found the mean length of thirty-two surviving nunnery churches in England to be 49.9 metres, with over half under 31 metres. The sample of Irish nunnery churches that can be

pp 50–8. **4** An exception is the survey of the Cistercian nunnery of Ballymore by Carville, "Cistercian nuns in medieval Ireland". See Barry, *Archaeology of medieval Ireland*, esp. pp 139, 157, for a general plea for detailed excavations of both the claustral buildings and the outer courts and surrounding manors of monasteries from medieval Ireland in general. **5** Stalley, *The Cistercian monasteries of Ireland*, p. 51. For the meaning of the word *cloister*, see Davies, "Introduction". **6** Leask, *Irish churches and monastic buildings*, I, pp 11–15. O'Keeffe, *An Anglo-Norman monastery: Bridgetown priory*, p. 50. **7** Robinson, *Geography of Augustinian settlement*, I, pp 155–63 and II, appendix 19, pp 397–8; Gilchrist, *Gender and material culture*, p. 45, for the use of the length of churches to determine relative wealth. Others to use these measurements are Greene, *Norton Priory*, pp 86–8, and Gallagher, "Planning of Augustinian monasteries in Scotland", pp 167–87. **8** Robinson, *Geography of Augustinian settlement*, I, pp 160–3.

Table 3. Size of surviving nunnery ruins

Name	*Date fd.*	*Value at dissolution*	*Length of cloister (m)*[9]	*Cloister area (m²)*	*Church length (m)*[10]	*Church breadth (m)*
Killone, Co. Clare	c.1240	£30	15.5/14[11]	217	39.32	10.97[12]
Kilcreevanty Co. Galway[13]		£34			36.5	17.37
Ballymacadane Co. Cork	15th c.[14]	n/a			27.13	6.09[15]
St Catherine d'Conyl Co. Limerick	c.1220	n/a	22.55	508	25.9	5.48[16]
Grace Dieu, Co. Dublin		£112			24.69	6.4[17]
Killeevy, Co. Armagh		£2			20.11	6.7[18]
Molough, Co. Tipperary		£6	19.8[19]	392	19.81	8.23[20]
Inishmaine, Co. Mayo		£3			18.29	10.97[21]
Clonmacnoise, Co. Offaly		n/a			12.19	5.79[22]
Ballynagallagh Co. Limerick		5s			n/a	2.7[23]
Killeenatrava, Co. Mayo		n/a			n/a	3.8[24]

9 The measurements here are in metric to enable comparison to Gilchrist's survey; data from Robinson needed for comparison has been converted from imperial to metric. **10** The measurements in this column are for total length. For those churches with a nave and a chancel, these have been added together. **11** Westropp, "Augustinian houses of Co. Clare", p. 129. The cloister is irregular; the measurements given are averages to enable comparison. **12** ITA survey, Clare East, Clarecastle parish, (1943), Clare County Library. These measurements are of the original size of the church; it was shortened in the fifteenth century, by the addition of an internal wall in the western end of the nave. The shortened measurements are (off square) 86'6" by 27'; 88' by 28' 2". **13** "OS Letters, Co. Galway, I", p. 10. The remains have deteriorated since O'Donovan's visit, and modern graves have obscured the outlines of the church structures. **14** But MacCarthy, "Ballymacadane Abbey", suggests that the building may be earlier than the fifteenth century. p. 13. **15** Hayes, "Ballymacadane Abbey", p. 141. **16** Westropp's measurements show a discrepancy between each wall, indicating that the structure is off centre. Westropp, in Wardell, "History and antiquities of St Catherine, Old Abbey", p. 54. **17** *Register of wills,* ed. Berry p. 211. **18** Chart, *Ancient monuments of Northern Ireland*, p. 77. **19** The cloister at Molough is rectangular and now has considerable infill of fallen and overgrown masonry; this measurement must be taken as a minimum estimate. **20** Power, *Waterford and Lismore*, pp 231–2. **21** Healy, "Two royal abbeys", p. 4. See also Leask, *Irish churches and monastic buildings*, II, pp 66–7. **22** de Breffny and Mott, *The churches and abbeys of Ireland*, p. 41. **23** Westropp describes the foundations of this church as being one of very small dimensions. See "A survey of the ancient churches in county Limerick" p. 449. **24** Only the west gable survived. See Knox, *History of Tuam*, p. 273.

measured is small, with the length of nine churches known along with the breadth of a further two. Comparison of the size of English and Irish nunneries shows that all the nunnery churches surviving in Ireland are smaller than the mean length of those in Gilchrist's study, although the smallest English nunnery church, Nunkeelling, at 14m was similar to the length of the Nuns' Church at Clonmacnoise. At least two Irish nunnery churches were narrower than Clonmacnoise, suggesting that they were also originally shorter.

When valuations made at the general suppression of the monasteries are added to the table of church measurements, it is clear that the surviving structures are not from the wealthier nunneries, with the exception of Grace Dieu. As Table 3 shows, wealth in the sixteenth century provides only a rough indicator of the size of the church and so of the relative status and size of the nunnery overall. It would be expected that the nunneries of Clonard, Lismullin, Timolin, Graney and Hogges would have been at least as large and probably larger than the surviving ruins at Killone and St Catherine d'Conyl, although not of the scale of the very large and wealthy English convents.

In order to place the size of the nunnery churches and cloisters into context, measurements of comparable male monastic houses need to be considered. Comparing the measurements of Irish monastic houses with Robinson's analysis of English and Welsh Augustinian houses, it is clear that most of the Irish Augustinian houses were similar in size to the smaller English houses.[25] In her analysis, Gilchrist finds that English nunnery churches are comparable in size to smaller male houses. These studies of English monastic building size reveal similar findings to the sample of male and female monastic houses in Ireland, where the nunnery churches are a comparable size to the smaller of the male houses.

Overall, these comparisons suggest that the foundation of these nunneries represented an investment to their founders roughly equivalent to many of the moderate or small Cistercian and Augustinian monasteries. The nuns may have had more difficulty attracting donations and managing their resources than monks did. The buildings in which they lived were not, however, necessarily inferior to many of the buildings in which monks lived. This is demonstrated particularly when the monastic buildings of one group are compared. The reformed orders of the Augustinians and Cistercians were introduced and patronised in Thomond as part of a distinct plan by the Ó Briain kings, particularly Donal Mór, in the late twelfth century. The surviving structures show signs of being constructed by either the same or a connected group of masons and sculptors, and so provide a group for analysis of differences in the sizes of the buildings.[26] Table 4 shows that the nunnery of Killone, founded as part of the Augustinian group of monasteries, was built with dimensions similar to the abbeys of Clare Abbey and Corcomroe. These houses can then be compared with other monastic houses of

25 See Appendix 19 in Robinson, *Geography of Augustinian settlement*, II, pp 397–8. **26** Mac Mahon, "The charter of Clare Abbey", pp 26–7, for the Augustinians; for other characteristics of the so-called "School of the West" see Leask, *Irish churches and monastic buildings*, II, pp 63–4ff.

the west, particularly the houses in Connacht under the patronage of the Uí Chonchobair kings.

Table 4. Comparison of surviving Thomond and Connacht monastic ruins[27]

Name Location	*Order*	*Founder*	*Date founded or refounded*	*Cloister area (m^2)*	*Church length (m)*	*Church Breadth (m)*
Abbeyknockmoy Co. Galway	Cist.[28]	Cathal Crobderg Ua Conchobair	1190	985	61.87	
Boyle, Co. Roscommon	Cist.		1148	1207	55	15
Corcomroe Co. Clare	Cist.	Donal Mór Ua Briain	c.1180	334	40	7
Ennis Friary Co. Clare[29]	OFM	Donnachad Cairprech Ua Briain	c.1247	481	39.34	7.7
Killone Co. Clare	OSA Nunnery	Donnachad Cairprech Ua Briain	c.1240	219	39.32	10.97
Clare Abbey Co. Clare[30]	OSA	Donnachad Cairprech Ua Briain		670	39.01	9.45
Kilcreevanty Co. Galway	AA Nunnery	Cathal Crobderg Ua Conchobair	c.1200		36.5	17.37
Clontuskert Co. Galway[31]	OSA	Uí Chealliagh	c.1140	110	32.5	8
Canon's Island Co. Clare[32]	OSA	Re-founded Ua Briain			25.9	7.08
O'Heynes' Church Kilmacduagh Co. Galway[33]	OSA	O'Heyne[34]			22.86	6.7
Inishmaine, Co. Mayo	AA Nunnery	Prob. Ua Conchobair	+1223		18.29	10.97

27 The references for the nunnery measurements are given in Table 3. **28** Leask, *Irish churches and monastic buildings*, II, p. 38, and Stalley, *The Cistercian monasteries of Ireland*, p. 240. **29** Westropp, "Ennis abbey", pp 135–54. The structure shows signs of rebuilding in the 15th century. **30** Westropp, "Augustinian houses of Co. Clare" p. 123. The original church length was divided into nave and chancel by the addition of a belfry in c.1460. **31** Fanning, "Excavations at Clontuskert priory", pp 97–170. **32** Westropp's plan in Royal Society of Antiquaries of Island visit to Canon's Island reported in RSAI Jn 1895. **33** Leask, *Irish churches and monastic buildings*, II, p. 70. **34** *Med. rel. houses Ire.*, p. 183, for summary of possible founders and patrons.

In this sample of monasteries from the west under Gaelic patronage it is clear that the Cistercian houses were built on a grander scale than the Augustinian houses, but within the Augustinian and Arroasian orders the three nunneries were of similar sizes to the men's houses. The nunneries, conceived as part of a larger plan of monastic houses to serve the needs of the kingdoms of Connacht and Thomond, probably were built to house similar numbers of religious as the men's houses, and given similar material support, at least at their foundation.

An aspect of the dimensions of the nunnery buildings that invites comparison is the size of the cloisters.[35] This is a useful measurement because it gives an indication of the size of the surrounding ranges and thus the number of religious people expected to use the cloister and ranges. A small cloister would result in small domestic ranges usually able to accommodate a limited number of residents. There were also other buildings within the monastic precinct which were used for accommodation of servants, labourers, bailiffs and other personnel. Nuns may have used these buildings if accommodation became too cramped in the cloister granges. There are three medieval nunneries in Ireland with extant cloisters: Killone, St Catherine d'Conyl and Molough.[36] Of these, Killone has the smallest cloister. The size of the churches of Killone and neighbouring Clare Abbey, however, are virtually the same at about 39m, indicating that when these two houses were founded they were built to accommodate similar numbers of monks and nuns. Killone, however, was extensively rebuilt in the fifteenth century, when the surviving domestic ranges were constructed and the church nave shortened by 13m. It is probable that the cloister itself was reduced in size when the new buildings were built and the church shortened. Such a reduction in size would have meant a reduction in the size of the domestic buildings, and suggests reduced numbers of nuns in the fifteenth century. Another possibility is that the rather sharp gradient at Killone meant that the cloister had to be relatively small.

The slope of the ground to the east and south towards Lake Killone meant that the convent was built with an unusual and structurally essential crypt. This means that the building rises up the hill from the low ground at the edge of the lake. The builders thus constructed the crypt to allow the church to be orientated to the east. This significant slope probably also necessitated the uneven shape of the north-facing cloister. Although monastic building is common in valleys leading to water, this slope contributed to considerable problems in designing the building.[37] The degree of architectural difficulty faced in order to ensure that the church and cloister were built to the general Augustinian plan suggests that the site was not chosen for the ease of construction. It can only be

35 Gallagher, "Planning Augustinian monasteries in Scotland" pp 170; 178–81. **36** The very small size of the sample means that no comparison with Gilchrist's theory of women's houses' affinity with north-facing cloisters can be made. Gilchrist had 58 nunneries in her sample, of which about a third had north-facing cloisters. See Gilchrist, "Blessed art thou among women", pp 213–17. **37** Carville, *The occupation of Celtic sites*, pp 25–9.

presumed that the lay founder, Donal Mór Ua Briain, and the ecclesiastical patron, the abbot of Clare Abbey, were involved in choosing the site and that its proximity to Clare Abbey as well as its seclusion must have made the deficiencies of the site worth the difficulties.[38]

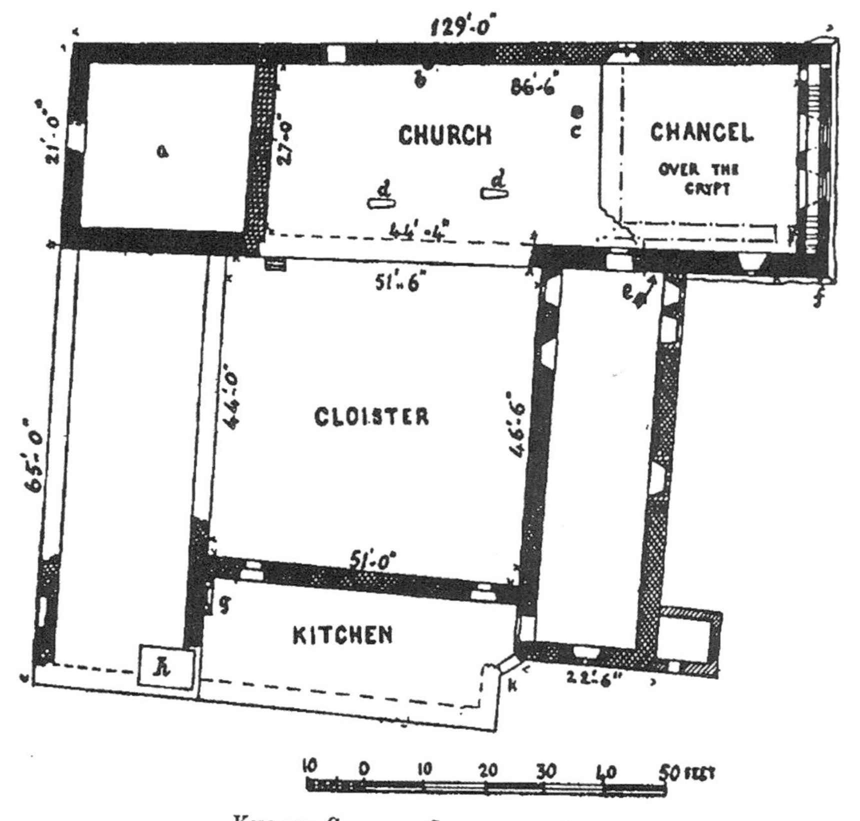

KILLONE CONVENT—SECTION AND PLAN.

(*a*) Stacpoole burial-place.
(*b*) Stoup.
(*c*) Font.
(*d*) Early Tombstone.
(*e*) Entrance to Stairs leading to Crypt.
(*f*) Corbel with Nun's Head.
(*g*) Lucas Monument.
(*h*) Daxon Monument.

Figure 6. Plan of Killone abbey
T.J. Westropp, reprinted from "Augustinian houses of Co. Clare: Clare, Killone and Inchicronan." *RSAI* Jn 30 (1900) p. 129. (Reproduced with permission of the Royal Society of Antiquaries of Ireland.)

The church at Killone has many stylistic features in common with other Augustinian houses in Thomond as well as other areas of the west of Ireland, and is dated by Leask to about 1225, while Westropp postulated an earlier date

38 O'Keeffe, *An Anglo-Norman monastery: Bridgetown priory*, p. 36 discusses similar problems at

Figure 7. East window at Killone abbey

of about 1190.[39] There is a particularly beautiful east window, as well as a damaged but still interesting example of a late Romanesque-type doorway leading from the cloister to the church. This door has similar carvings to those found at Clare Abbey, confirming the connections between the two houses.[40] The east window has a passageway between the walls leading to the roof, suggestive of the internal passageways in much larger churches and cathedrals.[41] The beauty and intricacy of the window underline the importance placed on the environment of the nuns of this royal foundation. (See Figure 7.)

Signs of wear and modification in the surviving structures also give indications of use over the centuries. When the church was shortened, the erection of an internal wall at the west end of the church created a small room. The priest or abbess could have used this as a living space, as it has the remains of a fireplace.[42] There are also signs of what may be either changes in fashion or usage of the church itself with considerable late medieval rebuilding of the north wall and insertion of a double lancet window that Westropp dates to the fourteenth century.[43] An unrecorded incident or incidents may have damaged the structure, necessitating the rebuilding of the convent itself. The fifteenth century saw an increase in monastic building works generally throughout the west of Ireland, accompanying an increase in interest and enthusiasm for monastic patronage. The inclusion of Killone in the widespread rebuilding of monasteries in the fifteenth century demonstrates interest in the continued presence of nuns and women's participation in the religious revival of the time.

At Killone the cloister was built by using a lean-to or overshot roof attached to the surrounding ranges, a relatively inexpensive model popular with English and Irish friaries and with monastic building in the west of Ireland.[44] Around the cloister traces of the three ranges survive, with the eastern range being the most extensive. This range was a double-storied building with doors to the cloister and to the crypt and a large doorway into the choir of the church that would have housed the night stairs. The windows in the upper storey are small, while the windows on the lower storey were unglazed with pivots for shutters.[45] This building is likely to have been the dormitory of the nunnery, and if the nuns followed the standard monastic plan, the lower storey would have been used for the chapter house and sacristy (Figure 8). The damaged inner wall of the south range survives, with the corner of a doorframe matching that of the east range, suggesting that the south range was built at the same time.[46] A photograph of

other sites. **39** Leask, *Irish churches and monastic buildings*, II, pp 63–4, and Westropp, "Augustinian houses of Clare", p. 131. **40** Gilmore, "Killone Convent", p. 24. **41** Such as Cashel and Newtown, Trim. See discussion by O'Keeffe, *An Anglo-Norman monastery: Bridgetown priory*, pp 124–5. **42** Westropp, "Augustinian churches of Clare", p. 128. Gilchrist, *Contemplation and action*, p. 134, notes other churches where a western chamber functioned as priest's quarters. **43** Westropp, "Augustinian churches of Co. Clare", p. 128. The features of the north door are not original, having been rebuilt in 1895. **44** See Gilchrist, *Contemplation and action*, p. 121. **45** Westropp, "Augustinian houses of Co. Clare" p. 132. **46** There are only mounds and some very low stones surviving of the north range.

Figure 8 Killone abbey today
This photo shows the roofless east range and the surviving remnants of the south and west ranges of the cloister. (Photograph by Margaret O'Flanagan.)

Figure 9. Killone abbey in the nineteenth century
The view is from across Lake Killone showing the eastern building and the remaining wall of southern wing tentatively identified by Westropp as a kitchen. (Lawrence Collection, 4472, National Library of Ireland, reprinted by permission.)

Killone taken in the late nineteenth century (Figure 9) shows the remains of the south range with two plain doorways leading to the cloister. This photograph also shows the slope of the valley leading to the lake, which necessitated the building of the crypt.

A nunnery obscured by an even thicker cloud of documentary silence than Killone is St Catherine d'Conyl. The ruins at St Catherine d'Conyl or Old Abbey include a smaller church than the one at Killone, and a larger cloister.[47] The small size of the church suggests that it was never intended to serve a large community of nuns. Their domestic buildings may have been more spacious than those at Killone. The relationship between the church and cloister is unusual, with the cloister opening from the west end of the church rather than the more usual south or less common north door. Gilchrist notes parallels of this unusual layout in a fourteenth-century Dominican convent in Kent and a thirteenth-century Franciscan convent in France, suggesting that this type of layout may have been acceptable in nunneries founded in the later period.[48] This does not fully explain the siting of St Catherine's, as its foundation in the early thirteenth century was not particularly late. According to Westropp, the oldest portion of the precinct buildings is the western range of the cloister, where three vaulted rooms survive with buttressing older than the cloister and used in its walls.[49] This suggests that the builders of the convent may have incorporated an existing building and this may have dictated the orientation of the church and cloister.

Until there is detailed excavation of the surrounding area and outbuildings of this site it is not possible to do more than speculate about the reason for siting the church in such an unusual position, but it is likely that the wishes of the founder would have had considerable weight and any existing buildings on the site would also have affected the decision.

Surviving features of the thirteenth-century buildings include north and south windows in the church which match a window from the refectory, and are common to Irish monastic buildings under English patronage at the time the convent was founded in the early thirteenth century.[50] There is a beautiful doorway at the west end of the church leading into the cloister, with side shafts and arches matching those of the piscina and recesses in the church, also dating to the early thirteenth century.[51]

There is evidence of late fifteenth-century rebuilding of the church and the building adjoining the refectory, which Westropp identifies as a kitchen, that fits with the date of the dissolution of the convent and conversion to other uses. It was at this time that the small east window of the church was inserted into a

47 When visited in summer 1995, the ruins were considerably obscured by ivy and nettles. **48** Gilchrist, *Contemplation and action*, pp 135–6. **49** Westropp in Wardell, "History and antiquities of St Catherine, Old Abbey", p. 53. Gilchrist puts all the claustral remains as thirteenth century, with the church late thirteenth century. See Gilchrist, *Contemplation and action*, p. 130. **50** Westropp in Wardell, "History and antiquities of St Catherine, Old Abbey", p. 55. **51** This doorway has been described and drawn by Westropp in Wardell, "History and antiquities of St Catherine, Old Abbey", p. 58.

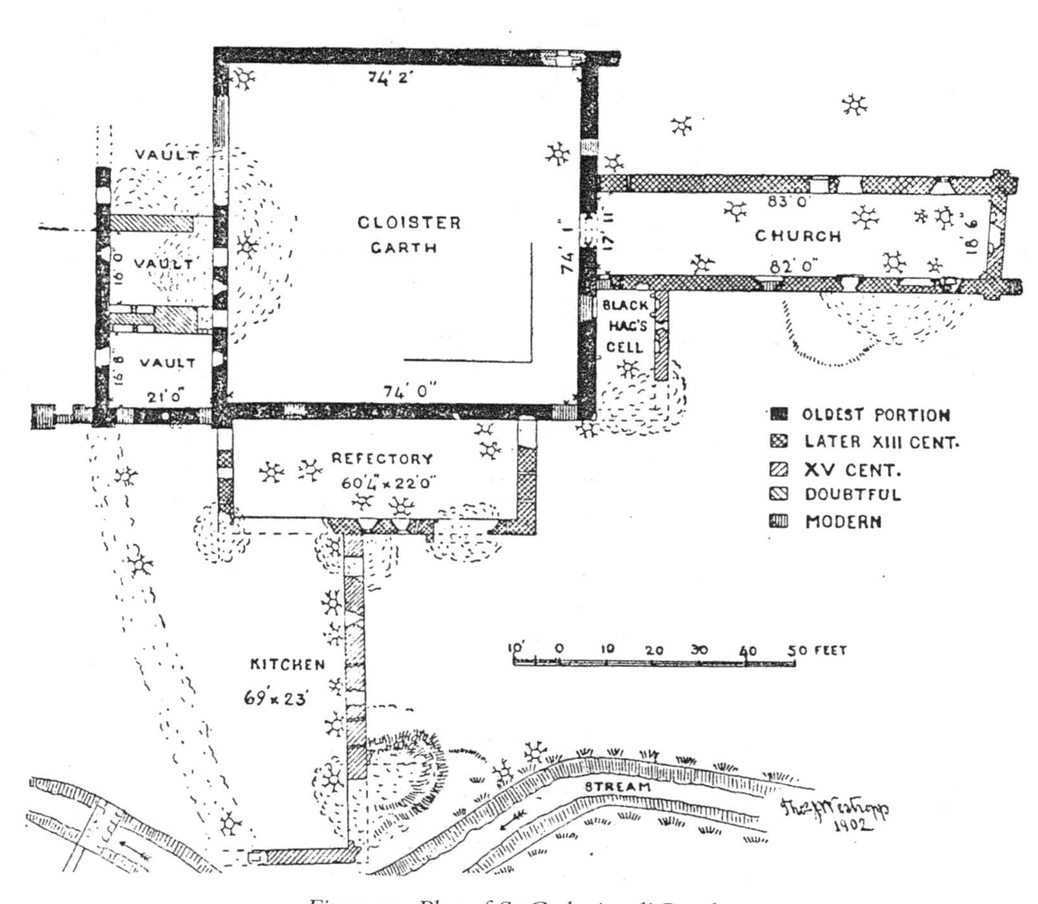

Figure 10. Plan of St Catherine d'Conyl
From T. J. Westropp reprinted from *RSAI Jn* 34 (1904) p. 54. (Reprinted with permission of the Royal Society of Antiquaries of Ireland.)

larger frame. Westropp also suggests that the windows and walls of the church were rebuilt at this time, and this may point to the buildings being in a state of disrepair prior to the suppression of the nunnery, lending credence to the complaints of the patron, the earl of Desmond, that the nuns were neglecting the church and its fabric.

St Brigid's at Molough has not had the attention of such an exact scholar as Westropp, which is unfortunate as it is, in many ways, a well-preserved site with traceable cloister, western range and church. It is situated in a quiet spot in the bend of the River Suir beside one of the ancient passes between Northern and

Figure 11. Western door of the church at St Catherine d'Conyl

Southern Deisi.[52] The extant church is smaller in length than that of Killone and St Catherine d'Conyl, while the cloister is larger than Killone's and smaller than St Catherine's. Its documented history is sparse and suggests that it was never a large or wealthy nunnery, with assets worth £6 at the dissolution and a moderate estate of 40 acres, a half-acre garden, one messuage in nearby Clonmel and an eelweir. It was probably always a modest nunnery with small numbers. The buildings themselves are thought to be thirteenth-century in date and are of rather plain design.[53] There is a tall double lancet east window in a well-preserved condition, and the door in the north wall has been restored with plain moulded stones, while the south door has been destroyed leaving only the space in the wall. There is also a double arched belfry at the western end of the church.

52 See map in *Life of St Declan*, and also note 87, p. 176. **53** Gilchrist, *Contemplation and*

The remodelling in the blocked lancet window in the south wall of the church may be medieval. It provided an opening on to an enclosed area that was possibly a later sacristy or priest's residence. All the extant buildings appear to be of similar date. The western range of the cloister buildings survives, showing it was a double-storied building with two rooms about 5.8m wide and 7.6m long. One of these rooms has a well-preserved narrow lancet light. It is possible that this west range was the guesthouse, as was usual in English nunneries. Gilchrist finds that west ranges often had superior quality masonry, reflecting the importance placed on hospitality by nunneries.[54] This may be a reason for the better survival of this range, as it was perhaps better-built originally or it continued to be used as accommodation of some sort after the dissolution of the nunnery and the destruction of the rest of the buildings. Without detailed archaeological survey and dating it is not possible to be certain of the function of the surviving structures. The significance of these ruins is that they show a solid though small structure, built around a cloister, suggesting that this nunnery was re-founded after the twelfth-century reforms and almost certainly by Anglo-Irish patrons, which is confirmed by the limited documentary evidence.[55] Overall, the architectural features of the extant buildings supports the few textual references to this priory: it was a small convent built by Anglo-Irish patrons along conventional lines. That no significant remodelling is obvious suggests that the structure was sufficient for the needs of the community throughout the medieval period.

A Gaelic Irish community of nuns, probably similar in size to that at Molough, worshipped in the small, late twelfth- or early thirteenth-century church at Inishmaine. There was a well-established male monastery there in the early medieval period.[56] Since there is very little known of this community, it is difficult to be sure when it became a women's house, although it was probably after the monastery was burned in 1227.[57] It is possible that nuns from the convent at Annaghdown were transferred there in the thirteenth century, although it might also have been a new foundation at about this time. There are features of the church which echo an earlier building, particularly the square-headed door in the north wall which may be from the destroyed male monastery, as the door structure is much earlier than other features of the building.[58]

The size of the church is comparable with the other Gaelic Irish churches built on the sites of early medieval nunneries such as Clonmacnoise and Killeevy, and smaller than the churches of the post-twelfth-century reform nunneries of St Catherine d'Conyl, Killone and Molough. At Inishmaine there are two chambers projecting at right angles to the chancel of the church that do not appear to have operated as side chapels. They may have been living quarters for either nuns or a priest, or perhaps one operated as a sacristy. A substantial, two-storied, late medieval gatehouse a short distance from the church may have functioned as fortified accommodation, a separate residence for the abbess or as

action, p. 121. **54** Gilchrist, *Gender and material culture*, p. 119. **55** See chapter 3. **56** See *Med. rel. houses Ire.*, p. 38. **57** *AFM*. **58** Wilde, *Lough Corrib*, p. 254.

a guesthouse. Large gatehouses have survived at other monastic sites, though not at nunneries. The large Augustinian monastery of Athassell (Co. Tipperary) has an impressive gatehouse some distance from the main entrance to the claustral buildings.[59]

There are no extant cloisters at Inishmaine, and while it is possible that they have not survived, it is also likely that standard Augustinian cloisters were never built. Accommodation and domestic buildings of nuns have survived particularly poorly, and although it is certain that Inishmaine had other domestic buildings, evidence for their structure and spatial relationship with the church and gatehouse must await archaeological excavation of the site. There are no cloisters extant at other Gaelic nunneries, such as Killeevy and Clonmacnoise, although their absence cannot be established definitively without detailed archaeological surveys. This may suggest that these Gaelic religious communities and their patrons favoured smaller churches with different domestic structures than the convents newly founded during the reform years. There is evidence of domestic buildings in the precinct of the nunnery at Temple Na Ferta in Armagh, a Gaelic house throughout its history. Since the excavation that discovered the foundation of the domestic buildings at Na Ferta was not able to extend beyond limited perimeters it is not known how these buildings related to others used by the nuns, none of which have survived.[60]

Nunneries were substantial buildings that were the administrative centres for large estates and provided accommodation for affairs of state or local government when the need arose. The choice of the abbess's house at Killeevy for the resignation of the archbishop of Armagh indicates that there was adequate guest accommodation for him and his party.[61] Separate residences for the head of monastic houses become common in the fourteenth and fifteenth centuries, and may have been a feature of many of the nunneries.[62] This development was associated with the changing role of the religious community and recognition of the high status of the abbess or abbot as the legal head of large estates. Separate quarters allowed the abbot of Holy Trinity, for example, to entertain potential patrons and officials whose good-will was essential to the smooth passage of the business of Holy Trinity through the legal and administrative systems of the colonial government.[63] In Kilculliheen, there also must have been significant guest accommodation either in the abbey precinct itself or very close by, as the court of the justiciar sat there at least twice in the early fourteenth century.[64]

59 O'Keeffe, *An Anglo-Norman monastery: Bridgetown priory*, pp 128–9. **60** Excavation by Quinn reported in "Medieval Britain and Ireland in 1984", p. 212. Also Lynn, "Recent archaeological excavations in Armagh City", p. 277, where he notes that there were two wells and a piece of Greek Porphry pottery found in one well, perhaps from a mosaic brought to Ireland by a pilgrim. **61** "Reg. Octavian" Nov. 10 1477, (NAI MS M 2822). **62** Greene, *Norton priory*, pp 145–6, for separate residences in male houses, and Gilchrist, "Community and self", p. 60, on separate space for abbesses, and guest houses. See O'Keeffe, *An Anglo-Norman monastery: Bridgetown priory*, p. 47, for Irish context. **63** *Account Roll of Holy Trinity, Dublin*, p. 94. **64** It is probable that it sat more often than this, however the extant records only cover a short

Contemporary descriptions of monastic buildings are disappointingly brief, but they do give some indication of the precincts of the nunneries whose buildings have completely or substantially disappeared. In 1310, Timolin had, along with its house and church, a walled close with a grange consisting of a mill, kiln and storage areas for corn, malt and wheat.[65] This layout is suggestive of the known structures of the Augustinian priory of Kells, in Co. Kilkenny, where there was a fortified court outside the walled enclosure of the church and cloister. This court also included a mill and a large space for the necessary farming activities.[66] At the dissolution, Timolin was described as having a "castle, and other houses, dwelling places of the nuns, which were necessary for the defence of the inhabitants and the farmer".[67] This reference to fortification is consistent with the known difficulties that Timolin faced with unrest and constant local fighting.[68]

Contemporary descriptions and surveys confirm the dissolution valuations of some nunneries that lacked the stone-built cloister ranges and churches of wealthier houses. The buildings in the precinct of the nunnery at Kildare were very small, described only as a small castle or "fortilage" with a chapel.[69] This may not represent the extent of the living quarters of the last nuns, who probably left sometime in the mid-fifteenth century, but it certainly suggests that the convent was not large enough to have left substantial buildings.[70] By 1550, the small nunnery at Killeigh consisted of only the walls of the chapel, and in 1569 its possession was a thatched house on its land.[71] Although this may not have been the only accommodation of the nunnery, it is probable that the nunnery at Killeigh was a very small house that may have shared its church with the nearby Augustinian monastery.[72]

Descriptions of nunneries known to have been well resourced confirm that they had substantial stone buildings. The precinct of the urban nunnery of St Mary del Hogges in Dublin consisted of a church with a bell-tower, dormitory, chapter house and "other buildings", suggesting that it was built around a cloister and probably had the standard arrangement of buildings before its demolition shortly after the dissolution.[73] The wealthy convent of Lismullin was described by the dissolution commissioners as having a church, cloister, dormitory and other buildings as well as a precinct with farm buildings.[74] The buildings of the site of Kilculliheen were taken over by the city of Waterford and put to numerous uses,

period. The court sat at Kilculliheen in October 1312 and February 1321. See NAI MS M 2750, pp 9, 18. **65** *Cal. justic. rolls Ire., 1307–1313*. **66** See the plan of excavations by Fanning in Empey, "The sacred and the secular", p. 150, and see O'Keeffe, *An Anglo-Norman monastery: Bridgetown priory*, pp 134–5. **67** *Extents Ir. mon. possessions* p. 171. **68** See chapter 5. **69** *Extents Ir. mon. possessions*, p. 163. **70** See chapter 5 for details of the dissolution of Kildare in the fifteenth century. **71** Cited in Fitzpatrick and O'Brien, *The medieval churches of County Offaly*, p. 88. **72** *Fiants Hen. VIII-Eliz., II*, p. 176. **73** *Cal. inquis. Dublin.*, p. 98. **74** *Extents Ir. mon. possessions,* p. 255. In 1985 when the site (SMR 32:24) visit was done there were only faint traces at the site of the nunnery, with traces of a cobbled surface and indistinct earthworks at the site. See *Archaeological Inventory Co. Meath*, p. 139.

and the leases reveal little more about the buildings than the dissolution commissioners' descriptions. In 1542, Waterford corporation leased the lands and buildings in separate parcels which included the Dortors, the small hall and kitchen to the east; the infirmary and great kitchen "with water within the kitchen"; the nuns' "late chamber" probably the chapter house; the steeple with the west chamber and cellar; mills, weir called the "mynchyn" weir; and the bake house, furnace and granaries.[75] This provides a picture of a large functioning convent built around a cloister with internal water supply for the kitchen, chapter house and dormitories, and a separate infirmary with its own kitchen.

The buildings in which religious women lived in medieval Ireland represented in material form their place within the local community. In many areas the nunneries would have been among the most substantial buildings in view. The walls of their enclosure marked these buildings as sacred, separate spaces set apart from, yet intrinsically part of, the landscape. The shape and character of these walls and the size and complexity of the buildings reveal some aspects of the surroundings in which religious women lived.

It was not only bare stone walls that surrounded medieval Irish nuns. Medieval conventual buildings were decorated with paint, wall hangings, pictures, statues and other religious images. The ornamentation used in European medieval nuns' churches and convent buildings has been studied in detail in recent years, and it has become recognised that the decoration and ornamentation contains important clues to the piety of the nuns and also to their sense of themselves as active religious women.[76] These are often the only remains of the self-expression of nuns and even if not their own personal choice, they were images that the builders of their churches wished them to see and reflect upon.

Iconography, images, paintings and statuary have survived poorly for Irish religious buildings and are complemented by few contemporary descriptions. What was spared at the general suppression and sale of monastic and church effects has fared badly since. Many people found practical uses for the materials from the deserted buildings, and items that could be reused or sold were taken from monastic sites.[77] In recent years, development pressures on land have led to predictions of widespread destruction of surviving archaeological remains. While

75 Quoted in Burke, "The nunnery of Kilculliheen", pp 14–6. All traces of the buildings were removed in about 1820 to build the Protestant church of Ferrybank. Carrigan, *The history and antiquities of the diocese of Ossory*, IV, p. 208. **76** See Bruzelius, "Hearing is believing", pp 83–91; Bruzelius and Berman, "Monastic architecture for women", pp 72–5; Hamburger, *Nuns as artists*. **77** Westropp, a friend of the later nineteenth-century owner of Old Abbey House adjacent to the site of St Catherine d'Conyl, noted that an arch from above the west door of the church had been removed in about 1840 and placed in the newly built summer-house; a block with ogee heads from a window of the church lay in the garden when he visited in 1875 and 1903, as did the stones of one window light of the now demolished upper story of the south cloister range; a window from the refectory was also reset in the summer-house; see Westropp in Wardell, "History and antiquities of St Catherine, Old Abbey", pp 60–2. He also recorded that the east window was said to have been lost in a game of dice in the early nineteenth century. See TCD MS 972 –1, f. 15.

most of the decoration of monastic buildings has been lost, enough remains of the decorative features to confirm that the buildings of Irish monks and nuns were decorated in styles that reflected their position in society. There have been substantial finds of window glass, floor tiles and pottery at Kells priory, and the Cistercian monastery of Jerpoint (Co. Kilkenny), the Cistercian house of Mellifont (Co. Meath) and other sites.[78] There is also documentary evidence that glass and other decorations were provided by patrons and founders. For example in the mid-fifteenth century Thomas, earl of Kildare, and his wife Johanna, donated the window glass as well as building the church and part of the cloister at the Franciscan convent of Adare.[79] Medieval frescos survive at Knockmoy, Holy Cross, Clare Island, Jerpoint, Cashel and Corcomroe.[80] There are remains of medieval religious sculpture throughout Ireland and a small number of free-standing statues, some still insitu.[81]

Just as the structural remains of medieval nunneries in Ireland have not survived well, neither has the decorative art associated with their convents, although future archaeological excavations will no doubt make important discoveries. The fragmentary evidence suggests that, like monasteries, nunneries were adorned with appropriate religious imagery and decoration. Pinholes for holding glass in the Romanesque double east window at Killone church survive, though no trace of any of the glass has come to light.[82] There is a recess in the south wall of the church at St Catherine d'Conyl that Westropp has suggested may have been intended to hold a picture[83] (Figure 11). A decorative piscina with small quatrefoil basin also survives in the south wall of the church at St Catherine d'Conyl (Figure 12). Kilculliheen owned a chalice and vestments at the dissolution and there were reports that the church plate from St Catherine d'Conyl was discovered in the late eighteenth century.[84]

So far, only one paving tile from a nunnery has been found and that was a tile found in Timolin graveyard, in the early twentieth century.[85] Floor tiles have been found in monastic sites from the Anglo-Irish dominated areas of Ireland, within the pale, south Leinster, and some Anglo-Irish ports and towns in

78 For an overview of archaeological excavations and relevant published discussions see Barry, *Archaeology of medieval Ireland*, pp 139–7. **79** Begley, *Diocese of Limerick* p. 359. **80** McGrath, "Materials and techniques of Irish medieval wall-painting", pp 96–124. **81** There are many examples: see Roe, "Illustration of the Holy Trinity", pp 101–50. **82** Westropp, "Augustinian houses of Co. Clare", p. 131. **83** Westropp in Wardell, "History and antiquities of St Catherine, Old Abbey", p. 56. **84** For Kilculliheen see *Extents Ir. mon. possessions*, p. 206. For the church plate of St Catherine d'Conyl apparently found in a small box in one of the gables and then given to Lord Cork, see Wardell, "History and antiquities of St Catherine, Old Abbey", p. 52. **85** Although the tile was found in the churchyard of the post-medieval parish church at Timolin and has been catalogued by Eames and Fanning as from a parish church, the medieval church here was the nunnery church, and it is almost certain that the tile came from the nunnery not a separate parish church. There is a vague reference to the tiles of St Mary del Hogges after its destruction by William Brabazon, where "the stones, tiles and timber" of the buildings were removed, but it is likely that this reference is to roofing tiles. *Extents Ir. mon. possessions*, p. 69.

Figure 12. Piscina in south wall of church at St Catherine d'Conyl

Munster and Ulster.[86] There is a complete absence of floor tiles from archaeological excavations of Gaelic Irish monastic buildings and it has been argued that the use of floor tiles was one of the cultural differences between monastic building in the English and Gaelic Irish areas.[87] That no other examples from

86 Eames and Fanning, *Irish medieval tiles*, pp 51–2. **87** Fanning, "Excavations at Clontuskert Priory", p. 161.

Figure 13. Tile from Timolin
From W. Fitzgerald, "An ancient church pavement tile from Timolin" *Kildare Arch. Soc.* Jn. 8 (1915), p. 328. (Reproduced with permission from County Kildare Archaeological Society.)

nunneries have survived is hardly surprising, with the most substantial nunnery ruins existing only in the areas outside the pale and outside strong Anglo-Norman influence. When the sites of nunneries within the pale are excavated it is probable that more examples of tiles and other decorative features will be found.

The Timolin tile had an impressed floral 4-foil within a four-quarter circles design on red clay which had been glazed in green, and has been dated to the fourteenth century by Fitzgerald.[88] The tile is one that required a pavement of adjoining tiles to complete the pattern and similar tile designs have been found at Dublin, Drogheda and Meath sites.[89] The discovery of the floor tile associated with Timolin strengthens the picture gained from documentary evidence that Timolin was a substantial and well-endowed convent of the Anglo-Irish community, able to afford the luxury of well-made tiles for its church, and that there was money available in the fourteenth century to complete a tiled pavement in the latest fashion.

Sculpture associated with the nunneries in Ireland is also rare. Probably the most famous is the sculptured decorations which adorn the fine Romanesque

88 The dating is confirmed by Eames and Fanning, *Irish medieval tiles*, pp 56–7. **89** Eames and Fanning, *Irish medieval tiles*, p. 90. The most recent discovery of insitu tiles are from the abbey of St Thomas, Dublin. See Walsh, "Archaeological excavations at the abbey of St Thomas the Martyr", pp 196–7.

arch and doorway at the nuns' church at Clonmacnoise. These are largely abstract designs, with some stylised figures, such as the human face and the exhibitionist female figure on the chancel arch.[90] There are also sculptured heads surviving at Killone, Killeigh and Grace Dieu.[91] The head at Killone was carved onto a corbel, situated on the upper exterior gable of the south-eastern angle of the church.[92] The nun's head from Killeigh is similar in many ways, although there is no information on where it was situated in the building itself.[93] The function of these sculptures is unclear, though decoration is likely. Gilchrist suggests that they may have represented either female founders or female saints, which is possible, but Killone was not founded by a woman and its patron saint was St John, so it is unlikely that this was the iconography of this head.[94] Since the sculpture at Killone is situated on the exterior wall, it may have been used as a way of marking the church as a nunnery church. Other sculptured heads appear in church architecture and were obviously for ornamental purposes. Sometimes they were grotesque in design, as is the one from St Catherine d'Conyl, formerly on the right-hand corbel of the west door of the church.[95] There were two small carved human heads on the wall on either side of the piscina at Ballymacadane.[96] The thirteenth-century eastern window at Killeevy has sculptured heads on the terminals of the dripstones.[97]

Carvings at Inishmaine are different in subject matter, with two carvings at the mouldings of the east window: one of a mounted figure and the other of two animals fighting. It is possible that carvings in the chancel arch were copied from this earlier building, as they were perhaps more suitable for a male monastery, or they may reflect the tastes of the sculptor or patron. The depictions of a man on horseback and the fighting animals have a more martial than contemplative association. There is however no intrinsic reason for them not to be in a nunnery.[98] There are also decorative carvings on the capitals of the columns of the chancel arch showing foliage on four and mythical beasts on one.

Aside from decorative sculpture, it is certain that the nunneries would have had religious sculpture in their churches. Westropp described a fluted font at

90 Manning, *Clonmacnoise*, p. 33. See photos of the human face as well as the arches on p. 32. **91** For the head at Grace Dieu see Archdall (1876) p. 86. It is still insitu, though much worn, at the site of the convent of Grace Dieu, in the grounds of Turvey House Golf Club, Co. Dublin. Private communication Colm Cullerton. **92** A drawing of the head appears in Gilchrist, *Contemplation and action*, p. 142, fig. 85. **93** There is drawing of this sculpture on the cover of the O'Brien and Sweetman comp. *Archaeological inventory of County Offaly*. **94** Gilchrist, *Contemplation and action*, pp 141–2. **95** See drawing and photographs by Westropp, in Wardell, "History and antiquities of St Catherine, Old Abbey", p. 58. The photograph is reproduced in Begley, *Diocese of Limerick*, p. 374. When Westropp visited this house in the late nineteenth century he reported that the head was the subject of "superstitious reverence" by the local people. See his notes, TCD MS 972–1, f. 15. In the *RSAI Jn* article he reported the tradition that kissing the figure on first visiting the buildings would bring good luck. **96** Mentioned in "Society outings" *Cork Hist. Soc. Jn* 49 (1944) p. 66 and described by Hayes, "Ballymacadane", p. 141. **97** Chart, *Survey of monuments Northern Ireland*, p. 77. **98** See drawings in Healy, "Two royal abbeys", pp 7–8.

Killone, which he dated to the fifteenth century.[99] Although a statue beside the well of St Columba near Calliaghstown (Co. Meath) is believed locally to be of that saint, analysis by John Bradley suggests that it was part of an altar piece, possibly of the three Magi. He dates the piece to around 1300, and tentatively suggests that it was from the nunnery at Calliaghstown.[100] This is a plausible explanation although it is unlikely that the nunnery at Calliaghstown was ever very large and a piece such as he describes would have been expensive, as it was well carved from English oolite. It is, however, not impossible that a wealthy patron donated the statue to the nunnery at Calliaghstown or that it came originally from another monastery altogether, perhaps the convent of Odder or one of the nearby male monasteries, and found its way to Calliaghstown sometime in the post-medieval period.[101]

Other iconography that would have been in nuns' churches was relics and reliquaries. Although there are many descriptions of reliquaries and relics in use in medieval Ireland, there are few of reliquaries at nunneries.[102] The cross of St Attracta, who founded the nunnery at Killaraght, was revered throughout the medieval period, although the nuns are not mentioned in relation to the cross. It seems that by the fifteenth century, and probably earlier, the relics of St Attracta, her cross and her cup, were in the control of lay keepers.[103]

There is a reference to churches near Armagh having holy images in them before they were burnt in 1557; these may have been Na Ferta or St Brigid's.[104] In the seventeenth century, a body was found at the site of Temple Na Ferta in Armagh, under the rubbish of the ancient nunnery. It was in a standing position with two crosses, one in front and one behind.[105] It was believed at the time to be St Lupita, sister of St Patrick, founder of the nunnery. It is likely that her tomb would have been the site of reverence and pilgrimage and would have added to the prestige of this nunnery, along with its other Patrician associations. This is borne out by the small fragment of Greek porphyry pottery found in one of the excavated wells at Na Ferta, probably brought there by a pilgrim.[105] The church at Na Ferta was obviously an important one, as it also housed a set of Italian panels which may have been brought to it by the fifteenth-century Italian primate of Armagh, Octavian del Palatio.[107]

Shrines and reliquaries were costly items and would usually have been commissioned when there was a specific donation or bequest to cover the cost. Only

99 See Westropp, "The churches of County Clare", p. 125. **100** Bradley, "A medieval figure at Calliaghstown", pp 149–52. **101** There are now no remains at Calliaghstown, however Archdall reports that "some years since" part of the chapel was uncovered while digging foundations. Archdall (1786) p. 519. **102** For general descriptions of reliquaries and relics in Ireland see Crawford, "Irish shrines and reliquaries", pp 74–93 and 151–76, and Lucas, "The social role of relics and reliquaries", pp 5–37. **103** Ó Floinn, *Irish shrines and reliquaries*, p. 30; *Cal. papal letters, 1404–15*, p. 45. **104** Jeffries, *Priests and prelates*, p. 66. **105** Archdall (1876), I, p. 49. **106** Lynn, "Recent excavations in Armagh city", p. 277. **107** These panels are described by Reeves, "The ancient churches of Armagh", p. 195, and see Jefferies, *Priest and prelates*, p. 66.

the wealthiest of lay patrons and monasteries could have commissioned most shrines.[108] There are several mentions of bequests to shrines in the surviving wills of the period: the image of Mary in the parish church of Lusk and a gold image of the Virgin Mary bequeathed to the main altar of Christ Church cathedral.[109] Brian, son of Owen Ruarc, and his wife Margaret, daughter of Ó Briain, commissioned the book shrine known as the shrine of St Caillen in 1530.[110] There are also some descriptions of shrines which were assessed at the dissolution, such as those from Limerick, where there were statues, "images", crosses, buttons and beads all made of silver and precious stones.[111] It is probable that nunneries would have received similar bequests for the shrines and statues in their churches as well as for the commissioning of reliquaries, although none have survived.

The decorations on seals were a medium through which the nunneries expressed their collective identity. There are several references to the use of seals, which demonstrates that the nunneries all had a conventual or chapter seal and probably a seal for the use of the prioress or abbess as well. In the record of a deed of the thirteenth century agreed between the city of Dublin and Matilda de Rupe, prioress of Graney, the seal of the chapter of Graney is mentioned.[112] Walter Chapfleur, abbot of St Mary, Dublin, refers to the thirteenth-century common seal of Lismullin in 1495.[113] There were also the seals of Renalda Ní Bhriain and her co-religious Caterine Ní Bhriain attached to Renalda's will of 1511.[114] The only surviving example of a nunnery seal that I am aware of is from St Mary del Hogges and is affixed to an indenture of Juliana, abbess of Hogges, in 1462 (Figure 14). The seal is on red wax with the letters LIVSCCM visible around the broken edges. The figures on the seal are the seated Virgin under the remains of a canopy with the Infant on her lap. The Virgin is turned and faces the Child, whose hand may be raised in benediction. To her left is a kneeling figure of an abbess, with covered head and crosier of her office, with arms raised towards the Virgin and Infant.

Similar images of the life cycle of the Virgin Mary on monastic seals were popular in Ireland. The priory seal of the Clunaic priory of Athlone is similar in many ways to the seal of Hogges. The upper half of the seal shows the Virgin Mary nursing the Infant Jesus in her left arm, while his right hand is raised in blessing. The lower half shows a priest at an altar saying mass. His left hand holds a chalice and his right is raised making the sign of the cross.[115] The image used

108 Some indications of costs survive: in 1344, Holy Trinity Dublin paid 17s to Brother John Savage for carving and ornamenting 18 images for a shrine. *Account Roll of Holy Trinity, Dublin* p. 98. **110** Register of wills, ed. Berry pp 51–53; *Book of Obits*, p. 69. **110** Crawford, "A descriptive list of Irish shrines and reliquaries", p. 154. **111** These descriptions are of the shrines of the churches of Holy Cross and St Sunday in Limerick, from BL Add MS 19,865, f. 69, and see Bradshaw, *Dissolution*, p. 102. **112** From the Dublin White Book, calendared in *Cal. anc. rec. Dublin*, I, p. 99. **113** *Ormond deeds*, IV, p. 321. **114** NLI MS D 1978. The seals are no longer extant. **115** Murphy, "On two monastic seals", p. 373. Other ecclesiastic seals with similar imagery are described in Vigors, "On an ancient ecclesiastical brass seal", pp 82–4;

Figure 14. Seal of Juliana, abbess of Hogges.

Detail from TCD MS 1207/224. (Reproduced with permission of the Board of Trinity College Dublin.)

by Juliana, abbess of Hogges, is that of the "Throne of Wisdom". Gilchrist has argued that this image was one of the most common used by English nunneries on their seals.[116] Bedos-Rezak finds in her study that the image of the seated Virgin and Child was the most common image used for monastic seals after about 1300, although she finds it is used predominantly by male houses.[117] This conventionality of Hogges in choosing this design for their seal shows that they were not isolated from the trends in English monastic houses or from other Irish monastic houses and that they saw themselves as part of the mainstream of religious expression.

There are few details of the internal goods and furnishings of nunneries before the dissolution and even then the descriptions can only be called laconic. One pre-dissolution description is from the small house of Termonfeckin which in the fifteenth century could boast only one chalice and one missal, although these would have been sufficient for the very small community that were in residence at the time.[118] Descriptions and valuations of the chattels of the nunneries give some indication of how they were equipped at the dissolution and generally indicate that the nuns lived in relative comfort. Although the dissolution commissioners did not record details of the furnishings in Irish

and Armstrong, "Some matrices of Irish Seals", pp 462–70. **116** Gilchrist, *Gender and material culture*, pp 146–7, and *Contemplation and action*, p. 144. **117** Bedos-Rezak, "French sigillographic sources", p. 9. **118** Reg. Octavian (PRONI, Belfast, MS DIO 4/2/9) f. 222 or 268. **119** Mc Neill, "Accounts of sums", p. 16.

monastic houses, they did record the sums of money that they received for the sale of chattels. These chattels included the price of vessels, jewels and ornaments of silver, bells, "superfluous" buildings, utensils and household furniture.[119]

Table 5. Value of chattels from nunneries at dissolution[120]

Name	*Total Value of estates*	*Value of chattels*		*Notes*
	£	£	s	
Lismullin, Co. Meath	109	73		4 bells not sold
Grace Dieu, Co. Dublin	112	51		
Odder, Co. Meath	36	38		
Kilculliheen, Co. Waterford	50	3		Vestments and chalices to parish
Molough, Co. Tipperary	6	7		

From the available figures it appears that the richer monastic houses also generally had chattels of greater value. As would be expected, this suggests that they had better quality fittings, furnishings, church plate and reliquaries than the poorer houses. Some monasteries with high total valuations at the dissolution returned low valuations for chattels. However, a number of different circumstances may have been operating for these houses. A common one may have been that the staff of the house had sold, given away, or kept for later personal use the chattels in anticipation of the arrival of the commissioners. Other monasteries may have been allowing the depreciation of the value of moveables for some time and these figures may be corroboration of the accusations that were rife about the mismanagement of some of the monastic houses at this time.[121] This is a likely explanation for the small value of the chattels of the wealthy nunnery of Kilculliheen.

Post-dissolution users of the estates of the nuns also probably kept many of the fittings. This appears to the be the case with Lismullin, when in 1571 Thomas Cusack bequeathed to the church of Trivet where he wished to be buried:

> the best clothe and vestments and other furniture, including a chalice, from the chapel of Lessmlen at the discretion of Lady Genet (his wife) … .[122]

120 Information from *Extents Ir. mon. possessions* and Mc Neill, "Accounts of sums", pp 11–37. **121** See the accusations against Elicia Butler, abbess of Kilculliheen, in chapter 7. **122** *Cal. inquis., Dublin*, p. 210.

Although there is no indication of the sources of these vestments, it is likely that Thomas, the brother of the last prioress as well as the commissioner who surveyed the lands and purchased the site of Lismullin, also kept or purchased for his own use valuable moveable property from the nunnery.

Nuns lived in furnished convents and worshipped in churches among religious decoration. Although little survives from nunneries in Ireland, enough remains to suggest that the inner environment of convents reflected the status and wealth of the convents. Prosperous establishments would have provided furnishings and religious items for the resident women that were similar to those in English and continental houses. There were many poor convents in Ireland. These, no doubt, had fewer material possessions, and these nuns would have lived in much simpler surroundings. The few examples of specific statuary and decoration indicate that the nuns in medieval Ireland had access to imagery consistent with the mainstream of medieval religious expression.

The stone walls of the nunnery buildings signalled the sharp boundary between lay and religious space. These walls were supposed to be inviolate, protecting the occupants from the harm and cares of secular life. Estates were donated to provide for the both the material well-being of the nuns and the services the nuns were expected to provide for the surrounding lay communities. The nunnery buildings were not, however, only those of cloister and church. The gardens, orchards and home fields were also visible structures signalling points of transition between the cloistered world of the nuns and the local community. The surroundings of the convent of Grace Dieu were described in the nineteenth century:

> In a field a short distance from the ruins … is a small sharply-conical moat, evidently once an ornament of the nunnery garden. From its base a very remarkable ancient narrow causeway leads into Swords … It was paved with a reddish stone and presents some curious small, yet elevated arches of bridges.[123]

This description of part of the ruins of Grace Dieu suggests both the physical boundary of the convent, marked in the landscape by the ornamental moat at a distance from the ruins, and the points of contact in that boundary between the nuns and their lay neighbours. The "ancient" well-built pathway with its bridges signalled the essential interactions between nunneries and laity, between the quiet nunnery garden and stone walls of the cloister and the busy town of Swords. These breaks in the boundaries provided physical points of contact between lay communities and nuns, and these points were essential to the functioning of convents within the lay communities.

123 D'Alton, *History of the county of Dublin*, p. 513. There are only a few stones remaining of the convent walls in the grounds of what is now Turvey House Golf Club. Personal communication from Colm Cullerton.

ESTATES

The bridge at Grace Dieu was also the liminal point between the buildings of the convent and their estates, the lands and resources that had been donated to them to maintain the nuns in their work of prayer and charity. Nunnery estates were invested with pious meaning by the donors of land and by the nuns, their servants, agents and tenants. They were the physical manifestation of both donors' pious generosity and the religious work of the nuns themselves. Although the estates were operated in ways similar to all medieval estates, the significance of ownership was never forgotten.[124] Donations from pious laity formed the boundaries of the nunnery estates and within these borders nuns interacted with different sectors of the community.

A favourable geographical position for convents was important to their long-term survival but the situation and capacities of estates were also essential ingredients for the material success of any religious institution. Studies of conventual economies in England and Europe have found that nunneries were often endowed with small, poor estates and remained relatively poor. While this has been seen by historians as evidence of the marginal position of medieval nuns, recently Oliva has argued that more isolated and poorer nunneries may have been exactly what the founders and the nuns themselves wanted in order to show their devotion to God in circumstances reflecting their ideas of poverty and piety.[125] This may have been the desire of the founders and some of the religious women, but for several nunneries in Ireland the marginal nature of their estates may have contributed to the eventual failure of their houses.

There have been significant scholarly studies of monastic estates within medieval Ireland, although none has concentrated on the estates of the nunneries.[126] Until there are more modern fieldwork studies of nunneries and their estates, knowledge of the creation and establishment of nunnery estates in medieval Ireland must remain based primarily on surviving textual sources.[127] However, given these limitations, there is much to learn about nunnery estates from the documents which they generated, documents of disputes and of normal practice such as leases and taxation assessments, and also extraordinary events such as the surveys conducted at the general suppression of religious houses in the sixteenth century.

124 For a discussion of this point and the gendered meanings of medieval monastic landscapes, see Gilchrist, *Gender and material culture*, pp 63 ff. **125** See Oliva, *Convent and community*, p. 10. See also McNamara, *Sisters in arms*, pp 272–4 for an overview of the overly harsh assessments of nuns' financial acumen by previous historians. **126** See, among others, Otway-Ruthven, "Medieval church lands of County Dublin", pp 54–73; Hennessy, "The priory and hospital of New Gate", pp 41–54; Mills, "Tenants and agriculture near Dublin", pp 54–63; Simms, "The geography of Irish manors", pp 291–326. **127** There has been a welcome beginning with local fieldwork based studies of nunneries by Carville, "Cistercian nuns in medieval Ireland", pp 63–84. She has also studied Graney and will publish the results of this study in the future.

Nunnery lands

The position and type of monastic lands were partly dependent on the wealth of donors, but also on the donors' and religious communities' expectations of the way of life that the estate was intended to support.[128] Income for most monastic estates, including nunneries', came from two distinct sources: landed property, usually referred to as the temporalities, and the income from churches, chapels, tithes, alms and offerings, referred to as the spiritualities.[129] Temporalities also consisted of rents from property that remained in the hands of the donor. These rents could either be the entire income from a property or any part of it.[130] There were advantages and problems with administering both forms of income that will be discussed in more detail later.

A familiar lack of source materials hampers the recreation of the estates of nunneries of medieval Ireland. But foundation documents of some nunneries survive, as do the dissolution surveys, and these, combined with scattered references in court proceedings over the centuries, mean that place names can be listed, even when the exact amount of land involved cannot be determined with accuracy.[131] Identifying medieval place names with their modern equivalent is also problematic, although Ireland's system of townland divisions whose names were often fixed by the medieval period is an advantage in identifying place.[132] Mapping estates of nunneries demonstrates that although holdings were not completely concentrated into single management units they were usually in the same general area as the home nunnery. A good example of this pattern is Kilculliheen (Co. Waterford), where the majority of the lands were within a twenty-kilometre radius.[133] This distribution pattern has also been found in smaller nunneries and monasteries in England, where the nunneries and monasteries with small estates and patrons from the local gentry tended to have estates within a fairly localised area. Larger monasteries and nunneries with patrons from a higher social class tended to have estates at a greater distance from the home nunnery or monastery.[134]

Many of the rural nunneries also held urban property. The priory of Grace Dieu held tenements in Drogheda and Dublin.[135] Molough in rural Tipperary

128 For a general discussion of the legal title to monastic lands and the feudal rights associated with them in the Anglo-Irish colony see Hand, *The church in the English lordship*, pp 23–5. **129** See Oliva, *Convent and community*, pp 27–31 and Kerr, *Religious life for women*, pp 234ff. **130** For a discussion of these "obit" rents which survived the sale or lease of the land see Scrase, "Working with British property records", p. 19. **131** For the problems inherent in recreating medieval monastic estates in England see Moorhouse, "Monastic estates", pp 29–32. For one method of representing a medieval monastic estate in Ireland see Hennessy, "The priory and hospital of New Gate", p. 42. For the different units of measures used in medieval documents see McErlean, "The Irish townland system", p. 320. **132** Barry, *Medieval moated sites*, p. 131 and McErlean, "The Irish townland system", p. 316, who both acknowledge that considerable caution needs to be exercised in using these sources. **133** See Hall, "Women and religion", p. 124. **134** This has been demonstrated for English Augustinian houses by Robinson, *Geography of Augustinian settlements*, I, pp 181, 315, 323, where he finds that over 75 per cent of land valued at over £5 lay within 10 miles of the home monastery. **135** *Alen's reg.*, p. 66; *Fiants Ire., Hen. VIII–Eliz., II*, p. 624.

held a messuage in the nearby town of Clonmel.[136] The nuns of Graney held lands in the city of Dublin from which they granted a portion of the rents to the citizens of Dublin in return for a fixed sum in the late thirteenth century.[137] Timolin also held land and rents in Dublin.[138] In England, the urban holdings of nunneries were probably used both as a source of rent and also places to store produce before sale, and as accommodation for nuns and staff who needed to conduct business in the towns.[139] Although there is no direct evidence of this in Ireland, it would be reasonable to assume that the nunneries used their urban properties in similar ways.

Urban nunneries also had a mixture of urban and rural property: for example, Hogges held the large manor of Calliaghstown (Co. Dublin) as well as rents, houses, gardens and plots within the Dublin town walls. Some of these rents were of considerable value, with, for example, over ten marks of rents from properties bequeathed to them in 1234.[140] The importance of the rural lands to the urban estates of Hogges is demonstrated by the value of the different properties at the dissolution. Even though the rural estates had been subject to deprecations from raiding Irish, they were still worth over £11 while the plots, gardens and rents in the city and suburbs of Dublin were worth about £6.[141] Urban nunneries also participated in the economy of the surrounding towns in which they held estates and where their tenants lived. In 1396 the town of Waterford successfully appealed against a license granted to the nuns of Kilculliheen to buy and sell goods within their demesne, which the appeal claimed was doing "great damage to the city of Waterford and its citizens".[142] Besides the obviously poor relations between Kilculliheen and the citizens of Waterford, this indicates that the economy of the nuns' demesne must have been of sufficient value for the loss of custom to be worth the expense of an appeal. It is also significant that the nuns had or wished to enter the market-driven economy of the area. The record does not reveal the form of commerce proposed; it may have been an annual fair or it may have been a more permanent market place.

Nunneries also earned income from feudal dues either donated specifically to them or associated with their lands.[143] Although there are no surviving records from nunnery manorial courts in Ireland, there are references to the courts included in the estates of the nuns of Kilculliheen, Graney and Lismullin.[144] The holder of the court was entitled to the fines and income from all the proceedings conducted there.[145] Feudal dues owed to Grace Dieu, for example, included such items as the fourth of every gallon of drink brewed for sale in the area of Crumlin in Dublin and the tithes of the fish and lambs of the manor of

136 *Fiants Ire., Hen. VIII-Eliz.*, II, p. 32. **137** *Cal. anc. rec. Dublin, I,* pp 98–9. **138** Berry, "History of the religious guild of St Anne's", p. 79. **139** Graves, "Stixwould in the Market-places", p. 227. **140** *Cal. doc. Ire., 1171–1251*, p. 327. **141** *Extents Ir. mon. possessions*, pp 69–71. **142** *Cal. pat. rolls, 1392–96*, p. 702. **143** For the importance of mills and dues such as rights of free common and the income generated by them see Eager, "Tristernagh priory", pp 29–31. **144** For Kilculliheen see *Book of Howth*, p. 366. Lismullin and Graney, in *Extents Ir. mon. possessions*, pp 73, 259. **145** Kerr, *Religious life for women*, pp 210–11.

Portrane.[146] Mills were not only essential for the home manor but also as a profitable source of income, by charges for the use of the mill to tenants. Water rights often accompanied grants of mills, and were essential for the smooth functioning of the mill and its income. Graney was granted both the mill of Ugressi and the water which flowed through it at its foundation.[147] Lismullin held several mills and Kilculliheen held five salmon weirs in the sixteenth century.[148] In Gaelic Irish communities and certain border areas nuns would also have held locally applied dues and services. In 1537, the prioress of Molough (Co. Tipperary), an area on the border of the Butler and Poer holdings which operated under a mixture of Gaelic and English customs, was extracting the common Gaelic in-kind payments of coyne and livery.[149] All these dues, services, rents and land formed the assets with which the nuns supported themselves to carry out the pious wishes of the founders and patrons and devote themselves to lives of prayer. Sufficient resources, efficiently managed, not only meant that these wishes could be fulfilled but also reflected on the more worldly prestige of patrons.

Value of monastic estates

All assets were not equal and the value of lands and estates were dependent on many different factors, including changing economic circumstances, changes in tenant base and depopulation due to war, and general instability. Comparing the value of monastic estates in medieval Ireland is fraught with problems, but it is possible to produce broad comparisons at two points: the ecclesiastical taxation ordered by Pope Nicholas IV and undertaken in about 1307; and the surveys conducted at the time of the general dissolution of the monasteries in 1539–40 and after. Both sets of data have problems that need to be understood before any analysis can take place. The ecclesiastical taxation was conducted in about 1307, with a further series of valuations in 1318–19 after the deprecations following the Bruce invasion, and then forwarded to the English exchequer in October 1323.[150] The surviving valuations include two valuations for the dioceses of Meath, Emly, Waterford, Cashel and Cork but do not cover the dioceses of Ossory, Ferns and part of Leighlin.[151] For the diocese of Ossory, a series of valuations for ecclesiastical taxations has been preserved in the Liber Ruber of the Bishops of Ossory, the first of which is probably from 1306–7, and the second probably from 1319.[152] However,

146 *Fiants Ire., Hen. VIII-Eliz*, II, p. 44 and *Extents Ir. mon. possessions*, p. 75. **147** *Pont. Hib.* I p. 137. Ugressi has not been identified. **148** The mill belonging to Lismullin and the holdings around it in Kilmartin were the subject of several court actions. See Calendar of Common Bench roll, Michaelmas 33 Ed I, (NAI MS RC 7/10), p. 377. For the salmon weirs belonging to Kilculliheen see Extents Ir. mon. possessions p. 204. **149** *The social state of the southern and eastern counties of Ireland*, p. 248. **150** For a discussion of the use of this valuation see Barry, *Medieval moated sites*, pp 128–32. The dating is not certain. Hand has argued for two sets of valuations in 1306 and about 1319–22 after the Bruce invasion; see Hand, "Dating of the early fourteenth-century ecclesiastical valuation", pp 271–4. **151** Barry, *Medieval moated sites*, p. 128. **152** The valuation and taxations which were forwarded to the Exchequer have been published in *Cal. doc. Ire., 1302–1307*, pp 302–23. For the first of the Liber Ruber valuations see

valuations for the diocese of Ferns, covering the county of Wexford, have not survived. There are also many omissions from the surviving valuation and it is often difficult to identify place names. When these problems are combined with the usual difficulties with deliberate undervaluation, the values from these surveys must be seen as imprecise at best.[153]

The surveys of monastic estates carried out in advance of the dissolution of the monasteries also suffer from problems affecting their interpretation.[154] The commissioners noted frequently that valuations were lower than normal due to war and "waste" of land, or that they could not visit certain areas because of hostile Gaelic Irish. This "waste" means that the normal dues raised on cultivated land could not be collected, perhaps because of conversion to pastoral uses of the land or to destruction and depopulation. There were also hidden incomes where land had been granted away in long leases prior to dissolution in return for cash "entry fines" to monastic superiors and not recorded in the dissolution surveys.[155] When the jurors could determine the value of monastic property they usually did not include the value of the home farm, the contents or chattels nor the church if it was parochial. Some valuations of furnishings and other moveable goods survive, and indicate that some of the convents had quite extensive contents when they were sold. The commissioners also did not fully survey large parts of the west of the country, although both the prominent convents of Killone (Co. Clare) and Kilcreevanty (Co. Galway) were surveyed.[156] While imprecise, these two groups of valuations offer the only points for which any comparison is possible and so must be carefully considered.[157]

Table 6 shows the values of the nunneries in 1307 and at the dissolution. The separate values recorded for rectories in column 3 are necessary because the sources record only the full value of the rectory, not the portion reserved for the nuns. The full valuation is given to provide a rough estimate of the relative value of rectories to the nunnery economies. Where the precise value of the nunnery's portion is known, this value is included under column 2.[158]

"Calendar of Liber Ruber of Ossory", pp 159–208, with selected extracts also published by Carrigan, *History and antiquities of Ossory*, IV, pp 363, 372, 375, 380, 384, 391. The second valuation has been published in full in *H.M.C. rep.* 10 app v. pp 234–42. For the dating of these valuations see Hand, "Dating of early fourteenth century ecclesiastical valuation," pp 273–4. **153** For a discussion of the difficulty using the taxation of Nicholas IV for English monastic estates, particularly the almost certain undervaluing of property, see Robinson, *Geography of Augustinian settlements*, I, p. 113. **154** For a general discussion of the problems of source material for the dissolution of the monasteries see Bradshaw, *Dissolution*, pp 17–18. **155** Bradshaw, *Dissolution*, pp 85–7. **156** For the progress of the dissolution in the kingdoms of Thomond and Connacht see Bradshaw, *Dissolution*, pp 169–75. **157** Valuations of the Franciscan and Dominican friaries, and the Hospitallers of Jerusalem, have not been included, The first two because they were not only usually inadequately surveyed, but also were founded and maintained in ways very different to the nunnery estates. The estates of the Hospitallers have likewise been excluded because of distinct differences in the ways that the estates were valued and managed. **158** For differences in calculating tithes and parochial dues between Gaelic and Anglo-Irish areas of Ireland see Nicholls, "Rectory, vicarage and parish in the western Irish Dioceses", pp 53–80, and Hand, *The church in the English lordship*, pp 20–1.

Table 6. Valuations of convents[159]

1. Convent	*2. 1306 values (£)*	*3. 1306 values of rectories (£)*	*4. Value at dissolution (£)*
Lismullin, Co. Meath	62	8	109
Graney, Co. Carlow	37	67▼	73
St John the Baptist, Cork	25[160]		Not known
Timolin, Co. Kildare	22	68	5
Kilculliheen, Co. Kilkenny	24[161]	5	50▼
Grace Dieu, Co. Dublin	7	61	112
St Mary del Hogges, Dublin	15	4	18▼
Kilcreevanty, Co. Galway	14	5▼	34[162]
Clonard/Odder, Co. Meath	0[163] 6	5	36
Killone, Co. Clare	2	4▼	40[164]
St Catherine d'Conyl, Co. Limerick	2[165]	8	Not known
St Mary's Clonfert, Co. Galway	2		Not known
Ballymore, Co. Westmeath	0.5		Not known
St Mary's, Down	Not known		16
Termonfeckin, Co. Louth	Not known		9
St Brigit, Molough, Co. Tipperary	Not known		6
Killeevy, Co. Armagh	Not known		2
Ardcarn, Co. Roscommon	Not known		2 (in 1589)
St Brigit, Kildare	Not known		2
Inishmaine, Co. Mayo	Not known		3 (in 1587)
St Peter's, Limerick	Not known		1

▼ = not all property valued.

159 All values are rounded to the nearest £ as given in the source. No attempt has been made to convert the values to any other currency. Sources unless otherwise indicated are *Cal. doc. Ire. 1302–1307*, for columns 2 and 3, and *Extents Ir. mon. possessions* for column 4. **160** This valuation is not that of the 1302–6 valuation, but the value of donations at the foundation in 1301. *Cal. doc. Ire., 1293–1301*, pp 363–5. **161** This is the value given in the ecclesiastical tax for Ossory, and includes the rector's portion of all rectories and chapels within the diocese. Some property was in other diocese and has therefore not been included. **162** "A list of the monasteries in Connacht, 1577", p. 34. **163** Temporalities of the abbess of Clonard did not suffice to support the nuns. **164** "A list of the monasteries in Connacht, 1577", p. 38. **165** The 1319 valuation showed that the nunnery did not suffice to support the nuns.

These comparisons give only broad indications of how nunnery estates fared between the early fourteenth and the sixteenth centuries. They do not take into account fluctuations in currency or land values. Localised conflict affected the value of monastic property largely through difficulties tenanting land in vulnerable positions and collecting rents from outlying estates and rectories. The other reason lands may have been described as "waste" was when land was turned over exclusively to pastoral uses.[166]

In order to assess the relative value of the nunneries the value of all the monastic and nunnery estates needs to be compared. A broad general comparison is possible only for the dissolution and the years immediately afterwards, when there are valuations for 110 monastic houses.[167] The wealthiest monastery surveyed at the dissolution was the granges of Colp and Duleek in Co. Meath with a value of £597, closely followed by the great monasteries of St Mary's and St Thomas', Dublin, with valuations of £538 and £452 respectively. There were twenty monasteries and convents with dissolution values over £100: these were the most stable houses and able to withstand the pressures of war and decline in patronage. They were clustered in rich arable lands within the English-dominated areas of Ireland, suggesting that not only did they have the best farming lands but were also the most effectively protected from the onslaughts of war and unrest. Two nunneries had values over £100: Lismullin with £109 and Grace Dieu with £112. This demonstrates their status as the wealthiest of the nunneries, with both their home manors and the majority of property situated well within the pale boundaries. Monastic houses valued between £100 and £50 were probably able to withstand the pressures and crises of sixteenth-century property management, although many were possibly in reduced circumstances. There were seventeen houses in this range, with many of these, including the two nunneries of Graney (£73) and Kilculliheen (£50), situated in the border areas of the pale or the Butler lordships.

There were forty-five monastic houses valued between £50 and £10 and these small houses may have been suffering the effects of depopulation and destruction of property. They tended to be situated in the march areas of the English Pale, or else in the Gaelic-controlled west where land was generally valued lower than in the east. There were four nunneries among this third group: Clonard/Odder (£36) and Hogges (£18), both with properties described as "waste" in the march, and Killone (£30) and Kilcreevanty (£34) in the Gaelic west. The proportion of nunneries in the group with the lowest income is slightly higher than in the more wealthy groups, with seven nunneries among the seventeen monasteries valued at less than £10. All these monasteries and convents would probably have been struggling to provide basic services and

166 Jefferies, *Priest and prelates*, p. 29. **167** These figures were calculated from *Extents Ir. mon. possessions*; Archdall (1786), "A rentall of Mounster and Connaught". For full details see Hall, "Women and religion", pp. 391–3.

maintain their estates. These comparisons demonstrate that by the end of the medieval period, nunneries in Ireland tended to have estates worth less than comparable monasteries. However, there were wealthy nunneries whose final incomes compared very favourably with the majority of male monastic houses, demonstrating that not all nuns were living in poverty.

Costs of supporting nuns

For these values to be meaningful some indication of the costs involved in managing convents and the numbers of nuns in residence would be useful.[168] Unfortunately, there are no internal accounts available for any nunneries in medieval Ireland. Estimates for the costs of running male monastic houses can be used with considerable caution as an indication of the costs of maintaining nuns in Ireland. In the 1340s, the Benedictine priory of Fore (Co. Westmeath) was taken into the control of the crown escheator because it was considered an alien priory as a dependency of St Taurin at Evreux.[169] The income for the priory was stated to be £20 2*s*. annually, supporting the prior, five monks and a servant. The prior was allowed 3*d*. daily, with the other monks allowed half that amount.[170] Although the priory was probably suffering restrictions on its income at this time, this does give some indication of costs for supporting religious people in a small monastic setting. Taking the amounts literally would mean that about £15 annually was spent on directly supporting this small community.

The fourteenth-century account roll for the priory of Holy Trinity in Dublin also gives some idea of the costs involved in running a large monastic house. The prior of Holy Trinity frequently entertained prominent men, often lavishly, however the other members of the convent appear to have lived less extravagantly. Some of the costs involved in feeding the monks can be calculated. For example it cost 5*d*. to provide ale for the dinner and supper of the convent on the Friday before Ash Wednesday in 1339. The numbers thus provided for are not given, but there were eleven canons in the priory in 1300 and eight in 1480.[171] On another occasion in 1344, the cost of feeding eight monks in bread, ale and meat was one crannoc of wheat, 8*d*. worth of ale and 6*d*. worth of meat.[172]

The few available records indicate that nunneries in Ireland were smaller than their English counterparts, although there is not the same range of securely dated evidence in Ireland.[173] Oliva has calculated numbers of nuns in Norwich nunneries and concludes that there were on average between 8.5 and twenty-one nuns in residence at any given time, with most nunneries averaging around eleven.[174]

168 Oliva, *Convent and community*, pp 90–9, details the financial arrangements for the nunneries in the diocese of Norwich. Although comparisons of income and expenditure are not relevant for the nunneries in Ireland, the overall impression of reasonable economic viability from often slender incomes is comparable. **169** *Med. rel. houses Ire.*, p. 106. **170** "Cat. pipe rolls, Ed. III", *PRI rep. DK* 53 (1926) pp 51–2. **171** Lydon, "Introduction" to *Account Roll of Holy Trinity, Dublin*, p. xix. **172** *Account Roll of Holy Trinity, Dublin*, p. 71. **173** Power, *Medieval English nunneries*, pp 117–25, outlines the expenses of some English nunneries. **174** Oliva, *Convent and community*, pp 38–45, for a discussion of her methods in

The personnel of the wealthy nunnery of Lismullin included a prioress, thirteen nuns, and a household of forty before the plague of 1348–9, while in 1367 the numbers had been reduced to a prioress, seven nuns, five girls being trained to be nuns either in that convent or others, and servants to the total of thirty-two people.[175] The nearest valuation to correspond with these figures is that of the ecclesiastical taxation of 1307, suggesting that on an income of approximately £62 Lismullin supported a prioress, thirteen nuns and forty staff. There are some other isolated figures for numbers of nuns in other convents in the fifteenth century when, during the episcopal visitation of the archbishop of Dublin in 1468, there were five nuns and the prioress at Grace Dieu, and three nuns and the prioress or abbess at Hogges.[176] These numbers are similar to the numbers of nuns who received pensions at the time of the dissolution. The values of the estates of Grace Dieu at the dissolution was £112, and for Hogges £18.

When the figures for the monks of Holy Trinity, Fore and other male communities are compared with the evidence for the nuns of Grace Dieu and Lismullin, it appears that the nuns were well provided for as long as their estates produced the assessed income.[177] The nuns of Hogges in the late fifteenth and early sixteenth centuries were less wealthy, and the smaller group of nuns living there may have experienced correspondingly lower living standards than the male monastic houses in Dublin. It is unlikely that the numbers of nuns, even at the wealthy house of Lismullin, ever reached much more than twelve or thirteen at any given time, although this cannot be conclusive especially for the large Gaelic-Irish nunneries such as Kilcreevanty and Killone, where there may have been more nuns in residence, particularly in the years following their foundation.

There were other costs involved in managing nunnery estates, such as the dues and taxes payable to various secular and ecclesiastical officials. While the fines and fees paid to crown officials were common to all landowners, convents and monasteries also owed fees to bishops. There is no way of knowing the full extent of nunneries' obligations for these legal fees and fines, but they are frequently mentioned in the surviving calendars of original rolls. In 1299, for example, the abbess of Odder owed 40*d.* in fines, while about 1304, the prioress of Lismullin owed 10s for fines in the county of Dublin. In 1341, Alianora, prioress of Lismullin, was fined 3*s.* 4*d.* for "making false claim", which usually meant they had lost a case.[178]

arriving at these averages. **175** *Calendar of inquisitions, miscellaneous, 1348–1377*, p. 236. **176** *Register of wills*, ed. Berry, pp 175–7. For comparison, at the time of the same visitation, the numbers at the other monastic houses in Dublin were: 6 canons, 1 sub-prior and 1 prior at the Priory of Holy Trinity (Christ Church cathedral) p. 172; 3 canons and the prior at the Priory of Holmpatrick; 4 canons, 1 sub-prior and 1 prior at the priory of All Hallows, p. 176; 9 monks, 1 sub-prior, 1 prior and 1 abbot at the monastery of St Thomas, Dublin, p. 177. **177** Preston, "The canons regular of St Augustine", p. 105, notes the paucity of evidence of numbers of male monastics and suggests that the numbers of Augustinian canons probably rarely rose above 10. **178** For Odder see *Cal. doc. Ire.,1293–1301*, p. 316. For Lismullin, "Cat. pipe rolls, Ed. III", *PRI rep. DK* p. 48.

Fees were owed to bishops for "relaxation" of visitation, procuration and a proportion of tithes.[179] Like their male counterparts, many of the nuns found that the charges owed to bishops were onerous.[180] The Cistercian nunnery of St Mary's at Down paid fees, including five marks in proxies and five marks in "refections", from an income recorded as £16 at the dissolution.[181] Wealthier nunneries paid correspondingly higher fees: Lismullin for example owed the bishop of Meath ten marks in 1254 for relaxation of visitation.[182] At the dissolution the procurations owed to church officials, the archbishop and local bishops were listed for Odder; they owed fees to the bishop and archdeacon of Meath and to the archbishop of Armagh.[183] The archbishops of Dublin may have felt the burden of care for nuns to be great. Archbishop Alen recorded the reason for the annual charge of four marks from the nuns of Grace Dieu as being because of their "weakness as a sex", indicating they needed extra care for their lack of discretion. The charge may also reflect a high degree of surveillance by the archbishops of Dublin.[184]

Convents had the additional charges of needing to pay for chaplains for their own church and for all the churches in their estates. Male monasteries were able to reduce some of these charges because some of their number were priests. At the dissolution, for example, Grace Dieu owed the chaplain for the convent church 53*s.* 4*d.* as well as 40*s.* for the curate at Tubber (probably Tober, Co. Wicklow) and 106*s.* 8*d.* for the curate at Westpalston (Co. Dublin).[185] The nunneries of Clonard/Odder and Termonfeckin owed similar sums to curates of their churches at the dissolution.[186]

Nunnery estates were designed to provide sufficient income for religious women to carry out the wishes of their patrons and pray for the communities who supported them. Some nunneries in Ireland were very wealthy, endowed with large estates and considerable resources. These prestigious houses reflected well on their patrons as well as the religious women themselves. Other houses were small and poorly resourced. This may have been because women religious were considered to be less worthy of patronage or the best parcels of land. It is also possible that the spiritual glory of living in religious poverty was the outcome intended by the original donors. The other factor in assessing the value and function of estates in medieval Ireland is the fluctuations in value of land and

179 See Preston, "The canons regular of St Augustine", pp 146–7 for details of the relationships between Augustinian canons and bishops over these fees. Also Ronan, *Reformation in Dublin*, p. 468. **180** Preston, "The canons regular of St Augustine", pp 146–7. **181** Archdall (1876), I, pp 262–3 n. 13 citing "The Terrier". The income at the dissolution was certain to be vastly reduced as all the monastic houses in Down were described as derelict when they were collated with the cathedral in 1513. See *Med. rel. houses Ire.*, p. 313. **182** "Lord Chancellor Gerrard's Notes", p. 253. **183** *Extents Ir. mon. possessions*, p. 262. **184** *Alen's reg.* p. 179. **185** *Extents Ir. mon. possessions*, p. 77. White identifies "Tober" as Tipperkevin, Kildare. However, there are many references to Tipperkevin in "Obligationes pro annatis diocesis Dublinensis, 1421–1520", pp 14–15 and none to "Tober" or to Grace Dieu. Tober, Wicklow is very close to holdings of Grace Dieu at Kineagh, Co. Kildare. **186** *Extents Ir. mon. possessions*, pp 235, 262.

resources over the three centuries between foundation and the dissolution. Estates which were sufficient for the needs of twelfth- and thirteenth-century nuns often became difficult to manage, cut off by changes in the composition of surrounding lay communities or devalued due to mismanagement or problems of local disturbances by the sixteenth century.

CHAPTER 5

Income, management and conflict

The estates donated to nunneries required religious women to be feudal landholders, engaged in maintaining, extending and defending their lands. Although estate management was not the stated purpose for the foundation of nunneries or the reason women joined convents, it was the most public aspect of their institutions and the one that has survived best in the archival evidence. Religious women were employers, landlords, legal supporters and opponents, holders of rectories, collectors of tithes. Nuns, especially superiors, had to act outside their walls, either physically or through the mediation of agents. This chapter will explore the methods employed by nuns to manage their estates and the effects of conflict, both legal and physical, on the viability of nunneries. Guardianship of these estates meant that nuns were required to interact with different sectors outside the nunnery walls and with officials of the government, ecclesiastical authorities and lay patrons.

MANAGING THE NUNNERIES' RESOURCES

Abbesses and prioresses were the hands-on managers of their estates, employing officials, such as bailiffs, stewards and attorneys, as well as labourers, to do much of the work.[1] Internal records from English nunneries suggest that as well as employing these agents, the abbesses and prioresses maintained significant personal control over receiving rents and dispensing produce for consumption, sale and distribution as alms.[2] The prioresses and abbesses of the convents in the Anglo-Irish areas of medieval Ireland were all, as far as can be determined, from the gentry of the surrounding communities.[3] Women of this class in England and Ireland were expected to be adept at managing estates either regularly or in the absence of their husbands and fathers.[4] In Gaelic Ireland, the women who were superiors of the large nunneries came from the local ruling families. Their brothers became chiefs, warriors and bishops, while their sisters made strategic

1 Venarde, *Women's monasticism*, pp 116ff. **2** Oliva, *Convent and community*, pp 76–90. **3** See chapter 6. **4** Archer, "How ladies ... who live on their manors", pp 152–4, details the sort of education and expectation of this class in England. There is no equivalent source for Ireland on which to base a comparison, but it is reasonable to assume that women of this class in the communities of Ireland were capable of and expected to manage similar resources.

marriage alliances, facilitating the complex and delicate weave of negotiation and contact between different familial groups. Although little is known of the education of these women, it must be assumed that they were educated to be capable of managing estates, employees and associated networks.[5]

In the surviving records, the most visible agents of the nunneries were their attorneys. Often these were canons attached in some way to the nunneries, as can be seen by the attorneys representing Lismullin in the late thirteenth and early fourteenth centuries.[6] After this time, the nuns of Lismullin seem to have employed professional lay lawyers in the courts, which probably indicates a change in the number of professional lawyers rather than a reduction in men working and living at the priory. The nuns of Timolin do not appear to have been represented by monks or canons, instead employing men like Philip le Poer and Peter FitzRoger as attorneys, probably professional lawyers, while the nuns and prioresses of Grace Dieu granted pensions to Thomas FitzSymons, advocate, and James Bath, "for good counsel" in 1538.[7] Although the nuns definitely employed other men, particularly as bailiffs and farm labourers, there are few references to them. Without internal working documents of the nunneries, the numbers, names and functions of their employees must remain obscure, with only chance references giving some of the details, such as that of Henry, clerk of Grace Dieu, whose violent death was recorded by the archbishops of Dublin.[8]

The employment of these men was a vital component of the nunneries' administration and there needed to be constant interaction between them and the nuns, usually represented by prioresses and abbesses, for the smooth running of the estates. Hints at difficulties between attorneys, bailiffs or other agents and the nuns appear rarely. In the judgement of one court action by Lismullin in the early fourteenth century, the comment was made that the land in question had already been lost by Henry, canon of Lismullin and advocate for the previous prioress.[9] Although the later case may have been no more than a hopeful action by the new prioress seeking to overturn a previous judgement, it is also possible that there was a breakdown in communication between the attorney and his employers or that the current prioress disagreed with the course taken by Henry and was seeking legal remedy. The meagre record does not elucidate further, but this case is one of the few where the professional relationship between advocate and prioress is more than baldly stated.

Extending estate boundaries

An important aspect of managing medieval monastic estates was not only caring for the initial endowments but also extending the estates to allow for expansion

5 For recent arguments about the achievements of women of this class see Fitzpatrick, "Mairgréag an-Einigh Ó Cearbhaill", pp 20–38; Kehoe, "Margaret Fitzgerald", pp 826–41; McKenna, "Was there a political role for women in medieval Ireland", pp 163–74. 6 Hall, "The nuns of the medieval convent of Lismullin", p. 62. 7 *Cal. inquis. Dublin*, p. 77. 8 *Alen's reg.*, p. 105. 9 Calendar of Common Bench Roll, 24 Ed I, Roll no. 26 (NAI RC 7/4), p. 220 and Calendar of Justices Itinerant Roll 29 Ed I, (NAI RC 7/8), pp 261–2.

or to offset the unpredictable effects of decline through agricultural disaster, war or pestilence. There is also evidence that donations continued through the centuries after foundation. This is consistent with Gilchrist's findings where she suggests that nunneries in England and France retained their position within the communities that supported them, with donations continuing right up to the dissolution.[10]

Donations received after the initial foundations of nunneries in Ireland reflect the local connections made and maintained by nuns. St Mary del Hogges received a handsome donation in the form of over 10 marks yearly rents from various properties of Margaret daughter of Richard Gillmichelle in 1234.[11] Although there are few records of donation of rents to Hogges, it is possible that like the hospital of St John the Baptist, in Dublin, Hogges was the recipient of rents from small land-holders during the course of the mid- to late thirteenth century and later.[12] Donations of rents tended to occur after the initial wave of foundations and since Hogges held many rents in Dublin at the dissolution, it is probable that it received a steady stream of donations after its initial foundation. There is an undated, although probably early thirteenth-century, grant to Timolin where Robert de Stanton gave land at "tres castellanos" which must have been near Timolin's other holdings as he also included a further two acres to ensure that they had access between their land and the new grant.[13] This grant indicates that there were strong ties between the nuns and the lay donor ensuring the donation was not only needed by the nuns but was accompanied by necessary access land. As this grant also seems to have accompanied the profession of the donor's daughter, Isabelle, the family probably were local.

Donations were not without their expenses to the recipients, especially after the promulgation of the statute of Mortmain, when the monasteries were obliged to pay not only for any hospitality for the donors, and for expenses of papal, episcopal and crown confirmations, but also licenses from the crown for exemption from the statute. These expenses could be onerous and needed to be set against the anticipated income of any donation or purchase.[14] In England patronage of convents and monasteries fell away during the fifteenth century in favour of patronage of guilds, fraternities and mendicant friars and the same trend can be observed in Ireland. Convents in the medieval colony of Ireland did continue to attract donations during this period, probably in a similar way to the English nunneries studied by Gilchrist. For example, in 1474 Eleanora, prioress of Swords, was granted 20*s*. yearly, and the abbess of Kilculliheen accepted the donation of the advowson of the church in 1392.[15]

10 Gilchrist, *Contemplation and action*, pp 107–8. **11** *Cal. doc. Ire., 1171–1251*, p. 327. **12** Hennessy, "Priory and hospital of New Gate", pp 45–6ff. **13** *Alen's reg.*, p. 306. **14** Scrace, "Working with British property records", pp 24–5 and Rabin, *Mortmain legislation*, pp 182–5. **15** For the donation to Eleanora see "Calendar of the Liber Niger Alani", p. 305. Swords must be Grace Dieu, which was located near Swords in Co. Dublin. For the donation to Kilculliheen see *A roll of the proceedings of the King's council, Ireland,* 1392–3, pp 152–4.

Evidence from wills shows that, although testators tended to favour male monastic houses, some income did accrue to nunneries from bequests. In 1276, Gilbert le Dycer left 2*s*. to the nuns of Hogges, and Joan, daughter of William Douce, left the nuns of St Mary del Hogges one mark in 1381.[16] In Limerick, the small nunnery of St Peter's attracted a bequest of one mark in the will of Martin Arthur, a prominent Limerick citizen, in 1376.[17] These figures are consistent with the findings of MacDonald in her study of bequests to nunneries in Yorkshire. In that study she found that although nunneries never received many bequests, there was a constant small number that lasted throughout the later medieval period.[18]

As internal documents for Irish nunneries do not survive, the record of purchases by nuns is haphazard and must underestimate the extent of their participation in the property market. It does appear that convents purchased and exchanged lands when necessary, but were not involved in large-scale expansion of their estates after their initial foundation. The nuns of Hogges may have been an exception, as they appear to have been active in property purchase and lease in Dublin itself. For example, in 1461, they purchased land in Dublin from Ralph de Piro and his wife Alicia.[19] The official records of many of the purchases and other exchanges by nuns were couched in terms that emphasize the poverty of the nunneries. Although this cannot be discounted as a reason for wishing to extend nunnery estates, it must also be taken with caution as appeals based on the poverty of nuns and monks were widespread enough to be commonplace in medieval legal and charter terminology.[20] Yet there were several factors that may have contributed to the chronic poverty and indebtedness of nunneries, one of which was that the nuns would rarely have worked the land themselves, relying on lay brothers and tenurial and hired labour.[21] So the pleas of the nuns for special consideration were likely to have been based at least in part on inability to extend their incomes by reducing payment for labour.

Nuns sometimes exchanged land to consolidate scattered estates, probably for ease of management. In the late thirteenth century, the nuns of St Mary del Hogges were granted three acres in Baggotrath in exchange for a plot of land in the suburbs of Dublin. This transaction may have been to benefit the donor, Robert Baggot, or it may have been to consolidate the nunnery's holdings.[22] Graney was given license to purchase land to the value of 20 marks in 1395, although there is no record of which land was purchased, whether it was worth this rather large sum, or how the nuns obtained the money to buy it.[23]

16 *Reg. St John Dublin*, p. 42 and Berry, "History of the religious guild of St Anne's", p. 47. **17** Begley, *The diocese of Limerick*, p. 351. **18** MacDonald, "Women and the monastic life in late medieval Yorkshire", pp 87–8. **19** *Alen's reg.* p. 305; "Calendar of Liber Niger Alani", p. 305. The entry in the Calendar notes the transfer of property as a gift, while *Alen's reg.* notes that the abbess and nuns paid 4 marks for the land, suggesting that it was more a purchase. **20** Robinson, *Geography of Augustinian settlements*, I, pp 186–7, outlines how some Augustinian monasteries cited poverty as reasons for needing to increase their stock of appropriated benefices. **21** Gilchrist, *Gender and material culture*, pp 85–6. **22** *Alen's reg.*, pp 146–7. **23** *Rot.*

Moving nunnery resources away from dangerous or untenanted lands in the marches was another motivation behind reorganising and consolidating estates. In 1392, Isabella Wolf, abbess of Kilculliheen, petitioned the Justiciar for permission to allow John Fylle, chaplain, to grant them the advowson of the church of Balitarstan, stating as reason "the great poverty of the house, and that their lands, tenements, rents and churches are for the greater part destroyed and laid waste as well by Irish enemies as English rebels".[24] Late in 1456, Fyna, abbess of Clonard and Odder, petitioned parliament for permission to exchange land in Calliaghstown (Collinstown, Co. Westmeath) for twenty acres of land in Dexterstown (Kilmessan, Co. Meath) and Jordanstown (near Tara, Co. Meath), closer to the home nunnery of Odder. The reason she gave for this request was that the lands in Calliaghstown were on the border of Meath and thus she was unable to collect the rents from it without great expense.[25] In this case her pleas were undoubtedly genuine as Calliaghstown was in contested country, and the usual fines required for this application were waived because of her poverty.

Other reasons besides poverty were given for wishing to increase property, the most usual being to improve services for the lay communities. In 1474, the nuns of Grace Dieu were given permission to purchase lands to the value of £20 to increase divine services and improve the conditions at their priory.[26] Jenet White, prioress of Termonfeckin, obtained permission to purchase lands the next year in order to increase the income of her priory, and Margaret Heynot, prioress of Lismullin, was granted permission to purchase lands to the value of £40 in order to augment divine services and hospitality in her priory.[27]

Nuns as landlords

When monastic estates were established in the twelfth and early thirteenth centuries, the nuns through their bailiffs farmed the home demesne and outlying granges. The founders of nunneries aimed to allow the religious women to be self-sufficient, and thus able to continue their lives of prayer. In reality, as the centuries wore on, farming practices changed with the rise of cash economies and labour hire, and from at least the fourteenth century managers of religious estates relied increasingly on leasing in return for fixed cash income.[28] The prevalence of these leasing arrangements in monastic estate management is indicated by Robinson's estimates that, by 1535, 85 per cent of the income of most of the Augustinian estates in England comprised fixed rents.[29]

pat. Hib., p. 153. For a discussion of the license system and how it worked in relation to the amounts given on the licenses see Brand, "The licensing of mortmain alienations", pp 127–8. It is possible that the 20 marks mentioned was an arbitrary and general figure which was designed to cover various contingencies. **24** *A Roll of the proceedings of the King's council in Ireland 1392–3*, pp 152–4. **25** *Statutes of Ireland, King Henry VI*, pp 404–7. **26** *Statutes of Ireland, 12–22 Edward IV*, pp 222–5. **27** *Statutes of Ireland, 12–22 Ed. IV*, pp 288–9, 420–1. **28** Gilchrist, *Gender and material culture*, pp 72–3; Moorhouse, "Monastic estates", pp 36–7; and Hare, "The monks as landlords", pp 82–95; Robinson, *Geography of Augustinian settlements*, I, pp 184, 292–5, for England. For Ireland see Graham, "The High Middle Ages", p. 77. **29** Robinson, *Geography of Augustinian settlements*, I, p. 299.

Leasing was used widely by nunneries in Ireland. The prioress of Timolin was entering into leases as early as 1220, when she leased lands in Dublin to David FitzJohn.[30] There is an indenture from 1462 between Juliana, abbess of St Mary del Hogges, and John Nicholl with his wife Juliana concerning land in Skinner's Street for the annual charge of 10p.[31] The nuns themselves leased this piece of land or one near it from the archbishop of Dublin for the sum of 4*s*.[32] Leasing and then subletting smaller divisions like this occurred frequently in urban and rural areas. In 1408, Lismullin was a free tenant of 137 acres of arable land in Betagheston (Co. Louth), holding the land from the Grange of Colp, only paying tithes of about 5*s*. an acre. They then placed their own tenants on the land, presumably to the profit of the convent.[33] Leases had to be periodically renegotiated to allow for either fluctuations in the value of the land or the death of leasees. In 1499, the prioress and nuns of Grace Dieu, for example, entered into a lease with Jenkyns Hancok of Swords whereby, in return for 13*s*. 4*d*. a year in two instalments, Hancok rented all the lands which had been previously leased by William Ffranchome in Co. Dublin.[34] The prioress of Grace Dieu entered into several lease agreements in the years before the dissolution. These deeds give some indication of the terms that the nuns might expect, although arrangements made under the shadow of the dissolution may have been substantially different to earlier leases. In 1529, the prioress granted the church, rectory and manor of Portrane to Walter Cusack, archdeacon of Dublin, and James Cusack of Portrane for the term of eighteen years for £8 per annum or forty measures of corn and forty measures of malt in lieu, at the choice of the prioress.[35] In this way the prioress retained some flexibility in how the rent might be paid and perhaps was able to compensate for fluctuating prices of commodities.

Leases could be obscured when "entry fines" or cash payments were made without record and then the transactions were described as gifts. The obscure reference to the Gascon knight who "obtained" two messuages and one carucate of land in Nuntown, (Ballynagalliagh, Co. Down) by the "gift" of the nuns of St Mary, Down, may be a reference to this sort of long-term lease rather than a sale or gift.[36] It is unlikely that nuns would give away land without some sort of return. Ballynagalliagh was listed in the survey of holdings of the nuns after the dissolution so it is more probable that lands were leased to the Gascon, rather then sold.[37]

Managing income from spiritualities

After the twelfth-century reforms throughout Ireland and the continent, the income from tithes and other dues collected on behalf of the church were increasingly viewed as property that should not be managed by the laity. Although there

30 *Reg. St John Dublin*, pp 110–11. **31** TCD MS 1207/224–(165). **32** TCD MS 1207 (149). **33** *Ir. cartu. Llanthony*, pp 180–4 and for discussion see Simms, "The geography of Irish manors", p. 300. **34** TCD MS 1207/257 (190). **35** *Cal. inquis. Dublin*, p. 77. **36** Archdall (1876), I, pp 262–3, n. 13. **37** BL MS Egerton 1774, f. 113v, gives the details of the Inquisition of 3 Ed IV.

continued to be lay control of rectories and advowsons in various guises throughout medieval Europe, there was also a shift of these resources away from lay land-holders to monastic houses and episcopal estates. In Ireland, the newly arrived Anglo-Normans generally distributed the tithes and advowsons of churches on their new holdings to bishops, monasteries and nunneries, while within Gaelic Ireland a similar movement during the twelfth and thirteenth centuries saw much of the income from tithes moving in the same way, although there were differences in the ways that spiritualities were organised. Presentation of vicars and division of tithes and parochial income was subject to local variation, but most would have followed the formula by which the nuns of Grace Dieu presented Gilbert de Kingston to Luke, archbishop of Dublin, for the vicarage of Killadreenan. He was to receive the "small" tithes and dues from the altar and graveyards of Killadreenan and its associated church of Newcastle, while the nuns would have the "great" tithes of wool and lambs of Newcastle and the land of Killadreenan. Gilbert was also responsible for the charges on the income that might be imposed by the bishop.[38]

Tithes and presentation rights of vicars were not only a source of income for nunneries. They also meant that the nuns may have been involved in different ways in the spiritual lives of lay communities. Although the presentation of vicars was purely formal in some areas, the nuns did have to negotiate with candidates for the positions and in some cases the nuns were also involved in providing certain services for the parishes in which they were involved. In Ireland there is little direct evidence of these sorts of activities, although in parishes in England nuns as rectors were sometimes expected to maintain different areas of the parish churches or provide for different feasts during the year.[39]

The estates of all the nunneries in medieval Ireland included some income from spiritualities. Lismullin held only one rectory, Kilpatrick (Co. Meath), at the dissolution.[40] This was due to the particular circumstances of Lismullin's foundation after the parish boundaries had been drawn up and the tithes donated to the Cistercian house of St Mary's, Dublin. Timolin and Graney, by contrast, were endowed with considerable wealth from rectories and tithes, again reflecting the circumstances of their foundation as the principal monastic houses established on their Anglo-Norman founders' lands. A confirmation of Graney's estates records that the founder, Walter de Riddlesford, donated all the churches of his barony of Bray, and this was the usual method of directing spiritual income to religious institutions.[41] The Gaelic Irish foundations of Kilcreevanty and Killone also extracted income from tithes and rectories, although there were differences in the ways that the tithes were calculated between Gaelic areas and the Anglo-Irish parochial system. Tithes in Gaelic Ireland were drawn from land rather than parishes, and divided between different recipients rather than considered in the

38 *Alen's reg.*, p. 77. See Jeffries, *Priests and prelates*, pp 28–31, for description and discussion of local variation in calculating "great" tithes and alterages. **39** Oliva, *Convents and community*, p. 149. **40** *Extents Ir. mon. possessions*, p. 257. **41** *Pont. Hib.*, I, p. 138.

fixed proportions which were customary in the English-dominated areas of the country.[42] Although income from spiritualities was important to nunneries, it was also important to other ecclesiastical estate holders and sometimes to lay landowners as well, often bringing the nuns into conflict with different interest groups.

Interactions with crown officials

As major landholders, nuns were required to participate in the complex arena of negotiations with the officials of the English government. The necessary contact with this bureaucracy involved the possibility of considerable expense and delays. The costs involved in conducting business with crown officials could be quite heavy: for example the large sum of 106*s*. 8*d*. was paid to John de Castro to go to England in 1339 on the business of the priory of Holy Trinity.[43] There were also the costs involved in keeping the officials of the government favourable. Holy Trinity paid 13*s*. 4*d*. to Richard de Deen, "by a settled agreement, that he should not injure the church on account of its temporalities in the absence of his master, nor incommode it in anything".[44] Much of the business of the monastic houses in Ireland could be, and often was, conducted through royal officials based in Ireland. The great abbeys of Kilculliheen, Clonard and Hogges were subject to the crown for permission to elect new abbesses, whereas the priories were usually subject solely to their local bishop.[45] The process undoubtedly led to considerable expense for the convents, as messengers to the royal court or the justiciar's office needed to be paid, as did the justiciar or bishop as well as the fines for the license and other documentation. There would also have been the expenses of travel for the abbess, prioress and their companions when they were required to appear in person to present their credentials to the bishop or justiciar.[46] In 1313, for example, the convent of Kilculliheen paid 40*s*. for the license the nuns needed to elect an abbess after the death of Joanna de Laundesay.[47] They were required to present guarantors of the fine, indicating that the nuns needed quite explicit business links with the lay communities to raise the funds necessary to finance the routine business of the convent.

The process could also be time-consuming even when all went normally. If the nuns made mistakes in procedure there were more delays.[48] The nuns of Clonard notified the king of the resignation of their abbess, Dervogyll, probably in October 1296.[49] He then sent letters to the justiciar and the nuns in early November 1296 notifying them of the issuing of the licence. The nuns held their election in early January, proceeded to Drogheda to meet the justiciar on 20 January, and gave him the necessary documentation under their chapter seal,

42 For the Gaelic system, see Nicholls, "Rectory, vicarage and parish in the western Irish dioceses", pp 53–80. **43** *Account Roll of Holy Trinity, Dublin*, p. 20. **44** Ibid., p. 94. **45** Kilculliheen, Clonard and Hogges were all founded by Irish kings and at the time of the conquest of Ireland, the patronage rights of their founders passed to the crown. See Milis, *L'ordre des chaniones règuliers d'Arrouaise*, p. 364. **46** Power, *Medieval English nunneries*, p. 44. **47** NAI MS KB 2/5 p. 23. **48** See Preston, "The canons regular of St Augustine", p. 156, for the delays and difficulties experienced by some male houses. **49** The date given in the

announcing that they had elected Gormlaith, daughter of Okerra, as abbess. They also needed the assent of the bishop of Meath, whose consent arrived in the second week of Lent (mid-February). The new abbess was then summoned to give her fealty. She had neglected to bring with her further documentation that the transfer of the temporalities would not disadvantage the crown. Once she did this, control of her lands was handed to her.[50] This process involved two journeys for the nuns, as well as the fees that would have been due for all involved, and took at least five months.

Other expenses associated with election of new abbesses were due to lost profits from estates during vacancies. Theoretically the estates of the convents held directly from the crown devolved to the king at the death of the office-holders. Once the new abbess or prioress was elected the estates were returned to her, but the profits during the vacancy were kept by the office of the crown escheator. Often the new election and the transfer of the temporalities occurred swiftly and would have resulted in minimal or no losses. In 1314, there were only five days recorded elapsing between the death of Mora, abbess of Clonard, and the transfer of the temporalities to Sibilla, the new abbess. In 1336, the abbacy of St Mary del Hogges was also only vacant a matter of days.[51] There are many references to the poverty of convents, where all the profits were used in the support of the nuns and there was little or none left over, and there may have been efforts made to expedite the processes to ensure that the nuns were not seriously disadvantaged by legal matters.

There was, however, the danger that the transfer of legal title to the nunnery estates from the escheator to the incoming abbess would be delayed, leading to diminution of income for the convent. This seems to have occurred in Kilculliheen in the final years of the thirteenth century, although the cause of the delay is not known. There may have been a dispute over the election or there may have been disagreement with the escheator over the title of lands, as occurred with the priory of Holy Trinity.[52] In 1292, the abbess of Kilculliheen was sending desperate and undoubtedly expensive messages to ensure that the abbey's estates were transferred to her care. In March, the bishop of Ossory sent letters on her behalf to the chancellor of England, asking for his intercession to the king to expedite the transfer of the convent's estates. Then in April she sent Robert FitzStephen bearing presents for the king to expedite the affairs of the convent. At about this time she also sent another formal request to the king.[53]

Although there is no report of the outcome of these intercessions, problems continued, with at least some of the abbey's estates in the hands of the escheator. From 1296 until at least 1306, the manor of Seneboth was in the hands of the

calendar of royal letter 3088, *Cal. doc. Ire., 1293–1301*, p. 117, is October 1295; it is more likely that the regnal year was misread, as *Cal. doc. Ire., 1293–1301*, no. 341, gives a calendar version of the patent roll entry which confirms the date as October 1296. **50** *Cal. justic. rolls Ire., 1295–1307*, p. 79. **51** "Cat. pipe rolls, Ed. II", *PRI rep. DK* 42 (1911) p. 19 and "Cat. pipe roll, Ed III", *PRI rep. DK* 44 (1912) p. 57. **52** *Account Roll of Holy Trinity*, p. xii. **53** *Cal. doc. Ire., 1293–1301*, p. 6; *Cal. doc. Ire., 1285–1292*, pp 480, 526.

escheator because of a vacancy in the abbacy.[54] There are two known abbesses of the convent at this time – Joan the abbess who was pleading with the crown in 1292, and died in 1300; then Mabilla, abbess by 1302.[55] Problems recurred in 1309–10, when the manor of Dysertmoon (Co. Kilkenny) was in the hands of the escheator: this probably corresponds to the vacancy caused by the death of Joanna de Landeley.[56] After Joanna's death, all the lands of Kilculliheen were taken into the care of the crown from 1310 until 1314, when they were handed to her successor Isabella de Keynes.[57] However, Dysertmoon was again in the hands of the escheator from 1315 until 1328.[58] All the estates of Kilculliheen were with the escheator at Isabella's death in 1335, although the issues were recorded as "worth nothing beyond the sustenance of the nuns" and so were quickly delivered to the prioress before the election of the new abbess. This swift management of the transfer of temporalities occurred again four years later with the death of the next abbess, Joanna.[59]

It is unclear from the bare accounts of the escheator what was happening with the sequestration of the profits of the manors of Seneboth and Dysertmoon when there were abbesses in office to take control. It may have been because they were manors tenanted by minors that the escheator ruled that the abbey could not be the effective feudal lord and so enjoy the profits. That the nuns were recognized as having some rights is suggested by the suit in 1308 against Abbess Johanna by Agnes de Rupe, widow of Henry de Rupe, the holder of the manor of Dysertmoon, for her dower.[60] The conflict between Kilculliheen and the escheator may have been the result of feuds that took many years to settle, as did the disputes between the priory of Holy Trinity and the escheator, later in the fourteenth century. There also may have been problems with the convent's title to the manors, which is suggested by the absence of both manors from the dissolution surveys. Whatever the cause of the disputes, the nuns were not able to enjoy the considerable profits that would have come from these estates at this time.

54 The accounts are for the profits of the manor of Seneboth, (possibly Shanbough, Co. Kilkenny) which was held by the minor son of Milo FitzPhilip. These rents should have gone to the abbey of Kilculliheen during the minority of the heir, but owing to the vacancy in the abbacy they went to the crown. "Cat. pipe rolls, Ed I", *PRI rep. DK* 38 (1906) pp 39, 79. **55** Joan as abbess *Cal. doc. Ire., 1285–92*, p. 480, her death recorded at *Cal. doc .Ire., 1293–1301*, pp 769–70. Mabilla was abbess in 1302–3. Calendar of Memoranda rolls, 31 Ed I, (NAI RC 8/1), pp 213–4, and Calendar of Common Bench rolls, 30 Ed I (NAI RC 7/9), pp 317, 383. **56** Joanna de Landesley described as late abbess in 1310 and 1312, "Cat. pipe rolls, 6 Ed. II", *PRI rep. DK* 39 (1907) p. 44. **57** "Cat. pipe rolls, 9 Ed. II", *PRI rep. DK* 39 (1907) p. 64. **58** Escheators accounts of Tristlemothan, see "Cat. pipe rolls, Ed. II", *PRI rep. DK* 39 (1907) pp 29, 40, 44, 59; *PRI rep. DK* 42 (1911) pp 14, 21, 38, 42, 44, 54; "Cat. pipe rolls, Ed. III", *PRI rep. DK* 44 (1912) pp 53, 60; *PRI rep. DK* 45 (1913) p. 45. **59** "Cat. pipe rolls, Ed. III", *PRI rep. DK* 44 (1912) p. 60 and *PRI rep. DK* 47 (1915) p. 62. **60** 2 Ed. II, cited in TCD MS 654 f. 28.

CONFLICT AND THE NUNNERY ESTATES

Nuns were a minority group within both the ecclesiastical and secular landscapes. They also occupied legal positions different to their lay sisters. Although they were accommodated within the legal systems of medieval Ireland, their marginal status made them vulnerable to legal and physical attack. The relationships that they built in the processes of estate management were crucial to the survival of their convents. In times of conflict, the ability of nunnery managers to extract income from their estates and ensure the safety of their dependants, employees and tenants was often dependent on their abilities to negotiate their position in the complex web of legal and personal relationships in medieval societies in Ireland. When these relationships broke down, the nuns were not able to enjoy the profits of estates that had been donated to them.

Defending temporal income

While little may be known about the daily management of nunnery estates, the frequency with which nunneries or their representatives appeared in secular courts in property cases speaks of attempts to maintain good estate management. Although vital to any analysis of the workings of these estates, records of disputes need to be read with caution and with the presumption of stability rather than chaos. It must be remembered that most of the nunneries, their abbesses and prioresses were successful in maintaining the boundaries around their convents sufficiently to ensure that there was space for women to live quietly, devoted to prayer, in communities that endured for hundreds of years.

Although some of the surviving legal records are so vague as to be almost meaningless, it is clear that nuns defended and initiated court actions throughout the medieval period. The details of many cases are lost, but enough emerge to allow analysis. One lengthy legal case involving the nuns of Lismullin in the fourteenth and fifteenth centuries was with the prior of Little Malvern in England over dues owed for land in Dunsink (Co. Dublin). The land had been granted to the convent at its foundation by Richard de la Corner, bishop of Meath.[61] The priors of Little Malvern subsequently demanded dues from the prioresses of Lismullin, based on Little Malvern's claim on the lands as part of the estate of their dependent priory, Castleknock, which led to court action stretching from at least 1297 until the early fifteenth century.[62] The dispute seems to have lasted until the cell of Little Malvern at Castleknock was sold to St Mary's, Dublin, in the fifteenth century. Part of Lismullin's holdings there had already been sold by Prioress Agnes in 1402.[63] The legal contest over the lands at Dunsink indicate the complexity of some of the stratagems needed by nuns to keep hold of their interest in lands donated for their use. When land titles were uncertain or when there were

61 "Unpublished medieval notitiae", p. 10. For further discussion of this case see Hall, "The nuns of the medieval convent of Lismullin", p. 63. **62** *Rot. pat. Hib.*, p. 174. **63** Ibid., p. 164; Varebeke, "The Benedictines of medieval Ireland", pp. 92–6.

difficulties with the initial donations, nuns needed to be able to devote considerable resources to ensure that their income was protected.

In another series of court actions in 1296 and 1301, the prioress of Lismullin was unsuccessful in defending her rights to income of the rent from land called Tarmsithyn, in Louth, which she claimed had been withheld from her by her tenant Richard de Parys and that his heirs were now alienating to her disadvantage.[64] In 1301 the judgment in this case was that the action had been previously lost by a canon of Lismullin.[65] In another case from 1300 involving a donation which was not honoured after the death of the donor, the prioress lost the case because it was found that since all concerned in the original donation were dead and the disputed rents had not been claimed for some time, she had no claim.[66] These actions underline the significance of maintaining favourable links with the lay communities who granted and tenanted the lands held by the nuns. They may also point to a newly appointed and vigorous prioress trying to re-establish the estates after the neglect of her predecessors, as there are a greater number of legal actions involving this prioress of Lismullin, Avicia de Howth, than for any other prioress. This, however, is possibly due more to archival survival than Avicia's litigious nature.

Nuns seem to have used many of the legal stratagems available to litigants in courts of law under the English system. In 1291 the nuns of Timolin were involved in a dispute over lands in Armacrenan, where they had been granted one carucate of land by John Cumin, archbishop of Dublin, in the late twelfth century.[67] It appears that they had purchased more land in the area in the late thirteenth century from Richard fitz Roger which was deemed contrary to the Statute of Mortmain and confiscated. The land was later returned and a license issued; however, it may have been this land that they were defending two years later. The records of the dispute are not very clear, but the nuns appear to have been using the well-known tactic of not attending court in an effort to thwart the collective action of the plaintiffs.[68] In the most complete surviving record, Joan de Waterford, the prioress, was accused of refusing to give up a tenement of the land and refusing to come to court with documentation to prove her case. It is not known how this dispute ended.

Hints at successful defence of property occasionally slip through the strong filter of sparse records. In a rather enigmatic comment, Archbishop Alen, referring to a survey of the episcopal manor of Portrane, noted the site of an old-court house and then that it "was alienated to the nuns of Grace Dieu under three seals of Walter and ill-done".[69] This is probably a reference to the

64 Tarmsithyn has not been identified. **65** Calendar of Common Bench Roll, no. 26, 24 Ed I (NAI RC 7/4), p. 220 and Calendar of Justices Itinerant Roll, no. 57, 29 Ed. I, (NAI RC 7/8), pp. 261–2. **66** Calendar of Common Bench Roll no. 48, 28 Ed I (NAI RC 7/7), pp. 141–3. For further details see Hall, "Necessary collaborations", p. 26. **67** *Alen's reg.*, p. 416. **68** *Cal. doc. Ire., 1285–1292*, pp. 396, 403, 423. For a brief summary of the difficulties in assuring attendance at court see "The Common Bench Plea Roll of 19 Edward IV", pp. 24–5. **69** *Alen's reg.*, p. 179.

confirmation of the nunnery's holdings in Portrane and grant of an extra two acres of pasture there by Archbishop Walter in 1490.[70] Seeking a confirmation of holdings is often a sign of insecurity felt by the land-holders, and the 1490 confirmation could have been the result of a threat to the nuns' tenure over the lands at Portrane, with the additional grant the result of a settlement with the archbishop. This suggests that the nuns of Grace Dieu were successful in maintaining and extending their rights to the manor, perhaps in the face of opposition from the archbishop.

Defending spiritual income

Difficulties with ecclesiastical authorities seem to have been a frequent problem for nunneries throughout medieval Europe. The curia moniales was viewed by many bishops as a burden requiring heavier supervision than that required by male monasteries. This may have coloured some of the adverse reactions from male ecclesiastical authorities faced by nuns in Ireland, or their difficulties may have stemmed from more direct conflicts of interest over valuable spiritual assets. Aside from the many advantages to administering rectories and other spiritual incomes, there were also problems for both nunneries and monasteries that held them.[71] Nuns needed to try and maintain good relations with the bishops, as episcopal confirmation of donation of any spiritual income was necessary for the donation to succeed. Bishops also brokered compromises between disputing parties, such as one in 1264 when Archbishop Fulk of Dublin intervened between Amicia, prioress of Grace Dieu, and John de la Hide over the rights of presentation to the rectory of Ballymadun. John relinquished his claim on the advowson and presumably the tithes, while keeping the right of presentation.[72] This sort of settlement was not unusual in the medieval colony and seems to have suited the parties involved. Bishops were also called upon to judge disputes over ownership of advowsons and rights of alienation where the heirs of a donor disputed a donation. For the small Cistercian nunnery of Ballymore, the donation of the advowson of the church of St Nicholas at Moyaghryth proved troublesome.[73] The prioress had to appear in court to defend her claims in 1302 and again when William Harold sued her in 1341.[74] She was able to prove to the bishop's satisfaction that she had been granted the church freely in alms and this appears to have been the end of the matter.[75]

Disputes over presentation rights of rectories resulting from confusion over ownership of land and its accompanying rights were not uncommon and sometimes brought nuns into open legal conflict with other ecclesiastical authorities. Confusion of this sort seems to have been at the heart of a dispute over the rectory and glebe lands of Dunbrin (Co. Laois) between the canons of St Thomas'

70 *Alen's reg.*, p. 251. **71** Robinson, *Geography of Augustinian settlements*, I, pp. 177–87, on the advantages and disadvantages of monasteries holding appropriated benefices and their incomes. **72** *Alen's reg.*, p. 100. **73** The rectory has not been identified, however it was probably close to the nunnery. **74** *Rot. pat. Hib.*, p. 9. **75** NLI MS 13, p. 117.

in Dublin and the prioress and nuns of Timolin. It is not clear on what basis the nuns laid claim to Dunbrin, but there is a record of its donation to the abbey of St Thomas by Milo de Stanton.[76] In 1213 the nuns and the abbey were in dispute over the rectory, and the subsequent inquiry suggests that the case was not so much over the rights to the benefice itself but over the lands belonging to the church.[77] The rectory remained in the possession of St Thomas' until the dissolution.[78] An agreement to another protracted dispute was reached in 1303, after at least two years of litigation, when Mabilla, abbess of Kilculliheen, and William, son of Walter le Bret, came to an agreement over the rights of presentation of the rectory of Nadan, in which the rectory was returned to the abbess's custody.[79]

Evidence of legal disputes generally exist only from areas within the ambit of English law, which fluctuated throughout the medieval period but was at its height in the late thirteenth century. The abbey of Kilcreevanty was therefore beyond the reach of the surviving records for most of its history, but records of disputes over property and presentation to rectories involving Kilcreevanty do survive from the thirteenth and fourteenth centuries. In 1260–1 Orlethe, abbess of Kilcreevanty, was in conflict with William Haket over an advowson. Unfortunately, there is no record as to which of the nunnery's many rectories was under discussion, nor whether William was a rival to the rights of presentation or a recalcitrant incumbent.[80] The abbess of this Ó Conchobair nunnery had no apparent difficulties in making use of the English legal system in her dispute, and as William's name is English, it is possible that the rectory in question was at that time in Anglo-Irish territory and this may have been the basis of the dispute.

The nuns of Kilcreevanty also used the courts when they were involved in a serious dispute with their episcopal superior, the archbishop of Tuam, in 1308. In February of that year, the abbess complained of undue visitations and exactions by the archbishop, who carried off goods and livestock by violence, and presented in her support the papal bull which allowed relaxation of visitation. The case was brought to the secular courts in Dublin the following year and although the court of the justiciar seemed to have found in her favour, she continued to have difficulty in receiving restitution for her losses and the case dragged on into the following year.[81] The nuns may have continued to have problems with the archbishop of Tuam as he was granted permission by the papacy to visit the convent in 1321, notwithstanding the exemption previously granted to the nuns.[82] This indicates that the nuns had to be compelled by legal means to admit

76 *Reg. St Thomas, Dublin*, p. 160. **77** *Pont. Hib.*, I, pp. 157–8. **78** "Rep. Viride Alen", p. 213. **79** Calendar of Common Bench Roll 30 E I, rolls no. 61 and 62 (NAI MS RC 7/9), pp. 248, 317, 383; Calendar of Memoranda rolls 31 E I (NAI MS RC 8/1), pp. 213–14. It does not appear to have been in the estates of the nuns at the dissolution; it is possible that the rectory was known by another name, or united with another of the abbey's rectories and so not included in the dissolution surveys. **80** Calendar of Justice Itinerant Roll no. 4, 45 Hen III (NAI MS RC 7/1), p. 387. **81** *Cal. justic. rolls, Ire., 1295–1307*, I, pp 48, 66, 113–4, 128. **82** *Cal. papal letters, 1305–42*, p. 212.

the bishop for visitation, suggesting that a serious breach remained between them. The nuns of Kilcreevanty were able to muster significant legal and material support for their dispute with the archbishop, although it seems that the reach of the Dublin court was not sufficient to ensure that their rights were protected.

Another area of dispute between convents and bishops was when foundation grants were upset and redirected to other churches and monasteries, particularly if later bishops declined to confirm donations or refused to allow the nuns' presentation of candidates for rectories. This may have occurred because the bishops disputed the ownership of the original donation, or they may have wanted lucrative rectories to go to their own monastic foundations or cathedral chapters. In 1318, there was a dispute between the nuns of Graney and the bishop of Leighlin over the rights of presentation of rectories at Dunleckny (Co. Carlow), into which the bishop intruded his own candidate. In this dispute the nuns seem to have been able to convince the court of their rights, and were awarded damages.[83] Richard de la Corner, the founder of Lismullin and bishop of Meath, had granted rectories in the Meath area to Lismullin. In 1322, Prioress Alianora Cusack of Lismullin had to sue, apparently unsuccessfully, the then bishop of Meath for the advowsons of the churches of Paynson-Dullard and Ardmulchan, which had been part of the original foundation by Richard de la Corner.[84] There was a further action in 1409, when the prioress appealed to the pope for the presentation rights to Ardmulchan that she claimed had been appropriated by the bishops of Meath. This demonstrates that the original donations were not eternally secure and were subject to the whims and desires of the heirs of the original donor, and that bishops often decided that nuns were not the appropriate custodians of spiritual income.

The archbishops of Dublin also redirected rectories away from nunneries in their diocese. Timolin was granted a number of churches in Norraghmore and Crokestown (Co. Kildare), the principal holdings of its founder Robert of Norragh. However, in 1191, John Cumin, archbishop of Dublin, granted them to St Patrick's cathedral in Dublin.[85] There is no record of any dispute over this, but it is possible that the doubts over titles to their assets prompted the nuns to seek confirmation of their property, including the disputed rectories, from Henry of London, archbishop of Dublin, in 1220. The nuns were successful in this case as the rectories were still in the control of Timolin at the time of the suppression of the convent when they finally passed into the hands of the archbishop of Dublin.[86] The nuns of Grace Dieu had also been granted several valuable rectories in Dublin by John Cumin, but these were redistributed by the next archbishop, who obtained a resignation of the nunnery's rights in these churches

83 Calendar of Common Bench Roll, 11 Ed. II, roll no. 122 (NAI MS RC 7/12), pp. 441, 501–2. The prioress was represented by an attorney for at least some of these actions. **84** *Cal. papal letters*, 1404–15, p. 163. **85** *Knight's fees*, p. 155. The editor, Brooks, thought that these advowsons had been permanently alienated away from the convent because they did not appear in the Extents Ir. mon. possessions, however none of Timolin's rectories appeared there, as they had already been appropriated to the archbishop. See "Rep. Viride, Alen". **86** *Alen's*

as well as some associated lands. The collective and archival memory of the nuns maintained their anger over this act and three centuries later Archbishop Alen rather ruefully commented that when he visited the priory in 1530, the "nuns made an outcry ... because they (the churches) were taken away unjustly".[87] These disputes do suggest that the nunneries in the archdiocese of Dublin were considered by some archbishops to be marginal and not capable of managing the estates that had been given to them.

Graney was involved in another long-running dispute with the cathedral of St Patrick over the rectory of Kineagh (Co. Carlow). This rectory was donated to both Graney, at its foundation in the early thirteenth century, and to the canons of St Patrick's at about the same time.[88] There followed litigation at various times after the fourteenth century between the canons of St Patrick's and the nuns. However, Graney's hold over the rectory, its chapels and lands was challenged from other quarters. In 1504 a papal bull directs an investigation into claims by the monks of St Thomas' Dublin in concert with certain laymen, including the earl of Kildare, to lands of the nunnery and also into the chapels associated with Kineagh.[89] The original of the bull survives and is endorsed with the comment that the lands in question were found to belong to Graney.[90] Six years later the nuns were again appealing to the papacy, claiming that the archbishop of Dublin had sequestered the income of Kinegh. The canons of St Patrick, however, did not cease their legal manoeuvres and in 1512 the canons alleged that the nuns were impeding their entry into Kineagh.[91] Finally an agreement was reached whereby the rectory was divided between St Patrick's and the nuns.[92] The litigation and disputes over this rectory and its lands endured for almost the entire lifetime of the convent and came from at least four separate challengers, necessitating many expensive legal battles.

The prioress and nuns of Graney continued to keep a watchful eye on their many other rectories, and they needed to engage in several legal actions to maintain their rights. Although the source of a dispute between Richard St Martin and the nuns is not clear from the fragmented record, a resolution was reached in 1230 whereby Richard leased the church of Turvil and paid one mark in their name to the church of Swords.[93] Graney also seemed to be having difficulty with the collector of papal dues, as in the early fourteenth century there is a reference to a dispute between Graney and the papal sub-collector Hugo de Calci.[94] This rather disparate evidence indicates that nuns in medieval Ireland needed to be vigilant in maintaining their rights to the estates that had been established to ensure their livelihoods. There were many other players who might prove anxious to disturb the boundaries of these estates.

reg., p. 7. **87** *Alen's reg.*, p. 49. **88** The notice of the donation to St Patrick's is in *Alen's reg.*, p. 60. **89** Ibid., notes the litigation which had been going on since before the time of Richard II. **90** TCD MS 1207/260 (201) and 315–4/ Misc. Vellum Deed 17. **91** *Cal. papal letters, 1503–13*, pp 430–1. **92** Ibid. The agreement which was reached is also detailed in "Rep. Viride Alen", p. 206. **93** "Calendar of the Liber Niger Alani", p. 317, and BL MS Egerton 1774, f. 283. **94** Boyle, *A survey of the Vatican archives*, p. 167, mentions that the letter which

It was not only with rivals to spiritual income that nuns had to contend: priests could and did take over rectories without the consent of the convents that held the rights of appointment. In order to bolster their positions claimants to rectories obtained confirmation of their appointments from the papacy. These were often preceded by complaints, which may have been spurious, registered against the incumbent. The role of the papal curia in these practices was to appoint investigators as well as to reclaim and redistribute deserted or neglected benefices.[95] It is probable that this occurred most often in areas where the holders of the rectories were unable to travel and that these priests may have been ministering to the immediate needs of the parishioners. It is difficult, however, to distinguish such cases from those where there was only intent to profit by appropriating the income from a benefice without ministering to the needs of the parishioners at all. There were also many instances of rivalry over benefices that reflect different local factions vying for office.[96] Both monasteries and nunneries suffered diminution of their incomes from these practices. Between 1475 and 1483, for example, there were several applicants, some obviously in direct rivalry, for the rectory of Ballyhancart (possibly Tankardstown) in Co. Limerick which was in the estate of Graney.[97] It is likely that little income reached the convent from these rectories by this time.

Distance from the home convent and the location of rectories in hostile areas also presented problems. In order to try and get some income from churches in unprofitable situations, the practice of leasing or farming was common. Even some leased properties were eventually lost, as the lessees were operating far from the home nunnery and there was little that could be done to redeem some leased rectories.[98] Graney held the rights to as many as five rectories in Co. Cork, which by the late fifteenth century were described as having been united "in perpetuity" and subject to leases "from time immemorial".[99] By this time the nuns were unlikely to have been receiving any income from their possessions in Cork as, in 1483, Eugenius Offailain was granted a papal dispensation for many crimes including taking the fruits from the parish churches of the abbess and nuns of Graney and Timolin.[100] It is likely that entrepreneurial priests or clerics may have been particularly interested in gaining access to rectories held by a distant convent, because such convents were unlikely to have been in a position to object. In 1487, Graney's churches in Cork were described as being in disrepair, with the roof and walls of the church at Brinny being in ruins.[101] At

mentions this quarrel was found as part of the cover of a volume of accounts. **95** The development of this system of papal provisions is outlined in Flanagan, "Papal provisions in Ireland 1305–78", pp. 92–103. For a summary of the background behind the appeals to the papacy for provision of benefices and other indulgences see Sughi, "The appointment of Octavian de Palatio", pp 146–50. **96** Walsh, "The clerical estate in later medieval Ireland", pp 363–5. **97** *Cal. papal letters, 1471–84*, pp 452, 831 and *Cal. papal letters, 1484–92*, pp 162–3. Probably Tankardstown, Co. Limerick. **98** See Robinson, *Geography of Augustinian settlements*, I, p. 189, for farming of rectories in England. **99** *Cal. papal letters, 1484–92*, p. 32. **100** *Cal. papal letters, 1471–84*, pp 452–3. **101** Ibid.

the dissolution the only reference to these rectories is a rather despairing note that there was a rectory in Munster "name unknown, which used to be farmed, now waste".[102]

Even when the appointed candidate was presented to the vicarage without problems over the nunneries' rights, he still may not have been able to take up his position owing to hostile conditions. If this occurred then the convent could not collect their dues from their priest nor their portion of the tithes. One relatively well-documented example concerns the rectory of Killadreenan (Co. Wicklow) held by Grace Dieu.[103] There are no problems recorded in 1421, when Maurice Standun became vicar after the death of the incumbent, John Brenach. When he in turn died in 1427, the nuns presented Philip Standun, but there was a dispute over this presentation, between the prioress and "a certain layman" that prevented Philip from taking up his position and he had to retire. He also did not take up holy orders within the appointed time limit. The next incumbent named is Maurice Machonairgy, who took up the position in 1438 and was succeeded by Odo Doiynac in 1462. In 1464, however, there is another record of dispute over this rectory with Patrick Standun claiming that he had been presented by the nuns of Grace Dieu after the death of Maurice. Another cleric, Dermot Yllamagayn, also seems to have had some sort of claim on this benefice. It is possible that the double presentation occurred because the office of prioress was vacant at the time, and the "laymen" took over the presentation. Odo resigned before 1464 and his place was taken by Patrick Machyncarigy. It is possible that this Patrick is Patrick Standun, or he may have been another Patrick who took over when the situation for Patrick Standun became untenable.[104]

These events suggest that there were rivals for the rights of presentation and that these rivals may have been local Gaelic Irish families. The area around Newcastle and Killadreenan in Wicklow at the time was being contested between Gaelic Irish and the Anglo-Irish inhabitants of the Pale. Grace Dieu remained Anglo-Irish throughout its history and this may have been one source of tension between the nuns who owned the rights and the local Gaelic Irish families. It has been suggested that the nuns of Grace Dieu, through the archbishop of Dublin, had an agreement with the Ó Byrne families of the area to continue the appointment of Anglo-Irish clergy and that this arrangement broke down in the early sixteenth century, when the nuns insisted on the appointment of English clergy while the archbishops were agreeing to compromise with appointments of candidates acceptable to the Ó Byrne families.[105] While there is no evidence to contradict this interpretation, there is also no evidence that the nuns acted as

102 *Extents Ir. mon. possessions*, p. 125. **103** The rectory, land and tithes of the area had been donated by John Cumin, archbishop of Dublin. See *Alen's reg.*, p. 31. **104** See *Cal. papal letters, 1417–31*, p. 520; "Obligationes pro annatis diocesis Dublinensis", pp 3, 8, 16, 19. Patrick Standun and Patrick Machyncarigy are the names used to refer to the parish at the same time, leading two scholars who examined the records to conclude that this was the same man with scribal error causing the confusion. Donnelly, "Incumbents of Killadreenan", pp 126–7. The bull with the resolution of the dispute is given on p. 139. **105** This argument is set out in

catalyst for this conflict: the nuns of Grace Dieu had managed to maintain their links with this contested region for many years and there is no indication that they had changed their policy. Whatever the reasons for the dispute, the archbishops of Dublin were constantly alert to opportunities to increase the income and influence of their office.[106] It is likely that there were local men who took advantage of both the distance between the nuns of Grace Dieu and their property and the unsettled conditions to take over the rectory.

The estates of the nunneries were essentially secular in the ways that they were managed internally and also in the methods used to maintain and defend their boundaries. Nuns used the secular courts to defend and initiate legal actions to maintain their rights to their assets, with some successes. As holders of spiritual income, the nuns needed to present vicars for the parish churches in their estates, and ensure that the income from the tithes and dues was collected and transferred to the home nunnery. These tasks were made difficult and in some cases impossible by hostile ecclesiastical authorities who challenged the ownership of some of the nuns' resources. Although there were court actions, appeals to the papacy and compromises brokered in many of the disputes involving nuns, different convents also lost control of some of their spiritual income over the centuries after their foundation to rival monastic houses and episcopal estates. Even when ownership by the nuns was maintained, great distance from the home nunnery and position in areas taken over by hostile lay communities meant that some nunneries lost considerable portions of their income base. However, legal challenges, rival claimants and hostile secular and ecclesiastical authorities were not the only hazards facing nunnery managers in medieval Ireland. The ever present threat of violence meant that nunneries and their estates were often vulnerable.

Violence and conflict

Medieval Ireland was an island affected at different times and in different ways by local warfare. This virtually universal experience is part of the backdrop to the history of any group or institution in Ireland. For some religious women, the background was brought violently to the fore when there were direct attacks with loss of life and property. For other religious women, the effects of war were seen in the loss of income from estates, either through attack on tenants' farms or through the inability to attract and maintain tenants in threatened areas. The march areas were not stable and were subject to changing conditions at any given point in the history of medieval Ireland. Nunneries and their estates founded in safe areas did not necessarily remain as protected or secluded as the founders would have wished.[107]

Ronan, "Killadreenan and Newcastle", p. 180. **106** Murray, "Archbishop Alen", p. 3. **107** Particularly useful in framing these comments is the work of R. Frame, particularly "The defence of the English lordship", pp 79–87.

Assessing the degree of depopulation and devastation due to war, and to what extent the nunneries were affected, is difficult. A comparison can be drawn by looking at the relative values of the properties by area at the dissolution. This is only a very approximate guide to the extent of war and waste due to depopulation, particularly because many houses had lands in more than one county. It does provide, however, a rough guide to the degree of widespread destruction and depopulation that affected most of the monastic estates in any given area. Analysis of the nunneries in the context of their area gives some interesting, though not unexpected, results. Nunneries and monasteries from the western parts of Ireland, under control of Gaelic kings and lords, tended not to be assessed by the dissolution commissioners and, where they were, the valuations were relatively poor, indicating both lower land values but also less accurate surveys. Monastic estates well within the pale boundaries, in the counties of Meath, Louth, Kildare and Dublin, were more thoroughly surveyed and also did not suffer as greatly from the decrease in rents and depopulation as other monastic houses. Monastic houses holding lands near to the borders of the pale not surprisingly show evidence of decline of value due to neglect and conflict. The nunneries that were particularly affected by this were Clonard (Co. Meath), Graney and Timolin (Co. Kildare). Timolin also held lands in Co. Wexford that was overrun by the O'Tooles and O'Byrnes by this time. The monasteries with lands in the relatively peaceful Butler lordship, in counties Kilkenny, Waterford and Tipperary, also held their value well, although border areas again suffered in value.

The full extent of the effects of war on the longevity of nunneries cannot be fully known. There were several nunneries that did not survive the thirteenth century and it is probable that some of these were destroyed physically or their viability was made untenable. Nuns sheltering in churches were vulnerable to attack, as occurred in the church of Emlagh in 1236, mentioned at the beginning of this book.[108] Emlagh's position suggests that it may have been a church affiliated with the nunnery of Kilcreevanty. The nearest convent site is that of Termonkeelin, probably founded after 1223, possibly with nuns from the small convents of Derrane and Roscommon. Without more details it is not possible to do more than speculate as to where the nuns who died at Emlagh were based. The demise of the houses of Derrane and Roscommon probably dates from this time and this incident may be associated with the abandonment of the two sites and the relocation of the nuns to Termonkeelin. There were widespread attacks on churches in Connacht during the advance of the Anglo-Normans in the early thirteenth century, and again in the later period, between rival branches of the Gaelic Irish kings.[109] One attack in 1224 was described as leaving "all Connacht wasted from Easroe to Clonuicknose, in so much as there was not in all these contreys the doore of a church left unburnt … "[110]

One house that was probably destroyed by war was the ancient foundation of Kildare. Although no longer having precedence over other nunneries nor power

108 *ALC* 1236. **109** *AFM* 1225; *AU* 1228. **110** *AClon.* 1224.

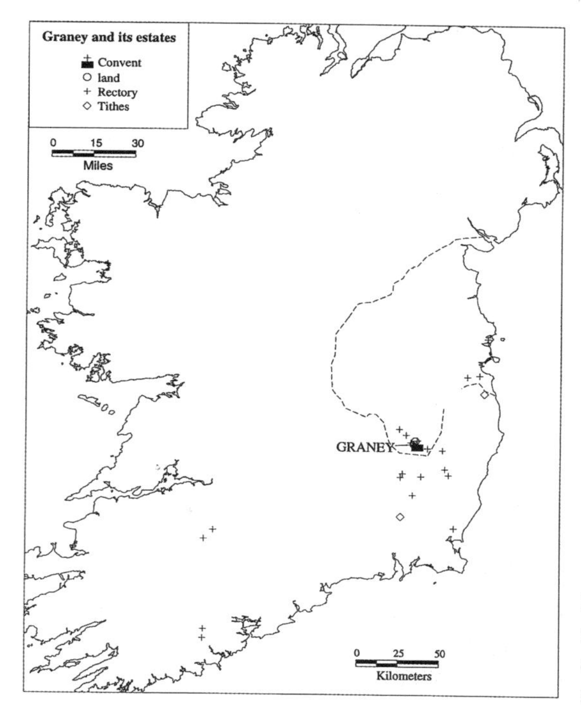

Figure 15. Holdings of Graney with the approximate boundary of the fifteenth-century pale marked

over bishops as the abbesses of Kildare had before the twelfth-century reforms, Kildare continued to function after the coming of the Anglo-Normans, and the eternal fire was still tended by the nuns in the "fyre house" adjacent to the cathedral of Kildare. It is probable that the nunnery was finally deserted in about 1447 when Christine Holby, a nun of Kildare, fled to Exeter where she applied for permission to be enclosed as an anchoress in a cell in the churchyard of St Leonard's. In the documentation of her request, the priory of Kildare is described as having been devastated and deserted, with the nuns dispersed to other houses.[111] Although the lands of Kildare were examined by the dissolution commissioners, it is likely that the nunnery had long been deserted.[112]

Other nunneries which suffered due to violence included the Gaelic nunnery at Clonmacnoise. There are very few records of the nunnery, but its fate must have been tied to the ancient precinct of Clonmacnoise, only a mile away. From about 1201, the annals of Clonmacnoise record heavy losses by the abbot and

111 *Register of Edmund Lacy*, II p. 394. **112** The evidence to support its continued functioning until the dissolution is late and not well documented. See the description by Stanyhurst of his visit to Kildare in the mid–sixteenth century, where he describes a vault-like structure which was the "fyre house". Stanyhust, *Description of Ireland*, p. 38.

bishop and the diocese become very poor.[113] It is certain that the nunnery was included in this pattern of decline. Other convents must have been affected by the many localized conflicts that were mentioned so frequently. The annals record in detail many of the wars and attacks that occurred throughout the medieval period. Some that may have affected known nunneries were the widespread attacks in Thomond in 1258–60 and the reported destruction of churches in the fifteenth century in Armagh, where "all the provisions of the churches of Armagh were carried away".[114] It is very unlikely that nunneries, their churches and estates escaped such widespread conflict and destruction of property, and the decline of several of the nunneries may be attributed to these causes.[115]

Clonard was forced to relocate completely in the late fourteenth century to one of its dependencies at Odder. The abbesses continued to use the title of abbess of Clonard and Odder, so they may have hoped to return when the area had stablised; however the site at Clonard was permanently abandoned.[116] They had been in an area of conflict on the borders of the lordship of Meath since the arrival of the Anglo-Normans. It is possible that the conflicts in the area contributed to the high number of abbesses elected within one period in the late thirteenth and early fourteenth centuries. Even after their relocation to Odder the nuns were unable to maintain connections with their estates in the area of the march and in 1456 obtained permission to exchange their property at Fore with smaller properties nearer to Odder itself.[117] The nuns at Odder were still troubled by the violence which surrounded them. Three of the nuns of Odder were called to serious account in 1470, when they were accused of harbouring Richard, son of Shane McThomas, who was convicted of theft. The nuns were successful in extricating themselves from this situation, claiming that they were unaware that Richard had committed any felony, nor had they harboured him in the way of which they were accused. However, they were required to petition parliament to stop proceedings against them.[118] This incident shows that nuns were not immune from the violence and lawlessness occurring throughout the colony of Ireland. Odder survived to the dissolution and although it did not remain the foremost nunnery or the richest, its survival is testament to the tenacity of the nuns and the willingness of the local communities to support them.

Nuns were also involved in conflict when their convents were used as places of refuge or escape by combatants. There is a rather romantic account, surviving

113 *AClon.* 1202, 1204, 1205, 1223, 1227 and see Gwynn, *The Irish church in the eleventh and twelfth centuries* p. 250. **114** *AI* 1258, 1260; *AFM* 1432. **115** The attacks on Thomond may have been one of the reasons why there are no records from Killone from the mid-thirteenth to the mid-fourteenth centuries. **116** By 1383, the abbess of Clonard was also called the abbess of Odder, so probably the transfer occurred after 1380. See *Med. rel. houses Ire.*, p. 314, citing communication with Brady. *Med. rel. houses Ire.*, p. 314, also cite "an unpublished extract from the Public Record Office in Dublin" where Thomas Preston pleads in 1407/8 that the nuns of Clonard had been forced to go to Odder because of Irish enemies. **117** *Statutes of Ireland Henry VI*, pp 405–6. **118** *Statutes of Ireland 12–22 Edward IV*, pp 338–41.

in a seventeenth-century history of Dublin, of how the nuns of St Mary del Hogges gave assistance to the English during the initial conquest of Ireland in the twelfth century. In this account eighty-six Englishmen were hidden from the Irish in the cloister of Hogges for eleven days until disguises could be made for them and they could escape. For this act of loyalty, the nuns received special treatment from King John in confirming their possessions.[119]

The estates and granges of the nuns were probably more vulnerable to direct attack and theft of goods than the nuns themselves. The threat of these attacks was more pronounced in areas of unrest in general, although it is generally only where the English law still was observed that records of attempts to gain some sort of restitution survive. From the end of the thirteenth century the nunneries of Timolin and Graney, situated near the areas of hostile Gaelic resurgence, were particularly vulnerable.[120] In 1297, the north grange of Timolin was robbed of livestock and cloth worth over twenty marks, by men described as "common criminals in the time of war".[121] In the same year, the nuns of Graney accused William and Gilbert de Chappelyn of theft of corn, although the jurors were reluctant to convict them because they were "of good fame".[122] The following year Thomas and Johanna Isrl' were charged with stealing corn from the prioress of Graney: Thomas was found guilty of this charge and of "being a common malefactor at the time of the disturbance" and fined, while Johanna was found not guilty.[123] In 1310, the nuns of Timolin were again troubled by three men: David and Peter, weavers of Moon, and John Baynguard, who were charged with climbing the walls of the close of the priory and stealing corn, malt and wheat worth 20*s*. from the grange, mill and kiln.[124] Later in 1315, Rathgar (Co. Dublin), a grange of the nuns of St Mary del Hogges, was attacked and six bulls, two cows and eight afers were stolen.[125] Losses such as these were probably common throughout the colony and beyond, and there is no indication that nuns and their properties were particularly targeted. The concentration of incidents over this period is probably related to better archival survival as well as greater penetration of English law at this time than later. Similar incidents probably occurred throughout the medieval period. Nevertheless, the problems for the nuns in managing their estates when they were subject to these very real threats must have been considerable.

As well as being directly threatened by the effects of conflict, the nuns, like all other inhabitants of the various communities of Ireland, were expected to contribute to the provisioning and maintenance of armies and fortifications. It is likely that for some convents this represented a substantial, if necessary, investment. The nuns of Grace Dieu were compensated over £8 by the crown for the corn taken from their estates and used to provision the castle of Mackynegan in 1276,

119 BL MS Add. 4813 ff. 51–2. **120** For discussion of the unrest in Co. Kildare see Lyons, *Church and society in County Kildare*, pp 115–16. **121** *Cal. justic. rolls Ire., 1295–1307*, pp 185, 187. **122** Ibid., p. 186. **123** Ibid., pp 196, 207. **124** *Cal. justic. rolls Ire., 1307–13*, pp 180–1. **125** Calendar of Justiciary rolls, Plea Roll 109, 9 Ed II (NAI MS KB 2/7), p. 44.

when the area was devastated by hostile Irish.[126] No doubt this was viewed as a necessary investment by the Anglo-Irish nunnery in protecting their estates, as Grace Dieu held the wealthy and vulnerable rectory of Newcastle MacKynegan and Killadreenan on the borders of Dublin and the hostile Irish of Wicklow. It was during this conflict that the area was described as "being uncultivated and devastated to such an extent that no profit could be obtained".[127] Investment by the nuns in the recovery of the area would have seemed money well spent.

In 1306 the nuns of St Catherine d'Conyl were forced to sue Maurice FitzPhilip, who had borrowed a horse from them to go to war with John FitzThomas, because, although he promised to return the horse immediately, he kept it for six months and took provisions for himself and his followers from the estates of the nuns to such an extent that the nuns' tenants were threatening to leave the land.[128] Although the loss of the horse would have been regarded as serious, the threat of tenants walking off land had the potential to devastate the nunnery's economy and may have been the catalyst for the court action.

In 1410, Margaret, prioress of Graney, had been given permission to sell produce to the Irish, enemies of the crown, because her priory was situated on the frontier of the march.[129] The nuns were evidently attempting to make the best of the existing situation and get some recompense from the Gaelic Irish lords whose incursions into previously Anglo-Irish-held land must have been impacting on their estates as much as the fighting between competing Anglo-Irish interests. The plight of the nuns of Graney was used in the accusations against Talbot by the earl of Ormond in 1422, when he charged that the nuns were relieved of over £40 worth of provisions for men and horses by Talbot and his men, because they were under the patronage of the earl of Ormond.[130] Such a huge extraction of provisions would have been an enormous burden on the nuns' estates and there are indications that these were not isolated instances for the abbey of Graney, which had its estates thoughout the contested areas around Castledermot and east towards Bray. Castledermot was in the middle of the area where the rebellious Fitzgeralds were based and Graney's crucial position was demonstrated by its swift dissolution and early reallocation to first Lord Grey then St Leger.[131] Archbishop Alen, in his survey of the diocese of Dublin in 1530, contrasted the current devastated state of the resources of Graney with the riches with which it had been endowed: "one after another have lately been brought into disorder from desertion and war because of strife upon the borders".[132] Finally in the years leading up to the dissolution, the position of Graney and Timolin, on the borders of the pale and on land under the control of the Mac Murrough Kavanaghs, was obviously tenuous in the minds of some,

126 *Cal. doc. Ire., 1252–84*, p. 259. **127** "Cat. of pipe rolls 16 Ed III", *PRI rep. DK* 53 (1926) p. 23. **128** Peyton's Survey, cited by Begley, *The diocese of Limerick*, I, p. 375. **129** *Rot. pat. Hib.* p. 196, and see Lyons, *Church and society in County Kildare*, p. 115. **130** Griffith, "The Talbot-Ormond struggle", p. 394. For more on the Talbot-Ormond conflict see Simms, "Bards and barons", pp 183ff. **131** Lyons, "Revolt and reaction", p. 44. **132** "Rep. Viride Alen", p. 206.

as a plan was put forward in which the Graney would be one of a handful of similarly placed religious houses which would be taken over by the crown and given to "young lords, knights and gentlemen out of England" in order to quell the unrest in the area.[133] Although nothing came of this plan, Timolin was suppressed before 1533 by the archbishop of Dublin, perhaps partly to improve his revenues by incorporating Timolin's rectories.[134] To a large extent, however, the lands of Timolin were probably unmanageable for their new owners as the area had been overrun by O'More, and the Anglo-Irish men who were eventually granted the sites and estates of the nunneries of Timolin and Graney were unable to take up possession.[135]

When the communities which supported the nuns were dispersed, the nunneries – though not necessarily directly attacked – became very vulnerable. Their lands were no longer tenanted or were occupied by hostile lay people, which prevented the collection of rents and tithes. The increased costs involved in these situations also contributed to the financial vulnerability of nunnery estates. The nuns of Termonfeckin, for example, had difficulties with their tenants and parishioners in about 1440, when the prioress, Elina, complained to the archbishop of Armagh that her parishioners in Kylclochir (Clogher, Co. Louth) did not pay their tithes, took away the harvest, allowed their animals access to the meadow of Callystown (Clogher, Co. Louth), made paths through growing corn and carried away property from her manor of Termonfeckin.[136] Here civil disobedience prevented the nuns from living their quiet pious lives; it necessitated the intervention of the archbishop and demonstrates that the nuns needed supporters, whether lay or ecclesiastical. It is possible that a scenario of this sort was also behind the sixteenth-century report that one of the chapels of Timolin had been all but destroyed because the parishioners preferred going to a neighbouring church for services.[137] Here the parishioners also withdrew their support from the nuns, taking their tithes and dues elsewhere; whether this was because of neglect by the nuns or political differences is not known, though both are possible.

In managing their estates, nuns had to cope with many specific difficulties over the course of the medieval period. Although vigorous superiors did attempt to defend nunnery assets, they were not always successful. For many this was not due to their gender so much as the vicissitudes of medieval land ownership and management. But it was particularly important for nuns, as non-combatant women, to preserve good relationships with the lay and ecclesiastical societies that surrounded them. Since so much of medieval life was based on personal relationships and negotiations, isolation and rupture of these relationships was potentially harmful to the nuns living within the boundaries of their convents.

133 Finglas, "A breviate", pp 44–5. **134** Murray, "Archbishop Alen", pp 1–2, and see Bradshaw, *Dissolution*, p. 43. **135** Bradshaw, *Dissolution*, pp 43, 73, 76. **136** *Reg. Swayne*, p. 183. **137** The chapel of Heyteley, which has not been identified but must have been near the church of Uske, where the parishioners preferred attending. "Rep. Viride Alen", p. 207.

Ensuring that the relationships necessary for successful management of their resources were maintained was not easy for medieval nuns. A closer and more intimate boundary than that of the estates separated them from lay communities, a boundary formed by the walls of their cloisters and reinforced by ideologies of enclosure, sequestion and separation.

CHAPTER 6

The permeable cloister

The stone walls of the conventual precinct provided a physical space in which the nuns lived and worked. This boundary separating lay and religious communities was not only made of stone walls, it was also reinforced with ideas about how religious women were to live and the extent of their interaction with the laity. When they entered the conventual walls they often chose local convents, or those where their relatives had previously lived. Within these walls the women lived together, sometimes in harmony, and at other times in obvious conflict. They were organized according to conventional medieval monastic hierarchies, living their lives under their religious vows while they provided services for the local lay communities, most importantly prayer, but also charity, hospitality and some education.

ENCLOSURE

Monastic enclosure had its origins in early Christian thought, and its theoretical basis was developed and refined throughout the medieval period. Usually referred to as the rules of the fact "enclosure", "cloister" or "claustration", these terms reinforce the fact that these boundaries were as solid and real as the stone walls of conventual buildings. Like any physical boundary, there were liminal areas in the ideology of enclosure, points where entry and exit were allowed or taken. It is in the combination of the theoretical rules with liminal points that the experience of the women who lived within these boundaries may be recovered, at least in part. It is often in the transgressions of enclosure that religious women emerge from their collective obscurity, and these brief appearances need to be analysed in the wider context of the societies from which they came and the religious rules under which they lived.

The medieval monastic cloister was a space designed for peace, tranquillity and concentration of the mind on God. It was both a physical space incorporated in the monastic building complex and a state of mind of individual religious people who lived within.[1] Although the cloister, both physical and theoretical,

1 For discussion of the spiritual meanings of cloister see Meyvaert, "The medieval monastic claustrum", pp 53–60 and Cassidy, "Cistercian monasteries", p. 6. For early ideas on enclosure

was common to male and female religious people, the ways these theories were developed and applied differed for men and women. Restrictions on the movement of all monastics are explicitly stated in all the surviving monastic rules, including the rules of St Benedict and St Augustine. By the later medieval period, in practice the restrictions were applied more strictly to nuns than to monks. There were also considerable difficulties in enforcing the dictates of enclosure on nuns, leading to repeated attempts to impose stricter regulations.[2]

The zeal of the Irish twelfth-century reformers in their introduction of the continental rules such as the Arroasian version of the Augustinian rule undoubtedly meant that nuns living under these rules were expected to be enclosed. These new rules affected men as well, with violation of enclosure by the Cistercian monks of Mellifont being one of the reformer Stephen of Lexington's many complaints about the laxity of the observance of the Cistercian rule.[3] It soon becomes clear that although there were restrictions on the movement of men in Irish reformed monasteries these were not considered to be as essential as those for women. In Ireland, although there is no record of ecclesiastical theorizing on claustration of religious women, some nuns at least were enclosed: as in 1260 the nuns of the Augustinian convent of Lismullin were described as being enclosed since their foundation.[4]

Developments in England during the thirteenth century suggest that enclosure for women was seen by canonists and reformers as not only necessary but often in need of urgent reform.[5] The concerns of church legislators, bishops and the papacy were deliniated most sharply in 1298, when the bull *Periculoso* was promulgated by Pope Boniface VIII.[6] This document declared that all nuns, no matter which rule they were following, or in which part of Europe they were living, were required to submit to strict claustration on pain of excommunication. They were no longer to permit the laity to enter their cloisters and were not allowed to leave except in certain restricted circumstances.[7] The most transparent reason for this emphasis on increased enclosure was no doubt the protection of the nuns and the surrounding lay population from the stain of sexual sin. Intact boundaries with few points of access for laity or points of

for women, see Hochstetler, "The meaning of the monastic cloister for women", pp 27–40. **2** There has been considerable interest in this subject. See, *inter alia* Schulenburg, "Strict active enclosure", pp 51–2, for definitions of monastic cloistering and for the lack of distinction in early rules between men and women monastics with regards to cloistering. Also see Johnson, "The cloistering of medieval nuns", pp 27–39, for differing interpretations of the contemporary meaning of cloister. For recent analyses of the reasons the medieval jurists used to justify the distinction between male and female claustration see Makowski, *Canon Law and cloistered women*, p. 126, and Medioli, "An unequal law", pp 139–43. **3** Stephen of Lexington as cited in Stalley, *The Cistercian monasteries of Ireland*, p. 18. **4** Papal letter dated 1260, the nuns were described as "sub clausura vivatis". *Vetera monumenta Hibernorum*, p. 86. See also *Pont. Hib.*, p. 137. **5** Power, *Medieval English nunneries*, pp 348–51 and Makowski, *Canon law and cloistered women*, pp 101–5. **6** Text of the bull Liber Sextus 3.16 De Statu reluarium *c.*un. "Periculoso" is translated by Makowski, *Canon Law and cloistered women*, pp 133–6. See p. 44, note 4, on the difficulties of terminology. **7** Brundage and Makowski, "Enclosure of nuns", p. 145.

departure for nuns was the guiding principal for this vision of enclosed spaces for nuns.

The legislation was acknowledged to be at considerable variance with the rules under which many women had entered religious life, sometimes leading to heated debate and dissent over the question of how these stricter rules were to be enforced in convents where the rules had been more lenient. It was also recognised that the legislation needed to be formally promulgated in all areas before it could be enforced. It is first mentioned in English episcopal registers soon after its inital promulgation, when Simon of Ghent, bishop of Salisbury, quoted it in full in a letter to the abbess of Wilton in late 1299.[8] Although there is no record of its official promulgation in Ireland, it is likely to have occurred at around the same time as in England. It may not be too fanciful to speculate that part of the problems that the abbess and nuns of Kilcreevanty had with the archbishop of Tuam in the early years of the fourteenth century may have been with his wish to enforce stricter controls on the nuns, including more frequent visitation than they had negotiated in 1223.[9]

The few surviving Irish episocpal documents reveal that bishops in Ireland were fully aware of their responsiblities with regard to enclosure of nuns and that they shared with bishops throughout Europe difficulties in reconciling the needs and desires of the nuns in their care with the rules they were expected to enforce. The most explicit attempt at enforcement comes in 1427 when John Swayne, archbishop of Armagh, on visitation at the convent of Lismullin, ordered that the nuns were to observe the rules of enclosure, the gates and other places of the convent were ordered shut and a copy of the *Periculoso* was appended to the order. There are two other undated entries in the episcopal register that order Lismullin to comply with enclosure, probably dated 1425 and 1427.[10] There is no extant evidence of whether the nuns obeyed his various commands, or what incidents provoked his ire. In the sixteenth century, Archbishop Alen of Dublin, when commenting on the convents of Timolin and Grace Dieu, noted that they were "quaram sexus fragilor, discretio minor et defensio debilor" and that they had both originally been "cloistral without a cloister and regulars without a rule", indicating his belief that his predecssors had been correct in imposing claustration and a strict rule upon these religious women.[11]

As was acknowledged by the many commentators on *Periculoso*, nuns were usually called upon to leave their conventual walls for the management of estates and general business, not seeking opportunities to sin. Management of large estates and negotiations with lay and ecclesiastical authorities for the continued prosperity of convent property necessitated the movement outside the boundaries

8 Power, *Medieval English nunneries*, p. 350, and Makowski, *Canon law and cloistered women*, p. 112. **9** There were also undoubtedly financial and property issues as well, with the archbishop allegedly seizing property violently and without authority. *Cal. justic. rolls Ire., 1307–13*, pp 113–14, and *Cal. papal letters, 1305–42*, p. 212, for the increased visitation granted to the archbishop of Tuam in 1321. **10** *Reg. Swayne*, pp 51–2. The entries to either side of the two undated entries give the approximate dates according to the editor. **11** *Alen's reg.*, p. 179.

of the convent walls by at least the abbess, and usually other office bearers in charge of kitchen and infirmaries.[12] Although superiors were required by *Periculoso* to appoint attorneys and proctors to engage in their official business, it appears in later commentaries that they were permitted to go in person to do homage for land.[13]

In Ireland, superiors of nunneries did appear in legal courts. In 1280, the abbess of Clonard herself went to Dublin over a suit of dower.[14] The abbess of Kilcreevanty, in her legal action against the archbishop of Tuam in 1308, is described as being present "in her own person" and the archbishop is represented by his attorney.[15] Possibly reflecting increased restrictions after the proclamation of *Periculoso*, in 1347 Margaret, prioress of Lismullin, was recorded being represented by her attorney in a court case because she "is not permitted by the rule of her order" to appear personally.[16] There were, however, variations in the movements of religious outside the cloister: in 1433, the prioress of Molough was one of several religious superiors who attended the court of the liberty of Tipperary rather than send proctors.[17] Nuns appear to been willing to try to use the rules to their advantage when they could, as when in 1506 the abbess of Kilcullliheen insisted that the rules of enclosure prevented her from attending a hearing into her management of a rectory.[18] On the eve of the dissolution in the 1530s there was a vacancy in the office of prioress of Termonfeckin, and the archbishop of Armagh was engaged in finding a successor. In his search for a suitable candidate, at least two nuns from Odder travelled to his court in Termonfeckin to discuss the situation with him and present documents detailing their house's claims to appoint the new prioress.[19]

While leaving the enclosure of the convent to conduct clearly defined business was probably accepted as necessary, visiting for social purposes was not seen by the episcopal authorities in the same light. Nuns of various communities throughout England and the continent strenuously resisted the rules of enclosure which shut them off from their friends and relatives outside the convent walls. Regulations were developed in England to try and counter the harshness of the ban, with visits of three to six days being officially tolerated. Even these restrictions were unwelcome, however, and proved impossible to enforce.[20] Nuns may also have found that different bishops interpreted rules and exemptions differently, probably leading to some confusion.[21]

12 See, among many others, Oliva, *Convent and community*, pp 34–7; Hamburger, "Art, enclosure and curia monialum", pp 108–10; McNamara, *Sisters in arms*, p. 388. **13** Brundage and Makowski, "Enclosure of nuns", pp 148, 154. **14** Calendar of Banco rolls, 8 Ed. I (NAI MS RC 7/1), pp 58–9. See also Calendar of Common Bench roll 8 Ed. I no. 6 (NAI, MS RC 7/2) pp 14, 41. In all these Isabelle is described as being represented by her attorney and the abbess is referred to as being present at the proceedings. In the last of the court appearances connected with this suit, the abbess is represented by her attorney, Robert Tarram (NAI MS RC 7/2), p. 52. **15** *Cal. justic. rolls Ire., 1307–13*, pp 113–14. **16** *Rot. pat. Hib.*, p. 51. **17** *Ormond deeds*, III, p. 91. **18** *Cal. papal letters, 1503–1513*, p. 424. **19** "Reg. Cromer", *Louth Arch. Soc. Jn. 8* (1933–6) pp 177–8. **20** Tillotson, "Visitation and reform", pp 5–10. **21** Power, *Medieval English nunneries*, p. 362 and Makowski, *Canon law and cloistered women*, p. 116.

Family connections remained important not just for the personal well-being of the nuns themselves but also for the maintenance of friendly relations with neighbouring lay communities and families who were the advocates and supporters of the convents. In order to maintain those relationships, attendance at family and community functions such as weddings was obviously considered important. Superiors of nunneries were important witnesses for ceremonies such as weddings, particularly if there was a possibility that there would be later questions as to their legitimacy. This may have been why the abbess of Kilculliheen attended the wedding of James Butler and Sadhbh Kavanagh in about 1470. Certainly, thirty years later her evidence was important in the protracted enquiries into the legitmacy of the marriage.[22] It is not clear whether she attended the wedding in her position as abbess or before her entry into religious life, but her status made her a significant witness and she may have been asked to attend the wedding in full knowledge of the weight her evidence would have in any future dispute over its legitimacy.[23] Nuns seem to have been respected witnesses in cases before ecclesiastical courts, and for their testimony to have value they also must have been expected to maintain relationships with lay families. In about 1455, Benmon ingen Omellan, described as abbess of St Brigid's, was called to give evidence before the archbishop of Armagh in a case where Felim McDomphnayll and Isabella ingen Neill were seeking dispensation to marry, even though they were within the prohibited degrees of affinity. Benmon's evidence proved that the couple were indeed related within the prohibited degrees of affinity. Her knowledge of the family relationships speaks of her being either a member of the family herself or having intimate knowledge of several generations of the Uí Néill.[24]

BREAKS IN THE CLOISTER BOUNDARY

It is likely that claustration was practised differently in various religious communities in medieval Ireland. The instances of explicit maintenance of claustration all come from nunneries in the Anglo-Irish areas. In Gaelic Ireland, where records are generally much poorer, there is no explicit mention of cloistering for nuns. It is also from Gaelic Irish nunneries that there is most evidence of nuns engaging in sexual liaisons, the avoidance of which was the explicit reason for strict claustration. In the ecclesiastical records these are recognised as lapses of chastity, but not usually referred to as lapses of enclosure; whether this is a result of ecclesiastical records avoiding a statement of the obvious or because enclosure was viewed as irrelevant is not clear.

22 *Ormond deeds* III, p. 297. The earls of Ormond were long-term patrons of Kilculliheen. See *Ormond deeds,* III, p. 139 for the payment of alms in 1443. **23** James and Sadhbh would have known that their marriage contradicted the rules of consanguinity, but the alliance was important for political and strategic reasons. **24** "Reg. Prene" (PRONI DIO 4/2/6) ff. 17v – 20, Reeve's transcripts (TCD MS 557/6) pp 414–19.

Sexual sin was the clearest manifestation of the breaking of cloister for medieval nuns. There is evidence from all over medieval Europe of nuns bearing children while enclosed within the safe and supposedly chaste boundaries of their convents.[25] There was considerable anxiety among medieval church writers about the prevelance of sexual sin within religious spaces, which undoubtedly led to heightened suspisicion of women and the perceived opportunities for sexual sin that their presence implied.[26] As Johnson has pointed out in her study of monks and nuns in medieval France, the rates of sexual sin for monks were probably greater, but sinning nuns were more easily recognized because of the visibility of pregnancy.[27] There was a tradition of support for nuns who found themselves sinning outside the cloister and who then repented. This support included the succour of any children and the readmittance of the women to the cloisters.[28] Religious women were not considered released from their vows even if they left the convents and lived secular lives.[29]

Although there were some real instances of pregnant nuns, there was also a very strong literary and moral tradition of the failings of nuns that must have influenced how religious and lay people viewed such nuns.[30] Wayward nuns have been the subject of many salacious and cautionary tales from the early medieval period onwards and their presence in literature is no guarantee that they existed in large numbers outside the imaginations of readers and writers. In the scant literature from Ireland describing nuns, there is a fifteenth-century example of the well-known story in which a nun left to "become a harlot" for fifteen years and was replaced in her convent by the Virgin Mary. When the nun returned, Mary forgave her and allowed her to return to her duties, "though thou didst break thy vow and riot in shame, thy black habit and the key in the holy house are not lost to thee".[31] Another exemplar, also based on a well-known story and probably originating in the Franciscan friary in Ennis, describes the nuns of a convent contriving to ensure that their abbess becomes pregnant. Her labour pains were then eased by the Virgin Mary, leaving the child to become a bishop.[32] There are different ways of interpreting these stories, including their function in Marian devotions, quite apart from any connection with nuns or nunneries. They indicate that in Ireland, as in the rest of medieval Europe, the topos of the sinning nun was a familiar one, which may have influenced how nuns who did sin saw themselves and were seen by others.

Reports of nuns who bore children also need to be analysed against the backdrop of attitudes to celibacy prevalent in medieval Ireland. The success of

25 Tillotson, "Reform and visitation", p. 9. **26** Elliot, "Sex in holy places", pp 6–34, and Daichman, "Misconduct in the medieval nunnery", pp 97–117, for general discussions. **27** Johnson, *Equal in monastic profession*, pp 114–19. **28** McNamara, *Sisters in arms*, pp 363, and 367. **29** Logan, *Runaway religious* pp 84–5ff. **30** For a general discussion of the overall medieval context see Elliott, "Sex in holy places", pp 6–34. **31** Pilib Bocht Óhuiginn, "Gach Maighdean go máthair Dé", quoted and discussed in O'Dwyer, *Mary*, p. 118. This was a common story throughout medieval Europe, originally found in Caesarius of Heisterbach. See McNamara, *Sisters in arms*, p. 368. **32** TCD MS 667, compiled about 1454. See Colker,

clerical marriages and inheritance of monastic and church offices in Ireland throughout the medieval period were of recurring concern to reformers both in Gaelic Ireland and elsewhere, although the frequent lack of concern with which clerical "concubinage" is mentioned suggests that there were few problems with it at community level.[33] There were periods of change, such as the twelfth century, when the reformers seem to have been successful, but from the fourteenth century onwards the frequency of reports of non-celibacy means that many parts of the church were effectively laicized as regards marriage and family inheritance of church office and property.[34] Both papal and episcopal registers contain many examples from the entire period, to the extent that one commentator has suggested that the papacy tacitly acquiesced to the situation in Ireland and quietly granted the many petitions for dispensation for illegitimacy as well as for irregularities of marriage alliances.[35]

There were still attempts to impose clerical celibacy within Ireland, as when John, bishop of Down, was excommunicated in 1440 because he refused to dismiss his "concubine", Letys Thomb.[36] The reports of the state of Ireland to the English government on the eve of the suppression of the monasteries and the Tudor expansion into Ireland contain several complaints about the sorry state of monastic houses, including the Cistercian house of Inislounaght in Co. Tipperary, where the abbot was using his "leman or harlot openly by daie and night to his pleasure and every monke of his havynge his harlot and household".[37] Many difficulties occurred because there was no formal provision for the women and children of churchmen and these were often brought to the fore in the everyday administration of church affairs, as after the death of Cornelius, bishop of Ardagh, when Katherine Offechayll and their son Cornelius refused to give up the horse, ring and cup which had belonged to the bishop.[38] These issues within the Irish medieval church are well known to historians but little attention has been paid to how they may have affected women religious.

Calculating whether sinning nuns were stigmatized by their local communities for breaking the rules of claustration or chastity is difficult given the paucity of the surviving documentation. The few surviving episcopal visitation records indicate that the cloistering of nuns and their possible sexual sins were one of the topics of investigation on visitations. When the archbishop of Armagh was in visitation at the convent of Termonfeckin, he found that one nun, Anna Owen or Onegan, was guilty of "incontinence" and sentenced her to the punishment

Trinity College Dublin: Descriptive catalogue, p. 1161. For the general background of this motif see Warren, "Pregnancy and productivity", pp 532–52. **33** Burrows, "Fifteenth century Irish provincial legislation and pastoral care", p. 57. Jeffries, *Priests and prelates*, pp 79–81. **34** See Nicholls, *Gaelic and gaelicised Ireland*, pp 107–11, for a summary of the evidence. **35** See Walsh, "The clerical estate", pp 365–6, and for a general overview of the problems which non-celibacy created for the medieval church in Ireland see Watt, *Church in medieval Ireland*, pp 185–93, and Nicholls, *Gaelic and Gaelicised Ireland*, pp 92–8. **36** *Registrum Iohannis Mey*, no. 37. **37** *The social state of the southern and eastern counties of Ireland*, p. 248. **38** *Reg. Swayne*, p. 38.

of seclusion in a private room, without lights, with necessities provided by the prioress who was to say the hours of the office with her. Anna was to remain in her room until the next visit of the archbishop.[39] Here the break in the boundary of cloister was to be punished by reinforcement of its power by enclosure in even stricter isolation, dramatically emphasizing the expected piety of religious women.

Most of the information we have of the sexual activities of nuns comes not from any complaints against the nuns themselves but from the dispensations which their children sought on entering ecclesiastical office.[40] Michael MacLacloyim OFM of the diocese of Armagh, for example, sought dispensation as the son of a nun in 1310.[41] Simon McGowand, a clerk from Armagh, was granted a papal dispensation in 1399 as he was the son of an Augustinian canon and a nun, probably from one of the two nunneries in Armagh itself.[42] Another monk, Patrick Ollealinx of the Cistercian abbey of Abbeyleix in Co. Laois, was granted a dispensation in 1523 as he was the son of a priest and a nun also of the order of St Brigid.[43] Identifying the women involved here is difficult as usually neither their names nor the names of their houses are mentioned, and even reference to their order may not be correct. Abbeyleix was close to Kildare where there was a nunnery dedicated to St Brigid that may have remained operational in some capacity after the dispersal of its nuns in the 1440s. The mother may also have come from one of the other nunneries dedicated to St Brigid such as Molough, in Tipperary, or Odder in Meath. Official censure of the men involved also yields some examples of religious women sinning: for example, the archbishop of Armagh gave dispensation in 1368 to a priest, Sir Roger Ogean of Down, for having had carnal knowledge with Matilda Stokys, a professed nun of the Down nunnery.[44]

The most complex of the examples of nuns proven to have borne children comes from Killone. Here it is likely that the convergance of Gaelic Irish attitudes to clerical celibacy as well as the realities of strong family involvement in conventual affairs all played their parts in a startling and possibly tragic family drama. The abbey of Killone was always under the patronage of the founder's family, the Uí Bhriain and all the known nuns were from the upper eschelons of this family, usually specified as the daughters of the kings of Thomond. There are three dispensations for clerics in the late fifteenth century which suggest that at least one and possibly two of the abbesses of Killone bore children from incestuous unions. Cornelius and Tatheus O Brien were clerics from Killaloe diocese who were granted dispensations, in 1482 and 1485 respectively, from the defect of their births which were as the result of fornication between their sister,

39 Reg. Octavian (PRONI MS DIO 4/2/9) f. 228a and TCD MS 557/10 pp 869–70. **40** On dispensations in general see Nicholls, *Gaelic and Gaelicised Ireland*, pp 93–4, and on the subject of papal dispensations for illegitimacy see Thompson, "The Well of Grace", pp 101–4. **41** *Cal. papal letters, 1305–42*, p. 72. **42** *Cal. papal letters, 1396–1404*, p. 252. **43** Reg. Pen. 69, fo. 40r. This reference and the information from it were kindly supplied to me by Dr M. Haren, who speculates that the convent of the nun involved was in Armagh. **44** *Reg. Sweteman*, no. 81, p. 84.

the abbess of Killone, and her father.[45] In 1501, another Ó Briain, Donald, was granted dispensation as the son of a bishop and an abbess, who were related in the second degree of consanguinity and the double second of affinity.[46]

It is probably reasonable to assume that dispensations would have been sought at the start of ecclesiastical careers, suggesting that there was an Ó Briain abbess of Killone in the 1460s and again in the 1480s who had children whilst in office. It is possible that the three men had the same mother, by her father and then her relative, the bishop. The father in question was possibly Conchobhar Mór mac Toirdhealbhaigh Ó Briain, king of Thomond between 1466 and 1496, although his brother Tadgh an Chomhaid who died in 1466 would be another candidate.[47] It is also possible, given the presumed age difference between the Donald and the elder two men, that they had different mothers, both of whom were abbesses of Killone. Since all the known abbesses of Killone were from the Uí Bhriain, this is possible. The wording of the dispensations is not totally conclusive as to whether the woman or women in question were abbesses at the time of the birth of the children, although it suggests that this was probably the case. The circumstances of the fathers, one a bishop and the other the father of their mother, ensured that the men would have needed dispensations anyway, so the mother or mothers may have entered the convent after the births of such children.

The name of one abbess from this time is known: Renalda Ní Bhriain, who died in 1510 and was probably a daughter of Tadhg an Chomhaid. She almost certainly did not enter the convent until around 1500.[48] Although she would be the right age, it is not likely she was the mother of any of the three clerics, as she was married to two Butler men and probably lived most of her adult life in the Butler territories around Tipperary.[49]

Notwithstanding the exact identity of the abbess or abbesses who bore children, the apparently lax conditions in which these women were cloistered suggests that they may have regarded celibacy in a similar light to the abbots of many Gaelic monasteries who openly supported wives and families and were succeeded in

45 Cornelius's dispensation is in Vatican Reg. Pen. 31, 217v; Tatheus's at Reg. Pen. 34, f. 273r. The Cornelius Oberynd, clerk of Killaloe and son of a nun OSA and an unmarried man referred to in 1483 *Cal. papal letters, 1471–84*, p. 131 is probably the same Cornelius. This case and that of Donald Ó Briain are discussed in Haren, "Social structures", pp 220–1. Dr Haren kindly supplied me with unpublished transcripts of the entries from the Penitentiary Registers. **46** Donald's dispensation is at Reg. Pen. 50, 345r and ASV L 1244 192v-196r and a later version is printed in calendar form in *Cal. papal letters, 1503–13*, pp 199–200. **47** Haren, "Social structures", p. 220, suggests that Conchobhar is the father involved. He also suggests that the three clerics had the same mother and gives the identification of the bishop as Toirdhealbhach mac Mathghamhna Ó Briain, bishop of Killaloe from 1483 until 1525. **48** Ó Dálaigh, "Mistress, mother and abbess", pp 60–1, where he argues that her father was Tadhg an Chomhaid who succeeded as head Ó Briain in 1459, because she was described as the daughter of O'Brien of Thomond at the time of her union with Sir John Butler which must have occurred in 1462. It is just possible, however, that she was promised to Sir John earlier than this or that she was actually the sister of Tadhg and the daughter of the previous O'Brien who died in 1459. **49** Ó Dálaigh, "Mistress, mother and abbess", pp 52–3.

ecclesiastic office by their sons. The duties of these abbots has always been assumed to be more as guardians of the monastic property than as spiritual leaders of their communities. The open acknowledgement of the paternity of the three Ó Briain clerics, their preferment to ecclesiastical careers and the fact that another Ó Briain abbess, Renalda, had private property to bequeath and also requested burial in the ancestral graveyard in the Franciscan friary in Ennis rather than in her convent all suggest that the office of abbess of Killone may have become substantially secularized by the end of the fifteenth century.

In favour of some sort of continued religious functioning of the convent and its nuns is the evidence of the surviving building structure, which shows signs of being altered in the fifteenth century, with the shortening of the church and the building of the substantial two-storeyed domestic building, almost certainly a dormitory and refectory for the nuns.[50] There is also a document from 1567 which recalls some of the services of Killone to the local community, including "relief for the poor, feeding and clothing the needy, naked, hungry and impotent". This same document, however, also suggests that the previous nuns used their income for "whoredom, gluttony and other kinds of excess and dissolute living".[51] Overall it is not possible to be conclusive about the extent of secularisation which occurred in the final years of Killone. The abbey may have been seen by the Ó Briains as a sort of refuge for their female relatives who needed to retire from the world when they were found to be embarrassingly with child or had passed their usefulness as political wives. In this case Killone would not have been unusual in the medieval world.

If the mother or mothers of the three Ó Briain clerics had been resident in the religious community of Killone at the time of the births, then the effectiveness of the cloister walls was obviously compromised. It is not possible at this distance to understand the feelings of the women involved, but the men who fathered these children – the abbess's father who was the secular ruler of the area, patron of the convent and descendant of the founder, along with the bishop, also a family member – were unlikely to have ever been able to be excluded from the cloister.[52] There are other instances where the man accused of sexual involvement with a nun is the bishop who should have been expected to ensure claustration; for example the abbot of Annaghdown, Thomas O'Malley, was dispensed from the impediment of being the son of a bishop and a nun in 1242.[53] In circumstances where the men who were supposed to have the power to ensure that the cloister was intact were the ones violating it, there is little doubt that the nuns could not have done anything to keep it intact.

50 Westropp, "The Augustinian convent of Killown", pp 409–10. **51** "A commentary on the nobility and gentry of Thomond, *c.*1567", pp 70–1. **52** For a discussion of the laws of consanguinity: father/daughter and brother/sister incest, see Nicholls, *Gaelic and Gaelicised Ireland*, pp 75–6, where he argues that the prevailing customs of separating children from birth families through fosterage may have lessened contact and loosened ties between parents and their biological children. **53** *Cal. papal letters, 1198–1304*, p. 232. As it is probable that the nunnery at Annaghdown closed in about 1223, the nun in question may have come from

Cloistering of nuns within Ireland, as in the rest of Europe, depended on the will of all involved to ensure that the boundaries, both physical and ideological, were recognized. If the nuns themselves did not wish to live within these boundaries and they had the support of the communities around them, then cloistering would have been problematic. Conversely, even when nuns wished to live quiet cloistered lives, if powerful men violated that wish, then the women would have been particularly vulnerable. Conflict could and did occur when nuns wished to enjoy more contact with their neighbouring communities than ecclesiastical authorities allowed.

THE PERMEABLE CLOISTER AT WORK

Most of the interactions between religious women and the lay communities around them occurred in the course of managing the convent estates or where individual nuns were known to have had sexual relationships with men. The permeable claustral boundary also permitted the rendering of services by the nuns to their supporters. Lay communities expected some return for their investment in maintaining religious women.[54] There was probably local variation in the services to the secular world by religious communities but these services came broadly under the headings of prayer, education and welfare. Female monastics could not provide the services of priests for masses out of their own numbers as their religious brethren could, but they were able to pray for patrons and to attract lay people who wanted burial in their grounds and churches and so the nuns must have been seen by many as able to provide a satisfactory service for their last and most important journey.

Prayers

Nunneries accepted bequests for anniversary masses, for which they needed to employ the necessary priests. In MacDonald's study of nuns in the wills of late medieval Yorkshire, she has found that testators who bequeathed money to nunneries did so in the expectation of prayers for their souls. She also argues that bequests to nunneries usually came from people with personal ties to the nuns.[55] Over time bequests for anniversary masses tended to become less profitable for the nunneries and this has been posited as one of the reasons for the poor financial situation of nunneries in the last centuries of the medieval period.[56] When Margaret Gillemichelle gave substantial grants to the abbey of St Mary del Hogges in 1234, for the saying of masses for her soul and the soul of Sir Alexander, anchorite of St Clement, the nuns would have employed priests to

nearby Inishmaine. **54** For a summary of these services and connection in European nunneries in general see McNamara, *Sisters in arms*, p. 388. **55** MacDonald, "Women and the monastic life in late medieval Yorkshire", pp 90–2. **56** Johnson, *Equal in monastic profession*, pp 111, 137.

say the masses, and the sisters themselves would have added their own prayers.[57] It is possible that the value of the bequest did not keep pace with the costs of providing masses, and meant that the nuns may have had to either decrease the number or frequency of the masses or redirect resources away from other parts of their estates in order to fulfil the terms of the bequest.[58]

A bequest or donation of a similar sort may have been the origin of the chantry at Termonfeckin parish church. It seems that in the late fifteenth century there was an arrangement that the chaplain of the chantry of the Virgin Mary would also perform services for the nuns at the priory of Termonfeckin in return for two days' sustenance by the parish and one day's from the nuns. This arrangement broke down in the early sixteenth century and the nuns did not wish to re-establish the services or the payment for the chaplain. After lengthy proceedings before the archbishop of Armagh's court, they were obliged to accept a compromise where they would pay for the chaplain one day a week and in return he would say mass for them four times a year.[59] Although there is little other direct evidence of these sorts of bequests to nunneries in Ireland, there is no reason to suppose that they did not occur.

Festivals and special masses were also held at convents, especially on the feast days of patron saints. These might be open to local parishioners and patrons as well as the religious community. Along with her many other grants, Margaret Gillemichelle donated money to maintain three wax lights at the mass for the Virgin Mary held "in the enclosure of the church" at St Mary del Hogges in Dublin.[60] Although no more is known about this mass, male monasteries in Dublin held special festivals and masses for their patrons saints. The Hospital of St John the Baptist, for example, held a parade, festival and mass on the feast day of its patron saint.[61] Some of the great civic pageants of Corpus Christi were probably performed on Hoggen Green, near to the nunnery of Hogges, although there is no evidence that the nuns took part in them.[62] These brief references suggest that nunneries may have been seen as part of the public religious life of urban areas.

Some of the nunneries in Ireland shared their churches with local parishioners, and possibly were called upon to provide prayers and other spiritual services for the parish communities.[63] In English nunnery churches shared with parishioners, the nuns usually worshipped in the choir with screens separating them from the

57 *Cal. doc. Ire., 1171–1251*, p. 327. **58** This was a common fate of bequests and donations for anniversary masses; for an example and discussion see Burgess, "A service for the dead", p. 185. **59** "Reg. Cromer", *Louth Arc. Soc. Jn 8* (1934) pp 176–9. **60** *Cal. doc. Ire., 1171–1251*, p. 327. **61** Archdall (1876), II, p. 61. For the civic festival of Corpus Christi in Dublin see Fletcher, "The civic pagentry of Corpus Christi", pp 73–84. **62** Fletcher, "The civic pagentry of Corpus Christi", p. 77, note 16. Nuns in Yorkshire were members of the York Corpus Christ Guild. See MacDonald, "Women and the monastic life in late medieval Yorkshire", pp 67–75. **63** Preston, "The canons regular of St Augustine", p. 177, has questioned the assumption that many Irish monastic churches were parochial and find evidence for only four Augustinian priory churches being parochial before the dissolution.

parishioners in the nave.[64] While internal divisions such as these have not survived in any of the nunnery churches in Ireland, there is other evidence that some nunnery churches were shared with parishioners, while others may have been attended by laity for regular or special services.[65] The nuns of Grace Dieu shared their church with the parish, and parishioners were buried in the graveyard attached to the church. In 1473 Cecily Langan stipulated in her will that she wished to be buried in the church of St Mary, Grace Dieu, and bequeathed livestock to be sold for cash, added to the church herds or used to provide food for alms.[66] Other nunnery churches described as parochial at the dissolution were Odder and Molough and Kilculliheen.[67] The nuns of St Catherine d'Conyl may also have shared church with the parish.[68] How the interactions between parishioners and nuns were played out is not really clear, although there were probably arrangements which meant sharing with the parish both the church and the cost of the priest.

The prioress of Termonfeckin seems to have taken an active interest in the parishes which surrounded her priory, possibly to provide spiritual direction but also because her priory was the recipient of some of the parish dues. There appears to have been considerable tension at different times with the parishioners of one of the parish churches appropriated to Termonfeckin, Kylclogher (Co. Louth). In 1440, the parishioners were refusing to pay tithes to the convent and in 1521 several of them were ordered by the prioress not to attend the parish church at Kylclogher, but to go to another of their churches at nearby Calliaghstown (Co. Louth). The parishioners appealed to the court of the archbishop, but unfortunately the case does not seem to have been concluded in the court.[69] This evidence suggests that the prioress of Termonfeckin and her nuns were closely involved in the practical management of the parishes where they held land, partially supporting the priests as well as collecting tithes and going so far as to direct parishioners to the church of the nuns' choosing.

Another aspect of the spiritual lives of nuns was their individual admission to the ranks of confraternities. In Yorkshire these contacts between nuns, usually superiors of convents, and the wealthy, prestigious confraternities and fraternities of city churches were common and MacDonald has postulated that besides the religious function of these associations, the nuns may have been looking to widen their spheres of influence, with some evidence that admission of the nuns to confraternities led to bequests to the nunneries from other confraternity members.[70] Although there is insufficient evidence for these sorts of associations

64 Gilchrist, *Gender and material culture*, pp 99–101, and *Contemplation and action*, p. 122, for the different types of arrangements found in English churches. **65** There is no evidence for this in female houses, although Preston has found evidence for male Augustinian houses. See Preston, "The canons regular of St Augustine", pp 181–5. **66** *Register of wills*, ed. Berry pp 65–6. **67** *Extents Ir. mon. possessions*, p. 206. **68** *Cal. papal letters, 1427–47*, pp 400–1. **69** *Reg. Swayne*, p. 183 and "Reg. Cromer", *Louth Arch. Soc. Jn.* 8 (1933–6) pp 186–7. **70** Mac Donald, "Women and the monastic life in late medieval Yorkshire", pp 67–75.

in Ireland, in the list of obituaries for Christ Church cathedral in Dublin, certainly the most prestigious confraternity in the area, there are the names of three nuns: Lady Alicia Bron, nun of Hogges; Lady Matilda, abbess of Hogges, and Lady Katerina Hakket, prioress of Grace Dieu.[71] These women may have wanted admission to the confraternity because of their family associations, for their own personal piety or to maintain relationships with the wider lay and religious communities.

Burials

The evidence of gravestones at the sites of medieval nunneries demonstrates that the grounds were used for lay burial and that wealthy patrons would expect burial within the church itself. Burial within the monastic church was reserved for prominent patrons and possibly members of the communities, and in return the patron might be assured of the prayers of the nuns to assure their spiritual health after death. In Yorkshire, a consistent minority of testators requested burial in nunneries, although the majority wished to be buried in their parish church. These testators probably had some sort of personal ties with the nunneries, usually relatives being resident as nuns there.[72] Gilchrist has also suggested that English nunneries may have been more egalitarian in their acceptance of laity for burial in their churches and graveyards than male monastic houses.[73] Although the evidence for burial within nunnery churches and graveyards in Ireland is scant, it is clear that burial patterns were probably similar to those found in English nunneries and in other monastic churches in Ireland. Some monastic churches and graveyards have been excavated in Ireland, and studies of these have found similar patterns to the monastic burial patterns in England. There is a predominance of older male burials in and around monasteries, as would be expected in male monastic houses, although there were also burials of some females and children, indicating that these monasteries incorporated a lay burial ground for benefactors and the surrounding lay population.[74]

It would then be expected that in nunneries there would be a specific section of the grounds, cloister or church where the nuns would be buried and an area for the laity in the graveyard, with prominent benefactors buried inside the church. Although there have been no excavations to date on nunneries in Ireland, it is possible to collate information from written sources describing the presence of burials at nunnery sites. Some of this information is no longer verifiable, and some relies on folk traditions, but these cannot be dismissed before detailed excavations are carried out. There were "coffin lid"-type early tombstones in the church at

71 *Book of Obits*, pp 82, 50, 71. **72** MacDonald, "Women and the monastic life in late medieval Yorkshire", pp 83–5. She finds approx. 1–3% of testators requested burial in nunneries. **73** Gilchrist, *Gender and material culture*, pp 58–61. **74** Some recent reports of monastic burials from excavations in Ireland include Halpin and Buckley, "Archaeological excavations at the Dominican priory, Drogheda", p. 193. For the monastic sites of St Mary's Dominican priory in Cork, St Saviour's Dominican Priory, Limerick, see Power, "A demographic study of human skeletal remains from historic Munster", pp 95–118.

Killone which were probably medieval and may have been for lay patrons, while the crypt beneath the east end of the church was supposed to have been used to bury members of the community.[75] Interestingly the two recorded deaths associated with Killone were both buried elsewhere. In 1252, Mór, daughter of Conchobar son of Tairdelbach Ó Briain and wife of Cormac Mac Carthaig, was buried at Killone; then later her body was transferred to a male monastic house.[76] When Renalda the abbess of Killone died she requested to be buried in her ancestral plot in the Franciscan friary at Ennis.[77] The reasons for this are not known, perhaps the Uí Briain preferred for the women of their families to be buried in ancestral plots rather than separated in nunnery burial grounds.

At St Catherine d'Conyl there was a medieval tombstone decorated with a Norman-type cross which may have been that of a member of the community or of an early patron.[78] The scant history of this nunnery has been enlivened by the story that a countess of Desmond was once buried beneath the altar of the church after she and her husband fled nearby Shanid castle during one of the many wars with the Butlers.[79] Although this narrative might be doubtful, the site of burial under the altar for a member of the patron's family and the use of the convent as a refuge are believable. There is a thirteenth-century effigy from the site of the convent of Timolin which is believed to be that of the founder Robert FitzRichard, lord of Norragh, although whether it was originally inside the church is now unknown.[80] Another headstone, probably from the late medieval or early modern period, was said to have been used as a well cover in the late nineteenth century in the grounds of Graney.[81] In a field beside Grace Dieu a thirteenth- or fourteenth-century tomb-slab was found, although it was not inscribed or decorated in such a way as to make any further identification possible.[82] Excavations of a field to the north of the site of the nunnery in 1988 found a cemetery within a large enclosure and the remains of many graves, along with domestic-type pottery, which is presumed to have been associated with the nunnery.[83] The cemetery, situated within three acres of orchard and garden at Grace Dieu, was mentioned in the description of the monastic holdings at the dissolution.[84] In 1569, the site of Kilcreevanty included a cemetery, although it is not known if the cemetery was for nuns and patrons or open to the parishioners.[85]

75 Westropp, "Augustinian houses of Co. Clare", p. 130. **76** *AI*. For discussion see Fry, *Burial in medieval Ireland*, pp 122, 173–4. She identifies the male house as Clare Abbey. **77** NAI MS D 1978. **78** For a description and drawing of the tombstone at St Catherine d'Conyl see Westropp, in Wardell, "History and antiquities of St Catherine, Old Abbey", p. 56. **79** Westropp, in Wardell, "History and antiquities of St Catherine, Old Abbey", p. 50, records this story as being current in the nineteenth century. however he gives no indication as to which Earl of Desmond is referred to. **80** Hunt, *Irish medieval figure sculpture*, p. 164 and plate I, Vol. II. Hartshorne, "Notes on a monumental effigy in the churchyard of Timolin", pp 131–4. **81** Fitzgerald, "The priory and nunnery of Graney", p. 380. **82** Harbison, "A medieval tombstone from Graney", pp 216–17. **83** Excavations carried out by M. Gowan within the Bord Gais Eireann pipeline corridor and reported in Gaimster, et. al., "Excavations in 1988", p. 228. **84** *Extents Ir. mon. possessions*, p. 73. **85** BL Egerton MS 1774, ff. 256–7.

Other finds of bones on the sites of medieval nunneries possibly represent medieval graveyards. There have been many reports of bones found on former nunnery sites subsequent to development and building work over the years. Bones were found on the presumed site of the nunnery of St John the Evangelist in Cork in the eighteenth century.[86] At the site of the church at Aghade, the small nunnery dependent on Hogges, there was an old baptismal font, a holy well and a graveyard described in the nineteenth century. The presence of the well suggests that the church site itself pre-dated the Norman period, and that it continued as a parish church throughout the medieval period, probably after the time that nuns were resident.[87] In the early nineteenth century, there was a small "old" graveyard attached to the ruined church at Ballynagallagh in Co. Limerick.[88] When a house was being built in the early nineteenth century on part of the site of Na Ferta, there were layers of human remains found, and when the site in Scotch Street Armagh was excavated in 1976, part of the early graveyard was discovered.[89] Although the nature of these graveyards is not always certain, and they may have held only nuns and patrons until after the medieval period, it is likely that at least the nunnery churches known to have been parochial would have had community graveyards attached. The presence of the nuns and their prayers would have enhanced the holiness of the cemetery and ensured the eternal protection of the dead.

Education

Educational services were also provided by some nuns in Ireland and these undoubtedly formed a part of their income. Recent estimates for English nunneries have suggested that there were never many children being educated in nunneries at any given time.[90] Most of the references to education in nunneries in Ireland concern convents in Anglo-Irish communities, so it is probable that Gaelic Irish nunneries would also have run schools of some sort. In one of Ware's later notebooks there is a reference suggesting the nuns of Hogges educated girls; he says that because the nuns of Hogges were considered to be elderly and thus staid, the women of Dublin entrusted them with their daughters.[91] St Peter's, Limerick, a small urban nunnery, was also reputed to have educated girls.[92] Both notices occur in late accounts without references to earlier material, and cannot be confirmed in contemporary sources, so they may represent later generations' assumptions that nuns would have educated girls.

There are also several contemporary reports of nuns operating schools, indicating that the education of children, particularly girls, was considered an

86 Smith, *The ancient and present state of Cork*, p. 383. **87** Comerford, *Collections from the dioceses of Kildare and Leighlin*, II, p. 117. **88** OS Letters, Co. Limerick (NLI Typescript copy), p. 107. **89** Reeves, "Ancient churches of Armagh", p. 203, for the description of the early discoveries of bones, and Lynn, "Recent archaeological excavations in Armagh City", p. 277, for the report of the 1976 excavation. **90** Educational services were also provided by nunneries in England. See inter alia, Power, *Medieval English nunneries*, pp 262–3ff, and Gardiner, "The English nobility and monastic education", pp 88–9. **91** BL Add MS 4813 f. 52. **92** Ó

important aspect of both the nunneries' economies and their social obligations. One of the services the group of early fourteenth-century Cork men wanted was a local house of nuns where "the knights and other free men might have their daughters brought up and maintained", as there was no other convent in the area.[93] As the history of the convent of the nunnery of St John's in Cork is very obscure, it is not known if the knights eventually did send their daughters to be educated with the nuns; however, the wording of the application suggests that education for girls was an expected and accepted service which nuns provided. In 1367 Lismullin had among its personnel five girls being trained to be nuns either in this house or others, and they may also have taken girls not necessarily destined for the cloister.[94] Odder was given an allowance in the 1530s by the crown for the care of children; whether these were their wards as holders of estates or young boys consigned to their care for education is not totally clear from the context.[95] Finally, in the shadow of the dissolution, Grace Dieu was one of six monastic houses which were commended to Cromwell by the lord deputy and council of Ireland to be spared because of "their value in educating men, women and children of the Englishry".[96] All these references suggest that some convents were engaged in providing education and care to young people, and that the nuns may have been particularly valued as educators who could be trusted to impart "English" values to girls. By the time of the dissolution, Bradshaw has argued, education, along with many other monastic services, was being provided by other sectors, with the sixteenth century seeing the increased establishment of secular schools which probably superseded the monastic ones.[97] However, secular schools may not have provided the same services for girls, and the nunneries may have continued to educate girls until the dissolution.

Welfare

Nuns, like monks, were expected to perform welfare services for the secular communities around them, including giving alms and supplying hospitality to travellers.[98] In English nunneries these services formed a distinct part of conventual expenditure and were carefully recorded in the cellarers' accounts.[99] Male monasteries in Ireland also allotted a portion of their income for alms. The canons of the priory of Holy Trinity, Dublin, for example, recorded a portion of their income in formal alms, as when on Holy Thursday 1344 Brother William Sterre was given 2*s.* 6*d.* to give out as alms.[100] Nunneries would have also received grants specifically for providing alms. The convent of St Mary del Hogges was to provide alms for the poor from the grant of 20*s.* annually from

Dalaigh, "Mistress, mother and abbess", p. 60. **93** *Cal. justic. rolls Ire., 1295–1307*, p. 155. **94** *Calendar Inquisitions post mortem, 1348–77*, p. 236. **95** *L.& P. Hen. VIII*, vol. 12, pt. 2, p. 465. **96** *L.& P. Hen. VIII*, vol. 14, pt. 1, p. 465. **97** Bradshaw, *Dissolution*, pp 222–6. **98** This was a universal expectation of monasteries in medieval Europe. See Leclerq, "Hospitality and monastic prayer", pp 5–10. **99** Power, *Medieval English nunneries*, pp 121–2; Thompson, *Women religious*, pp 42–3; Tillotson, "Visitation and reform", p. 18. **100** *Account Roll of Holy Trinity, Dublin*, p. 102.

lands of Margaret Gillemichelle in 1234, suggesting that the nuns were able to be quite generous with their almsgiving and that they were already involved in hospitality at this time.[101] Without foundation and other charter evidence for the majority of nunneries, it is not possible to be sure of the amounts donated for the specific provision for the poor, however nuns did allocate some of their resources for alms even when this caused considerable difficulties. In 1476, one of the reasons that Jenet White, prioress of Termonfeckin, used to support her request for relief from feudal dues on her lands was that she gave hospitality for the poor people and was thus reduced to poverty herself.[102] A similar reason was advanced by Margaret Heynot, prioress of Lismullin, for her request for permission to purchase more lands in order to continue to finance the usual operations of her priory.[103] Although such explanations may have been formulaic, there is no reason to suppose that the nuns of these houses did not provide hospitality and alms for the poor. When a writer in 1567 lamented the deplorable morals of the late nuns of Killone, he was forced to admit that "some relief was had there for the poor, feeding and clothing the needy, naked, hungry and impotent" and that since the dissolution of the nunnery these services were no longer provided from the income of the nunnery estates.[104] Another way that nuns might be able to support the laity was through corrodories or renting their properties cheaply to needy people. St Peter's, Limerick, possibly rented its gardens and cottages in Limerick to deserving widows and others.[105] The main evidence for corrodories in medieval Ireland is from the Hospitaller house at Kilmainham. It is probable, however, that nunneries were also involved in providing these services, although no evidence of such has so far been found.[106] Although the evidence for nunneries' contribution to lay communities is not as detailed as it is for English nunneries, there is sufficient evidence available to establish that the nunneries in Ireland were an important part of their communities and provided valued services.

RELIGIOUS WOMEN AND THEIR FAMILIES

One of the most obvious links between nunneries and local lay communities was through the personal connections of their nuns: to state the obvious, nuns came from lay families. The family background of medieval nuns is often difficult to ascertain. Nuns in Ireland, like the rest of Europe, would ideally have been expected to be from families with some material resources to provide for their maintenance, either through "dowry" grants or other patronage of the house.

101 *Cal. doc. Ire., 1171–1251*, p. 327. **102** *Statutes of Ireland, 12–22 Edward IV*, pp 420–1, 457. **103** *Statutes of Ireland, 12–22 Edward IV*, pp 288–9. **104** "A commentary on the nobility and gentry of Thomond", pp 70–1. **105** Ó Dálaigh, "Mistress, mother and abbess", p. 60, suggests that the nuns rented cottages and gardens to deserving widows. The inquisition he cites, however, includes both men and widows in equal numbers renting the properties. There is no way of knowing if these people were particularly deserving or poor. **106** Massey, *Prior Roger Outlaw*, pp 13–20.

Nuns also would have usually been expected to be literate to the same degree as other women of their class.[107] It appears that the family background of nuns in the English areas of medieval Ireland corresponded with the family background of most English nuns. Generally the nuns were from prominent, though not usually aristocratic, families of the English colony.[108] It is possible that women from Anglo-Irish magnate families who wished to become nuns were accommodated in the aristocratic English nunneries, as their families would have held considerable estates in England as well as Ireland.

The family backgrounds of some of the nuns in Ireland can be ascertained when their surnames are compared with surnames of known families. This is obviously an approach based to a large degree on speculation, as the nuns themselves are rarely mentioned in any family documents.[109] At Kilculliheen there were nuns with surnames from prominent local families such as Poer, Cantwell and Butler.[110] Another nun, Katherine Mothing, was possibly related to Nicholas Mothing, chancellor of St Canice's cathedral, who witnessed the definitive sentence of deposition against Elicia Butler, Katherine's predecessor as abbess.[111] The abbess of Hogges in 1361 was Margarete de Broun, who may have been a relative of William Broun, escheator of Ireland in the mid-fourteenth century.[112] Jonet Preston, a nun at Hogges in 1468, may have been from the family descended from Roger de Preston, a justice of the common bench in Dublin in the mid-fourteenth century.[113] One nun from Grace Dieu, Elizabeth Tanner, may be from the family of Robert Tanner, mayor of Dublin in 1339.[114] The last prioress of Molough in Co. Tipperary, in an area dominated by the Poer or Power family, was Joan Power.[115] The nuns of the wealthy house of Lismullin were from a similar mixture of prominent local families, with two members of the Cusack family – Elianora in the early fourteenth century and Mary at the dissolution. Another nun at Lismullin at the dissolution was Jenetta Barnwell, possibly from the Barnewall family based then at Drimnagh, near Dublin, but soon to take over the estates of Grace Dieu.[116] The prioress of Termonfeckin from about 1467 until at least 1480, Jenet White, may have been related to a prominent local family, including perhaps Alice White, a widow who in the early

107 Johnson, *Equal in monastic profession*, pp 144–5. For a discussion of dowry grants and the difficulty of ascertaining these, see Thompson, *Women religious*, pp 187–9. **108** There has been some debate about the class of the majority of English nuns; for a summary of the protagonists see MacDonald, "Women and the monastic life in late medieval Yorkshire", pp 43–5. **109** See Appendix 1. **110** Desiderata le Poer, abbess who resigned in 1277, *Cal. doc. Ire., 1252–1284*, p. 245; Elinia/Elicia Butler, abbess or abbesses from *c.*1478 until after 1540, and Anastasia Cantwell, nun at the dissolution, *Extents Ir. mon. possessions*, p. 206. **111** Katherine is also referred to as Isabelle in some documents. For an account of Nicholas see Graves and Prym, *The history, architecture and antiquaries of St Canice*, pp 266–7. **112** For Margarete de Broun, see BL MS 4789, f. 19v; for William Broun, see *Account Roll of Holy Trinity*, Dublin, p. 178. **113** *Register of wills*, ed. Berry, p. 177 and *Account roll of Holy Trinity, Dublin*, p. 184. **114** Elizabeth Tanner, *Cal. papal letters, 1404–1415*, p. 395; see *Account Roll of Holy Trinity, Dublin*, p. 155, for notes on Robert Tanner, mayor of Dublin. **115** *Extents Ir. mon. possessions*, p. 336. **116** *Extents Ir. mon. possessions*, p. 260; for information on the Barnewalls, see *Account roll of Holy*

fifteenth century held land in Callystown (Co. Louth), where the nuns of Termonfeckin also held lands and the rectory.[117] Alsona Plunket, probably from the prominent Meath family of that name, died in 1535 as prioress of Termonfeckin.[118]

Some family names recur over several generations in the nunneries of the pale, indicating that women and their families looked to the convent which had housed family members previously, or that the women chose to join the convent closest to them geographically and therefore best known to them and to their families.[119] There are three Hackett women recorded as being nuns of Grace Dieu at the same time in 1468: the prioress Elena, Joan and Katherine, who later became prioress.[120] Margarete de Broun, abbess of Hogges in the mid-fourteenth century, may have been related to Alicia Bron, also a nun of Hogges.[121] At Graney, there are two women of the de Rupe family: Matilda, who was prioress in the late thirteenth century, and Christina, prioress before 1317.[122] These women were probably from the local de Rupe family, descendants of Eustace de Rupe, prominent patron of the nunnery and feudal tenant of the founder, Walter de Riddlesford.[123] In the sixteenth century the last two prioresses of Graney were Elizabeth and Agidia Wale, who were probably related.[124] At Odder in 1467 there were two nuns with the same surname, Isabella and Margery Bermingham, who may have been from the same family as Thomasina Bermingham, prioress of Lismullin twenty years earlier.[125] Anne de Mandeville, prioress, and Margaret de Mandeville, of the nunnery of Down, are mentioned in the same year in 1353.[126] These women may have been from the prominent Mandeville family who provided several constables of Ulster.[127]

There were many other nuns whose families are obscure, probably meaning that they were local people who could afford the luxury of a daughter who was a nun, but were not of the wealthier gentry. Few of the entry dowry charters and other evidence of family finances of these women have survived. When Isabelle, relative of Robert FitzRichard, entered the convent of Timolin, she came with

Trinity, Dublin, p. 176 and Cullerton, "From barrow boy to viscount", pp 5–6. **117** White is a common name around Louth. See the entries under this name in *Dowdall deeds*. For Alice White's holdings at Callystown, see *Dowdall deeds*, p. 151. **118** "Reg. Cromer", *Louth Arch. Soc. Jn.* 10, pp 177–8. **119** This has been found in many studies of medieval nuns. See for example McNamara, *Sisters in arms*, pp 287ff, and Oliva, *Convent and community*, pp 52–61. **120** *Register of wills*, ed. Berry, p. 175. Katherine Hacket, prioress, is listed as a member of the confraternity of Christ Church cathedral. There is no date given for her death in the list of obits. *Book of Obits*, p. 71. **121** Alicia Bron's undated obit is recorded in *Book of Obits*, p. 82. It is possible that she is the same woman whose name is recorded as Alicia Vroun or Groun in *Cal. papal letters, 1342–1362*, p. 470. **122** *Cal. anc. rec. Dublin*, pp 98–9. **123** Brooks, "de Ridelisfords", pp 127–8. Eustace de Rupe married one of Walter de Riddlesford's daughters Sonanda and witnessed several charters. **124** Fitzgerald, "The priory and nunnery of Graney", p. 376, and Archdall (1786), pp 316–17, citing the Chief Remembrancer. **125** Isabella and Margery, see *Statutes of Ireland, 1–12 Edward IV*, pp 338–41; Thomasina, see TCD MS 654 f. 117v. **126** *Cal. papal letters, 1342–1362*, pp 503, 509. **127** See "Abstracts of Manderville deeds", pp 3–5, for brief a summary of the Mandeville family primarily in the fifteenth and sixteenth century. For the Mandevilles in Louth see Smith, "Tenure and locality", p. 31.

an amount of land and castles donated by Robert de Start or Stanton, who may have been her brother.[128] One nun of Grace Dieu, Amicia, was the co-heiress to land with her sister when she entered the convent in the later years of the thirteenth century, suggesting that she was of a prosperous family.[129] Such details suggest that these women were from families in the prosperous burgess or small land-holding class who could afford the luxury of endowing a daughter for the convent rather than for marriage and may have welcomed closer ties with the convents.

The known names of nuns and religious women from Gaelic Ireland are almost always from the ruling families, although difficulty in identifying different members of the same very wide kin groups obscures relationships, as does the tendency of later genealogists to omit unmarried females from their research. From the few known names of the great Gaelic nunneries of the later medieval period, it would appear that the nunneries were staffed by members of the same kin groups and were almost certainly all relatives. All the known names from the nunnery of Kilcreevanty are Uí Chonchobair and the nuns of Killone were all Uí Bhriain.[130] The three known abbesses in the fifteenth and sixteenth centuries of Killevy, in Co. Armagh, are from the Ó hAnluain family, who dominated the area surrounding the convent.[131] At Clonard, between its foundation in the late twelfth century and the early fourteenth century when the names became English, there were three abbesses from the family of the founder, Ó Maíl Sechnaill, and some of the other abbesses, only known by first names, were probably from this family as well.

There is more detailed information about the families of very few nuns. Records about two of the Ó Briain abbesses of Killone have survived because they were mothers of children who later felt it was important to prove their identities. Renalda Ní Bhriain's first son was fathered by John Butler, later sixth earl of Ormond, in 1462 and became known as James Dubh Butler. She later married another Butler, Richard, baron of Knockgraffon in Co. Tipperary, and had at least one other son, Thomas. It is probable that she lived at Knockgraffon until after her first son's death in 1496 at the hands of Piers Butler, later eighth earl of Ormond.[132] It is the connections with the Butlers which have ensured the survival of evidence for Renalda and her later retirement to Killone.[133] Her will is witnessed by another nun surnamed Ó Briain, Caterine, who is described as a nun and devotee of Renalda's. Renalda's later successor as abbess of Killone,

128 There is no date for this donation, but it was probably twelfth- or thirteenth-century, prior to the laws of Mortmain which would have complicated such a donation. *Alen's reg.*, p. 306. **129** Amicia and her sister Matilda were heirs of Robert son of Roger; since Amicia, as a nun, could not inherit, the land passed to Matilda and then to her nephew John fitz Richard. These events occurred *c.*1280 and were recorded for 1302. See "Calendar of common bench roll, T 30 Ed. I, roll 63" (NAI RC 7/9), p. 440. **130** See Appendix 1 for names and references. **131** See Appendix 1 for references, for the Ua hAnluain see O'Sullivan, "The march of south-east Ulster", p. 57. **132** Neely, "The Ormond Butlers of County Kilkenny", pp 107–8 and Ó Dálaigh, "Mistress, mother and abbess", pp 52–3. **133** NLI MS D 1978, and she is noted in the genealogies of the Butlers as the mother of James Dubh and Richard

Ónora, also a member of the Uí Bhriain, later married Sir Ruaidrí Ó Seachnasaigh, and their warring grandchildren were later quick to point out that she was a nun at the time of the birth of her elder children.[134] She was likely to have been a relatively young woman at the time of the dissolution, and may have married either before or soon after it became clear that Killone was to be dissolved.[135] Renalda's retirement at Killone and Ónora's marriage must have occurred under Ó Briain protection, demonstrating the importance of family relationships to religious women.

Mary Cusack was the sister of Sir Thomas Cusack, later chancellor of Ireland.[136] His job in the 1540s was as one of the commissioners surveying the monastic properties within the Pale.[137] He then acquired the priory of Lismullin with all its holdings and established his main residence there. Elicia Butler, abbess of Kilculliheen in the early sixteenth century, was also well connected, as the sister of Piers Butler, later eighth earl of Ormond and the effective controller of the vast Ormond territories from the death of his father, the seneschal of the earlier absentee Earls.

Information on some women can be found in papal dispensations for various faults. Some women were illegitimate or unable by some other difficulty with the canonical legality of their birth to take up office with their convents. They then, like so many of their brothers throughout medieval Ireland, appealed for papal dispensation.[138] It is possible that these women may have entered conventual life because their illegitimacy rendered them unsuitable as wives, but this is unlikely given the large numbers of men who sought such dispensations at the time, indicating that Anglo- and Gaelic Irish communities had a fairly relaxed attitude to the strict legalities of marriage laws, except when these came headlong into conflict with the laws of the church in preferment for ecclesiastical office. The number of women known to have been dispensed for illegitimacy is not large. Those whose names are known come mostly from the later medieval period, when records are better preserved, and also when papal dispensations were both easier to obtain and more readily used in Ireland. In 1446/7 for example, Gormelina Ní Chonchobair, nun of Kilcreevanty, was granted dispensation for being daughter of uncanonically wed parents.[139] Dispensations were not

Butler's son. **134** The dispute between the descendants of Ónora occurred in 1616. *Cal. pat. rolls Ire., Jas. I.*, p. 301, and *The genealogies, tribes and customs of Hy-Fiachrach*, p. 379. **135** There is no record of her age, but one of the witnesses to the legitimacy of her grandchildren was her sister, who was described as being over 80 years of age in 1616 – therefore born not long before the dissolution of the monasteries. With serial and concurrent marriages common among Gaelic leaders at the time, it would not have been unusual for siblings to be widely separated in age, but this does suggest that her sister would have been a young woman in the 1540s. **136** Maria Cusack from Odder is probably the same woman as Mary Cusack, prioress of Lismullin. However, there were several branches of the Cusack family in the area and there is no direct proof that they were the same woman. **137** See "Accounts of sums", p. 12; see also Bradshaw, *Dissolution* p. 103. **138** Dispensations would also have been available from bishops, but since episcopal records have survived so poorly, the records extant are from papal archives. **139** *Cal. papal letters, 1447–55*, p. 351.

restricted to Gaelic Irish nuns, but also included several women with Anglo-Irish names. Alice Groun or Vroun, nun of Hogges, was granted a dispensation because of illegitimacy in 1352.[140] Margaret Tuyt, nun of Clonard in 1409, and Elizabeth Tanner of Grace Dieu in 1412, were dispensed as being the daughters of priests and unmarried women, while in 1511 Joanna Barrett, nun of Lismullin, was dispensed as the daughter of a lay woman and a canon.[141] These women would not have been prevented from becoming nuns by their illegitimacy but would not have been eligible for higher office without the dispensations. There is no further mention of any of these women; however, it may be safe to assume that some, if not all, of them did succeed to office within their nunneries.

Apart from names, there is little else known of the lives of nuns in convents in medieval Ireland. Although some were young when professed – Mary Cusack was probably less than thirty at the dissolution and Elicia Butler was also possibly young when she entered Kilculliheen – the nuns' ages on entering religious life are not known nor their life expectancy inside the convent walls.[142] The nuns of Hogges and Kilculliheen were traditionally supposed to be aged over thirty at their profession, and preferably widows, although little else is known about them.[143] Nuns were expected to live out their lives within their convents, and there are some prioresses and abbesses who retired because of old age. The communities also housed both young novices and children or adolescents being educated or cared for before life outside the convent. These, together with lay corrodarians, and retired and elderly nuns, would have made for communities of mixed abilities and experiences. As argued in the previous chapter, the number of nuns in the nunneries in Ireland is difficult to ascertain with any certainty, but they were small compared to English nunneries and may never have had more than a dozen nuns at any one time, usually far less.[144]

Office bearers

All the nunneries in Ireland had a prioress or abbess as superior, depending on the legal status of the convent, and usually it is the abbess or prioress who is named in the sources.[145] Whether the other offices usually occupied in monastic houses were also filled in nunneries in Ireland is not really known.[146] The great abbeys of the English areas of Ireland, St Mary del Hogges, Clonard and

140 *Cal. papal letters, 1342–62*, p. 470. She may have been surnamed Broun and so related to Margarete Broun, abbess of Hogges in 1361. **141** *Cal. papal letters, 1404–15*, pp 159, 395. For Johanna Barrett, see Haren, "Social structures", p. 218. **142** For discussion and evidence about Elicia's identity and age see Chapter 7. **143** This is not from a contemporary source, but from notes made by James Ware, BL Add MS 4813, f. 50. For Kilculliheen see Burke, "The nunnery of Kilculliheen", p. 10. The source for Burke's information is not given, and he may have assumed that since the nuns of Hogges were older then the nuns of Kilculliheen, dependent on Hogges at its foundation, were also. **144** See chapter 5. Oliva, "Counting nuns", pp 37–8 which demonstrates that the average for the nunneries of Norwich was between 8 and 20 with most about 10. **145** See Preston, "The canons regular of St Augustine", pp 84–6, which notes the often rather fluid differences between status as priory and abbey. Generally Arroasian houses were known as abbeys and Augustinian were known as priories. **146** Preston, "The canons regular of St Augustine", pp 96–101, notes the internal

Kilculliheen, did fill the office of prioress as well as abbess during the thirteenth and fourteenth centuries and probably later as well. The abbey of St Mary del Hogges also probably had a sub-prioress at this time.[147] The prioress of Hogges succeeded as abbess on at least two occasions and since this was a recognized path of promotion it is likely that this occurred more often than surviving records indicate.[148] In 1271, the prioress R. requested permission to elect a successor for Agneta, and then in 1277 the abbey was reporting the death of their abbess, Roesia, who was probably the same woman.[149] Margaret is called prioress in 1295, and then is referred to as abbess in 1297, with her death recorded in 1309.[150] The abbey of Kilculliheen also had both abbess and prioress, with references to the prioress requesting permission to elect abbesses from 1264 until 1300.[151] There are also prioresses reported for Clonard from about 1282 until 1326.[152] At least one of these prioresses probably succeeded as abbess: Sibil was prioress in 1295, then Sibyl, daughter of McGoyhan, was abbess from about 1319 until 1326.[153] The dates represented here are due to archival survival and do not suggest that there were no prioresses earlier or later. It is likely that the office of prioress survived throughout the medieval period.

organisation of male Augustinian houses in Ireland, although she acknowledges that she is hampered by a lack of sources for definitive analysis, p. 96. **147** The prioress or sub-prioress was often noted at the time of election of new abbesses. R. prioress, 1271 – *Cal. doc. Ire., 1252–84*, p. 153; prioress in licence to elect new abbess in 1309, see *Cal. pat. rolls, 1307–13*, pp 193–4; in 1386/7 see *Rot. pat. Hib.*, p. 149; sub-prioress noted in 1408/9, *Rot. pat. Hib.*, p. 192. Other named holders of the office of prioress are Margaret, prioress in 1295, see TCD MS 654 f. 106v. Cecilia, prioress in 1336–1340, TCD MS 654 f. 78v. **148** Some references to these women are difficult to decipher, since they are later notes and calendars of originals. It is certain that sometimes the offices of prioress and abbess were confused in the sources, probably because most of the convents in Ireland were officially priories and headed by prioresses. For example, Madden's notes gives Cecilia as a prioress of St Mary del Hogges in 1336 until 1340 on one page and on another page refers to Cecilia as abbess for the same dates, then there are references to a Cecilia as abbess in the Record Commissioners' calendars in 1336. This could be referring to two women named Cecilia occupying the offices of prioress and abbess at the same time, however since both sources are not contemporary it must also be a probability that one was mistaken. Since the references in the Calendars are to court cases where it was customary for the legal head of the convent to appear, it is most likely that Cecilia was abbess, not priores, at this time. See TCD MS 654 f. 78v; 106v and the "Calendars of De Banco roll 10 Ed III" (NAI. RC 8/20), p. 115 and "Calendar of Mem' Sacc 10 Ed III", pp 418–19. **149** *Cal. doc. Ire., 1252–84*, p. 248. **150** TCD MS 654 f. 106v; "Calendar of common bench roll, 24 Ed I, no. 22", (NAI RC 7/3), p. 285; her death *Cal. pat. rolls, 1307–13*, pp 193–4. **151** *Cal. doc. Ire., 1252–84*, pp 121, 245, 253, 444. *Cal. doc. Ire., 1285–92*, p. 145; *Cal. doc. Ire. 1293–1301* p. 357. TCD MS 654 f. 111v has a doubtful reference beside the name of Ismay of Kilculliheen, which could be prioress or more probably a surname such as Poer. **152** *Cal. doc. Ire., 1252–84*, pp 436; 511; *Cal. doc. Ire., 1285–92*, pp 109, 177, 184, 194; *Cal. doc. Ire., 1293–1301*, p. 117; *Cal. pat. rolls, 1307–13*, pp 290–1; *Rot. pat. Hib.*, p. 23; *Cal. pat. rolls, 1324–7*, p. 251. **153** Sibil the prioress is recorded in 1295. *Cal. doc. Ire., 1293–1301*, p. 117. Sibil daughter of McGoyhan was elected abbess sometime between 1317 and 1320, "Cat. Pipe rolls, Ed. II" p. 19; a Sibil, abbess, died in 1326. *Cal. pat. rolls, 1324–27*, p. 251.

At Kilculliheen the pension lists at the dissolution reflect what was probably the different status of the nuns, with the abbess receiving the highest pension, then three nuns who received £6 between them. The two other nuns in the list were the deposed abbess, Elicia Butler, who received 53*s.* 4*d.*, and Anastasia Cantwell with 46*s.* 8*d.* Although this cannot be proved, it is possible that the difference in Anastasia's pension was that she held the office of prioress and so was accorded greater rights than the other nuns named.[154] The pension lists for Hogges and Clonard/Odder are not as clear, with only the abbess of Hogges mentioned, while at Odder the abbess received her pension and, of the three other nuns, one received 20*s.* and the other two 40*s.*[155] These differences could reflect office holders, or they could also reflect differences in seniority or in the amount of property brought to the nunnery at profession.

Usually the office of prioress or abbess was for life, but there were a number of instances recorded where the office was declared vacant for reasons other than the death of the incumbent. The most usual of these was when the infirmities of old age made retirement necessary. So in 1450 Joan, abbess of Kilculliheen, retired because she was "so old and weak that she cannot rule and administer" the convent.[156] It is likely that elderly retired nuns were supported within the convent until their deaths as they were in English and European convents. At the dissolution Elicia Gaal was described as the "late" abbess and was still in residence at Kilculliheen to receive her pension. There were, however, many other reasons which might necessitate the resignation of an abbess. In English nunneries there is ample evidence that nunnery superiors sometimes found that their rule was ineffective because of dissension within the ranks of the nuns, forcing the resignation of the head of the house.[157] There are several instances where this may have occurred in the nunneries of Ireland, though the lack of any evidence besides the requests for permission to elect new officers usually makes definitive judgment impossible. In the convent of Kilculliheen, the abbess Desiderata le Poher resigned in 1277.[158] Only five years later, the next abbess, Mabila de Curcy, also resigned and appears to have been replaced by Desiderata, who finally died in 1287, a full ten years after her initial resignation.[159] There are many scenarios which would fit these facts, including the illness and then recovery of Desiderata. It is also possible that Desiderata resigned because of factional disagreements within the nunnery and then came into favour again and her successor was forced into resignation. At Clonard in the troubled years of the close of the thirteenth century, the declining fortunes of the Ua Máel Sechlainn family were possibly influential in the deposition of Fingola ni Melgahlin in 1284. It is likely that her father was Art na gCaislean Ua Maél Sechlainn, who fought for years against the English in Meath.[160] However, as she died shortly

154 *Cal. pat. rolls Ire., Hen. VIII-Eliz.*, I, p. 61. **155** *Extents Ir. mon. possessions*, pp 72, 262. **156** *Cal. papal letters, 1447–55*, p. 508. **157** Power, *Medieval English nunneries*, pp 46–57. **158** *Cal. doc. Ire., 1252–84*, p. 245. **159** *Cal. doc. Ire., 1252–84*, p. 444; *Cal. doc. Ire., 1285–92*, p. 145. **160** Brady, "The nunnery of Clonard", p. 4.

afterwards, her removal from office may have also been to do with infirmity.[161] In October 1288, the nuns of Clonard notified the crown that they had elected Burgenilda as abbess; but shortly afterwards they were forced to report her resignation.[162] There is no other available evidence as to the circumstances in this instance, and again the sudden illness of Burgenilda may have necessitated her resignation, but the possibility that her election was not welcomed by significant sections of the convent must also be entertained.

The abbess of Temple Na Ferta in Armagh seems to have become the victim of a faction or party who wished to take over her position. Although the details are scanty, in 1430 Mary ingen Mcumab appealed to the archbishop of Armagh to help her protect her position from unnamed persons.[163] In the context of the divided province of Armagh this perhaps suggests that her difficulties were with local, well-connected people. The province of Armagh was effectively divided in the fifteenth century and the archbishop governed the Irish section through deputies, although he was still recognized by the laity and ecclesiastics in the area *inter hibernicos*.[164] Because of this, Archbishop Swayne directed his letter supporting the abbess to David McGillade, prior of the Culdees of Armagh. There is no indication of the result of his efforts, but it is probable that Mary was facing an internal revolt which threatened to deprive her of office, possibly supported by powerful factions among the church and laity of Armagh. Kilculliheen was the convent embroiled in the best documented case of internal dissension, which resulted in the abbess, Elicia Butler, being deprived of office in 1531. The circumstances surrounding this will be discussed in greater detail below.

Nunneries not only had to cope with internal dissension. There were also problems with discipline and diminishing numbers. These were more common in the religious houses in later medieval Ireland when the political landscapes were constantly changing and there was considerable decrease in incomes because of desertion and destruction on estates. Breakdown in celibacy is one of the most-often cited indicators of the strife-ridden state of later medieval monastic houses in Ireland. As noted above, although there were obviously many instances where monastic men and women broke their vows of celibacy, there is also evidence that in some parts of the country, particularly in the Gaelic areas, cleric and monastic celibacy was not viewed as being a priority in selection of personnel to staff clerical vacancies.[165] It is likely then that charges of immorality

161 *AClon*. 1286. **162** The date she resigned is not clear. The calendar entries give Oct 16 1288 [Patent rolls. 16 Ed I, m. 4] as the date of her election and then June 10 [Royal letters 2836] and July 12 1288 [Patent rolls 16 Ed I. m. 10] as the date of her resignation. The latter is probably misdated, however she is described as being "recently elected" in this report, so it was certainly shortly after her election, probably the following year. *Cal. doc. Ire. 1285–92*, pp 177, 184, 194. **163** *Reg. Swayne* p. 128. **164** For discussion of this situation see Watt, *Church in medieval Ireland*, pp 202–4, and "Ecclesia inter Anglicos et inter Hibernicos", pp 46–64, and now Jeffries, *Priests and prelates*. **165** Watt, *Church in medieval Ireland*, p. 186 ff. For a discussion of the cultural differences between Anglo-Irish and Gaelic Irish ecclesiastics on hereditary succession to office see Simms, "Frontiers in the Irish church", pp 178–83.

based on lack of celibacy were usually based on other considerations and were often linked with lax administration of monastic estates and used to oust nuns, priests and monks who did not measure up to standard.

Assessing these charges is made all the more difficult because of the long-acknowledged propensity for Irish clerics to appeal for provision of benefices to the papacy in order for offices to be declared vacant and a more suitable appointment made. Since these appointments were usually made in favour of the complainant there is considerable evidence of abuse of this system and doubt as to the validity of some of the charges made.[166] There are two instances of complaints related to late medieval nunneries. Kilculliheen was the subject of a complaint by the patron Sir James Butler, third earl of Ormond, in 1427 in which he complained that the nuns of the house led "dissolute, unreligious and immodest" lives and that "very many inconveniences and scandals had arisen and more were feared".[167] James wanted to establish a collegiate church on the site and endow it with the convents assets. At about the same time, in 1432, James, earl of Desmond, complained about the convent of St Catherine d'Conyl in similar terms, claiming that the nuns lived dissolute lives and that the only remaining nun had married and been deprived of her office by the bishop of Limerick.[168]

Although the complaint against Kilculliheen did not result in disbanding of the house, the convent at St Catherine d'Conyl probably was suppressed.[169] There was a tradition in the early nineteenth century among the people living nearby that St Catherine d'Conyl had been suppressed prior to the Reformation and that the last prioress, a FitzGerald, had remained at the convent, taking up witchcraft and fortune-telling, and living to a great age in the sacristy of the church, known afterwards as the "Black hag's cell" because her face was quite black with age.[170] There are several possible historical explanations for this tradition, including that part at least of the story was derived from the Irish name for the site, Monasternagalliaghduffe – Monastery of the black nun, with subsequent blurring of the meaning between the Irish word for nun and for hag or old woman.[171] It is also quite possible that the story is true in its details about a nun staying on after the dissolution of the nunnery.

Other religious women

So far religious women considered have all been professed nuns living in recognized institutions. This is, however, a rather restricted category of religious

166 "Rome running" as it was called has been long recognised as rife within the Irish church., See also Watt, *Church in medieval Ireland*, pp 188–93, and Nicholls, *Gaelic and Gaelicised Ireland*, pp 96–7, 102–5. **167** *Cal. papal letters, 1417–31*, p. 522. **168** *Cal. papal letters, 1427–47*, pp. 400–1. **169** The date the convent was dissolved is unclear; the date of the complaint of Desmond is 1432, while the date at which Alan Olongsichh was appointed to the rectory of the "suppressed order of nuns of St Catherine de Oconil" before 1429. "Obligationes pro annatis diocesis Limiricensis", p. 111 and note 21. **170** Wardell, "History and antiquities of St Catherine's Old Abbey", pp 50–1. **171** For the different possibilities of meanings for the word "caílleach" and the conflation of meaning between nun and hag see Ní Dhonnchadha,

women, excluding many women who lived religious lives. Women living as nuns in private homes are well attested in other parts of Europe throughout the medieval period. In the Lowlands, many of these women eventually joined or followed the women who were known as Beguines.[172] Although there is no evidence for any sort of similar women's religious movement in Ireland, there are instances of individual women who were not members of any of the recognised convents. To some extent this may be due to survival of evidence, since the annalists and some papal records often did not mention the convent to which nuns belonged, and most of these women living outside institutions would not have been noticed by contemporary record keepers. This may be the explanation for the way Isabella Palmer was described on her death in 1347. She was a wealthy Kilkenny woman who died at the age of seventy, reportedly a virgin though having been married several times.[173] Her material support for the Franciscans of Kilkenny suggests that she was a pious woman who may have lived under private vows. Often privately vowed religious women were only noticed because they were in some sort of difficulty, as in 1401 when Margaret Ballagh of Galway appealed to the king because, although she had taken a vow of chastity in her youth, she was now subject to harassment by "evilly disposed" people.[174] If Margaret was of the Anglo-Irish merchant class of Galway, as her name suggests, there would have been few opportunities for following a religious life in a recognised nunnery. The nearest convent was the Gaelic-Irish house controlled by Ó Conchobair at Kilcreevanty and its small dependencies, which were probably closed to her.

The convent to which other women may have belonged can now sometimes be guessed from their name and location. So when Duibhessa, a daughter of Ruairdí Uí Conchobair and wife of Cathal Mac Diarmait, died a nun in 1230, she may have been living in Kilcreevanty where others from her extended family became nuns.[175] Other women cannot be placed firmly within the orbit of any particular nunnery. Bean-Midhe, daughter of MacMaghnusa, died as a nun in 1362, and may have belonged to a convent, or she may have lived as a nun privately.[176] Another is Finemhain, daughter of MacThomas, who died a "devout nun" in 1442.[177]

There were also women who were described as anchorites or hermits in both Gaelic and Anglo-Irish areas. In 1300, Roesia de Naungles, an anchorite, sued Adam de Trym for debt in the court of the justiciar at Dublin. Although her place of residence was not recorded it is likely to have been in or near Dublin.[178] There were other known recluses attached to churches within Dublin and some of these were women. Robert de Moenes, a prominent Dublin citizen, bequeathed money in 1326 to a female recluse at St Paul's, as well as money to two male

"Caillech", pp 93–4. Augustinian nuns wore black habits; see for example Clark-Maxwell, "The outfit for the profession of an Austin Canoness", p. 119. **172** The literature on the Beguines is large. See in general McNamara, *Sisters in arms*, pp 239–42 ff, for an overview. **173** *The annals of Ireland by John Clyn and Thady Dowling*, 34. **174** Cited in "Irish material in the class of Chancery warrants", p. 160. See also *Cal. pat. rolls, 1399–1401*, p. 409. **175** *AFM; AConn.; ALC* note her death. **176** *AU.* **177** *AU.* **178** *Cal. justic. rolls Ire., 1295–1307*, p. 313.

recluses at different churches.[179] Two other religious women were left money in Robert's will, and were described as sororibus minoribus, which usually refers to Franciscan nuns.[180] These women may also have been living as recluses attached to a church or to the Franciscan friary in Dublin, as there is no record of a community of Poor Clares in Dublin. Outside Dublin there were also women living as hermits: Gormalaigh, daughter of David O Duibhgen and wife of Brian Mac Aedacain, was an anchorite, attached to the Premonstratensian Canons of Trinity Island, Loch Cé, when she died.[181] Some anchorites were also supported by nunneries, living on their granges or attached to dependent churches. The anchorite Felicia lived on property belonging to the convent of Grace Dieu.[182] The nuns of Hogges were obliged to use the church courts in order to remove an anchorite named Maria from their church of Aghade and grange at Kilselli.[183] Women may also have continued to live as anchorites on land owned by nunneries, such as at Fore; in an area where nuns were recorded in the twelfth century and since then owned by Clonard, there was a house known in the sixteenth century as the "domus anchoristarum".[184]

In other parts of the country there are less tangible signs that women lived as vowesses or as recluses. Vowesses were usually women who took vows of chastity and piety after their widowhood and lived in private.[185] In St Canice's cathedral there is an early fourteenth-century incised gravestone of a woman who by her dress could be either a nun or a vowess.[186] It is possible that she was a nun of Kilculliheen, since this was the only significant convent in the diocese of Ossory. It is also possible that she was a recluse or vowess attached to the cathedral. Less definite evidence for religious women living in private homes comes from the old name for part of the castle at Moygara in Sligo, where the northwest tower was known as Teach na calliagh or house of the nun, and may refer to a time when a religious woman lived there. However, it is not possible to give a firm date to this, and it may refer to a woman who lived there after the dissolution of her convent, possibly Killaraght on the other side of Lough Gara or possibly from the post-medieval period when there were few opportunities for women to follow religious lives in Ireland. Given the difficulties with the meanings of the word "calliagh" it may also mean the house of the widow or veiled one, which may suggest that it was used as the home not of a nun but of a widow.[187]

There were other avenues open for women who wished to serve God in a religious institution besides the expensive option of choir nuns or the precarious one of recluse. There were a number of hospitals and hospices in Ireland, as in

The court was sitting in Dublin, it is not recorded where Roesia lived. **179** TCD MS 1207/85–26. **180** Ibid. **181** *AConn.* 1437. **182** NLI MS 13, f. 143; also discussed by Archdall (1786), p. 131. Betham's extracts from the rolls puts the date for Felicia's suit at 1308. Dublin Genealogical Office, MS 190, p. 25. **183** BL Egerton, MS 1774, f. 152. **184** *Fiants Hen. VIII-Eliz*, III, p. 453. **185** Erler, "English vowed women", pp 155–203 and Cullum, "Vowesses", p. 21. **186** Hunt, *Irish medieval figure sculpture*, I, p. 184. **187** O'Rorke, *History of Sligo*, II, pp 364–5 and for the multiple meanings of calliagh see Ní Dhonnchadha, "Caillech"

other parts of medieval Europe, which were staffed by men and women who took religious vows and followed a religious rule, while working tending the elderly, sick and poor who lived in or visited their houses.[188] The largest and best-documented of these houses is the Hospital of St John the Baptist outside the Newgate in Dublin, where the brothers and sisters followed the Augustinian Rule as Fratres Cruciferi.[189] This house was established by a married couple, Aelred Palmer and his wife, before 1188, when both took monastic vows and lived in their foundation.[190] The name of one woman who followed them shortly afterwards is known: Emeline, relative of Robert de Aveneio, entered the hospital as a nun in about 1190 accompanied by a generous grant of lands.[191] The sisters worked there alongside the brothers throughout its history, although there are very few mentions of them after the close of the thirteenth century.[192] The women probably cared for women inmates and possibly also did the expert weaving of ecclesiastical vestments for other Dublin houses which was undertaken at this priory.[193] Other hospitals which accepted women as members of staff were St John the Baptist's priory at Ardee; St John the Baptist, Drogheda, and the hospital and priory of St Leonard's, Dundalk, where it is thought that the women who staffed the little hospital of St Mary Magdalene were transferred in the late twelfth century.[194] There was also a leper hospital of St Mary Magdalene in Wexford which was staffed by men and women. It was founded by Strongbow before 1176, and there are references to the sisters as well as brothers in 1389 and 1408.[195]

Both the hospitals of St John the Evangelist, Waterford and Cork, were dependencies of the Benedictine monastery of St Peter's, Bath, and were staffed by monks and sisters.[196] The hospital of St John in Waterford also seems to have had a dependency known as St Leonard, where four brothers and four sisters lived.[197] It is not entirely clear from the foundation charter, issued by Robert Bottiller in 1468, whether the women were considered to be carers or among the destitute needing care.[198] In practice there was probably not much difference between the two categories, as inmates of most hospitals were required to live

pp 89–94. **188** The history of hospitals in England is interesting and has parallels with the ways in which hospitals were established and maintained in Ireland. See Gilchrist, *Gender and material culture*, pp 172–6. **189** *Med. rel. houses Ire.* pp 208–9 and 212. **190** *Pont. Hib.*, I, pp 61–3. **191** *Reg. St John Dublin*, pp 172–3. **192** The grant of alms from the crown in 1334 mentions only the 155 sick tended by the prior and brethren. *Cal. pat. rolls, 1330–34*, p. 552. **193** It is not certain how the work within hospitals staffed by men and women was divided; Gilcrhist, *Contemplation and action*, p. 16, suggests that sometimes women would do more of the physical care for inmates than male staff. For the weaving, see Archdall (1872) II, p. 61. **194** For the priory at Ardee see *Med. rel. houses Ire.*, p. 210, and Archdall (1786), p. 446; the brothers and sisters of St John the Baptist Drogheda are mentioned in a charter in *Reg. Trist.*, pp 25–6. For St Leonard's see *Med. rel. houses Ire.*, pp 212–13, see also Curran, "The priory of St Leonard, Dundalk", pp 138–9. **195** NLI MS 13, f. 141. See also Archdall (1786) p. 820 and Lee, *Leper hospitals* p. 59. **196** *Reg. St Saviour*, pp 206–7, 213–5. For the dependency of Cork with two brothers and two sisters see "Cat. Pipe rolls, Ed. III", *PRI rep. DK* 44 (1912) p. 30. **197** Power, "The priory of St John the Evangelist, Waterford", 81–97. **198** Power, "The priory of St John the Evangelist, Waterford", p. 83 suggests that they were destitute and under a quasi-religious rule and were often only admitted under recommendation of the patrons. Margareta Herbard, for instance, entered the hospital with the rents from land. Whether this was similar to an entry dowry or as corrodory is not entirely clear, but it probably made little practical difference, as from the wording of the charter Margareta was intending to stay in the hospital for life.[199] Although there is no record of any religious women serving at the priory and hospital of St John the Baptist at Kells, there survives a medieval sculpture from the priory graveyard which represents a woman in the habit of a nun and holding a staff.[200] It is thus possible that this priory did accept women religious, or that religious women who were not attached to other nunneries were buried in the graveyard. There was a small nunnery at Kells in the twelfth century which was a dependency of Clonard, although it is presumed to have failed in the thirteenth century. Hunt dates the figure in the graveyard as thirteenth century, so it may be from this small nunnery rather than the hospital.

There were also hospices and hospitals which were staffed entirely or almost entirely by women living under a monastic rule. There is one reference to a leper hospital in Tipperary which was under the care of Agnes in 1312. This may have been a short-lived establishment, however there is a townland near Tipperary town known as Spittle field, which usually indicates it was the site of a leper house.[201] At Ballynagalliagh near Drumcliffe, Co. Sligo, there was a chapel where several nuns caring for the sick and poor were living in 1426.[202] Drumcliffe was an early Irish religious centre for hospitality, with the erenagh, Amhlaibh O Beollain, who died in 1225, praised as the principal holder of hospitality and guest houses in Ireland.[203] The hospital staffed by nuns there possibly cared for women and children, with the nuns being subject to Kilcreevanty, as land and tithes from Ballynagalliagh and Drumcliffe were among the possessions of Kilcreevanty in the early seventeenth century.[204] The convent at Killaraght also probably supported a hospital, although almost nothing is known about it.[205] Some women may have established hospitals which lasted only during their lifetime. One example of this may have been when Saive ingen Oconnolan sought permission in 1456 to establish a hospice in the church lands at Donoghmore and to live "continently".[206] From these scattered references it seems likely that women who wished to live as religious women and care for the sick could do so in many parts of medieval Ireland, in private houses or on church lands. It is likely that many more did so than have left any historical trace, particularly in the Gaelic Irish areas where so few medieval records have survived.

needing care. For the difficulty of distinguishing between nun and inmates see Thompson, *Women religious*, p. 38. **199** *Reg. St Saviour*, pp 153–7. **200** Hickey, "A medieval stone at St John's cemetary", pp 104–5, and Hunt, *Irish medieval figure sculpture*, I, p. 206. **201** The reference to Agnes, guardian of the leper house, is in one of the Record Commissioners' Calendars. "Calendar of justiciary rolls, 6 Ed. II" (NAI MS KB 2/4), p. 384. As this is the only reference, it may be corrupt and refer not to an Agnes but to a variant of a male name. **202** "Obligationes pro annatis diocesis Elphinensis", p. 6. **203** *Med. rel. houses Ire.*, p. 34, and ALC. **204** *Cal. pat. rolls Ire., Jas. I*, p. 179, the place names identified by Knox, *History of Tuam*, p. 284. **205** O'Rorke, *History of Sligo*, p. 371. **206** *Registrum Iohannis Mey*, p. 324.

Other women, most notably significant patrons of monasteries, settled in or near male monasteries and lived in pious retirement, not necessarily under any specific rule, though probably with spiritual guidance from the monastic staff. This was a common practice among French Cistercian houses where women patrons were likely to obtain places in which to retire and seek spiritual counsel in the time before death.[207] The earliest known Anglo-Norman woman to retire in this way was Basilia, sister of Strongbow and significant patron of St Thomas's in Dublin, who retired there around 1200.[208] Gerald of Wales, that anxious moral critic, roundly denounced the admission of benefactresses to the Cistercian house of St Mary's in Dublin.[209] Women such as Duvcovlagh, daughter of Conor Mac Dermot, who died in the monastery of Boyle in 1231, may have been living there in retirement, or may have gone there in her last illness to take on the monastic robes and so enjoy the advantages of a monastic in death.[210] Some women retired to monasteries and may have died in the habit of the monastic as many men did. One such woman was Ailbh, who retired to Lisgoole in 1477.[211]

The Third Order of the Franciscans arrived in Ireland in the fifteenth century and was enthusiastically adopted particularly by the Gaelic Irish.[212] Papal letters about the Third Order in Ireland were addressed to both men and women, including permission in 1454 for the foundation of a house of the Third Order for brothers and sisters at court in Co. Sligo.[213] Gwynn and Hadcock – following other historians of the Franciscans – argue, however, that there were no women involved until the post-medieval period.[214] Nuala Ó Conchobair, who was a patron of the Franciscans at Killeigh in Co. Offaly, lived "a life of piety and retirement as their neighbour" until her death in 1447.[215] She may have lived as a Tertiary, however there was a small Augustinian nunnery near the friary at Killeigh and she is likely to have retired there.[216] Fionnghuala, daughter of Conchobar Ó Briain, was eulogized for her charity and piety on her death in 1528 and spent the last twenty-one years of her life "in the robe of the Third Order, practicing piety, charity and good works towards God and the world".[217] It is possible that she followed the rule of the Third Order and lived privately. Walter Lynch gave his daughter a house, near the church of St Nicholas, Galway, afterwards known as the "house of the poor nuns of St Francis". Walter's daughter may also have lived there privately following the rule of the Tertiaries.[218] So although there were no recorded foundations for female Tertiaries in Ireland, individual women probably lived according to this Rule, seeking spiritual guidance from Franciscan friars. Other less well-connected women probably did so as well. But their deaths went unrecorded by the annalist.

207 See Berman, "Women as donors", p. 54. **208** *Reg. St Thomas, Dublin*, p. 111. The deed which states her donations in return for burial and retirement is probably dated to around 1200. **209** Giraldus Cambriensis, *Opera*, IV, p. 179. **210** *AFM* 1231 The annals do not specifically say that she took on the habit, as they do when Tadhg, son of Brian mac Andrias mac Brian Lughnech mac Toirdhelhach Mor, did. See *ALC* 1302. **211** *AU* cited in *NHI* II, p. 436. **212** For a summary of the Third Order Secular, see Watt, *Church in medieval Ireland*, p. 199. **213** Mooney, "Franciscans in Ireland", p. 90. *Med. rel. houses Ire.*, pp 264–6. **214** See also Conlan, *Franciscan Ireland*, p. 94. **215** *AFM* 1447. **216** Fitzpatrick and O'Brien, *Medieval churches of Offaly*, p. 88. **217** *AConn.* 1528. **218** Mooney, "Franciscans in Ireland", p. 131.

CHAPTER 7

Elicia Butler and Kilculliheen[1]

Connections between religious women and lay communities operated on many levels within and across the carefully delineated boundaries of the cloister and conventual estates. Throughout this discussion of nuns in medieval Ireland, the fragmentary evidence has been allowed to accumulate so that the small pieces fit together to form a whole able to bear analysis. There are few individual women who emerge from the collective obscurity cloaking medieval religious women from both Gaelic and Anglo-Irish Ireland. One who does stand out in contrast to her quieter sisters is Elicia Butler, the well-connected abbess of Kilculliheen who was deposed in 1531 for behaviour which incited her nuns into open rebellion. Elicia Butler and the community of Kilculliheen in the late fifteenth and early sixteenth centuries provide a case-study of how nuns interacted together and with lay society in the management of their convent and estates. The reason for highlighting Elicia and her religious sisters is not only that their story encapsulates most effectively the themes examined in this book, but also because there is more information about them than about any other group of individual nuns. Even with the more abundant records for this period, there remain significant gaps which invite speculation rather than definitive arguments.

The evidence for the downfall of Elicia Butler is found in a formal deposition and sentence handed down from the court of Milo de Baron, bishop of Ossory, who reported the charges to the archbishop of Dublin and then to the secular authorities.[2] There were also civil charges for offences against the statutes of provision and praemunire laid against her, of which the only surviving evidence is found in a calendar version of the pardon granted to her.[3] Milo convicted Elicia on charges of impropriety including squandering the resources of the convent, celebrating the holy offices after she had been excommunicated for failure to pay episcopal dues, striking her nuns hard enough to draw blood, having a liaison with a monk of a neighbouring house which resulted in the birth of a child, consorting with powerful lay friends and also with ordering the

1 I wish to thank Mrs Margaret Phelan for her kindness and generosity in sharing with me her knowledge of Elicia Butler's tomb and the architecture of St Canice's cathedral. 2 *Ir. mon. deeds, 1200–1600*, pp 178–81. A partial translation of the deposition was published by Mulhullond, "The trial of Alice Butler, abbess of Kilculliheen", pp 45–6. The reports of the charges to the archbishop of Dublin and crown are at *L.& P. Hen. VIII*, vol. 14, pt 2, p. 115. 3 *Cal. pat. rolls Ire. Hen. VIII-Eliz.*, I, p. 2.

assault of a young man. This accumulation of offences was allegedly brought to the notice of the bishop by the other nuns of the convent, in particular Katerine Mothing, only after the nuns had been forced to leave their convent to seek help in finding food and clothing at the houses of powerful lay families, and the public rumour of the squandering of the benefices and neglect of the buildings of Kilculliheen had reached the bishop's ears. Charges such as these were not uncommon in the turbulent world of ecclesiastical hierarchy where accusers were often then given preference for the office vacated. Although there are no other cases surviving in such detail as Elicia's, there is no reason to think that other religious women were immune either from such attacks nor from the temptation to behave in ways which might invite accusation.

Who was Elicia Butler?

In order to make some sense both of these accusations and the world in which Elicia and her sister nuns lived, some investigation into Elicia's identity and life is needed. In 1478, a papal dispensation was granted to one Elinia Butler. Her offences were that she formed a liaison with a man with whom she was related within the prohibited degrees, later married another man and had children by both. There is a papal dispensation dated 1469 for the marriage of Richard Poer of Lismore and Elena Botlier who were related within the prohibited degrees of affinity. They had already had children. It is possible that this is the Elina/Elicia Butler who later entered Kilculliheen.[4] After the death of her husbands she was professed a nun and entered the convent of Kilculliheen, although her profession was irregular, receiving the veil not from her abbess nor from the bishop of Ossory "but from another bishop (sed ab alio antistite)". She was, however, absolved from these irregularities and granted permission to obtain any office including that of abbess within the convent.[5] Later in that year, she was sued by the papacy for being behind in paying dues owed after the deprivation of office of Alsona Elene, abbess of Kilculliheen, probably since 1450.[6] Although she is described in this document as a nun (moniales), the substance of the notice is that she has taken over as abbess of the convent, perhaps somewhat irregularly. An Elicia Butler is next visible in 1501, when she is one of the witnesses called to give evidence to Oliver Cantwell, bishop of Ossory, that she had been present at the wedding in 1468 of Sir James Butler and Sadhbh Kavanagh, daughter of Diarmait Mac Murchadha, and that their son Piers Butler was born subsequent to this marriage.[7] This hearing was important within the context of Piers's ambitions for the earldom of Ormond, because he had two older brothers whom he was trying to have declared illegitimate and therefore unable to inherit the title from their cousin Sir Thomas Butler, the seventh earl. Also present at this hearing and listed as first was the lady abbess of Kilculliheen.[8]

4 *Cal. papal letters, 1458–71*, pp 687–8. 5 *Cal. papal letters, 1471–84*, p. 636. 6 "Obligationes pro annatis diocesis Ossoriensis", p. 12. 7 *Ormond deeds*, III, p. 298. 8 *Ormond deeds*, III, p.

In the 1532 civil pardon, Elicia Butler is stated to be also known as "Alice the nun".[9] "Alice the nun" has been identified by Butler genealogists as being a third child born prior to the legitimate marriage of James and Sadhbh, making her the sister of Piers.[10] It is tempting to identify this Elicia with the earlier Elinia, first because the names are sufficiently similar for scribes to have misread them, and second because the accusation that Elinia was professed irregularly by a bishop other than the bishop of Ossory is repeated in the trial against Elicia where she is accused of being irregularly professed by the bishop of Waterford, instead of the bishop of Ossory. The imputation that Elicia imposed herself on the abbacy is suggested by both the notice of dues owed to the papacy in 1478 and also from her civil pardon from the statutes of provisions and praemunire, usually used against ecclesiastics who went to the papacy for preferment in benefices.[11] If Elicia and Elinia are the same person and if she is "Alice the nun", sister of Piers, then her presence at the wedding of James Butler and Sadhbh Kavanagh was essential in order that she be declared legitimate. If these theories are accurate, Elicia must have been born sometime between 1455 when James and Sadhbh were married within the prohibited degrees of kinship and 1468 when the papal dispensation for the marriage was granted. Since she is described in 1478 as having had unions with two men and at least two children she must have been born towards 1455, making her in her late teens or early twenties when she entered the convent and in her seventies when she was deposed in 1532. She was still alive nine years later to receive a pension at the dissolution in 1541.[12] It would be equally interesting if Elicia and Elinia were different women, both from the Butler family. If this latter possibility is carried through we would have two women from the same important family who entered the abbey of Kilculliheen under irregular circumstances, pointing to significant familial influence in obtaining admission to the convent in violation of the rights of the bishops of Ossory. Although it is possible that Elicia Butler, abbess of Kilculliheen in 1531, is not the Elinia Butler mentioned in papal correspondence in 1478, for the rest of this discussion this identification will be assumed.

The career path of Elinia Butler was not unusual within the late medieval Irish church. As has been noted in previous chapters, in a world where canonically approved marriages were often seen as an impediment to the delicate web of alliances between families, it is not surprising that a woman of the Butler family would be involved with a man to whom she was too closely related for the liaison to be canonically approved, nor that she was subsequently married to another man. In another branch of the Butler family, an important alliance with the Ó Briain kings of Thomond was achieved by the birth of the son of Renalda daughter of the Ó Briain king and John Butler, later sixth earl of Ormond.

297. **9** *Cal. pat. rolls Ire. Hen. VIII-Eliz.*, I, p. 2. **10** T. Blake Butler (NLI MS 12025 f. 2 and *passim*) lists the evidence and identifies Elinia with Elicia and Alice the Nun. Graves and Prym, *History, architecture and antiquities of St Canice's*, p. 267, identifies Alice the nun with Elicia abbess of Kilculliheen. **11** Bradshaw, *Dissolution*, p. 18. **12** *Extents Ir. mon. possessions*, p. 206.

Renalda went on to marriage with another member of the Butler family, before retiring to the Ó Briain convent of Killone in Thomond.[13] That Elicia Butler entered Kilculliheen at presumably such a young age may indicate that there were problems with the marriage, the husband and children may have died, or she may have been repudiated by her husband and any children brought up by her husband's family.[14] Her entry into the convent would not have necessitated papal pardons for her irregular alliances with men, but her elevation to any office would have done.

Elicia's presumed prompt accession to the abbacy is signalled by the demand for her to pay the fines for her entry into the office. It was probably family influence which was instrumental in bringing about her entry into the convent and her swift election to the position of abbess. Since she did not receive the veil from either the abbess of Kilculliheen or the bishop charged with the care of the nuns, it is most likely that her entry and election were opposed by both the abbess, Alsona Elene, and the bishop of Ossory. Kilculliheen was under the patronage of the earls of Ormond. Elicia's father, Sir James Butler, was the powerful resident seneschal of the earls of Ormond and it is unlikely that he would act against their interests. Elicia's intrusion may have been an attempt by Ormond's supporters to gain or regain control of the nunnery. Although this is a likely scenario, the family politics of the Butlers, like most other large and powerful families in medieval Ireland, meant that it is not clear to which branch of the family Elicia was aligned. She may have been supported by her powerful father, her ambitious brother Piers, or by either one of his older brothers slighted in the pursuit of the title by Piers. There are also the men by whom Elicia had children, either of whom may have supported her directly or through their families, as there is ample evidence that some women in medieval Ireland became more ardent supporters of their husbands' families than their own birth families.[15] Since there is so little direct evidence the limits of the speculation about Elicia's family alliances are to some extent the limits of the imagination, although on balance it is likely that she had the support of Piers at the end of her life.

The entry into the convent of a woman like Elicia/Elinia Butler who had passed her usefulness in the tapestry of marriage alliances was also not unusual. As detailed in the previous chapter, there was a long tradition of secularization of monastic offices within Ireland, and of application to Rome for provision to office based on accusations of impropriety or other sins. The surviving papal documentation for Elinia Butler is consistent with this course of events, where an applicant would obtain any dispensations necessary and would also lodge complaints about the incumbent of the office or benefice claimed. All of these

13 See above. **14** Simms, "The legal position of Irishwomen", pp 98–9; for some examples of women also see Simms, "Women in Norman Ireland", pp 18–19, and Cosgrove, "Consent, consummation and indissolubility", pp 96–7ff. **15** Piers himself gained a powerful and supportive wife with his marriage to Margaret Fitzgerald, daughter of the earl of Kildare, but

procedures required powerful backing and money with which to pay all the necessary fines and fees of the advocates, scribes and officials involved. Whatever Elinia's personal ambitions or piety may have been, she still would have required a high level of ecclesiastical and lay support in her entry into Kilculliheen.

If the identification of Elinia and Elicia is correct, it appears that she may not have kept the office of abbess for all the years between 1478 and 1531, which again suggests that there were different factions within the convent, possibly contributing to the management difficulties. In 1501, when the witnesses for the marriage of James Butler and Sadhbh Kavanagh were called, the abbess of Kilculliheen is listed, as is an Elicia Butler.[16] This may refer to another Elicia Butler, as it was a common name within the family, or it may indicate that there was another abbess at the time.[17] An Elicia Gaal appears on the pension list as "late abbess" in 1540. At what point she was abbess is not mentioned. She may have been in office after Elicia Butler and been succeeded by Katherine Mothing, the abbess who surrendered the convent in 1540.[18] This evidence is slight and inconclusive and it serves as a reminder that although there is more known about this period in Kilculliheen's history than in other convents, there are still very large gaps in our knowledge of even the basic names and dates.

Elicia Butler and the boundaries of the convent of Kilculliheen

Elicia Butler moved broadly within two of the spheres in which religious women have been located in previous chapters of this thesis. She was accused of mismanaging the internal relationships between the nuns and allowing or even causing them to cross the borders of their convent boundaries and move into the lay world beyond. These faults were combined with poor relationships with ecclesiastical officials and too-close ties with lay families. As well as this, she was charged with mismanaging the conventual estates to the extent that they were seriously decaying.

As has been argued in the last chapter, women living in nunneries did not always live together in harmony. If the accusations against Elicia Butler have any substance, the community at Kilculliheen was under severe stress by the 1530s. The nuns testified that, Elicia, "laid violent hands on the professed nuns of her convent, to the extents of shedding blood"; the bishop questioned the nuns as to whether this rough treatment was meted out in the course of her duties as abbess, and the nuns replied that it was not through any desire to correct that Elicia struck them, but from quarrelling and fighting.[19] The violence and bloodshed were apparently not the issue, but the motivation provoking it,

always a supporter of her husband's claims when they conflicted with her birth family's. See Kehoe, "Margaret Fitzgerald", p. 826. **16** *Ormond deeds*, III, p. 297. **17** See family trees and list of Margaret's and Piers's children in Kehoe, "Margaret Fitzgerald", pp 834, 839. **18** In the dissolution records, the last abbess is named variously as Isabella and Katherine Mothing. Since Katherine is known to have been at the convent during the trial of Elicia it is reasonable to assume that it is Katherine that is referred to. *Cal. pat. rolls Ire., Hen. VIII-Eliz.*, I, p. 61, refers to Katherine Mothing and p. 137 refers to surrender by Isabella Mothing. **19** *Ir. mon. deeds,*

indicating that quarrelling was not acceptable behaviour for an abbess, though correcting her nuns, even with violence, might be considered appropriate.

That this discord may have been overlooked or corrected privately is indicated by the emphasis within the deposition on the public knowledge of the internal affairs of the convent. The boundary surrounding the cloister, built upon the understanding that peaceful prayer was the work and function of the nuns, was in effect breached by the "loud, scandalous and public rumour", which reached the ears of the bishop himself. These rumours and scandal were intensified by the breaking of the physical enclosure of the nuns, with Elicia and the nuns all being described as wandering outside the convent walls and in the "houses of powerful lords and other friends, against the observed rule of said nuns … ".[20] Elicia was also accused of fornication with a monk and bearing a child. If the identification of Elicia with Elinia is correct then this accusation would have been very old news by the 1530s, when Elicia must have been in her seventies. It is this accusation added to all the other diverse charges which strongly suggests that the nuns and the bishop were gathering together every possible charge against Elicia, rather than relying on whatever was the catalyst for their actions. Although attendance at legal proceedings, even important dynastic weddings, might be overlooked by the bishops of Ossory, the breaches of enclosure by Elicia and her fellow nuns were obviously considered to be too flagrant to be ignored.

Not only was Elicia apparently unsuccessful at maintaining good relations with the nuns in her convent, her way of conducting the business of the convent had evidently been a thorn in the side of the bishops of Ossory for some time. Besides her irregular profession by the bishop of Waterford, another of the charges against her was that she had continued to celebrate the divine office in an irregular manner even after she was excommunicated by Oliver, late bishop of Ossory, for non-payment of rents and dues. Oliver Cantwell was bishop of Ossory between 1487 and 1527, so these charges were also several years old in 1531 and may have been one of the factors in prompting Milo to appoint managers for the convent's affairs.[21] Appointing administrators for conventual business was usually only undertaken when there were internal management problems.[22]

Other evidence of financial mismanagement at Kilculliheen in the late fifteenth and early sixteenth centuries probably means that Kilculliheen was suffering from long-term poor management by the 1530s and that Milo was attempting to avert financial problems in the convent. It is only in passing that it is recorded in 1488 that the nuns of Kilculliheen, who held the rights of presentation of Dysertmoon (Co. Kilkenny), had not presented a vicar there for some time and that the rectory was being held illegally by another party.[23] Difficulties with managing rectories were quite common by the fifteenth

1200–1600, p. 179. **20** *Ir. mon. deeds, 1200–1600*, p. 179. **21** *Ir. mon. deeds, 1200–1600*, p. 180. **22** Power, *Medieval English nunneries*, pp 229–36, for the appointment of custos for nunneries. **23** *Cal. papal letters, 1484–92*, p. 122.

century. There were also evidently considerable problems in 1506, when the pope ordered the abbess of Kilculliheen to give up the rectory of Rathpatrick (Co. Waterford). The papacy argued that this rectory had been vacant for long enough to revert to the papacy, however the nuns were not prepared to relinquish it.[24] There may have been local resistance to the nuns' administration and installation of their candidate to the vicarage. They also may have attempted to circumvent this opposition by obtaining confirmation of their right to hold the rectory only twelve years before.[25] However, since Rathpatrick is very close to the nunnery itself, the problems may have been more to do with the failure of the nuns to provide for any candidate at all, or with difficulties reconciling rival factions within the convent. The pope ordered that the abbess herself attend the hearing "notwithstanding Boniface VIII's restrictions on judicial procedures and the two days restriction of the general council".[26] This was certainly recognition of the practical necessity of the abbess conducting business herself; it also probably reflects the stratagems employed by the abbess to avoid an unwelcome lawsuit, and using *Periculoso* as an excuse not to attend what would have been a difficult legal hearing. Other evidence that the financial viability of Kilculliheen had been reduced was that although the estate was worth £50 at the dissolution, there were only £3 worth of chattels to be sold by the commissioners.[27] The accusations levelled at Elicia Butler for squandering the assets of the nunnery and making her nuns ask their secular friends for support may have had a great deal of substance if the chattels of the relatively wealthy abbey had been reduced to this rather small amount at the dissolution.

The nuns of Kilculliheen and their friends beyond the cloister

The reference to the "friends" to whom the nuns turned in their hour of need demonstrates that lay neighbours could be involved in the internal divisions within convents and that outside tensions could be replicated inside the cloister itself. There are a few hints about the identity of these friends. The names of two of the nuns are the same as those of two of the officials of St Canice's cathedral. Katherine Mothing was one of the main accusers of Elicia. Her success as Elicia's rival is demonstrated by her elevation to the office of abbess, sometime before 1541 when the house was dissolved. The first witness to the document which reported Elicia's trial was the chancellor of St Canice's cathedral, Nicholas Mothing, one of a prominent Kilkenny family. It is likely that there was a family connection between Katherine and Nicholas.[28] Another of the nuns who testified against Elicia was Anastatia Cantwell, who may have been related to the previous bishop of Ossory, Oliver Cantwell. There are many Cantwells in the Kilkenny area, some of whom were prominent members of the clergy, including

24 *Cal. papal letters, 1503–13*, pp 424–5. **25** "Obligationes pro annatis diocesis Ossoriensis", p. 25. **26** *Cal. papal letters, 1503–13*, p. 424. **27** "Sales of chattels", pp 11–37, and *Extents Ir. mon. possessions*, p. 206. **28** Graves and Prym, *History, architecture and antiquities of St Canice's*, pp 266–7. Nicholas Mothing died in 1568 and was buried in the cathedral.

Patrick, archbishop of Cashel in 1455, and John, precentor of Cashel around 1483.[29] Anastatia's success after the deposition of Elicia is hinted at by her larger pension at the dissolution and suggests that she may have been a prioress or other official.[30] These specific links cannot be proven conclusively; however, the wording of the deposition strongly suggests that, whatever the identity of the "friends" to whom the nuns turned, they seem to have supported them materially, as the nuns describe themselves as being reduced to poverty and penury without food and clothing because of the incompetence of Elicia's management of the convent's resources.

It is not certain that Elicia had the support of her powerful brother, but there are several factors which suggest that she did. That Piers and his wife, Margaret Fitzgerald, offered some sort of protection to Elicia is indicated by a reference in the letter written by Milo, bishop of Ossory, to the archbishop of Dublin, in which Milo states that Elicia left for England soon after the accusations were made and charges could be laid only after her return. He then states that Elicia "has no cause to fear the earl or lady of Ossory".[31] Their support may also explain how Elicia was able to secure a civil pardon for her offences and even explain why she was the subject of the deposition at all. Bradshaw, in his discussion of the monasteries in Ormond on the eve of the dissolution, argues that it was the Butler interests in the abbeys of St Katherine's in Waterford and Athassel in Tipperary that may have provoked investigations into their internal affairs by locals hostile to increasing Butler control.[32] He also suggests that the Ormond Butlers were opposed to abbess Elicia, and it is possible that they were opposed to her abbacy without necessarily withdrawing their support totally. Alternatively, the charges against Elicia were sufficiently serious that her powerful brother could not wholly prevent her excommunication or her demotion from the office of abbess. The other evidence for Ormond Butler support is from Elicia's tomb in St Canice's cathedral. The tomb which has been identified as hers is a very expensive one, almost certainly made by the O Tunney family of sculptors who also made the tombs of Sir Piers Butler and Margaret Fitzgerald.[33] Although the date of Elicia's death is unknown, it must have been after that of Piers who died in 1539, and may have been after Margaret's in 1542.[34] If she is Piers's elder sister, then she would have been elderly at the time of the dissolution and her death presumably occurred sometime in the 1540s. If the tomb is hers, she must have been accepted back into the Butler family, and her tomb paid for either from her own estates or more likely by her nephews. The iconography of the tomb indicates that she carried to her death associations of her profession and office.

29 *Ormond deeds*, III, pp 116, 255. **30** She was granted 46*s.* 8*d.*, *Extents Ir. mon. possessions*, p. 206; this was a smaller amount than that granted to Elicia Butler, and see previous chapter for discussion of the ways that the various offices may have been filled in convents in Ireland. **31** *L.& P. Hen. VIII,* vol. 14, pt 2, p. 115. **32** Bradshaw, *Dissolution*, pp 20–1. **33** See Phelan, "An unidentified tomb", pp 43–4. **34** Kehoe, "Margaret Fitzgerald", p. 837.

Figure 16. Tomb of Elicia Butler, St Canice's Cathedral, Kilkenny.
Photograph by Margaret O'Flanagan. (Reproduced by kind permission of the Dean and Chapter of St Canice's Cathedral, Kilkenny.)

The effigy itself is not dressed in the robes of an abbess, nor does it carry the staff of office; however she is dressed as would be appropriate for a vowess, which is reasonable considering that she died after the dissolution of her abbey and after she had been demoted.[35] The side panels of the altar tomb may not be original or they may have been separated from the top and then reassembled in the nineteenth century. They are, however, appropriate for a woman who wished to emphasise her piety and religious profession. The side panels show female saints, including St Catherine and St Mary Magdalene, as well as a bishop and an archbishop. There may have also been another panel which has been separated from the tomb and is particularly interesting as it shows an abbess with staff and the Butler coat of arms displayed prominently.[36] This abbess may be an image of Elicia herself or it may be St Brigid displayed as a patron of one of the Butler family.[37] These symbols on her tomb suggest that she may have kept her vows

35 Her dress has meant that she has not previously been identified as a nun, however, as Phelan has argued, such an expensive tomb could not have been commissioned by anyone of the "humbler sort". Phelan, "An unidentified tomb", p. 40. **36** This panel is believed by Phelan to have originally belonged to Elicia's tomb. See Phelan, "An unidenified tomb" p. 42. **37** Hunt, *Irish medieval figure sculpture*, I, p. 193, II, plate 316, identifies this figure as St Brigid,

after the dissolution of her abbey. Certainly it indicates that she and her family were eager to ensure that she was remembered as a religious woman, even after the dissolution of her abbey and her demotion from office.

However justified the complaints against her appear in the documents, it is worth emphasizing that the image of Elicia as a forceful and ultimately incompetent woman is recorded in hostile sources. She steered a course through treacherous shoals of family influence and local politics in the arena outside her convent walls and brought that tension within the confines of the cloister. Maintenance of connections with the influential family members meant that outside tensions could enter the convent. The intrusion of a member of a powerful family could upset the balance within a convent and play havoc with the management of the conventual resources. Whether Elicia Butler was as incompetent as her accusers suggest or whether she was responding to the demands put upon her by her secular family at the expense of her religious community is not now known. That the community of Kilculliheen was divided in the early sixteenth century is certain and that those divisions were supported, if not initiated, by powerful secular interests is clear from the available evidence. The boundaries so carefully established in the twelfth century by powerful families were breached in the sixteenth by other important families.

however it may also be a representation of Elicia's former office. See Phelan, "An unidentified tomb", p. 42. Hunt's commentary places the Butler coat of arms on plate 315, rather than plate 316. The unidentified female in plate 315 could be a representaion of a vowess, nun or abbess rather than a saint, as Hunt suggests.

sweeping in his dismissal of the relevance of religious women. Reasons for the early surrender of nunneries may be that convents could not provide ecclesiastical careers to the relatives of local rulers in the way that male houses could, while nunnery estates were probably always in the de facto control of the ruling families through their daughters. The nunneries were thus easy targets for Gaelic rulers looking for monasteries they could dissolve to appease the crown officials and demonstrate their loyalty without great sacrifice. How this affected the local communities who supported and may have depended on the nunneries for social and religious services is not known.

Other convents, such as Kilculliheen, undoubtedly had been suffering problems of mismanagement and internal conflict. While the declining numbers evident at other nunneries such as Termonfeckin and St Mary del Hogges in Dublin indicate that some nunneries were part of the overall decline in general monastic standards, the lack of internal records from nunneries precludes any definitive pronouncements on either the extent or the diminution of their role in lay societies. There have recently been suggestions that English nunneries did not share the fate of many of their male counterparts in being marginalized by their lay supporters by the sixteenth century, and largely retained their local support until the dissolution.[8] The value local lay communities placed on the services of Irish convents at the dissolution can be glimpsed for some; for example, there was a plea for Grace Dieu to be one of a number of monasteries in the Anglo-Irish community to be exempt from dissolution because it provided educational services.[9] The backhanded compliment paid to Killone in 1567, where the lack of services the nuns had previously provided was lamented, also suggest that the nuns at this convent were valued by their local community.[10]

Once the convents were closed, the nuns had to find their way in secular society. Studies of English nuns after the dissolution have shown that although some married, others remained single with their pensions as their only support. A few banded together and continued to live communally, supporting themselves on their pooled resources.[11] Their pensions tended always to be less than comparable male monastics, even though the pensions of the men had been calculated with their ability to supplement them with employment as priests in mind. It has thus been argued that ex-nuns in the sixteenth century suffered considerable financial hardship, compared with ex-monks.[12]

Pensions granted to nuns in Ireland have not been analysed in detail by scholars. In his discussion of monastic pensions Bradshaw confines his remarks on the adequacy of pensions to those of male monastics, who were expected to

Dissolution, p. 176. **8** Berman has suggested that English nunneries continued to receive bequests from wealthy men and women to support prayers throughout the latter medieval period. Berman, review of *Gender and material culture*. **9** *L. & P. Hen. VIII*, vol. 14, pt. 1, p. 465. **10** "A commentary on the nobility and gentry of Thomond", pp 70–1. **11** Bettey, *Suppression of the monasteries in the west country*, pp 115 and 111, for the example of some of the nuns of Shaftsbury continuing to live together in houses leased from the estate. **12** Bettey, *Suppression of the monasteries in the west country*, pp 110–19.

take up employment as curates and priests under the new regime. Like the monastic pensions granted in England, the pensions for ex-religious in Ireland were calculated using several factors, the most significant being the size and value of the estates of the houses, along with the length of service and position within the monastery. Bradshaw's analysis reveals that pensions of over £10 for monastic superiors were quite generous, and those few superiors who received over £40 were doing very well. He points out that fifteen of the thirty-four pensions awarded to male superiors were for £6 or under.[13] Only one nunnery superior received a pension over £10: Mary Cusack of Lismullin, who headed one of the wealthier nunneries. As she was also the sister of Sir Thomas Cusack, one of the dissolution commissioners and the leesee of Lismullin's estates, these connections undoubtedly helped her to the generous pension. Other than Mary, the pensions of the nuns were similar in value to most of those granted to monks and canons from the smaller and less wealthy monasteries. The biggest difference between men and women receiving pensions was that the men were also often granted vicarages and those that were not were no doubt expected to apply for the curacies and vicarages vacant after the withdrawal of the monasteries.

As well as the adequacy of monastic pensions, the reliability of payment is also difficult to detect. Historians have detailed some of the taxes and fines that were levied on even the smallest English pensions, reducing the actual value of the pensions considerably. Many English pensions ceased after 1552, although there were still religious living after this date. How they survived is not known. Although they had fewer opportunities for employment than their religious brethren, some English nuns ran schools and there is evidence that they held on to their status as nuns or ex-nuns long after the dissolution.[14] With the state of

Table 7. Pensions awarded to nuns at the dissolution[15]
All amounts are rounded to the nearest £.

House	*Number of pensions granted*	*Pension of superior*	*Pension of other nuns*	*Total estate value*
Grace Dieu, Co. Dublin	5	6	2	112
Lismullin, Co. Meath	4	16	2	109
Kilculliheen, Co. Waterford	5	5	2 3	50
St Mary del Hogges, Dublin	1	6		18
Odder, Co. Meath	4	6	2 1	36
Termonfeckin, Co. Louth	2	1	0.5	9

13 Bradshaw, *Dissolution*, pp 133–5, based on figures from *Cal. pat. rolls Ire. Hen. VIII-Eliz.* pp 59–63. **14** Oliva, *Convent and community*, pp 200–4. **15** References are to *Extents Ir. mon.*

Irish records it is not possible to be certain when the pension payments to ex-religious ceased; certainly they were still paid in 1562.

The lives of a few of the last medieval Irish nuns can be traced after the 1540s. Ónora Ó Briain, the last abbess of Killone, married profitably to Ruaidrí Ó Seachnasaigh, possibly even before the dissolution of her convent.[16] All the religious houses in Connacht were subject to dissolution by Ó Briain himself and he received most of the confiscated lands as part of a deal with the English government, so it is hardly surprising that Ónora found a comfortable life after the dissolution of her convent. Since the marriage was respectable, it was almost certainly a family arrangement, suggesting she had few material problems adjusting to life outside the cloister. Sir Thomas Cusack, the powerful brother of Mary, the last prioress of Lismullin, owed his sister considerable sums of money that he was either reluctant to repay or had some difficulty repaying.[17] She is described as being "of Lismullin" in one document, so she probably settled on the estate after the dissolution. There is no mention of her marriage, so it is likely that she remained unmarried and lived on her pension when she received it.[18] She is not mentioned in her brother's will of 1571, perhaps indicating her death between May 1570 and his death in April 1571 or that he believed that she was adequately provided for with the repayment of the £100 he owed her. There is nothing recorded for the rest of the nuns of Lismullin, except that in 1562 both Mary Cusack and one of her nuns, Anne Weldon, were still in receipt of their pensions.[19]

Local tradition believes that some of the Grace Dieu nuns continued to live at their manor of Portrane with the collusion of the lessee, Isabella Walsh, and the new owner of Grace Dieu, the Barnewall family.[20] This arrangement is believed to have continued until 1577, when a further inquisition found the prioress in possession of the manor.[21] The evidence for this is not, however, completely certain. Archdall interpreted the inquisition of 1577 to mean that the nuns were still living there, whereas the text he cites reads more sensibly in the past tense, that is, that the prioress had leased the manor before the dissolution, not that she was still living there. Bradshaw suggests that the collusion of the Barnewalls, who were granted the home convent and manor of Grace Dieu, would also have been necessary for this arrangement to work.[22] Local and family tradition agree that once Patrick Barnewall took over the convent and demolished some of its

possessions; *Cal. pat. rolls Ire. Hen. VIII-Eliz.* vol I. pp 59–62, and *Fiants Ire., Hen. VIII-Eliz.*, I, pp 14–25. **16** See above. **17** It is also possible that he was withholding the money rather than borrowing it. See Mac Curtain, "Women, education and learning in early modern Ireland", p. 164. **18** *Cal. inquis. Dublin*, p. 202, summarises Thomas's debts to his sister. They are outlined in more detail in the Record commissioners' calendars of "Deeds and wills extracted from Inquisitions Exchequer Series, Eliz I-James I, Co. Dublin" (NAI MS RC 10/2) pp 444–8. Thomas Cusack's will of 1570 does not mention Mary but does mention his "poor" sister Maude. See *Cal. inquis. Dublin*, pp 210–12. For discussion see Gallwey, "Cusack family", p. 312. **19** "Report on recent acquisitions in the Bodlein Library", p. 70. **20** Bates, *Donabate and Portrane, a history*, pp 26–8. **21** Archdall (1786) pp 217–18, Moran's notes in Archdall (1876) give the details of the inquisition of 18 Eliz. **22** Bradshaw, *Dissolution*, p. 197.

buildings to construct his new manor, the last prioress cursed him and all his family, and when the nuns were driven away their cries of sorrow and distress could be heard for miles.[23] Although this may be thought to argue against continued support by the Barnewalls for the nuns, local tradition believes that Patrick's son, Christopher, did continue to give them his protection.[24] Overall, this evidence suggests that the surviving nuns did live together without any status and with the help of local families. This type of arrangement occurred in England and it may have happened elsewhere in Ireland for convents where there is little or no surviving information. Some nuns, anchorites and hospital workers must have continued with their religious vows and their community work privately and faded into an obscurity they no doubt sought, away from the glare of the dissolution commissioners' investigations.

When these women left their convents, they were entering a landscape where religious behaviour and practice were being redrawn, although substantial change was still many years away. While the buildings of the old churches and convents where medieval Irish women lived their lives and practised their religion often survived, the individual voices of these women were swept away. Today there are few reminders of what must have been the ever-present pious practices of medieval Irish women – some convent ruins, some grave stones, a meagre collection of facts recorded in ancient documents. Yet these women were part of the medieval religious world: they worshipped, lived and died in accordance with their communities' religious beliefs and practices and around the boundaries, both physical and ideological, that they and their communities built and maintained.

23 On the curse see Cullerton, "From barrow boy to viscount", p. 5. The story of the nuns' cries of sorrow has been widely reported. See among others Power, *Life of Frances Power Cobbe*, I, p. 9. **24** Colm Cullerton, personal communication.

APPENDIX ONE

Convents in medieval Ireland

Date	*Dedication, Convent, Modern county*	*Order*	*Dependent*	*Founder*	*Later patron*	*Dissolved*
+500	St Brigit, Molough Co. Tipperary	Celtic to OSA		Daughters of Cannich	Butlers	1540
–500	Temple-Breed Temple-na-Ferta Co. Armagh	Celtic		St Patrick		1562?
?500	St Brigit, Kildare Co. Kildare	Celtic to OSA		St Brigit		1460+?
?500	Killevy Co. Armagh	Celtic		St Monenna		1542
?500	Killaraght, Co. Sligo	Celtic	?Kilcreevanty	St Attracta		1591?
–578	St Mary, Annaghdown Co. Galway	Celtic to AA	Clonard to Kilcreevanty	St Brendan		1223+?
?600	Addrigoole Co. Laois	Celtic to AA	Kilculliheen	St Finbarr	David FitzMilo	1240+
1026	St Mary, Clonmacnoise Co. Offaly	Celtic to AA	Clonard to Kilcreevanty		Derbforgaill, wife of Tigernán Ua Ruairc	1500+
?–1142	Mellifont, Co. Meath	?Cist.				1228
+1144	St Mary, Derrane Co. Roscommon	AA	Kilcreevanty			1223+
–1144	St Mary, Kells Co. Meath	AA	Clonard			1400–
+1144	St Brigit or Kilbride Co. Meath	AA	Clonard			1400–

➤

Date	Dedication, Convent, Modern county	Order	Dependent	Founder	Later patron	Dissolved
+1144	St Mary, Termonfeckin Co. Louth	AA	Clonard	Donnchad Ua Cerbaill, King of Airgialla and Áed Ua Cáellaide, Bp of Airgialla.		1539
+1144	St Mary, Clonfert Co. Galway	AA	Kilcreevanty	St Malachy		1540
c.1144	St Brigit, Odder Co. Meath	AA	Clonard to	St Malachy Independent		1539
c.1144	St Mary, Clonard Co. Meath	AA		Murchad Ui Maelsechlain		1540–
1146	St Mary del Hogges, Dublin	AA	Clonard to Independent	Diarmait Mac Murchada	Crown	1536
c.1146	Lusk, Co. Dublin	Arroaisan	St Mary del Hogges then Clonard.	Diarmait Mac Murchada		1195
1150?	Inishlounaght, Co. Tipperary	?Cist.				1228
1151	Aghade, Co. Carlow	AA	St Mary del Hogges, Dublin	Diarmairt Mac Murchada		1500–
1151	St Mary de Bello Portu, Kilcullliheen Co. Waterford	OSA	St Mary del Hogges and Clonard to Independent	Diarmait Mac Murchada	Earls of Ormond	1540
–1171	Tagmon, Co. Wexford	AA	St Mary del Hogges	Diarmait Mac Murchada		1330–
?1171	St Peter, Limerick	OSA	Killone	Uí Bhrian		1541
?1180	Jerpoint, Co. Kilkenny	?Cist.				1228
c..1240	St John or Killone, Co. Clare	OSA		Uí Bhrian		1540+
+1195	St Mary, Calliaghstown, Co. Meath	AA	Clonard			1500–

➤

Date	*Dedication, Convent, Modern county*	*Order*	*Dependent*	*Founder*	*Later patron*	*Dissolved*
+1195	St Mary, Grace Dieu, Co. Dublin	AA		John Cumin, Archbishop of Dublin		1539
+1195	St Mary, Drumalgagh, Co. Roscommon	AA	Clonard to Kilcreevanty			1543?
+1195	Killeigh, Co. Offaly	AA	?Clonard		O Conor Faly	*c.*1569?
1199	St Mary, Timolin, Co. Kildare	AA		Richard Calf, Baron of Norragh		1530
−1200	St Mary, Downpatrick	Cisterican to Benedictine		Bagnal		1513−
1200	St Mary, Graney, Co. Kildare	AA		Walter de Riddlesford		1539
1218	St Mary, Ballymore, Co. Westmeath	Cist.		Walter de Lacy		1470?
?1218	St Mary, Derry	Cist.		Turlough Leinighs of Strabane Castle		1512−
*c.*1200	Kilcreevanty, Co. Galway	Benedictine to AA		Cathal Crobderg Ua Conchobair		1543
+1223	Termonkeelin Co. Roscommon	AA	Kilcreevanty			1543+
−1223	St Mary, Cloonoghil, Co. Roscommon	AA	Kilcreevanty			1543?
−1223	St Mary or Killinmulrooney, Co. Roscommon	AA	Kilcreevanty			1543?
+1223	Inishmaine, Co. Mayo	AA	Kilcreevanty			1546+
+1223	Killeenatrava, Co. Mayo	AA	Kilcreevanty	Cong Abbey		1560?

➤

Date	*Dedication, Convent, Modern county*	*Order*	*Dependent*	*Founder*	*Later patron*	*Dissolved*
+1223	Ballynagalliagh, Co. Sligo	AA	Kilcreevanty			1562
–1223	St. Mary, Ardcarn, Co. Roscommon	AA	Kilcreevanty		Clarus Mag Mailin 1243	1590?
1240	Holy Trinity, Lismullin, Co. Meath	OSA		Richard de la Corner and Avice de la Corner		1539
–1261	St Catherine de O'conyl, Co. Limerick	OSA		Grandfather of Thomas fitzMaurice	Earl of Desmond	1428–
1283	Ballynagallagh, Co. Limerick	OSA	Killone	Fitzgibbon	Uí Briain in fifteenth century	1548
1297	St John the Baptist, Cork	Benedictine to OSA		Agnes de Hareford with de Barrys		1540?
–1385	Carrick-on-Suir, Co. Tipperary	OFM				1542–?
–1385	St Anne, Youghal, Co. Cork	OFM				1542?
–1440	Annagh, Co. Mayo	AA	Kilcreevanty	Walter de Burgo		1543?
1450	Ballymacadane, Co. Cork	OSA		Cormac Mac Carthy Mac Tiege, Laider.		1539?
1511	Galway	OFM		Walter Lynch		

APPENDIX TWO

List of all the names of individual women

connected with nunneries in medieval Ireland found in the course of research

Notes on listing: The names are given in the spelling of the original sources. Dates are those of the source, rather than the dates of election, death or lifespan, unless otherwise noted.

Ballymore [Loughswedy, Plary]

1417	Margaret, prioress	*Cal. papal letters*, 1417–31, p. 83.
1427	Joan, prioress	*Cal. papal letters*, 1417–31, p. 571.

Clonard/Odder

1196	Agnes, granddaughter of Ua Máel Sechlainn, sister of Derbforgaill, died	*ALC*; Brady, "Clonard", p. 4; Dugdale, *Monasticon*, pp 1043–4.
1282	Agnes, abbess, died	*Cal. doc. Ire., 1252–84*, p. 436.
1284	Fingola ni Melaghlin, abbess, deposed	*Cal. doc. Ire., 1252–84*, p. 511.
1286	Felicia, abbess	*Cal. doc. Ire., 1285–92*, p. 109; AClon.
1288	Mariote, prioress	*Cal. doc. Ire., 1285–92*, p. 184.
1288	Burgenilda, abbess	*Cal. doc. Ire., 1285–92*, pp 194, 177.
1295	Sibil, prioress	*Cal. doc. Ire., 1293–1301*, p. 117.
1295	Derborgyll, resigned abbess	*Cal. doc. Ire., 1293–1301*, p. 117.
1297–1310	Gormlaith, daughter of O Kerra	*Cal. just. rolls. 1303–10*, p. 79; *Cal. pat. rolls 1307–13*, pp 290–1.
1313–18	More daughter of Ua Maelechlainn, abbess	"Cat. pipe rolls", *PRI rep. DK* 39 (1907) p. 44; 42 (1911) p. 19. *Rot. pat. Hib.* p. 23.
1319–26	Sibilla, daughter of McGoyghan, abbess	"Cat. pipe rolls" *PRI rep. DK* 42 (1911) p. 19; *Cal. pat. rolls, 1324–7*, p. 251.
1344–55	Joanna, abbess	TCD MS 654, f. 106r; *Rot. pat. Hib.* p. 50; BL. MS 4789, f. 18v.
1355	Matilda O'Daly abbess	BL MS 4789, f. 18v.

Clonard/Odder (cont.)

1381	Johanna, abbess	Rot. pat. Hib., p. 107.
1383	Matilda Methe, late abbess	*Med. rel. houses, Ire.*, p. 313.
1385	Johanna, abbess	*Rot. pat. Hib.* pp 120, 131.
1405	Mabilla, former abbess	TCD MS 654, f. 124v.
1405	Joanna, abbess	TCD MS 654, f. 91r.
1405	Maria, abbess	TCD MS 654, f. 124v
1409	Margaret Tuit, nun	TCD MS 654, f. 124v; *Cal. papal letters, 1404–15*, p. 159.
1417	Joan, abbess	TCD MS 654, f. 124v.
1455–67	Fyna, abbess	TCD MS 654, f. 124v; *Statute rolls of the parliament of Ireland, Henry VI*, p. 406.
1467	Isabella Leyns, abbess	*Statute rolls of the parliament of Ireland, 1–12 Edward IV*, pp 338–41.
1467	Margery Bermingham, nun	*Statute rolls of the parliament of Ireland, 1–12 Edward IV*, pp 338–41.
1467	Isabella Bermyngham, nun	*Statute rolls of the parliament of Ireland, 1–12 Edward IV*, pp 338–41.
1479–82	Elizabeth, abbess	TCD MS 654, f. 124v.
1511	Elizabeth, abbess	TCD MS 654, f. 124v; BL Add. MS 4791, f. 199v.
1525–40	Margaret Silk, abbess	TCD MS 654, f. 124v.; "Reg. Cromer", *Louth Arch. Soc. Jn.* 10 (1941–4) pp 177–8; *Fiants Ire., Hen. VIII-Eliz.*, I, p. 15.
1535	Maria Cusack, nun	"Reg. Cromer", *Louth Arch. Soc. Jn.* 10 (1941–4) pp 177–8.
*c.*1540	Matilda Hancock, nun	*Extents Ir. mon. possessions*, p. 262; *Fiants Ire., Hen. VIII-Eliz.*, I, p. 15.
*c.*1540	Margaret Mape, nun	*Extents Ir. mon. possessions*, p. 262; *Fiants Ire., Hen. VIII-Eliz.*, I, p. 15.
*c.*1540	Joan Stanny, nun	*Extents Ir. mon. possessions*, p. 262; *Fiants Ire., Hen. VIII-Eliz.*, I, p. 15.
*c.*1540	Johanna Tancy[1]	*Fiants Ire. Hen. VIII-Eliz.*, I, p. 15.

Down

1353	Anne de Mandeville, prioress	*Cal. papal letters, 1342–62*, p. 509.
1353	Margaret de Mandeville, nun	*Cal. papal letters, 1342–62*, p. 509.

1 This could be the same woman as the previous entry.

Down (cont.)

1368	Matilda Stokys, nun	*Reg. Sweteman*, p. 84.
1462	Christina, prioress	"Reg. Prene", TCD MS 557/6, p. 237.
1462	Alicia, once prioress	"Reg. Prene", TCD MS 557/6, p. 237.

Grace Dieu, Co. Dublin

1235	Africa, prioress	"Calendar of the Liber Niger Alani", p. 419.
1294	Petronella, prioress	TCD MS 654, f. 106v; NAI RC 7/3, p. 255.
1301	Annabella, prioress	TCD MS 654, f. 106v.
1302	Amicia, heir of Robert son of Roger	NAI RC 7/9, p. 440.
1307–8	Isolda, prioress	TCD MS 654, f. 106v.
1359	Roysia, prioress	TCD MS 654, f. 106v.
1363–4	Mariota Wassra, prioress	TCD MS 654, f. 106v.; BL Add. MS 4791, f. 17.
1391–5	Elizabeth Tharn, prioress	TCD MS 654, f. 106v
1404–18	Margrina Traham, prioress	TCD MS 654, f. 106v.
1412	Elizabeth Tanner, nun	*Cal. papal letters, 1404–15*, p. 395.
1444–55	Elizabeth, prioress	TCD MS 654, f. 106r.
1466	Alison Cauod, nun	*Cal. papal letters, 1458–71*, p. 541.
1468	Elena Hacket, prioress	*Register of wills*, ed. Berry, p. 175.
1468	Alson Taylour, nun	*Register of wills*, ed. Berry, p. 175.
1468	Margaret Warde, nun	*Register of wills*, ed. Berry, p. 175.
1468	Katherine Hacket, nun, later prioress	*Register of wills*, ed. Berry, p. 175; *Book of Obits*, p. 71.
1468	Joan Hacket, nun	*Register of wills*, ed. Berry, p. 175.
1468	Anne Gelluys, nun	*Register of wills*, ed. Berry, p. 175.
1474	Alianora, prioress	Moran's notes, Archdall (1872) citing King's Collectanea, p. 136.
1475	Ellen, prioress	*Statute rolls of the parliament of Ireland 12 & 13–21 & 22 Edward IV*, pp 223–4.
1499	Margaret, prioress	TCD MS 1207/257/190.
1540–77	Alyson White, prioress	TCD MS 654, f. 106r, Archdall (1786) pp 217–8, *Fiants Ire., Hen. VIII-Eliz.*, I, p. 17.
1540	Margaret Cestre/ Coscrowe nun	*Extents Ir. mon. possessions*, p. 77; *Fiants Ire., Hen. VIII-Eliz.*, I, p. 17.

➤

Grace Dieu, Co. Dublin (cont.)

1540	Thomasina Dermen, nun	*Extents Ir. mon. possessions*, p. 77; *Fiants Ire., Hen. VIII-Eliz.*, I, p. 17.
1540	Katherine Eustace, nun	*Extents Ir. mon. possessions*, p. 77; *Fiants Ire., Hen. VIII-Eliz.*, I, p. 17.
1540	Alison Fitzsymond, nun	*Extents Ir. mon. possessions*, p. 77.

Graney

+1267–84	Matilda de Rupe. prioress	*Calendar of ancient records of Dublin*, I, pp 98–9.
1302	Amabilla, prioress	NAI RC 7/9 p. 281.
1317	Cris' de Rupe, once prioress	NAI RC 7/12 pp 501–2.
1385	Elizabeth, prioress	NAI M 2653, p. 52.
1409	Margery, prioress	Rot. pat. Hib., p. 196.
1531	Gylis, prioress	*Crown surveys of lands, 1540–1 with the Kildare rental*, p. 243.
–1535	Elizabeth Wale, prioress	Fitzgerald, "The priory and nunnery of Graney", p. 376.
1535	Agidia Wale, prioress	Archdall, (1789) pp 316–17; *Fiants Ire., Hen. VIII-Eliz.*, I, p. 13.

St Mary del Hogges

12th century	? Mor, sister of Lorcáin Ua Tuathail	BL Add. MS 4813, f. 51v–52.
March 22, 1271	Margaret, abbess, died	*Cal. doc. Ire., 1252–84*, p. 153.
Oct. 29, 1271	R., prioress Agneta, abbess	*Facsimiles of Ireland* II, LXXIV
1277	Roesia, abbess, died	*Cal. doc. Ire. 1171–1251*, p. 248.
1288	Isolde de la Hide, abbess, died	*Cal. doc. Ire., 1285–92*, p. 172.
1291–d.1309	Margaret, prioress/abbess	TCD MS 654, f. 106v.; NAI RC 7/4 p. 440; *Cal. pat. rolls 1307–13*, pp 193–4.
1309–30	Joanna de Arundell, abbess[2]	TCD MS 654, f. 78v; NLI MS 760, p. 284; NAI RC 8/15, pp 164, 198.
1336–40	Cecilia, ?prioress then abbess	TCD MS 654, f. 78v; NAI RC 8/20, pp 63; 115; 418–19.
1342–5	Margaret, abbess	TCD MS 654, f. 78v; "Cat. pipe roll", PRI rep. DK 54 (1927) p. 23.

2 The references to Joanna de Arundel date to 1309 and 1310, there are then references for 1318–30 to a Joanna, as abbess. This may refer to two different women named Joanna.

St Mary del Hogges (cont.)

1352	Alice Groun or Vroun, nun	*Cal. papal letters, 1342–62*, p. 470.
–1361	Alise Tirrell, ?once abbess	BL MS 4789, f. 19v.
1361	Margarete de Broun, abbess	BL MS 4789, f. 19v.
1379–d. 1409	Alica, abbess	TCD MS 654, f. 106v and 78v; *Rot. pat. Hib.*, p. 192.
1462–8	Juliana Walshe, abbess	TCD MS 1207/224–165; *Register of wills*, ed. Berry, p. 177.
1468	Jenet Darsys, nun	*Register of wills*, ed. Berry, p. 177.
1468	Alson Cruce, nun	*Register of wills*, ed. Berry, p. 177.
1468	Jonet Preston, nun	*Register of wills*, ed. Berry, p. 177.
1522–35	Margaret Graydon, abbess	TCD MS 654, f. 78v.
1535	Margareta Hubard, nun	"Reg. Cromer", *Louth Arch. Soc. Jn* 10 (1941–2) pp 177–8.
no date	Alicia Bron, nun	*Book of Obits*, p. 82.
no date	Matylda, abbess	*Book of Obits*, p. 50.

Kilcreevanty

before 1223	Orata, abbess	*Pont. Hib.* I, pp 239–43.
1261–96	Orlath[3]	TCD MS 654 f. 111r. ; NAI RC 7/1, p. 387; 426. *AClon. Cal. justic. rolls. Ire., 1295–1307*, pp 113–14.
1301	Finnghuala, daughter of Fedhlim O Connor, abbess, died.	ALC.
1325	More, abbess	Archdall, (1876), II, p. 219, note 21.
1446–7	Gormelina Yngnyconchar, nun	*Cal. papal letters, 1447–55*, p. 351
1543	Dervorgilla O Connor, abbess	Archdall, (1786), p. 799.

Kilculliheen

1264	Ellen, abbess, died	*Cal. doc. Ire., 1252–84*, p. 121.
1277	Desiderata le Poer, abbess, resigned	*Cal. doc. Ire., 1252–84*, p. 245.
1277– 82	Mabilla de Curcy, abbess, elected 1277 and resigned 1282.	*Cal. doc. Ire., 1252–84*, pp 253, 444.

→

3 This could refer to two different women.

Kilculliheen (cont.)

1287	Desiderata le Poher, died	*Cal. doc. Ire. 1285–92*, p. 145.
1291	Mabilla Comyn, abbess, died	*Cal. doc. Ire. 1285–92*, p. 490.
1292–*c*.1300	Joan, abbess	*Cal. doc. Ire. 1285–92*, p. 480; *Cal. doc. Ire. 1293–1301*, p. 357.
1302–07	Mabilla, abbess, died	NAI RC 7/9, p. 383; RC 8/1, pp 213–14.
1308–13	Joan Landeley, abbess, died	TCD MS 654, f. 111v; TCD MS 671, f. 28; BL Add MS 4791, f. 4v; NAI KB 2/5, p. 23; "Cat. pipe rolls", *PRI rep. DK* 39 (1907) p. 44.
1314–17	Isabella de Keynes, abbess	NLI MS 760, pp 321, 326; "Cat. pipe rolls", *PRI rep. DK* 39 (1907) p. 64.
1336	Isabella, abbess, died	"Cat. pipe rolls", *PRI rep. DK* 44 (1912) p. 60.
1342	Joanna, abbess, died	"Cat. pipe rolls", *PRI. rep. DK* 47 (1915) p. 62.
1350	Ismay, prioress	TCD MS 654, f. 111v.
1392	Isabelle Wolf, abbess	*Proceedings of the King's council Ireland, 1392–3*, pp 152–4.
1400	Joanna, abbess	Archdall, (1876) II, p. 326, note 12.
1450	Joanna, abbess,[4] resigned	*Cal. papal letters, 1447–55*, p. 508.
1450	Alsona Lang, abbess	*Cal. papal letters 1447–55*, p. 508.
c.1478	Alsona Elene, abbess deposed [?same woman as above]	"Obligationes pro annatis diocesis Ossoriensis", p. 12.
1478	Elinia Botiller, abbess[5]	*Cal. papal letters, 1458–71*, p. 636; "Obligationes pro annatis diocesis Ossoriensis", p. 12.
1531–40	Elicia Butler, abbess,[6] deposed, also known as Alice the nun.	*Ir. mon. deeds, 1200–1600*, p. 178; *Cal. pat. rolls Ire. Hen. VIII-Eliz.*, I, p. 2.; *Cal. state papers 1509–73*, p. 50; *Extents Ir. mon. possessions*, p. 206.
1540	Isabella or Katherine Mothing, abbess	*Extents Ir. mon. possessions*, p. 206; *Cal. pat. rolls Ire. Hen. VIII-Eliz.*, I, pp 61,137.
1540	Elicia Gaal, late abbess	*Extents Ir. mon. possessions*, p. 206.
1540	Egidia Fitz-John, nun	*Extents Ir. mon. possessions*, p. 206.
1540	Anastasia Cantwell, nun	*Extents Ir. mon. possessions*, p. 206.

➤

4 It is possible that these two entries refer to the same woman, but over fifty years as abbess seems a little unlikely so they have been listed as two. **5** The circumstances regarding the deposition of Alson Lang and the election of Elinia Botillier are not immediately clear; see Chapter 7. **6** It is probable that this Elicia is the same woman as Elinia Botillier; see Chapter 7.

Killevy

1540	Anne Clerc, nun	*Extents Ir. mon. possessions,* p. 206.
1454	Benmy ingen Mcdonochy Ohanlowan. prioress, died	*Registrum Johannis Mey* p. 371.
1454	Alicia engen Mcdonochy Ohanlowan, prioress, elected	*Registrum Johannis Mey* p. 371.
1542	Alicia ingen McDonchey Ohanlon. prioress	Archdall, (1786) p. 782.

Killone

1252	Mór, granddaughter of Turlough O Brien, wife of Cormac Mac Carthaigh, died at Killone.	*AI.*
1259	Slaine, daughter of Donnchad Cairbreach, abbess, died.	*AI.*
1350	Dubcollaighig O Brien, abbess, died	"Fragmentary annals from the west of Ireland", p. 153.
*c.*1460	Daughter of Conchobhar Mór Ó Briain, abbess	Haren, "Social structures", p. 220, citing Vatican Reg. Pen. 31, f. 217v and Reg. Pen. 34, f. 273r.
*c.*1480	relative of Toirdhealbhach MacMathghamhna Ó Briain, bishop of Killaloe.	Haren, "Social structures", p. 220, citing Reg. Pen. 50, f. 345r and Cal. papal letters, 1503–13, pp 199–200.
*c.*1500–10	Renalda Ní Bhriain ?daughter of Tadgh an Chomhaid Ó Briain, abbess.	NLI MS D 1978.
1510	Caterina Ní Bhriain, nun	NLI MS D 1978.
*c.*1540	Honora ny Brien, last abbess	*The genealogies, tribes and customs of Hy-Fiachrach*, p. 378.

Lismullin

1240–69[1]	Avicia de la Corner, founder and ?1st prioress.[7]	"Unpublished medieval notitiae and epistolae"; NAI RC 7/1, p. 463.
1250–69	Roesia, prioress	TCD MS 654, f.117v; NAI RC 7/1, p. 463.
1275–95	Alda or Aude, prioress	TCD MS 654, 117v; NAI RC 7/2, pp 95ff.; NAI RC 8/1, p. 162; NAI RC 7/3 pp 213, ff.

➛

7 Whether Avicia de la Corner was first prioress is not certain; it is also possible that these references are to two women of the same name.

Lismullin

1295–1318	Amica or Avicia de Houthe, prioress	TCD MS 654, f.117v.[8]
1319–41[9]	Elianora or Alianora Cusack, prioress	TCD MS 654, f.117v; BL Add. MS 4791, f. 8.; NAI RC 8/14, p. 561; 8/15, pp 47ff; 8/19, pp 200ff.
1347–61	Margaret, prioress	TCD MS 654, f. 117v; NAI MS M 2652, p. 30; *Rot. pat. Hib.*, p. 51.
1368	Katherine, prioress	*Cal. pat. Rolls, 1367–70*, p. 123.
1379	Agnes, prioress	TCD MS 654, f. 117v.
1390	Katherine, prioress	TCD MS 654, f.117v.
1398–1430	Agnes, prioress	TCD MS 654, f. 117v; *Rot. pat. Hib.*, pp 164, 174, 255.
1446	Thomasyna Birmyngham, prioress.	TCD MS 654, 117v.
1465–78	Margaret Huynot, prioress	TCD MS 654, f. 117v.; *Statute rolls of the parliament of Ireland, 1–12 Edward IV*, pp 379, 709–11; *Statute rolls of the parliament of Ireland 12 & 13–21 & 22 Edward IV*, p. 289; Archdall (1786), p. 556.
1511	Joanna Barrett, nun	Reg. Pen. 56, f. 828v cited by Haren, "Social Structures".
1540	Jenetta Barnwell, nun	*Extents Ir. mon. possessions*, p. 260.
1540	Alison Eustace, nun	*Extents Ir. mon. possessions,* p. 260.
1540–62	Anne Weldon, nun	*Extents Ir. mon. possessions*, p. 260; 'Rawl. A 237' p. 70.
1535–70	Mary Cusack, prioress[10]	*Extents Ir. mon. possessions*, p. 260; "Rawl. A 237", p. 70; NAI MS RC 10/2, pp 444–6.

Molough

1289	Juliana, prioress	BL MS 4789, f. 24.
1540	Joan Power, prioress	*Extents Ir. mon. possessions*, p. 336; *Fiants Ire., Hen. VIII-Eliz.*, I, p. 34.

➛

8 There are many more references to Amicia or Avicia de Houthe than listed, most of them in the Record Commissioners calendars of the proceedings of the crown courts. NAI RC 7/3–7/12; 8/1 and 10. **9** It is possible that there were two prioresses named Elianora who succeeded one another. The references to Elianora Cusack are all in the earlier years of this time-span so the Elianora named in 1337 and 1341 may be a different woman. **10** Probably originally a nun from Odder.

Termonfeckin

*c.*1440	Elina, prioress	*Reg. Swayne*, p. 183.
1467–80	Jenet White, prioress	*Statute rolls of the parliament of Ireland 12 & 13–21 & 22 Edward IV*, p. 421; "Reg. Cromer", *Louth Arch. Soc. Jn* 8 (1935) pp 169–71.
1480	Anna Onegan, nun	"Reg. Octavian", TCD MS 557/10 pp 869–70.
at least 1519–35	Alsona Plunket, prioress, died.	"Reg. Cromer", *Louth Arch. Soc. Jn 8* (1935) pp 176–8.
1540	Margaret Hubarde, prioress	*Cal. pat. rolls Ire., Hen. VIII-Eliz.*, I, p. 61.
1540	Ann Gaydon, nun	*Cal. pat. rolls Ire., Hen. VIII-Eliz.*, I, p. 61.

Timolin

t. King John	Lecelina, relative of Richard, Lord of Norragh	"Rep. Viride, Alen", p. 207.
*c.*1200	Lucie, prioress	*Chart. St Mary's, Dublin*, II, pp 18–19.
1289–1300	Joan de Waterford, prioress	*Cal. doc. Ire. 1285–92*, pp 423, 396, 403, 423; NAI RC 7/7, pp 60–1, 210; TCD MS 654, f. 128v.
1347–58	Lucia Chamberleu, prioress	TCD MS 654, f.
128v. 1362–5	Mabilla, prioress	TCD MS 654, f. 128v.
1367–8	Rhoesice, prioress	TCD MS 654, f. 128v.
1395	Isabella, prioress	TCD MS 654, f. 128v.
1401–18	Rosina/Roesia, prioress	TCD MS 654, f. 128v; NAI CB 1/5.
1445	Annisa, prioress	TCD MS 654, f. 128v.
1495–1518	Ellen Wulf, prioress	*Crown surveys of lands, 1540–1 with the Kildare rental begun in 1518*, pp 239–40.
no date	Eglantina, prioress	*Alen's reg.*, p. 306.
no date	Isabella, daughter of Robert de Start, nun	*Alen's reg.*, p. 306.

Other Religious Women

1190	Emeline, relative of Robert de Avencio, entered the Hospital of St John the Baptist, Dublin	*Reg. St John Dublin*, pp 172–3.

→

Other Religious Women (cont.)

1230	Duvesa, daughter of Roderic [Uí Chonchbair] and wife of Cathal MacDermot, died a nun[11]	*AConn.; ALC.*
1291	Beatrice, prioress of 'Balielan' probably St Catherine d'Conyl.	NAI RC 7/3, pp 26, 195.
1297	Agnes de Hareford, recluse and founder of St the Baptist, Cork	*Cal. just. rolls, 1295–1307*, p. 154; Dugdale, *Monasticon*, p. 1020; *Cal. doc. Ire., 1293–1301*, p. 365.
1300	Roesia de Naungles, anchorite	*Cal. just. rolls. 1295–1303*, p. 313.
1334–	Edda, prioress of Tagmon	"Cat. of pipe roll 8 Ed III", *PRI rep. DK* 44 (1912) pp 29–30.
1382	Bean-Midhe, daughter of Mac Maghnusa, a nun, died	*AU.*
15th century	Felicia, anchorite at Ballymudon	Archdall (1786), p. 216.
1430	Mary ingen Mcumab, abbess of Na Ferta, Armagh	*Reg. Swayne*, p. 128.
1437	Gormalaigh, daughter of David O Duibgennain, wife of Brian Mac Aedacain, and ultimately an anchorite	*AConn.*
1442	Finemhian, daughter of MacThomas, a devout nun, died	*AU.*
1447	Christine Holby, nun of Kildare	*Register Edmund Lacy*, II, p. 394.
1455	Benmon Ingen Omellan, abbess of St Brigid, probably in Armagh	"Reg. Prene", TCD MS 557/6 pp 414–16.
1456	Saive ingen Oconnolan, desiring to live continently, founded a hospice in Donougmore	*Registrum Johannis Mey*, p. 324.
1472	Honor Ni Carthaigh, abbess of Ballymacadane	Hayes, "Ballymacadane", pp 141–3.
1528	Finnguala, daughter of Conchobar O Briain, spent twenty-one years in robes of Third order, died	*AU.*

11 Possibly at Killcreevanty or one of its dependencies.

Bibliography

ADDITIONAL ABBREVIATIONS

Arch. Soc.	Archaeological society.
Cork Hist. Soc. Jn	*Journal of the Cork historical and archaeological Society.*
IER	*Irish Ecclesiastical Record.*
IHS	*Irish Historical Studies.*
Jn	*Journal.*
RIA Proc. C	*Royal Irish Academy Proceedings,* Part C.
RSAI Jn	*Royal Society of Antiquaries of Ireland, Journal.*
UJA	*Ulster Journal of Archaeology.*

UNPRINTED SOURCES

Belfast

Public Records Office Northern Ireland

MS DIO/4/2	Registers of archbishops of Armagh.

Dublin

Geneological Office, Dublin

MS 190–192	Extracts from the rolls.

National Archives of Ireland

CB 1	Common bench rolls.
KB 2	Calendars of justiciary rolls.
M 2542, 2645, 2652–3	Extracts from justiciary rolls.
M 2750	Places of justiciary sittings.
RC 7	Calendar of commonbench and plea rolls.
RC 8	Calendar of Memoranda rolls.
RC 10	Deeds and wills extracted from inquisitions – Exchequer Series

National Library of Ireland

MS 13	Collectanea de rebus Hibernia, transcribed by W. Harris.
MS 105	Materials for Irish ecclesiastical history, compiled by J. Lyons.
MS 676	Collections for Monasticon Hibernicon, compiled by M. Archdall.
MS 760	Extracts from the Pipe rolls compiled Sir W. Betham.
MS D 1978	Will of Renalda ny Briain.
MS 12025	Butler family history, compiled by T. Blake Butler.

Typescript of Ordnance Survey letters.

Trinity College

MS 557	Transcripts of the registers of the archbishops of Armagh
MS 579	Collectanea de rebus monasticia Hibernicae.
MS 653	Sternes' "Collectanea de rebus Hibernica".

MS 654	John Madden, "Extracts from the registers of several monasteries".
MS 671	John Madden, "Notes from records in Bermingham Tower".
MS 971	T. J. Westropp, "Notebook".
MS 972	T. J. Westropp, "Monastic and heraldic notes on Clare, Meath etc.
MS 1207	Miscellaneous Dublin deeds".

Ennis

Clare County Library

Irish Tourist Authority Survey, Clare East, Clarecastle parish (1943).

London

British Library

Add. MS 4789	James Ware, "Extracts from monastic registers etc".
Add. MS 4791	James and Robert Ware "Excerpts from rolls, registers, and histories, mainly concerned with ecclesasitical history".
Add MS 4813	James Ware, "Collections concerning religious houses in and around Dublin".
Add MS 19,865	Papers relating to the Sexton family of Limerick.
Add. MS 43,769	Extracts from the rolls concerning the Delafield family.
Egerton MS 1774–5	M. Archdall, *Monasticon Hibernicon* with notes by M. Mason.
Egerton MS 1783–6	*The Whole Works of James Ware*, revised and improved by W. Harris (1739–46) with notes by A. Cooper, Ab. Newcome, M. Archdall, J. Beresford and J. Lodge.

PRINTED SOURCES

"A commentary on the Nobility and Gentry of Thomond, *c.*1567", ed. K.W. Nicholls, *Irish Genealogist* 2 (1968) pp 65–73.

"A list of the Monasteries in Connacht, 1577", ed. K.W. Nicholls, *Galway Arch. Soc. Jn.* 33 (1972) pp 28–43.

A roll of the proceedings of the King's Council in Ireland 1392–3, ed. J. Graves (London, 1877).

"Abstracts of Manderville deeds", ed. P. Connolly, *Analecta Hibernica* 32 (1985) pp 3–26.

Account roll of the Priory of Holy Trinity, Dublin 1337–1346, ed. J. Mills (Dublin, 1891), rept. with introduction by J. Lydon and A. Fletcher (Dublin, 1996).

Acts of Archbishop Colton in his metropolitan visitation of the dioceses of Derry, AD MCCCXCVII with a rental of the see estates at that time, ed. W. Reeves (Dublin, 1850).

Aithdioghluim dána: A miscellany of Irish bardic poems, ed. and trans. L. McKenna (Dublin, 1939, 1940).

"An unpublished charter of Raymond le Gros", ed. E.StJ. Brooks, *RSAI Jn* 69 (1939) pp 167–9.

"Ancient Irish deeds and Writings etc", ed. J. Hardiman, *RIA Trans* (1828) pp 2–93.

Ancient Irish deeds and writings from the twelfth to seventeenth centuries, ed. J. Hardiman (Dublin, 1826).

Annala Connacht: the annals of Connacht 1224–1544, ed. A.M. Freeman (Dublin, 1844, rpt. 1970).

Annála rioghachta Eireann: Annals of the kingdom of Ireland from the earliest period to the year 1616 by the Four Masters, ed. and trans. J. O'Donovan (Dublin, 1851).

Annala Uladh: Annals of Ulster 431–1541, ed. W.M. Hennessy and Bartholomew MacCarthy (Dublin, 1887–1901).

"Annals of Christ church", ed. A. Gwynn, *Analecta Hibernica* 16 (1946) pp 324–9.

Annals of Ireland: three fragments copied from ancient sources by Dubhaltach Mac Firbisigh', ed. and trans. J. O'Donovan, *Miscellany Irish Archeological Celtic Society* (Dublin, 1860).

"Archbishop Cromer's register", ed. L.P. Murray and Aubrey Gwynn, *Louth Arc. Soc. Jn.* 7 (1929–30) pp 516–24; 8 (1933–6) pp 38–49, 169–88, 257–74, 322–51; 9 (1937–40) pp 36–41, 124–30; 10 (1941–4) pp 116–27, 165–79.

Archeological Inventory Co. Meath, comp. M. Moore (Dublin, 1987).

Bernard of Clairvaux, Life of St Malachy of Armagh, trans. H.J. Lawlor (London, 1920).

Book of Howth, vol. 6, *Calendar of Carew manuscripts, preserved in the archiepiscopal library at Lambeth*, ed. J.S. Brewer and W. Bullen (London, 1873).

Books of survey and distribution, ed. R.C. Simington, 4 vols (Dublin, 1944–67).

"Brussels MS 3947: Donatus Moneyus Provincia Hiberniae St Francisican", ed. B. Jennings, *Analelcta Hibernica* 6 (1934) pp 12–138.

Calendar of ancient deeds and muniments preserved in the Pembroke estate office, Dublin. (Dublin, 1891).

Calendar of Archbishop Alen's register, c.1172–1534, ed. C. McNeill (Dublin, 1950).

"Calendar of documents contained in the chartulary commonly called Dignitas Decani of St Patrick's Cathedral", ed. J.H. Bernard, *RIA Proc.* C 25 (1904–5) pp 481–507.

Calendar of documents relating to Ireland, ed. H.S. Sweetman, and G.F. Hancock (London, 1875–86).

Calendar of entries in the papal registers relating to Great Britian and Ireland: Papal letters, ed. W.H. Bliss, et.al. ed. (London and Dublin 1893–).

Calendar of inquisitions formerly in the office of the Chief Rememberancer of the Exchequer prepared from the manuscripts of the Irish Records Commissioners, ed. M. Griffith (Dublin, 1991).

Calendar of inquisitions post mortem (London, 1904–74).

Calendar of justiciary rolls of Ireland 1295–1307, comp. J. Mills (Dublin, 1905–14).

Calendar of patent and close rolls of chancery of Ireland. Henry VIII to 18th Elizabeth, ed. J. Morrin (Dublin 1861).

Calendar of the ancient records of Dublin, ed. J.T. and R.M. Gilbert (Dublin, 1889–1922).

Calendar of the Gormanston register (c.1175–1397), ed. J. Mills and M.J. McEnery (Dublin, 1916).

Calendar of inquisitions miscellaneous (chancery) (London, 1916–69).

Calendar of the justiciary rolls or the proceedings of the court of the justiciar of Ireland, I–VII Edward II prepared under the direction of H. Wood and A.E. Langman, ed. M. Griffith (Dublin, 1957).

"Calendar of the Liber Niger Alani", ed. G.T. Stokes, *RSAI Jn* 23 (1893) pp 303–420.

"Calendar of the Liber Niger and Liber Albus of Christ Church, Dublin", ed. H.J. Lawlor, *RIA Proc.* C 27 (1908) pp 1–93.

"Calendar of the Liber Ruber of the diocese of Ossory", ed. H.J. Lawlor, *RIA Proc.* C 27 (1908–9) pp 159–208.

"Calendar of the register of Archbishop Fleming", ed. H.J. Lawlor, *RIA Proc.* C 30 (1912–13) pp 94–190.

"Calendar of the register of Archbishop Sweteman", ed. H.J. Lawlor, *RIA Proc.* C 29 (1911–12) pp 213–310.

Calender of Ormond deeds 1172–1603, ed. E. Curtis (Dublin, 1932–43).

Calendar of patent rolls (London, 1906–).

"Catalogue of great rolls of the pipe of the Irish exchequer – Edward I", *PRI rep. DK* 36 (1904) pp 22–77; 37 (1905) pp 24–55; 38 (1906) pp 29–104.

"Catalogue of great rolls of the pipe of the Irish exchequer – Edward II", *PRI rep. DK* 39 (1907) pp 21–74; 42 (1911) pp 11–78.

"Catalogue of great rolls of the pipe of the Irish exchequer – Edward III", *PRI rep. DK* 43 (1912) pp 15–67; 44 (1912) pp 18–61; 45 (1913) pp 24–56; 47 (1915) pp 19–77; 53 (1926) pp 17–54; 54 (1927) pp 21–64.

"Catalogue of great rolls of the pipe of the Irish exchequer – Henry III", *PRI rep. DK* 35 (1903) pp 29–50.

"Catalogue of the mayors, provosts and bailiffs of Dublin city, 1229–1447", ed. H.F. Berry *PRIA Proc.* C 25 (1904–5) pp 21–106.

Chartularies of St Mary's abbey, Dublin with the register of its house at Dunbrody and annals of Ireland, ed. J.T. Gilbert (London, 1884).

Council books of the Corporation of Waterford 1662–1700 together with 9 documents of 1580–82, ed. S. Pender (Dublin, 1964).

Crede Mihi: the most ancient book of the archbishops of Dublin before the reformation, ed. J.T. Gilbert (Dublin, 1897).
Crown surveys of lands, 1540–1 with the Kildare rental begun in 1518, ed. G. Mac Niocaill (Dublin, 1992).
Documents on the affairs of Ireland before the King's council, ed. G.O. Sayles (Dublin, 1979).
Dowdall deeds, ed. C. McNeill, and A.J. Otway–Ruthven (Dublin, 1960).
Dugdale, William, *Monasticon Anglicanum: A history of the abbies and other monasteries, hospitals, friaries, and cathedrals and collegiate churches with their dependencies in England and Wales; also all such Scotch, Irish and French monasteries as were in any manner connected with religious houses in England*, ed. John Caley, Henry Elles and B. Bandinel (London, 1846, orig pub. 1672).
Ecclesiastical antiquities of Down, Connor and Dromore consisting of a taxation of those dioceses compiled in the year MCCCVI, ed. W. Reeves (Dublin, 1847).
Extents of Irish monastic possessions 1540–1, from manuscripts in the Public Record Office, London, ed. N.B. White (Dublin, 1943).
Finglas, P., "A breviate of the getting of Ireland and the decaie of the same. Made by Patrick Finglas Squire, Cheife Baron of the Exchequer in King Henry VIII's time", in *Hibernica or some ancient pieces relating to Ireland never hitherto made publick*, ed. Walter Harris (Dublin, 1747).
"Fragment of a lost register of the diocese of Clogher", ed. H.J. Lawlor, *Louth Arch. Soc. Jn.* 4 (1918) pp 226–57.
"Fragmentary annals from the west of Ireland", ed. E.J. Gwynn, *RIA Proc. C* 37 (1925–7) pp 149–57.
Giolla Brighde Mac Con Midhe, *The poems of Giolla Brighde Mac Con Midhe*, ed. and trans. N.J.A. Williams (Dublin, 1980).
Giraldus Cambriensis, *Topographia Hibernia – The history and topography of Ireland*, trans. John J. O'Meara (Dublin and Atlantic Highlands, NJ, 1982 2nd ed).
Giraldus Cambriensis, *Opera*, ed. J.F. Dimock (London, 1867).
Grace, J., *Annales Hibernicae*, ed. R. Butler (Dublin, 1842).
"History of the religious guild of S. Anne's in St Audoen's church, Dublin, 1430–1740", ed. H.F. Berry, *RIA Proc.* C 25 (1904–5) pp 21–106.
Irish Exchequer payments 1270–1446, ed. P. Connolly (Dublin, 1998).
Irish fiants of the Tudor soveriegns during the reigns of Henry VIII, Edward VI, Phillip and Mary and Elizabeth I (Dublin, 1994).
"Irish material in the class of Ancient Petitions (S.C. 8) in the PRO London", ed. P. Connolly, *Analecta Hibernica* 34 (1987) pp 1–106.
"Irish material in the class of Chancery warrants", *Analecta Hibernica* 36 (1995).
Irish monastic and episcopal deeds 1200–1600, transcribed from the originals preserved at Kilkenny Castle, with an appendix of documents of the sixteenth and seventeenth centuries relating to monastic property after the dissolution, ed. N.B. White (Dublin, 1936).
Irish patent rolls of James I: facsimile of the Irish Record Commission's calendar prepared prior to 1830 (Dublin, 1966).
John of Salisbury, Historia *Pontificalis*, ed. and trans. Majorie Chibnall (London, 1956).
Knights' fees in counties Wexford, Carlow and Kilkenny, ed. E. StJ. Brooks (Dublin, 1950).
"Late medieval Irish annals: two fragments", ed. K.W. Nicholls, *Peritia* 2 (1983) pp 87–102.
Leabhar Chlainne Suibhne: An account of the MacSweeny families in Ireland with pedigrees, ed. P. Walsh (Dublin, 1920).
Liber exemplorum ad usum praedicantium seculo XIII compostitus a quodam fratre minore Anglico de provincia Hibernia, ed. A.G. Little (London, 1908, rpt. 1966).
Life of St Declan of Ardmore and Life of St Mochuda of Lismore, ed. and trans. P. Power, Irish Texts Society 16 (London, 1914).
"List of Irish material in the class of Chancery Files (Records) C. 260 P.R.O. London", ed. P. Connolly, *Analecta Hibernica* 31 (1984) pp 1–18.
Lives of the Saints from The Book of Lismore, ed. W. Stokes (Oxford, 1890).

"Lord Chancellor Gerrard's notes of his report on Ireland", ed. C. McNeill, *Analecta Hibernica* 2 (1931) pp 93–291.
Martyrology of Donegal, trans. J. O'Donovan, ed. J. Todd and W. Reeves (Dublin, 1864).
Material for the history of the Franciscan province of Ireland 1230–1450, ed. E.B. Fitzmaurice and A.G. Little (Manchester, 1920).
McNeill, C., "Calendar of Harris" "Collectanea de Rebus Hibernicis", *Analecta Hibernica* 6 (1934) pp 248–450.
McNeill, C., "Report on recent acquisitions in the Bodlein Library", *Analecta Hibernica* 1 (1932).
Miscellaneous Irish annals (1114–1437), ed. S. Ó hInnse (Dublin, 1947).
"MS. Rawlinson A. 237. The Bodlein Library, Oxford", *Analecta Hibernica* 3 (1932) pp 151–218.
Notes of the Liber Primus Kilkenniensis, ed. C. McNeill (Dublin, 1927).
O'Flaherty, R.A., *Chorograhical description of west or h-lar Connaght, written 1684*, ed. J Hardiman (Dublin, 1846).
"Obligationes pro annatis diocesis Ardfertensis 1421–1517", ed. J. O'Connell, *Archivium Hibernicum* 21 (1958) pp 1–51.
"Obligationes pro annatis diocesis Casellensis 1433–1534", ed. L. Ryan and W. Skehan, *Archivium Hibernicum* 28 (1966) pp 1–32.
"Obligationes pro annatis diocesis Clonfertensis 1413–1531", ed. P.K. Egan, *Archivium Hibernicum* 21 (1958) pp 52–74.
"Obligationes pro annatis diocesis Cloynensis 1413–1526", ed. D. Buckley, *Archivium Hibernicum* 24 (1961) pp 1–30.
"Obligationes pro annatis diocesis Corcagiensis 1421–1526", ed. A. Bolster, *Archivium Hibernicum* 29 (1970) pp 1–32.
"Obligationes pro annatis diocesis Darensis, 1413–1521", ed. A. Coleman, *Archivium Hibernicum* 2 (1913) pp 39–72.
"Obligationes pro annatis diocesis Dublinensis, 1421–1520", ed. A. Coleman, *Archivium Hibernicum* 2 (1913) pp 1–37.
"Obligationes pro annatis diocesis Elphinensis 1426–1548", ed. G. Mac Niocaill, *Archivium Hibernicum* 22 (1959) pp 1–27.
"Obligationes pro annatis diocesis Fernensis 1413–1524", ed. J. Ranson, *Archivium Hibernicum* (1955) pp 1–15.
"Obligationes pro annatis diocesis Laoniensis 1421–1535", ed. D.F. Gleeson *Archivium Hibernicum* 10 (1943) pp 1–103.
"Obligationes pro annatis diocesis Limiricensis, 1426–1519", ed. M. Moloney, *Archivium Hibernicum* 10 (1943) pp 104–62.
"Obligationes pro annatis diocesis Lismorensis, 1426–1529", ed. P. Power, *Archivium Hibernicum* 12 (1946) pp 15–61.
"Obligationes pro annatis diocesis Ossoriensis, 1413–1531", ed. T.J. Clohosey, *Archivium Hibernicum* 20 (1957) pp 1–37.
"Obligationes pro annatis diocesis Rossensis, 1432–1533", ed. J. Coombes, *Archivium Hibernicum* 29 (1970) pp 33–48.
"Old Latin deeds in the library of Trinity College", ed. J.G. Smyly, *Hermathena* 66 (1945) pp 25–39; 67 (1946) pp 1–30; 69 (1947) pp 31–48; 70 (1947) pp 1–21; 71 (1948) pp 36–51; 72 (1948) pp 115–20; 74 (1949) pp 60–7.
"On some Irish deeds", ed. J. Todd, *RIA Proc. C* 7 (1857–61) pp 15–9.
Ordnance Survey memoir of Londonderry, ed. T. Colby (Dublin, 1837, rpt. Limavady, 1990).
Pontifica Hibernica, ed. M. Sheehy (Dublin, 1962).
Red Book of Ormond, ed. N.B. White (Dublin, 1932).
"Regestrum Monasterii fratrum praedictarum de Athernry", ed. A. Coleman, *Archivium Hibernicum* 1 (1912) pp 201–21.
Register of the abbey of St Thomas' Dublin, ed. J.T. Gilbert (London, 1889).
"Register of the chantry of St Saviour's, Waterford (BM Harl 3765)", ed. G. Mac Niocaill, *Analecta Hibernica* 23 (1962) pp 137–222.

Register of wills and inventories of the diocese of Dublin in the time of Archbishops Tregury and Walton 1457–1483, ed. H.F. Berry (Dublin, 1898).
Registrum Iohannis Mey, archbishop of Armagh 1443–1456, ed. W.G.H. Quigley and E.F.D. Roberts (Belfast, 1972).
Registrum de Kilmainham: register of chapter acts of the hosptial of St John of Jerusalem in Ireland 1326–39, ed. C. McNeill (Dublin, 1932).
Registrum monasterii B.V. Mariae de Tristernagh ... register of the priory of Tristernagh, ed. M.V. Clarke (Dublin, 1941).
Registrum Prioratus Omnium Sanctorum juxta Dublin, ed. R. Butler (Dublin, 1845).
Rerum Hibernicarum scriptores veteres, ed. C. O'Conor (Buckingham, 1814–26).
"Returns at dissolution of County Louth monasteries", trans. M. O Farrell, *Louth Arch. Soc. Jn* (1929–32) pp 45–52.
Rotulorum patentium et clausorum cancellarie Hibernicae calendarium, ed. E. Tresham (Dublin, 1828).
"Rotulus clausus de anno 48 Ed III – a reconstruction", ed. E. Dowse and M. Murphy, *Analecta Hibernica* 35 (1992) pp 89–154.
"Some unpublished texts from the Black Book of Christ Church, Dublin", ed. A. Gwynn, *Analecta Hibernica* 16 (1946) pp 281–338.
Stanyhurst, R., Description of Ireland, in *Chronicles*, ed. R. Holinshed (Facs. of 1807–8 edtion, New York, 1965), vol. IV.
Statute rolls of the parliament of Ireland 12 & 13–21 & 22 Edward IV, ed. J. Morrissey (Dublin, 1939).
Statute rolls of the parliament of Ireland, Henry VI, ed. H.F. Berry (Dublin, 1910).
Statute rolls of the parliament of Ireland, 1–12 Edward IV, ed. H.F. Berry (Dublin, 1914).
Statutes, ordinances and acts of parliament of Ireland, King John to Henry V, ed. H.F. Berry (Dublin, 1907).
Stephen of Lexington, Letters from Ireland 1228–9, trans. Barry W. O'Dwyer (Kalamazoo, 1982).
"Survey of the Memoranda rolls of the Irish Exchequer 1294–1509", ed. J. Lydon, *Analecta Hibernica* 23 (1966) pp 49–134.
The "Digniatas Decani" of St Patrick's Cathedral, ed. N.B. White (Dublin, 1957).
The annals of Clonmacnoise, being the annals of Ireland from the earliest period to 1408, trans. C. Mageoghagan and ed. D. Murphy (Dublin, 1896).
The annals of Inisfallen (MS Rawlinson B 503), ed. S. Mac Airt (Dublin, 1951).
The annals of Ireland by John Clyn and Thady Dowling together with the annals of Ross, ed. R. Butler (Dublin, 1849).
The annals of Loch Cé: a chronicle of Irish affairs 1014–1590, ed. W.M. Hennessy (London, 1871).
"The annals of Nenagh", ed. D.F. Gleeson, *Analecta Hibernica* 12 (1943) pp 155–64.
"The annals of Tigernach", ed. W. Stokes, *Revue Celtique* 16 (1895) pp 374–419, 17 (1896) pp 6–33, 119–263, 337–420, 18 (1897) pp 9–59, 150–97, 267–303.
The Black Book of Limerick, ed. J. Mac Caffrey (Dublin, 1907).
The Book of Obits and Martyrology of the cathedral church of the Holy Trinity, commonly called Christ Church, Dublin, ed. J.C. Crosthwaite, and J.H. Todd (Dublin, 1844), rpt. *The registers of Christ Church cathedral, Dublin*, ed. R. Refaussé with Colm Lennon (Dublin, 1998) pp 37–86.
"The charters of the Cistercian abbey of Duiske", ed. C.M. Butler and J.H. Bernard, *RIA* Proc. C 35 (1918) pp 1–188.
The Civil Survey 1654–1656, ed. R.C. Simington, 10 vols (Dublin, 1931–61).
"The commonbench plea roll of 19 Edward IV (1479–80)", ed. S. Ellis, *Analecta Hibernica* 31 (1984) pp 21–60.
The Dublin guild merchant roll 1190–1265, ed. P. Connolly and G. Martin (Dublin, 1992).
The genealogies, tribes and customs of Hy-Fiachrach commonly called O'Dowd's country, ed. and trans. J. O'Donovan (Dublin, 1844).
The Irish cartularies of Llanthony prima and secunda, ed. E. StJ. Brooks (Dublin, 1953).
"The Irish memoranda rolls: Some unexplored aspects", ed. P. Connolly, *Irish Economic & Social History* 3 (1976) pp 66–74.

The medieval pilgrimage to St. Patrick's Purgatory: Lough Derg and the European tradition, ed. M.J. Haren and Y. Pontfancy (Enniskillen, 1988).
The Red Book of the earls of Kildare, ed. G. Mac Niocaill (Dublin, 1964).
The register of Edmund Lacy, bishop of Exeter 1420–1455, ed. G.R. Dunstan (Torquay, 1963–72).
The register of John Swayne, archbishop of Armagh and primate of Ireland. 1418–1439, ed. D.A. Chart (Belfast, 1935).
The register of Milo Sweteman, archbishop of Armagh, 1361–1380, ed. B. Smith (Dublin, 1996).
The register of the hospital of St John the Baptist, Dublin, ed. E. StJ. Brooks (Dublin, 1936).
"The registrum novum: a manuscript of Holy Trinity cathedral the medieval charters", ed. M. Sheehy, *Reportorium Novum* 3 (1961–4) pp 249–81; 4 (1965) pp 101–33.
"The Reportorium Viride of John Alen, archbishop of Dublin, 1533", ed. N.B. White, *Analecta Hibernica* 10 (1941) pp 171–222.
The social state of the southern and eastern counties of Ireland in the sixteenth century ... ed. H.J. Hore and James Graves (Dublin, 1870).
The song of Dermot and the earl, ed. and trans. G.H. Orpen (Oxford, 1892).
Thesaurus Palaeohibernicus: A collection of Old-Irish glosses, scolia prose and verse, ed. W. Stokes and J. Strachan (Cambridge, 1901–03).
Ulster and other Irish maps c.1600, ed. G.A. Hayes (Dublin 1964).
"Unpublished medieval notitiae and epistolae", ed. M. Sheehy, *Collectanea Hibernica* 4 (1964) pp 7–17.
Vetera monumenta Hibernorum et Scotorum, ed. A. Theiner (1864).
Visio Tnugdali: The vision of Tnugdal by Brother Marcus, ed. and trans. J.-M. Picard (Dublin, 1989).
"Visitations of the dioceses of Clonfert, Tuam and Kilmacdough 1565–67", ed. K.W. Nicholls, *Analecta Hibernica* 26 (1970) pp 144–58.
Vitae sanctae Hiberniae. ed. C. Plummer (Oxford, 1910).

SECONDARY SOURCES

Archdall, M, *Monasticon Hibernicum or an history of the Abbies, Priores and other religious houses in Ireland* (London, 1786).
——, *Monasticon Hibernicum or an history of the Abbies, Priores and other religious houses in Ireland,* edited and expanded by P.F. Moran (Dublin 1876).
Archer, R., "'How ladies ... who live on their manors ought to manage their households and estates': Women as landholders and administrators in the later middle ages", in *Women as a worthy wight: Women in medieval English society, 1200–1500,* ed. P.J.P. Goldberg (Gloucester, 1992) pp 149–81.
Archer, R. and B.E. Ferme, "Testamentary procedure with special reference to the Executrix", *Reading Medieval Studies* 15 (1989) pp 3–33.
Armstrong, E.C.R., *Irish seal-matrices and seals* (Dublin, 1913).
——, "Some matrices of Irish seals", *RIA Proc.* C 30 (1912–1913) pp 451–76.
Barrett, A., "Books for nuns: Cambridge University Library MS Additional 3042", *Notes and Queries* n.s.44 (1997) pp 310–19.
Barron, C., "The parish fraternities of medieval London", in *The church in pre-reformation society: Essays in honour of F.R.H. Du Boulay,* ed. Caroline M. Barron and Christopher Harper-Bell (Woodbridge, 1985) pp 13–37.
Barry, T.B., *The archaeology of medieval Ireland* (London, 1987).
——, *The medieval moated sites of south-eastern Ireland: Counties Carlow, Kilkenny, Tipperary and Wexford* (Oxford 1977).
Bates, P., *Donabate and Portrane, a history* (Drogheda, 1988).
Bedos-Rezak, Brigitte, "French sigillographic sources for the history of women", in *Medieval women and the sources of medieval history,* ed. Joel T. Rosenthal (Athens, GA., 1990) pp 1–36.

Begley, J., *The Diocese of Limerick: ancient and modern* (Dublin, 1906).

Berman, C., Review of *Gender and material culture. The archaeology of religious women*, by Roberta Gilchrist. *Medieval Review* 95.08.02.

——, "Men's houses, women's houses: the relationship between the sexes in twelfth century monasticism", in *The medieval monastery*, ed. A. MacLeish (St Cloud, Minn. 1988) pp 43–52.

——, "Women as donors and patrons to southern French monasteries in the twelfth and thirteenth centuries", in *Worlds of medieval women: Creativity, influence and imagination*, ed. C.H. Berman, S.W. Connell and J. Rothschild (Morganstown, 1985) pp 53–68.

Bethell, D., "English monks and Irish reform in the eleventh and twelth centuries", *Historical Studies* 8 (1971) pp 111–35.

Bettey, J.H., *The suppression of the monasteries in the West Country* (London, 1989).

Biancalana, Joseph, "Widows at common law: the development of common law dower", *Irish Jurist* 23 (1988) pp 255–329.

Bigger, F.J., "Inis Cholthrann on Lough Ree: its history and antiquities", *RSAI Jn* (1900) pp 69–90.

Bishop, T.A.M., "Monastic demesnes and the statute of mortmain", *English Historical Review* 49 (1934) pp 303–6.

Bitel, Lisa, *Land of women: Tales of sex and gender from early Ireland* (Ithaca and London, 1996).

——, "Women's donations to the churches in early Ireland", *RSAI Jn* 104 (1984) pp 5–23.

——, *Isle of Saints: monastic settlement and Christian community in early Ireland* (Ithaca and London, 1990).

——, Women's monastic enclosures in early Ireland: a study of female spirituality and male monastic mentalities', *Jn of Medieval History* 12 (1986) pp 15–36.

Blake, M.J., "Knockmoy abbey", *Galway Arch. Soc. Jn.* 1 (1900) pp 65–85.

Board of Public Works, *Historical and descriptive notes with ground plans etc of the ecclesiastical remains of Sligo abbey* (Dublin, 1914).

Bond, C. James, "Water management in the rural monastery", in *The archaeology of rural monasteries*, ed. R. Gilchrist and H. Mytum (Oxford, 1989) pp 83–112.

Boyle, L., *Survey of the Vatican archives and its medieval holdings* (Toronto, 1972).

Bradley, John, "A medieval figure at Calliaghstown, Co. Meath", *RSAI Jn* 110 (1980) pp 149–52.

Bradshaw, B., "Nationalism and historical scholarship in modern Ireland", *IHS* 26 (1989) pp 329–51.

——, *The dissolution of the religious orders in Ireland under Henry VIII* (Cambridge, 1974).

Brady, C. ed. *Interpreting Irish history: the debate on historical revisionism 1938–1994* (Dublin, 1994).

Brady, C., "Political women and reform in Tudor Ireland", in *Women in early modern Ireland*, ed. Margaret Mac Curtain and Mary O'Dowd (Edinburgh, 1991) pp 69–90.

Brady, J., "The nunnery of Clonard", *Ríocht na Mídhe* 2 (1960) pp 4–7.

Brand, Paul, "King, church and property – the enforcement of restrictions on alienation into mortmain in the lordship of Ireland in the later middle ages", *Peritia* 3 (1984) pp 481–502.

——, "The formation of the parish: the case of Beaulieu, county Louth", in *Settlement and society in medieval Ireland: studies presented to F.X. Martin OSA*, ed. J. Bradley (Kilkenny, 1988) pp 261–76.

——, "The licensing of mortmain alienations in the medieval lordship of Ireland", *Irish Jurist* 21 (1986) pp 125–44.

Bhreathnach, E., "Medieval Irish history at the end of the twentieth century: unfinished work", *IHS* 32 (2000) pp 260–71.

Bridgett, T.E., *Blunders and forgeries* (London, 1890).

Brooks, E.StJ., "Fourteenth century monastic estates in Meath. The Llanthony cells of Duleek and Colp", *RSAI Jn* 83 (1953) pp 140–9.

——, "The de Ridelisfords", *RSAI Jn* 81 (1951) pp 115–38; 82 (1952) pp 45–61.

——, "The family of Marisco", *RSAI Jn* 61 (1931) pp 22–38; 89–112, 62 (1932) pp 50–74.

Brundage, James A. and Elizabeth M. Makowski, "Enclosure of nuns: the decretal Periculoso and its commentators", *Jn of Medieval History* 20 (1994) pp 143–55.

Bruzelius, C., "Hearing is believing: Clarissan architecture, *c.*1213–1340", *Gesta* 31 (1992) pp 83–91.

Bruzelius, C. and Constance Berman, "Introduction: Monastic architecture for women", *Gesta* 31 (1992) pp 72–5.

Buckstaff, Florence Griswold, "Married women's property in Anglo-Saxon and Anglo-Norman law and the origin of common-law dower", *Annals of the American Academy of political and social sciences* 4 (1893–4) pp 233–64.

Burgess, Clive, "A service for the dead: the form and function of the anniversary in late medieval Bristol", *Transactions of Bristol and Gloucestershire Arch. Society* 105 (1987) pp 183–221.

——, "Late medieval wills and pious convention: testamentary evidence reconsidered", in *Profit, piety and the professions in later medieval England,* ed. Micheal Hicks (Gloucester, 1990) pp 14–33

Burgess, Clive and B. Kümin, "Penetential bequests and parish regimes in late medieval England", *Jn of Ecclesiastic History* 44 (1993) pp 610–30.

Burke, W.P. "The nunnery of Kilculliheen", *Jn of the Waterford and South East of Ireland Arch. Soc.* 8 (1902) pp 9–17.

Burrows, M., "Fifteenth century Irish provincial legislation and pastoral care", in *The Churches, Ireland and the Irish,* ed. W.J. Sheils and D. Woods (Oxford, 1989) pp 55–67.

Butler, G., "Red Piers Butler of Ormond", *Jn of the Butler Society* 1 (1968) p. 38

Butler, L., "Medieval urban religious houses", in *Urban Archaeology in Britain,* ed. J. Schofield and R. Leech (London, 1987) pp 167–76.

——, "The archaeology of rural monasteries in England and Wales", in *The archaeology of rural monasteries,* ed. R. Gilchrist and H. Mytum (Oxford, 1989) pp 1–28.

Carrigan, William, *The history and antiquities of the diocese of Ossory* (Dublin, 1905).

Carville, G., "Cistercian nuns in medieval Ireland: Plary Abbey, Ballymore, Co. Westmeath", in *Hidden springs: Cistercian monastic women.* Vol III. *Medieval religious women,* ed. J.A. Nichols and L.T. Shank (Kalamazoo, 1995) pp 63–84.

——, *The occupation of Celtic sites in medieval Ireland by the Canons regular of St Augustine and the Cistercians* (Kalamazoo, 1982).

Champneys, A.C., *Irish ecclesiastical architecture* (London and Dublin, 1910, rpt. Shannon, 1970).

Chart, D.A., *A preliminary survey of the ancient monuments of Northern Ireland* (Belfast, 1940).

Clarke, H.B., "Urbs et suburbium: beyond the walls of medieval Dublin", in *Dublin and beyond the pale: studies in honour of Patrick Healy,* ed. Conleth Manning (Dublin, 1998) pp 45–58.

——, ed., *Medieval Dublin: making a metropolis* (Blackrock, 1990).

——, ed., *Medieval Dublin: The living city* (Blackrock, 1990).

Clark-Maxwell, W.G., "The outfit for the profession of an Austin Canoness at Lacock, Wilts. in the year 1395 and other memoranda", *Archaeological Jn* 69 (1912) pp 117–24.

Clay, M., *The medieval hospitals of England* (London, 1966).

Cochrane, R., "Abbey Knockmoy, County Galway: notes on the building and frescoes", *RSAI Jn* 34 (1904) pp 244–53.

Cogan, An., *The diocese of Meath: ancient and modern* (1862–70. Revised Dublin, 1993).

Colker, M., *Trinity College Dublin: descriptive catalogue of the medieval and renaissance manuscripts* (Aldershot, 1991).

Comerford, M., *Collections from dioceses of Kildare and Leighlin* (1883–6).

Comerford, R.V., *Religion, conflict and coexistence in Ireland: Essays presented to P.J. Corish* (Dublin, 1990).

Conlan, Patrick, *Franciscan Ireland* (Mullingar, 1988).

Connolly, P., "The medieval plea rolls – an introduction", *Irish Archives: Jn of the Irish Society for Archives* (Spring 1995) pp 3–11.

Conwell, E.A., *A ramble around Trim: amongst its ruins and antiquities* (Dublin, 1872).

Cooke, Kathleen, "The English nuns and the dissolution", in *The cloister and the world: Essays in medieval history in honour of Barbara Harvey,* ed. John Blair and Brian Golding (Oxford, 1996) pp 287–301.

Corish, P., "Women and religious practice", in *Women in early modern Ireland*, ed. M. Mac Curtain and M. O'Dowd, (Edinburgh, 1991) pp 212–22.
Cosgrove, A., "Consent, consummation and indissolubility: some evidence from medieval ecclesiastical courts", *Downside Review* 109 (1991) pp 94–104.
——, "The Armagh register: an under explored source for late medieval Ireland", *Peritia* 6–7 (1990 for 1987–8) pp 307–20.
Cosgrove, A. ed., *New history of Ireland*. vol. II *Medieval Ireland* (Oxford, 1987, 1992)
Cotter, F., *The Friars Minor in Ireland from their arrival to 1400*, ed. Roberta A. McKelvie, (St Bonaventure, New York, 1994).
Cowell, G.Y., "St Brigid and the cathedral church of Kildare", *Kildare Arch. Soc. Jn.* 2 (1896–1899) pp 235–52.
Cownie, E., *Religious patronage in Anglo-Norman England 1066–1135* (Woodbridge, Suffolk, 1998).
Craig, M., *The architecture of Ireland from the earliest times* (London and Dublin, 1982).
Crawford, H.S., "A descriptive list of Irish shrines and reliquaries", *RSAI Jn* 53 (1923) pp 74–93 and 151–76.
Cullerton, C., "From barrow boy to Viscount, the story of Matthew Barnwall", *History Ireland* 7: 4 (1999) pp 5–6.
Cullum, P., "And hir name was charité: women and charity in medieval Yorkshire", in *Woman is a worthy wight: women in medieval English society 1200–1500*, ed. P.J.P Goldberg (Gloucester, 1992) pp 182–211.
——, "St. Leonard's Hospital, York: the spatial and social analysis of an Augustinian Hospital", in *Advances in monastic archaeology*, ed. R. Gilchrist and H.Mytum (Oxford, 1993) pp 11–18.
——, "Vowesses and female lay piety in the province of York, 1300–1500", *Northern History* 32 (1996) pp 21–41.
Cunningham, B., "Women and Gaelic literature, 1500–1800", in *Women in early modern Ireland*, ed. M. Mac Curtain and M. O'Dowd (Edinburgh, 1991) pp 147–59.
Curran, A., "The priory of St Leonard, Dundalk", *Louth Arch. Soc. Jn* 17: 3 (1971) pp 131–40.
Curran, M.J., "Dublin diocesan archives", *Reportorium Novum* 2:1 (1958) pp 1–2.
D'Alton, E.D., *History of the archdiocese of Tuam* (Dublin, 1928).
D'Alton, J., *History of the county of Dublin* (Dublin 1838).
Daichman, G.S., "Misconduct in the medieval nunnery: fact, not fiction", in *That gentle strength: Historical perspectives on women in Christianity*, ed. L.L. Coon, K.J. Jaldane and E.W. Sommer (Charlotteville, 1990) pp 97–117.
Davies, W., "Introduction", *The Cloister Symposium,* Gesta 12 (1973).
de Breffny, B. and George Mott, *The churches and abbeys of Ireland* (London, 1976).
de Burgo, T., *Hibernica Dominicana* (1762).
de Paor, L., "Excavations at Mellifont Abbey, Co. Louth", *RIA Proc.* C 68 (1969) pp 109–64.
de Paor, A., "The status of women in medieval Ireland", *University College Galway Women's Studies Review* 3 (1995) pp 69–79.
Degler-Spengler, B., "The incorporation of Cistercian nuns into the order in the twelfth and thirteenth centuries", in *Hidden springs: Cistercian monastic women Medieval religious women*, vol. III, ed. J.A. Nichols and L.T. Shank (Kalamazoo, 1995) pp 85–134.
Dickenson, J.C., "English regular canons and the continent in the twelfth century", *Transactions of the Royal Historical Society* 5th series 1 (1951) pp 71–90.
Dinn, R., "Monuments answerable to men's worth: Burial patterns, social status and gender in late medieval Bury St Edmunds", *Jn of Ecclesiastic History* 46 (1995) pp 237–55.
Dobson, B., "Citizens and chantries in late medieval York", in *Church and city 1000–1500, Essays in honour of Christopher Brooke*, ed. D. Abulafia, M. Franklin and M. Rubin (Cambridge, 1992) pp 311–32.
Donahue, C., "Female plaintiffs in marriage cases in the court of York in the later middle ages: What can we learn from the numbers", in *Wife and widow in medieval England*, ed. Sue Sheridan Walker (Chicago, 1994) pp 183–214.

Donnelly, N., "Incumbents of Killadreenan and the archdeacons of Glendalough in the fifteenth century", *RSAI Jn 23* (1893) pp 123–39.
Dowd, J., *History of Limerick*, ed. Cian O Carroll (Dublin, 1990).
Duffy, E., *The stripping of the altars: traditional religion in England, 1400–1580* (New Haven, 1992).
Duffy, S., *Ireland in the middle ages* (London, 1997).
——, "The first Ulster plantation: John de Courcy and the men of Cumbria", in *Colony and frontier in medieval Ireland: Essays presented to J.F. Lydon*, ed. T.B. Barry, R. Frame and K. Simms (London and Rio Grande, 1995) pp 1–27.
Duffy, S., ed. *Atlas of Irish history* (Dublin, 1997).
Dunning, P.J. "Irish representatives and Irish ecclesiastical affairs at the Fourth Lateran Council", in *Medieval studies presented to Aubrey Gwynn*, ed. J.A. Watt, J.B. Morrall and F.X. Martin (Dublin, 1961) pp 90–113.
——, "The Arroasian order in medieval Ireland", *IHS* 4 (1944–5) pp 297–315.
Dyer, C., "Gender, archeology and documents", in "Review article: Gender and material culture *The archaeology of religious women*", R. Gilchrist et al. *Cambridge Archaeological Jn* 6 (1996) pp 122–4.
Eager, B., "Tristernagh Priory: The establishment of a colonial monastic house in the lordship of Meath, *c.*1220", in *The churches, Ireland and the Irish.* ed. W.J. Sheils and D. Woods (Oxford, 1989) pp 25–36.
Eames, E. and T. Fanning, *Irish medieval tiles: decorated medieval paving tiles in Ireland with an inventory of sites and designs and a visual index* (Dublin, 1988).
Edwards, R. Dudley, "The king of England and papal provision in fifteenth–century Ireland", in *Medieval studies presented to Aubrey Gwynn*, ed. J.A. Watt, J.B. Morrall and F.X. Martin (Dublin, 1961) pp 265–80
Egan, P., "The Augustinian Priory of St.Mary, Clonstuskert O Many", *Galway Arch. Jn.* 22 (1946–7) pp 1–14.
Elkins, S., *Holy women in twelfth century England* (Chapel Hill, 1988).
Elliott, D., "Sex in holy places: An exploration of a medieval anxiety", *Jn of Women's History* 6: 3 (1994) pp 6–34.
Ellis, S., *Reform and revival, English government in Ireland, 1470–1534* (Woodbridge, 1984)
——, "'More Irish than the Irish themselves?' the 'Anglo-Irish', in Tudor Ireland", *History Ireland* 7 no. 1 (Spring 1999) pp 22–6.
——, "Historiographical debate: representations of the past in Ireland: whose past and whose present"? *IHS* 27 no. 108 (Nov. 1991) pp 289–308.
Empey, C.A., "Conquest and settlement patterns of Anglo-Norman settlement in north Munster and south Leinster", *Irish Economic and Social History* 8 (1986) pp 5–31.
——, "Medieval Knocktopher: a study in manorial settlement", *Old Kilkenny Review* NS 4 (1982) pp 329–42; 5 (1983) pp 441–52.
——, "The Butler lordship", *Jn of the Butler Society* 1 (1970–1) pp 174–87.
——, "The sacred and the secular: the Augustinian priory of Kells in Ossory 1193–1541", *IHS* 24 (1984) pp 131–51.
Erikson, A., *Women and property in early modern England* (Routledge, 1992).
Erler, M.C., "English vowed women at the end of the middle ages", *Medieval Studies* 57 (1995) pp 155–203.
Everson, P., "Rural monasteries within the secular landscape", in *The archaeology of rural monasteries*, ed. R. Gilchrist and H. Mytum (Oxford, 1989) pp 141–6.
Fanning, T., "Excavations at Clontuskert Priory, Co. Galway", *RIA Proc.* C 76 (1976) pp 97–169.
Fenning, H., "The Dominicans of Trim: 1263–1682", *Ríocht na Midhe* 3 (1963) pp 15–23.
Fitzgerald, W., "An ancient church pavement tile from Timolin", *Kildare Arch. Soc. Jn.* 8 (1915) p. 328.
——, "Narraghmore and the barons of Norragh", *Kildare Arch. Soc. Jn.* 7 (1912–14) pp 242–65.
——, "Notes on Lady Margaret Fitzgerald who married Pierce, 8th earl of Ormonde in 1485", *Kildare Arch. Soc. Jn.* 8 (1915–7) pp 503–11.

——, "The priory and nunnery of Grany, Co. Kildare", *Kildare Arch. Soc. Jn* 7 (1912–14) pp 373–81.
——, "Timolin", *Kildare Arch. Soc. Jn.* 2 (1896–9) pp 413–25.
Fitzpatrick, E., Mairgréag an-Einigh Ó Cearbhaill, "The best of the women of the Gaiedhil", *Kildare Arch. Soc. Jn.* 18 (1992–3) pp 20–38.
Fitzpatrick, E. and C. O'Brien, *The medieval churches of County Offaly* (Dublin, 1998).
Flanagan, M.T., *Irish society, Anglo-Norman settlers, Angevin kingship: interactions in Ireland in the late twelfth century* (Oxford, 1989).
——, "St Mary's Abbey, Louth, and the introduction of the Arroasian observance into Ireland", *Clogher Rec.* 10 (1979–80) pp 223–34.
Flanagan, U.G., "Papal letters of the fifteenth century as a source for Irish history", *Proceedings of the Irish Catholic Historical Committee* (1958) pp 11–15.
——, "Papal provisions in Ireland 1305–78", *Historical Studies* 3 (1961) pp 92–103.
Fleming, P.W., "Charity, faith and the gentry of Kent 1422–1529", in *Property and politics in later medieval English history*, ed. Tony Pollard (Gloucester, 1984) pp 36–58.
Fletcher, A.J., "The civic pagentary of Corpus Christi in 15th and 16th century Dublin", *Irish Economic and Social History* 23 (1996) pp 73–96.
Flood, W.H. Grattan, "St Brigid's Priory, Clonsilla", *IER* 20 (1922) pp 138–44.
Flower, R. and M. Dillon, *Catalogue of Irish manuscripts in the British Museum* (London, 1953).
Ford, A., *The Protestant reformation in Ireland*, 1590–1641 (2nd edition, Dublin, 1997).
Frame, R., *English lordship in Ireland 1318–1361* (Oxford, 1982).
——, "Les Engleys nées en Irlande": The English political identity in medieval Ireland', *Transactions of the Royal Historical Society* 6th ser. 3 (1991) pp 83–103.
——, "Military service in the lordship of Ireland 1290–1360: Institutions and society on the Anglo-Gaelic frontier", in *Medieval frontier societies*, ed. Robert Bartlett and Angus MacKay (Oxford, 1989) pp 101–26.
——, "The defence of the English lordship, 1250–1450", in *A military history of Ireland,* ed. Thomas Bartlett and Keith Jeffrey (Cambridge, 1996) pp 76–98.
French, K.L., *The people of the parish: community life in a late medieval English diocese* (Philadephia, 2001).
Fry, S., *Burial in medieval Ireland, 900–1500: a review of the written sources* (Dublin, 1999).
Gaimster, M., S. Margeson and T. Barry compiled, "Medieval Britain and Ireland: excavations in 1988", *Medieval Archaeology* 33 (1989).
Gallagher, D.B., "The planning of Augustinian monasteries in Scotland", in *Meaningful architecture: social interpretations of buildings*, ed. M. Lococ (Aldershot, 1994) pp 167–87.
Gallwey, H., "The Cusack family of Cos Meath and Dublin", *Irish Genealogist* 5 (1974–9) pp 298–313; 464–70; 591–600; 673–84.
Gardiner, E.J., "The English nobility and monastic education *c.*1100–1500", in *The cloister and the world: essays in medieval history in honour of Barbara Harvey*, ed. John Blair and Brian Golding (Oxford, 1996) pp 80–94.
Gilchrist, R., "Blessed art thou among women: the archaeology of piety", in *Woman is a worthy wight: women in medieval English society 1200–1500*, ed. P.J.P Goldberg, (Gloucester, 1992) pp 212–26.
——, *Contemplation and action: The other monasticism* (London, 1995).
——, "Community and self: perception and use of space in medieval monasteries", *Scottish Archeology Review* 6 (1989) pp 55–64.
——, *Gender and material culture: the archaeology of religious women* (London, 1994).
——, "The archaeology of medieval English nunneries: a research design", in *The archaeology of rural monasteries,* ed. R. Gilchrist and H. Mytum (Oxford, 1989) pp 251–60.
——, "The spatial archaeology of gender domains: a case study of medieval English nunneries", *Archaeological Review from Cambridge* 7 (1988) pp 21–8.
Gillespie, R., *Devoted people: Belief and religion in early modern Ireland* (Manchester, 1997).
Gilmore, H., "Killone Convent", *The Other Clare* 6 (1982) pp 22–5.

Glynn, J.A., "Knockmoy Abbey, County Galway", *RSAI Jn* 34 (1900) pp 239–53.
Goaley, M., *Monastic ruins at Annaghdown, Co. Galway* (Annaghdown, 1974).
Gold, P.S., *The lady and the Virgin: Image, attitude, and experience in twelfth century France* (Chicago, 1985).
Golding, B., "Burials and benefactions: An aspect of monastic patronage in thirteenth-century England", in *England in the thirteenth century*, ed. W.M. Ormrod (Woodbridge, 1985) pp 64–75.
Graham, B.J., "Medieval settlements in County Meath", *Ríocht na Midhe* 5 (1974) pp 40–67.
——, "The high middle ages *c.*1100–1350", in *An historical geography of Ireland* ed. B.J. Graham and L.J. Proudfoot (London, 1993) pp 58–98.
Graham, B.J. and L.J. Proudfoot, "A perspective on the nature of Irish historical geography", in *An historical geography of Ireland*, ed. B.J. Graham and L.J. Proudfoot (London, 1993) pp 1–18.
Graves, Corburn V., "Stixwould in the market-places", in *Medieval religious women. Distant Echoes*, vol. I, ed. J.A. Nichols and L.T. Shank (Kalamazoo, 1984) pp 213–36.
Graves, James and J.G.A. Prym, *The history, architecture and antiquities of the cathedral church of St Canice, Kilkenny* (Dublin, 1857).
Greene, J. Patrick, *Medieval monasteries* (London and New York, 1992).
——, *Norton Priory. The archeology of a medieval religious house* (Cambridge, 1989).
Griffith, M.C., "The Talbot-Ormond struggle for control of the Anglo-Irish government 1414–47", *IHS* 2 (1940–1) pp 376–97.
Gwynn, A. *Anglo-Irish church life the fourteenth and fifteenth centuries. History of Irish Catholicism*, vol. 2, part 4 (Dublin and Sydney, 1968).
——, "The early history of St Thomas' Abbey", *RSAI Jn* 84 (1954) pp 1–35.
——, *The Irish church in the eleventh and twelfth centuries*, ed. G. O'Brien (Dublin, 1992).
——, *The medieval province of Armagh from 1460–1546* (Dundalk, 1946).
——, "The origins of St Mary's Abbey, Dublin", *RSAI Jn* 74 (1949) pp 110–25.
——, *The twelfth century reform. History of Irish Catholicism*, vol. 2, part 1 (Dublin and Sydney, 1966).
——, "Towards a new 'Monasticon Hibernicum'", *Proceedings of the Irish Catholic Historical Committee* (1958) pp 24–8.
Gwynn, A. and R.N. Hadcock, *Medieval religious houses: Ireland* (Dublin, 1970).
Hadcock, R.N., "The origin of the Augustinian order in Meath", *Ríocht na Midhe* 3 (1964) pp 124–31.
Hall, D., "Necessary collaborations: Religious women and lay communities in medieval Ireland, *c.*1200–1540", in *Female experiences: Essays in Irish women's history*, ed. Diane Urquhart and Alan Hayes (Dublin, forthcoming) pp 15–29.
——, "The nuns of the medieval convent of Lismullin, Co. Meath and their secular connections", *Ríocht na Midhe* 10 (1999) pp 58–70.
——, "Towards a prosopography of nuns in medieval Ireland", *Archivium Hibernicum* 53 (1999) pp 3–15.
Halpin, A. and L. Buckley, "Archeological excavations at the Dominican Priory, Drogheda, Co. Louth", *RIA Proc.* C 95 (1995) pp 175–253.
Hamburger, J., "Art, enclosure and the Curia Monialium: Prolegomena in the guise of a postscript", *Gesta* 31 (1992) pp 108–34.
——, *Nuns as artists: The visual culture of a medieval convent* (Berkeley, 1997).
Hand, G., "Dating of the early fourteenth-century ecclesiastical valuation of Ireland", *Irish Theological Quarterly* 24 (1957) pp 271–4.
——, "English law in Ireland, 1172–1351", *Northern Ireland Legal Quarterly* 13 (1967) pp 393–422.
——, *English law in Ireland 1290–1324* (Cambridge, 1967).
——, "Material used in Calendar of documents relating to Ireland", *IHS* 12 (1960) pp 99–104.

——, *The church in the English lordship, 1216–1307. A History of Irish Catholicism* vol. 2, pt. 3 (Dublin and Sydney, 1968).
——, "The Psalter of Christ Church, Dublin (Bodl. MS Rawlinson G 185)", *Reportorium Novum* 1 (1956) pp 311–22.
Harbison, P., "A medieval tombstone from Graney", *Kildare Arch. Soc. Jn.* 17 (1987–91) pp 216–7.
——, *Pilgrimage in Ireland: The monuments and the people* (Syracuse and London, 1992).
Hardiman, James, *History of the town and county of Galway* (Dublin, 1820).
Harding, V., "Burial choice and burial location in late medieval London", in *Death in towns: urban responses to the dying and the dead 100–1600*, ed. S.Bassett (Leicester, 1992) pp 119–35.
Hare, J.N., "The monks as landlords: The leasing of the demenses in southern England", in *The church in pre-reformation England*, ed. C. Barron and C. Harper-Bill (Woodbridge, 1985).
Haren, M.J. "Social structures of the Irish church: A new source in papal penitentary dispensations for illegitimacy", in *Illegitimität im Spämittelalter. Schriften des Historischen Kollegs. Kolloquien*, 29, ed. L. Schmugge (Munich, 1994) pp 207–26.
——, "The religious outlook of a Gaelic lord: a new light on Thomas óg Maguire", *IHS* 25 (1986) pp 195–7.
Harris, B., "A new look at the reformation: Aristocratic women and nunneries 1450–1540", *Jn. of British Studies 32* (1993) pp 89–113.
Hartshorne, A., "Notes on a recumbent monumental effigy in the churchyard of Timolin", *Kildare Arch. Soc. Jn. 1* (1891–5) pp 131–4.
Harvey, B., *Living and dying in England 1100–1540: The monastic experience* (Oxford, 1993).
Hayes, J.P., "Ballymacadane Abbey, Co. Cork", *Cork Hist. Soc. Jn.* 3 (1894) pp 141–3.
Hayman, S., *Notes and records of the ancient religious foundations at Youghal, Co. Cork and its vicinity* (Youghal, 1854).
Healy, J., "Two royal abbeys by the western lakes – Cong and Inishmaine", *RSAI Jn 35* (1905) pp 1–20.
Heath, P., "Urban piety in the later middle ages: The evidence of the Hull wills", in *The church, politics and patronage in the fifteenth century*, ed. B. Dobson (Glouceseter, 1984) pp 209–34.
Helmholz, R.H., "Married women's wills in later medieval England", in *Wife and widow in medieval England*, ed. Sue Sheridan Walker (Chicago, 1994) pp 165–82.
Hennessey, M., "Parochial organisations in medieval Tipperary", in *Tipperary: History and society: Interdisciplinary essays on the history of an Irish county*, ed. W. Nolan and Thomas McGrath (Dublin, 1985) pp 71–91.
Hennessy, M., "The priory and hospital of New Gate: the evolution and decline of a medieval monastic estate", in *Common ground: Essays on the historical geography of Ireland presented to T. Jones Hughes,* ed. W.J. Smyth and K.Whelan (Cork, 1988) pp 41–54.
Herity, H., "The layout of Irish early Christian monasteries", in *Irland und Europa, Ireland and Europe, Die Kirche im Frühmittelalter, The early church.* ed. P. Ní Chatháin and Michael Richter (Stuttgart, 1984).
Herlihy, D., "Land, family and women in continental Europe 701–1200", *Traditio* 18 (1962) pp 89–120.
Hewson, G.J., "Sheela-na-Guira", *RSAI Jn* 22 (1892) pp 437–8.
Hickey, E., "A medieval stone at St John's cemetery, Kells", *Ríocht na Midhe* 5:4 (1974) pp 104–5.
——, *Clonard: The story of an early Irish monastery 520–1202* (Leixlip, 1998).
——, "Monument to Sir Thomas Cusacke", *Ríocht na Midhe* 5: 1 (1975) pp 75–91.
——, "St Mary's abbey and the church at Skryne", *RSAI Jn.* 82 (1952).
——, *Skryne and the early Normans* (Meath, 1994).

Hicks, M., "Chantries, obits and almshouses: the Hungerford foundations 1325–1478", *The church in pre-reformation England*, ed. C. Barron and C. Harper-Hill (Woodbridge, Suffolk, 1985) pp 123–42.

Hochstetler, D., "The meaning of monastic cloister for women according to Caesarius of Arles", in *Religion, culture and society in the early middle ages*, ed. T.F.X. Noble and J.J. Contreni (Kalamazoo, 1987) pp 27–40.

Hunt, J., *Irish medieval figure sculpture 1200–1600: a study of Irish tombs with notes on costume and armour* (Dublin and London, 1974).

Hymans, P.R., "The charter as a source for the early common law", *Jn of Legal History* 12 (1991) pp 173–89.

Jefferies, Henry A., *Priest and prelates of Armagh in the age of reformations, 1518–1558* (Dublin, 1998).

Jennings, B., "The chalices and books of Kilconnell Abbey", *Galway Arch. Soc. Jn.* 21 (1944) pp 63–70.

Johns, S., "The wives and widows of the earls of Chester, 1100–1252: The charter evidence", *Haskin Society Jn* 7 (1995) pp 117–32.

Johnson, P., *Equal in monastic profession: Religious women in medieval France* (Chicago, 1991).

——, "The cloistering of medieval nuns: Release or repression, reality or fantasy", in *Gendered domains: rethinking public and private in women's history*, ed. D.C. Hely and S.M. Reverby (Ithaca N.Y. and London, 1992) pp 27–39.

Joyce, P.W., *Irish place names explained, rpt in Book of Irish names, first, family and place*, ed. R. Coglan et. al (New York, 1989).

Joyce, W.StJ., *The neighbourhood of Dublin: its topography, antiquities and historical association* (Dublin 1912).

Kearney, J., *Killeigh and Geashill (Co. Offaly): A pictorial record* (Tullamore, 1990).

——, *The long ridge: Towards a history of Killeigh parish* (Tullamore, 1992).

Kearns, M., "The abandoned canopy", *The Other Clare* 21 (1997) pp 14–5.

Kehnel, A., "The lands of St Ciarán", in *Clonmacnoise studies.* vol. 1, ed. H.A. King (Dublin, 1998) pp 11–17.

Kehoe, I., "Margaret Fitzgerald, wife of Piers Butler, 8th Earl of Ormond and 1st Earl of Ossory", *Old Kilkenny Review* NS 4 (1991) pp 826–41.

Kelly, J.P., "The priory of Lismullin", *Ríocht na Midhe* 3 (1961) pp 53–6.

Kerr, B.M., *Religious life for women, c.1100–c.1350: Fontevraud in England* (Oxford, 1999).

King, H.A., "Late medieval crosses in County Meath c.1470–1635", *RIA Proc.* C 84 (1984) pp 79–115.

Knox, H.T., *Notes on the early history of the dioceses of Tuam, Killala and Achonry* (Dublin, 1904).

Langrishe, R., "Notes on Jerpoint Abbey, Co. Kilkenny", *RSAI Jn* 36 (1906) p. 190.

Lawlor, H.J., "The genesis of the diocese of Clogher", *Louth Arch. Soc. Jn.* 4 (1917).

Leask, H., *Irish churches and monastic buildings* (Dundalk 1955–60).

——, "The Augustinian abbey of St Mary the Virgin, Cong, Co. Mayo", *Galway Arch. Soc. Jn.* 19 (1940–41) pp 107–18.

Leclerq, L., "Hospitality and monastic prayer", *Cistercian Studies* 8 (1973) pp 3–24.

——, "La monachisme fèminin au moyen áge", *Cistercian Studies* 1 (1980) pp 445–58.

Lee, Gerald A., *Leper hospitals in medieval Ireland* (Dublin, 1996).

Lenihan, M., *Limerick: its history and antiquities* (Cork, 1866, rpt. 1967).

Lennon, C., "The chantries of the Irish reformation: the case of St Anne's Guild, Dublin, 1550–1630", in *Religion, conflict and coexistence in Ireland*, ed. R.V. Comerford, M. Cullen, J.R. Hill and C. Lennon (Dublin, 1990) pp 6–25.

Lewis, S., *Topographical dictionary of Iree English in medieval Ireland. Proceedings of the first joint meeting of the Royal Irish Academy and the British Academy*, Dublin 1982 ed. J. Lydon (Dublin, 1984) pp 1–26.

Lynch, A., "A calendar of the reassembled register of John Bole, archbishop of Armagh 1457–71", *Seanchas Ard Machas* 15 (1992) pp 113–85.
——, "Religion in late medieval Ireland", *Archivium Hibernicum* 36 (1981) pp 3–15.
Lynn, C. J., "Excavation in the Franciscan Friary church, Armagh", *UJA* 38 (1975) pp 61–80.
——, "Recent archaeological excavations in Armagh city: An interim report", *Seanchas Ard Machas* 8 (1977) pp 275–80.
Lyons, M.A., *Church and society in County Kildare, c.1470–1547*, (Dublin, 2000).
——, "Revolt and reaction: The Geraldine rebellion and monastic confiscation in County Kildare 1535–1540", *Kildare Arch. Soc. Jn.* 18 (1992–3) pp 39–60.
McAuliffe, M, "The lady in the tower: The social and political role of women in tower houses", in "*The fragility of her sex"? Medieval Irishwomen in their European context*, ed. C. Meek and K. Simms (Dublin, 1996) pp 153–62.
Mac Carthy, Charles J.F., "Ballymacadane Abbey", *Cork Examiner* 9 March 1935 p. 13.
McCotter, P., "The sub-infeudation and descent of the Fitzstephen/Carew moeity of Desmond", *Cork Hist. Arch. Soc. Jn.* 101 (1996) pp 64–106; 102 (1997) pp 89–106.
Mac Curtain, M., "Women, education and learning in early modern Ireland", in *Women in early modern Ireland*, ed. M. Mac Curtain and M. O'Dowd (Edinburgh, 1991) pp 160–78.
Mac Curtain, M. and M. O'Dowd, "An agenda for women's history I: 1500–1800", *IHS* 28 (1992) pp 1–19.
McEneaney, E., "The government of the municipality of Waterford in the thirteenth century", *Decies* 13 (Jan 1980) pp 17–27.
McErlean, T., "The Irish townland system of landscape organisation", in *Landscape archeology in Ireland*, ed. Terence Reeves-Smith and Fred Hammond (Oxford, 1983) pp 315–40.
McGrath, M., "The materials and techniques of Irish medieval wall painting", *RSAI Jn* 117 (1987) pp 96–124.
McKenna, E., "The gift of a lady: women as patrons in medieval Ireland", in *Women in renaissance and early modern Europe, ed. C. Meek* (Dublin, 2000) pp 84–94.
——, "Was there a political role for women in medieval Ireland? Lady Margaret Butler and Lady Eleanor MacCarthy", in *"The fragility of her sex"? Medieval Irishwomen in their European context*, ed. C. Meek and K.Simms (Dublin, 1996) pp 163–74.
Mac Kenna, J.E., "The Franciscan Abbey of Creevelea, Co. Leitrim", *UJA* 5: 4 (1899) pp 190–201.
McLaughlin, M.M., "Looking for medieval women: an interim report on the project – 'Women's religious life and communities AD500–1500'", *Medieval Prosopography* 8 (1987) pp 61–91.
Mac Mahon, Michael, "The charter of Clare abbey and the Augustinian province of Co. Clare", *The Other Clare* 17 (1993) pp 21–8.
McNamara, J., *Sisters in arms: Catholic nuns through two millennia* (Cambridge, Mass. and London, 1996).
McNeill, C., "Hospital of St. John without the New Gate, Dublin", *RSAI Jn* 51 (1925) pp 58–64.
——, "The Hospitallers of Kilmainham and their guests", *RSAI Jn* 54 (1924) pp 15–39.
——, "Accounts of sums realised by sales of chattel of some suppressed Irish monasteries", *RSAI Jn* 52 (1922) pp 11–37.
——, "Some Drogheda gilds and properties", *Louth Arch. Jn. 6* (1928) pp 239–46.
——, "The suppression commission of 1539 and religious houses of Co. Louth", *Louth Arch. Jn.* 5 (1923) pp 161–4.
McNeill, T., *Castles in Ireland: Feudal power in a Gaelic world* (London and New York, 1997).
Mac Niocaill, G., "Aspects of Irish law in the late thirteenth century", *Historical Studies* 10 (1976) pp 25–42.
——, "The contact of Irish and common law", *Northern Ireland Legal Quarterly* 23 (1972) pp 16–23.
——, "The interaction of laws", in *The English in medieval Ireland*, ed. J. Lydon (Dublin, 1984) pp 105–18.

Magery, M.P., *The transforming power of nuns: Women, religion and cultural change in Ireland, 1750–1900* (New York & Oxford, 1998).
Makowski, E., *Canon law and cloistered women: Periculoso and its commentators 1298–1545*, (Washington, D.C. 1997).
Martin, F.X., "The Augustinian friaries in pre-reformation Ireland", *Augustiniana* 6 (1956) pp 346–84.
——, "The Irish Augustinian reform movement in the fifteenth century", in *Medieval studies presented to A. Gwynn*, ed. J.A. Watt, J.B. Morrall and F.X.Martin (Dublin, 1961) pp 230–64.
Mason, E., "The role of the English parishioner, 1100–1500", *Jn of Ecclesiastic History* 27 (1976) pp 17–29.
——, "Timeo barones et donas ferentes", in *Religious motivation: biographical and sociological problems for the church historian*, ed. D.Baker (Oxford, 1978) pp 61–75.
Massey, E., *Prior Roger Outlaw of Kilmainham, 1314–41* (Dublin, 2000).
Manning, C., *Clonmacnoise* (Dublin, 1994).
Map of Monastic Ireland (Dublin, 1979).
Medioli, F., "An unequal law: the enforcement of clausura before and after the Council of Trent", in *Women in renaissance and early modern Europe*, ed. C. Meek (Dublin, 2000) pp 136–52.
Meigs, S., *The reformations in Ireland: Tradition and confessionalism, 1400–1690* (Dublin, 1997).
Meyvaert, P., "The medieval monastic claustrum", *Gesta* 12 (1973) pp 53–60.
Milis, L.M., *L'ordre des chaniones règuliers d'Arrouaise. Son historie et son organisation de la foundation de L'Abbaye-mère (vers 1090) la fin des chaptres annuels (1471)* (Bruges, 1969).
Mills, J., "Tenants and agriculture near Dublin in the fourteenth century", *RSAI Jn* 21 (1890–1) pp 54–63.
——, The Norman settlement in Leinster – the cantred near Dublin', *RSAI Jn* 24 (1894) pp 161–75.
Milne, G., *St Bride's church London: Archeological research 1952–60 and 1992–5* (London, 1997).
Mitchell, L.E., "The lady is a lord: Noble widows and land in thirteenth-century Britain", *Historical Reflections/Reflexions historiques* 18 (1992) pp 71–98.
Monck Mason, W.H., *The history and antiquities of the collegiate and cathedral church of St Patrick's near Dublin from its foundation 1190 to 1819* (Dublin, 1820).
Mooney, C., "Irish church in the sixteenth century", *IER* 99 (1963) pp 102–13.
——, "Irish Franscican libraries of the past", *IER* 60 (1942) pp 215–28.
——, "The Franciscans in Ireland", *Terminus* 8 (1954) pp 66–9, 84–7, 105–8, 126–8, 150–53, 180–2; 9 (1954) pp 193–5; 10 (1954) pp 245–50; 11 (1955) pp 5–9, 39–41, 85–9, 128–32; 12 (1956) pp 14–17, 40–4.
——, *The church in Gaelic Ireland: thirteenth to fifteenth centuries. History of Irish Catholicism*, vol. 2, part 5 (Dublin 1966).
Moore, A., "The cell of the canonesses regular of St Augustine at Clonoghill", *Old Athlone Society Jn* 1 (1969) pp 15–6.
Moorhouse, S., "Monastic estates: their composition and development", in *The archaeology of rural monasteries,* ed. R. Gilchrist and H. Mytum (Oxford, 1989) pp 29–82.
Mortimer, R., "Religious and secular motives for some English monastic foundations", in *Religious motivation: Biographical and sociological problems for the church historian*, ed. D. Baker (Oxford, 1978) pp 77–85.
Mount, C., "Five early Bronze Age cemeteries in Brownstown, Graney West, Oldtown and Poopluck, Co. Kildare and Strawhall, Co. Carlow", *RIA Proc.* C 98 (1998) pp 25–99.
Mulhulland, J., "The trial of Alice Butler, abbess of Kilculiheen", *Decies*, Old Waterford Society 25 (Jan 1984) pp 45–6.
Mullarkey, T., "St Mary's Abbey, Devernish: An architectural survey", *Clogher Record* 4 (1960–61) pp 9–15.

Murphy, B., "The status of the native Irish after 1331", *Irish Jurist* 2 (1967) pp 116–38.
Murphy, D., "Townland survey of Co. Louth: Termonfeckin", *Louth Arch. Jn* 21 (1985–8) pp 398–406.
——, "On two monastic seals lately come into the possession of the academy", *RIA Proc.* C 3 (1893–6) pp 371–3.
Murphy, M., "Balancing the concerns of church and state: The archbishops of Dublin, 1181–1228", in *Colony and frontier in medieval Ireland: essays presented to J.F. Lydon* (London, 1995) pp 41–56.
——, "Ecclesiatical censure: an aspect of their use in thirteenth century Dublin", *Archivium Hibernicum* 44 (1989) pp 89–97.
——, "The high cost of dying: an analysis of pro anima bequests in medieval Dublin", in *The church and wealth*, ed. W.J. Sheils and D. Wood (Oxford, 1987) pp 111–22.
Murray, J., "Archbishop Alen, Tudor reform and the Kildare rebellion", *RIA Proc.* C 89 (1989) pp 1–16.
Murray, L., "Archbishop Swayne's visitation of Meath (A.D. 1428)", *IER* 22 (1923) pp 240–6.
Neary, A., "The origins and character of the Kilkenny witchcraft case of 1324", *RIA Proc.* C 83 (1983) C pp 333–50.
Neely, W.G., "The Ormond Butlers of County Kilkenny, 1515–1715", in *Kilkenny: History and society. Interdisciplinary essays on the history of an Irish county*, ed. W. Nolan and K. Whelan (Dublin, 1990) pp 107–26.
Ní Dhonnchadha, M., "Caillech and other terms for veiled women in medieval Irish texts", *Éigse* 28 (1994–5) pp 71–96.
Ní Mharcaigh, M., "The medieval parish churches of south-west Co. Dublin", *RIA Proc.* C 97 (1997) pp 245–96.
Ní Shéaghdha, *N. Collectors of Irish manuscripts: motives and methods* (Dublin, 1985).
Nicholls, K., "Anglo-French Ireland and after", *Peritia* 1 (1982) pp 370–403.
——, "Irishwomen and property in the sixteenth century", in *Women in Early modern Ireland*, ed. M. Mac Curtain and M. O'Dowd (Edinburgh, 1991) pp17–31.
——, *Gaelic and Gaelicised Ireland in the middle ages* (Dublin, 1972).
——, *Land, law and society in sixteenth-century Ireland* (Dublin, 1976).
——, "Rectory, vicarage and parish in the western Irish dioceses", *RSAI Jn* 101 (1971) pp 53–84.
——, "Worlds apart? The Ellis two-nation theory on late medieval Ireland", *History Ireland* 7 no. 2 (Summer 1999) pp 22–6.
Nichols, J., "The architectural and physical features of an English Cistercian nunnery", *Cistercian Ideals and reality*, ed. J. Sommefledt (Kalamazoo, 1978) pp 319–28.
——, "The internal organization of English Cistercian nunneries", *Cîteaux* 30 (1979) pp 23–40.
——, "Why found a medieval Cistercian nunnery", *Medieval Prosopography* 12:1 (1991) pp 1–28.
Ó Cléirigh, C., "The O'Connor Faly lordship of Offaly, 1395–1513", *RIA Proc.* C 96 (1996) pp 87–102.
Ó Conbhuí, C., "The lands of St Mary's Abbey, Dublin", *RIA Proc.* C 62 (1961–3) pp 21–86.
Ó Corráin, D., *Ireland before the Normans* (Dublin, 1972).
Ó Cróinín, D., *Early medieval Ireland 400–1200* (London, 1995).
Ó Dálaigh, B., "Mistress, mother and abbess, Renalda Ní Bhrian", *North Munster Antiquarian Jn* 32 (1990) pp 50–63.
O'Dowd, M., "Women and the law in early modern Ireland", in *Women in renaissance and early modern Europe*, ed. C. *Meek* (Dublin, 2000), pp 95–108.
Ó Floinn, R., *Irish shrines and reliquaries of the middle ages* (Dublin, 1994).
Ó hÉailidhe, P., "The cloister arcade from Cook Street, Dublin", in *Settlement and society in medieval Ireland: Studies presented to F.X. Martin OSA*, ed. J. Bradley (Kilkenny, 1988) pp 377–420.
O'Brien, C. and P.D. Sweteman ed., *Archaeological inventory of County Offaly* (Dublin, 1997).
O'Dwyer, B., "Gaelic monasticism and the Irish Cistercians *c.*1228", *IER* 108 (1967) pp 19–28.

——, *The conspiracy of Mellifont, 1213–1231: an episode in the history of the Cistercian order in medieval Ireland* (Dublin, 1970).
——, "The impact of the native Irish on the Cistercians in the thirteenth century", *Jn of Religious History* 4 (1966–7) pp 287–301.
O'Dwyer, P., Mary: *A history of Irish devotion* (Dublin, 1988).
——, *Towards a history of Irish spirituality* (Dublin, 1995).
O'Keeffe, T., *An Anglo-Norman monastery: Bridgetown priory and the architecture of the Augustinian canons regular in Ireland* (Cork, 1999).
O'Rorke, T., *History of Sligo town and county* (Dublin, 1890).
O'Sullivan, D., "The monastic establishments of medieval Cork", *Cork Hist. Soc. Jn* 48 (1943) pp 9–18.
O'Sullivan, H., "The march of south-east Ulster in the fifteenth and sixteenth century", in *The borderlands: Essays on the history of the Ulster-Leinster border,* ed. Raymond Gillespie and Harold O'Sullivan (Belfast, 1989) pp 55–74.
O'Sullivan, W., "A finding list of the manuscripts of James Ware", *RIA Proc.* C 98 (1998) pp 69–99.
——, "Ussher as a collector of manuscripts", *Hermathena* 88 (1956) pp 34–58
Oliva, M., "Aristocracy or meritocracy? Office holding patterns in late medieval English nunneries", *Studies in Church History* 27 (1990) pp 197–208.
——, "Counting nuns: A prosopography of late medieval English nuns in the diocese of Norwich", *Medieval Prosopography* 16 (1995) pp 27–55.
——, *The convent and community in late medieval England: Female monasteries in the diocese of Norwich, 1350–1540* (Woodbridge, Suffolk, 1998).
Ordinance Survey of Ireland, Dublin c840–c1540: the medieval town in the modern city (Dublin, 1978).
Orpen, G.H., *Ireland under the Normans* (Oxford, 1911–20).
——, "Mottes and Norman castles in Ireland", *EHR* 22 (1907) pp 228–54; 440–7.
Otway-Ruthven, A.J., "Parochial development in the rural deanery in Skreen", *RSAI Jn* 94 (1964) pp 111–22.
——, "The medieval church lands of County Dublin", in *Medieval Studies presented to Aubrey Gwynn*, ed. J.A. Watt, J.B. Morrall and F.X. Martin (Dublin, 1961) pp 54–73.
——, "The native Irish and English law in medieval Ireland", *IHS* 7 (1950–1) pp 1–16.
——, "The organisations of Anglo-Irish agriculture in the middle ages", *RSAI Jn* 81 (1951) pp 1–13.
Parker, C., "Paterfamilias and Parentela: The le Poer lineage in fourteenth century Waterford", *RIA Proc.* C 95 (1995) pp 93–117.
Parrey, Y., "'Devoted disciples of Christ': early sixteenth-century religious life in the nunnery at Amesbury", *Historical Research* 67 (1994) pp 240–9.
Paterson, T.G.F and O. Davies, "The churches of Armagh", *UJA* 3rd Series 3 (1940) pp 82–103.
Pedersen, F., "Did the medieval laity know the canon law rules on marriage? Some evidence from fourteenth century York cause papers", *Medieval Studies* 56 (1994) pp 111–52.
Phelan, M.M., "An unidentified tomb in St Canice's Cathedral, Kilkenny", *Old Kilkenny Review* 48 (1996) pp 40–4.
Platt, C., *The monastic grange in medieval England* (London, 1969).
Postles, D., "Choosing witnesses in twelfth-century England", *Irish Jurist* 23 (1988) pp 333–46.
——, "Heads of religious houses as administrators", in *England in the thirteenth century*, ed. W.M. Ormond (Stamford, 1991).
——, "Lamps, lights and layfolk: 'popular' devotion before the Black Death", *Jn of Medieval History* 25 (1999) pp 97–114.
Power, C., "A demographic study of human skeletal remains from historic Munster", *UJA* 57 (1997 for 1994) pp 95–118.
——, "The human remains of 19–20 Cove St Cork City", *Cork Hist. Soc. Jn* 102 (1997) pp 79–88.
Power, E., *Medieval English nunneries c.1275–1535* (Cambridge, 1922).

Power, F., *Life of Frances Power Cobbe by herself* (London, 1894).
Power, P., "The priory, church and hospital of St John the Evangalist, Waterford", *Waterford and South East Ireland Arch. Soc. Jn* 2 (1896) pp 81–97.
——, *Waterford and Lismore: A compendious history of the united dioceses* (Dublin & Cork, 1937).
Quinn, J.F., *History of Mayo*, ed. Brendan Quinn (Ballina, 1993).
Rabin, S., *Mortmain legislation and the English church 1279–1500* (Cambridge and New York, 1982).
Rae, E., "Irish sepulchral monuments of the later middle ages", *RSAI Jn* 100 (1970) pp 1–38; 101 (1971) pp 1–40.
——, "The sculpture of the cloister of Jerpoint abbey", *RSAI Jn* 96 (1966) pp 59–104.
Reade, G.H., "Cill-Sleibhe-Cuillinn founded by St Darerca alias Moninne, about 518", *RSAI Jn* 6 (1867) pp 93–102.
Reeves, W., "On the townland distribution of Ireland", *RIA Proc.* 7 (1857–61) pp 473–90.
——, "The ancient churches of Armagh", *UJA* 2nd Series 2 (1896) pp 194–204; 3 (1897) pp 193–5; 6 (1900) pp 24–33.
Robinson, D.M., The *geography of Augustinian settlement in medieval England and Wales* (Oxford, 1980).
Roe, H.M., "Funerary monuments of south-east Ireland", in *Dublin and beyond the pale: Studies in honour of Patrick Healy* ed. Conleth Manning (Dublin, 1998) pp 209–18.
——, "Illustrations of the Holy Trinity in Ireland 13th to 17th centuries", *RSAI Jn* 109 (1979) pp 101–50.
Ronan, M.V., "Anglo–Norman Dublin and diocese", *IER* 5th series 45 (1935) pp 148–64, 274–91, 485–504, 576–95; 46 (1935) pp 11–30, 154–71, 257–75, 377–93, 490–510, 577–96; 47 (1936) pp 28–44, 144–63, 459–68; 48 (1936) pp 170–93, 378–96; 49 (1937) pp 155–64.
——, "Killadreenan and Newcastle", *RSAI Jn* (1933) pp 172–81.
——, "Lazar houses of St Laurence and St Stephen in medieval Dublin", in *Essays and studies presented to Professor Eoin MacNeill on the occasion of his seventieth birthday, May 15th, 1938*, ed. John Ryan (Dublin, 1940) pp 480–9.
——, *Reformation in Dublin* (Dublin, 1926).
——, "Religious customs of Dublin medieval guilds", *IER* 26 (1925) pp 225–47, 364–81.
Rosenthal, J.T., ed. *Medieval women and the sources of medieval history* (Athens, GA, 1990).
Rousseau, C.M., "Pope Innocent III and familial relationships of clergy and religious", *Studies in Medieval and Renaissance History* 14 (1993) pp 105–48.
Schulenburg, J.T., "Strict active enclosure and its effects on the female monastic experience (c. 500–1100)", in *Distant echoes: Medieval religious women* 1, ed. J.A. Nichols and L.T. Shank (Kalamazoo, 1984) pp 51–86.
——, "Women's monastic communities, 500–1100: Patterns of expansion and decline", *Signs* 14 (1989) pp 261–92.
Scrase, A.J., "Working with British property records, the potential and the problems", in *Power, profit and urban land: land ownership in medieval and early modern European towns* ed. Finn-Einar Eliassen and G. Ersland (Aldershot, 1996) pp 15–38.
Seymour, StJ.D., *The diocese of Emly* (Dublin, 1913).
Sharpe, R., *Medieval Irish saints' lives – An introduction to Vitae Sanctorum Hiberniae* (Oxford, 1991).
Sheehan, M., *Marriage, family and law in medieval Europe*, ed. James K. Farge (Toronto, 1996).
Simms, A., "The geography of Irish manors: the example of the Llanthony cells of Dulleek and Colp, County Meath. With an appendix by John Bradley", in *Settlement and society in medieval Ireland: Studies presented to F.X. Martin OSA*, ed. J. Bradley (Kilkenny, 1988) pp 291–326.
Simms, K., "Archbishop of Armagh and the O'Neills", *IHS* 19 (1974) pp 38–55.
——, "Bards and barons: The Anglo-Irish aristocracy and the native culture", in *Medieval frontier societies*, ed. Robert Bartlett and Angus MacKay (Oxford, 1989) pp 177–98.
——, *From kings to warlords: The changing political structure of Gaelic Ireland in the later middle ages* (Suffolk, 1987).

——, "Frontiers in the Irish church: Regional and cultural", in *Colony and frontier in medieval Ireland: essays presented to J.F. Lydon*, ed. TB. Barry, R. Frame and K. Simms (London and Rio Grande, 1995) pp 178–216.

——, "The legal position of Irish women in the later middle ages", *Irish Jurist* (1975) pp 96–111.

——, "Women in Gaelic society during the age of transition", in *Women in early modern Ireland*, ed. Margaret Mac Curtain and Mary O'Dowd (Edinburgh, 1991) pp 32–42.

——, "Women in Norman Ireland", in *Women in Irish society*, ed. Margaret Mac Curtain and Donncha Ó Corráin (Dublin, 1978) pp 14–25.

Smith, B., *Colonisation and conquest in medieval Ireland: The English in Louth, 1170–1330* (Cambridge, 1999).

——, "Tenure and locality in north Leinster in the early thirteenth century", in *Colony and frontier in medieval Ireland: Essays presented to J.F. Lydon*, ed. T.B. Barry, R. Frame and K. Simms (London and Rio Grande, 1995) pp 29–40.

Smith, C., *The ancient and present state of Cork* (1750, rpt Cork, 1815).

Smith, R.M., "Some thoughts on 'hereditary and propriety' rights in the land under customary law in thirteenth and early fourteenth century England", *Law and History Review* 1 (1983) pp 95–128.

——, "Women's property rights under customary law: some developments in the thirteenth and fourteenth centuries", *Transactions of the Royal Historical Society* 5th series, 35 (1985) pp 165–94.

Smyth, W.J., "A pluralities of Irelands: Regions, societies and mentalities", in *In search of Ireland: A cultural geography*, ed. B. Graham (London & New York, 1997) pp 19–42.

Stalley, R.A., *Ireland and Europe in the middle ages: Selected essays on architecture and sculpture* (London, 1994).

——, Irish Gothic and English fashion', in *The English in medieval Ireland*, ed. J. Lydon (Dublin, 1984) pp 65–86.

——, "Mellifont Abbey: A study of its architectural history", *RIA Proc.* C 80 (1980) pp 263–354.

——, "Sailing to Santiago: Medieval pilgrimage to Santiago de Compostella and its artistic influence in Ireland", in *Settlement and society: Studies presented to F.X. Martin, OSA* ed. John Bradley (Kilkenny, 1988) pp 397–420.

——, *The Cistercian monasteries of Ireland: An account of the history, art and architecture of the white monks in Ireland from 1142 to 1540* (London and New Haven, 1987).

——, "The medieval sculpture of Christ Church cathedral, Dublin", *Archaeologia* 106 (1979) pp 107–22.

Steuer, S., "Family strategies in medieval London: Financial planning and the urban widow, 1123–1473", *Essays in Medieval Studies* 6 (1999) http://www.luc.edu/publications/medieval/vol12/12ch6.html.

Stubbs, W.C., "Weavers' guild", *RSAI Jn 49* (1919) pp 60–88.

Styles, P., "James Ussher and his times", *Hermathena* 88 (1956) pp 12–33.

Sughi, M., "The appointment of Octavian de Palatio as archbishop of Armagh, 1477–8", *IHS* 31 (1998) pp 145–64.

Sweetman, P.D., "Archaeological excavations at Abbeyknockmoy, Co. Galway", *RIA Proc.* C 87 (1987) pp 1–12.

Thompson, B., "From, 'alms' to 'spiritual services': the function and status of monastic property in medieval England", in *Monastic Studies* II, ed. J. Loades (Bangor, 1991) pp 227–61.

——, "Habendum et Tenendum: lay and ecclesiastical attitudes to the property of the church", in *Religious belief and ecclesiastical careers in later medieval England*, ed. C. Harper-Bell (Woodbridge, 1991) pp 197–238.

——, "Monasteries and their patrons at foundation and dissolution", *Transactions of the Royal Historical Society* 6th series, 4 (1994) pp 103–26.

Thompson, J.A.F., "The Well of Grace: Englishmen and Rome in the fifteenth century", in *The church, politics and patronage in the fifteenth century*, ed. B. Dobson (Gloucester, 1984) pp 99–114.

——, "Piety, charity in late medieval London", *Jn of Ecclesiastic History* 16 (1965) pp 178–95.

Thompson, S., "The problem of the Cistercian nuns in the twelfth and thirteenth centuries", in *Medieval women*, ed. D. Baker (Oxford, 1978) pp 227–52.

——, "Why English nunneries had no history: A study of the problems of the English nunneries founded after the conquest", in *Distant echoes: Medieval religious women*, ed. J.A. Nichols and L.T. Shank (Kalamazoo, 1984) pp 131–50.

——, *Women religious: The founding of English nunneries after the Norman conquest* (New York, 1991).

Tillotson, J., "Visitation and reform of the Yorkshire nunneries in the fourteenth century", *Northern History* 30 (1994) pp 1–21.

Varebeke, H.J de, "The Benedictines of medieval Ireland", *RSAI Jn* 80 (1950) pp 92–6.

Venarde, B., *Women's monasticism and medieval society: Nunneries in France and England 890–1215* (Ithaca and London, 1997).

Vickers, N., "The social class of Yorkshire medieval nuns", *Yorkshire Arch. Jn.* 67 (1995) pp 127–32.

Vigors, P.D., "On an ancient ecclesiastical brass seal of the diocese of Leighlin", *RSAI Jn* (1895) pp 82–4.

Walsh, C., "Archaeological excavations at the abbey of St Thomas the Martyr, Dublin", in *Medieval Dublin I*, ed. S. Duffy (Dublin, 2000) pp 185–202.

Walsh, K., "The clerical estate in later medieval Ireland: alien settlement or element of conciliation?" in *Settlement and society in medieval Ireland: Studies presented to F.X. Martin OSA*, ed. J. Bradley (Kilkenny, 1988) pp 361–78..

Walsh, P., "The dating of the Irish annals", *IHS* 2 (1940–1) pp 355–75.

Wardell, R., "The history and antiquities of St Catherine's Old Abbey, Co. Limerick" with appendix by T.J. Westropp, "The conventual buildings", *RSAI Jn* 34 (1904) pp 41–64.

Ware. J., *Equitis aurati de Hibernia et antiquitatibus ejus, disquitiones 1654* in *Collection of tracts and treaties illustrative of the natural history and antiquities and the political and social state of Ireland* (Dublin, 1860–1).

——, *The history and antiquities of Ireland*, in *The whole works of Sir James Ware concerning Ireland*, vol. II, ed. and trans. W. Harris (Dublin 1764).

Warren, Ann K., *Anchorites and their patrons in medieval England* (Berkely, 1986).

Warren, N.B., "Pregnancy and productivity – The imagery of Female monasticism within and beyond the cloister walls", *Jn of Medieval and Early modern studies* 28 (1998) pp 532–52.

Waterman, D.M., "St Mary's Priory, Devenish: Excavation of the east range, 1972–4", *UJA* 42 (1979) pp 34–50.

Watt, J., "Ecclesia inter Anglicos et inter Hibernicos: Confrontation and coexistence in the medieval diocese and province of Armagh", in *The English in medieval Ireland,* ed. J.F. Lydon (Dublin, 1984) pp 46–64.

——, *The church in medieval Ireland* (2nd edition Dublin, 1998).

——, *The church in the two nations in medieval Ireland* (Cambridge, 1970).

——, "The medieval chapter of Armagh Cathedral", in *Church and city 1000–1500, Essays in honour of Christopher Brooke*, ed. David Abulafia, Michael Franklin and Miri Rubin (Cambridge, 1992) pp 219–48.

——, "The papacy and Ireland in the fifteenth century", in *The church, politics and patronage in the fifteenth century*, ed. B. Dobson (Gloucester, 1984) pp 133–45.

Webster, C.A., *The diocese of Cork* (Cork, 1920).

Westropp, T.J., "A description of the ancient building and crosses at Clonmacnoise", *RSAI Jn* 37 (1907) pp 277–306.

——, "A survey of the ancient churches in the county of Limerick", *RIA Proc.* C 25 (1904–5) pp 327–480.

——, "Augustinian houses of Co. Clare: Clare, Killone and Inchicronan", *RSAI Jn* 30 (1900) pp 118–35.

——, "Ennis abbey and the O'Brien tombs", *RSAI Jn* 25 (1895) pp 135–54.

——, "Foundation charter of Forgy Abbey, Co. Clare", *RSAI Jn* 22 (1892) pp78–9.
——, "St Mary's Cathedral, Limerick", *RSAI Jn* 28 (1898) pp 35–48.
——, "The Augustinian convent of Killown near Ennis", *RSAI Jn* (1891) pp 409–10.
——, "The churches of County Clare and the origin of the ecclesiastical divisions in that county", *RIA Proc.* C 6 (1900–2) pp 100–80.
Wilde, W.R.W., *Lough Corrib, its shores and islands with notices of Lough Mask* (Dublin, 1867).
Yorke, B., "Sisters under the skin? Anglo–Saxon nuns and nunneries in Southern England", *Reading Medieval Studies* 16 (1990) pp 95–117.
Youngs, S., J. Clare and T. Barry comp., "Medieval Britian and Ireland in 1984", *Medieval Archaeology* 29 (1985).

UNPUBLISHED THESES

Cassidy, M.E. "Cistercian monasteries: monastic spaces and their meanings", PhD thesis, University of Melbourne, 1998.
Hall, D., "Gender and sanctity in the hagiography of early medieval Irish women", MA thesis, University of Melbourne, 1993.
——, "Women and religion in late medieval Ireland", PhD thesis, University of Melbourne, 2000.
MacDonald, A.C., "Women and the monastic life in late medieval Yorkshire", PhD thesis, Oxford University, 1997.
Preston, Sarah, "The canons regular of St Augustine in medieval Ireland: An overview", PhD thesis, University of Dublin, 1996.

Index